Basic Facts
about the
United Nations
2014

United Nations Department of Public Information
New York

Basic Facts about the United Nations

Published by the United Nations Department of Public Information
New York, New York 10017, United States of America

Revised edition
Copyright © 2014 United Nations
All rights reserved

ISBN: 978-92-1-101279-8
eISBN: 978-92-1-056166-2
United Nations publication
Sales No. E.13.I.6

Front cover: A Syrian girl plays with a young child in the Akçakale refugee camp in southern Turkey, housing some 10,000 refugees. (26 September 2012, UNHCR/A. Branthwaite)

Cover design: Graphic Design Unit, United Nations, New York

Printed in the United States of America

Basic Facts about the United Nations

FOREWORD

Since 1947, *Basic Facts about the United Nations* has served as a trusted guide to the Organization. This new edition introduces readers to the structure and history of the entire United Nations system, and provides essential details about its latest efforts to address the challenges of our times.

The United Nations, since its inception, has challenged nations to resolve disputes peacefully and avoid the destruction unleashed by armed conflict. That same imperative—to build a landscape of peace—drives our efforts to conquer poverty and hunger and our pursuit of human rights, justice and environmental protection. In addressing these global issues, we are compelled to work as citizens not of any one nation alone but of our one, shared planet.

The peace and security challenges covered in this volume highlight the need for international cooperation. Civil war in the Syrian Arab Republic has resulted in massive refugee flows and regional instability. In the Republic of South Sudan—the newest and 193rd member of the United Nations—lingering security and development issues necessitated the deployment of a new peacekeeping operation. The United Nations has also established peacekeeping missions in Mali and the Abyei region of Sudan. In the Democratic Republic of the Congo, the UN brokered a new framework agreement that embodies a regional approach to the long-standing cycles of violence. Alongside new approaches to peacekeeping, the Organization continues to strengthen preventive diplomacy, mediation and other steps to avert conflict in the first place.

The Organization's commitment to the Millennium Development Goals (MDGs) has helped the world meet targets to reduce extreme poverty, increase access to drinking water and improve conditions for millions of slum-dwellers. As we strive to finish the job and build on MDG successes, we are also looking to define a post-2015 development agenda that is every bit as inspiring. Discussions on the agenda will culminate in 2015 with a set of goals for sustainable development to carry our work forward. That same year is also the deadline by which Member States have pledged to complete a new legally binding agreement on climate change.

The human family now numbers 7 billion members—a population milestone reached in 2011. In an interdependent world, people and countries alike need an effective institution that can uphold universal values, address shared threats and seize common opportunities. *Basic Facts about the United Nations* shows how the Organization is laying the foundations for a better future for people everywhere. I know of no better introduction to our work than this reliable handbook.

Ban Ki-moon
Secretary-General of the United Nations
New York, 27 August 2013

CONTENTS

II. INTERNATIONAL PEACE AND SECURITY

III. ECONOMIC AND SOCIAL DEVELOPMENT

IV. HUMAN RIGHTS

V.   HUMANITARIAN ACTION

VI.   INTERNATIONAL LAW

APPENDICES

LIST OF ACRONYMS

CTBTO	Preparatory Commission for the Comprehensive Nuclear-Test-Ban Treaty Organization
DESA	Department of Economic and Social Affairs
DFS	Department of Field Support
DGACM	Department for General Assembly and Conference Management
DM	Department of Management
DPA	Department of Political Affairs
DPI	Department of Public Information
DPKO	Department of Peacekeeping Operations
DSS	Department of Safety and Security
ECA	Economic Commission for Africa
ECE	Economic Commission for Europe
ECLAC	Economic Commission for Latin America and the Caribbean
ECOSOC	Economic and Social Council
ESCAP	Economic and Social Commission for Asia and the Pacific
ESCWA	Economic and Social Commission for Western Asia
FAO	Food and Agriculture Organization of the United Nations
IAEA	International Atomic Energy Agency
IASC	Inter-Agency Standing Committee
IBRD	International Bank for Reconstruction and Development
ICAO	International Civil Aviation Organization
ICSID	International Centre for Settlement of Investment Disputes
IDA	International Development Association
IDPs	Internally displaced persons
IFAD	International Fund for Agricultural Development
IFC	International Finance Corporation
ILO	International Labour Organization
IMF	International Monetary Fund
IMO	International Maritime Organization
IPCC	Intergovernmental Panel on Climate Change
ITC	International Trade Centre
ITU	International Telecommunication Union
MDGs	Millennium Development Goals
MIGA	Multilateral Investment Guarantee Agency
NEPAD	New Partnership for Africa's Development
NGOs	non-governmental organizations
OCHA	Office for the Coordination of Humanitarian Affairs
OHCHR	Office of the United Nations High Commissioner for Human Rights
OIOS	Office of Internal Oversight Services
OLA	Office of Legal Affairs

OPCW	Organisation for the Prohibition of Chemical Weapons
UNAIDS	Joint United Nations Programme on HIV/AIDS
UNCDF	United Nations Capital Development Fund
UNCTAD	United Nations Conference on Trade and Development
UNDP	United Nations Development Programme
UNEP	United Nations Environment Programme
UNESCO	United Nations Educational, Scientific and Cultural Organization
UNFPA	United Nations Population Fund
UN-HABITAT	United Nations Human Settlements Programme
UNHCR	Office of the United Nations High Commissioner for Refugees
UNICEF	United Nations Children's Fund
UNICRI	United Nations Interregional Crime and Justice Research Institute
UNIDIR	United Nations Institute for Disarmament Research
UNIDO	United Nations Industrial Development Organization
UNITAR	United Nations Institute for Training and Research
UNODA	United Nations Office for Disarmament Affairs
UNODC	United Nations Office on Drugs and Crime
UN-OHRLLS	Office of the High Representative for the Least Developed Countries, Landlocked Developing Countries and Small Island Developing States
UNOPS	United Nations Office for Project Services
UNRISD	United Nations Research Institute for Social Development
UNRWA	United Nations Relief and Works Agency for Palestine Refugees in the Near East
UNSSC	United Nations System Staff College
UNU	United Nations University
UNV	United Nations Volunteers
UN-Women	United Nations Entity for Gender Equality and the Empowerment of Women
UNWTO	World Tourism Organization
UPU	United Nations Postal Union
WFP	World Food Programme
WHO	World Health Organization
WIPO	World Intellectual Property Organization
WMO	World Meteorological Organization
WTO	World Trade Organization

ABOUT THIS EDITION

B asic Facts about the United Nations, published regularly since 1947, serves as the definitive introduction to the UN and its family of related institutions and agencies. Over the years, Basic Facts has expanded the scope and depth of its coverage as the Organization has broadened its commitment to meet the urgent needs of an ever more populous and complex world. At the same time, the book has remained true to its roots as a comprehensive yet concise guide to this leading world body. Continuing that tradition, this 2014 edition outlines the current structure of the UN system and explains how each individual part contributes to achieving key international goals.

Basic Facts begins by recounting the origins of the United Nations and providing an overview of the wider system of UN institutions and agencies. Successive chapters describe the Organization's efforts to advance international peace and security; enhance economic and social development in an environmentally sustainable manner; protect human rights and eliminate discrimination; provide humanitarian relief to refugees, displaced persons and those affected by natural and man-made disasters; and develop and standardize international law. These chapters portray an Organization unique in its ability to mobilize collective action to meet the challenges facing our world.

Also functioning as a practical handbook, Basic Facts includes appendices providing essential information on UN membership; current and former UN peacekeeping missions; and the observance of UN decades, years, weeks and days. It also contains contact information for UN information centres, services and offices, and lists selected UN websites.

This edition has been thoroughly updated to reflect significant recent developments in the world and within the UN itself. Photographs illustrate how various UN system bodies have partnered with local institutions—and local people—to help save and improve lives everywhere. Coverage has been streamlined to provide a clearer, more focused picture of today's dynamic and effective UN. Developments concerning new and continuing peacekeeping and peacebuilding missions are discussed, but situations in states or regions in which the UN has ended its security presence are no longer treated. Likewise, details concerning past UN programmes and conferences have been replaced by information on newer entities such as UN-Women, and on activities such as the United Nations Conference on Sustainable Development (Rio+20). This edition covers the important work completed by the Trusteeship Council as a principal UN organ, however, as the Council's operations have been suspended, coverage has been condensed and consolidated in the chapter on peace and security.

Although officially produced by the UN Department of Public Information, Basic Facts about the United Nations 2014 incorporates material provided by UN system offices, programmes, agencies and institutions throughout the world. Their input has been essential in bringing Basic Facts to researchers, students and the public at large, and they deserve thanks for their contributions to this book and for their efforts to strengthen the United Nations and improve the lives of the world's poorest and most vulnerable people.

All data presented in this book are current as of 31 March 2013 unless otherwise noted. For the latest information on UN activities throughout the world, please visit:

—the official website of the United Nations (*www.un.org*);

—the UN News Centre (*www.un.org/news*);

—the *Yearbook of the United Nations* (*unyearbook.un.org*), the Organization's authoritative reference work, providing an in-depth and historical presentation of UN goals and activities;

—the *UN Chronicle* magazine (*www.un.org/wcm/content/site/chronicle*), providing a thematic perspective on issues of global concern.

The flag of the United Nations at the Organization's Headquarters in New York. (26 April 2013, UN Photo/Rick Bajornas)

The United Nations System

UN Principal Organs

General Assembly

Security Council

Economic and Social Council

Secretariat

International Court of Justice

Trusteeship Council[6]

Subsidiary Bodies

Main and other sessional committees

Disarmament Commission

Human Rights Council

International Law Commission

Standing committees and ad hoc bodies

Subsidiary Bodies

Counter-terrorism committees

International Criminal Tribunal for Rwanda (ICTR)

International Criminal Tribunal for the former Yugoslavia (ICTY)

Military Staff Committee

Peacekeeping operations and political missions

Sanctions committees (ad hoc)

Standing committees and ad hoc bodies

Funds and Programmes[1]

UNCTAD United Nations Conference on Trade and Development

- **ITC** International Trade Centre (UNCTAD/WTO)

UNDP United Nations Development Programme

- **UNCDF** United Nations Capital Development Fund
- **UNV** United Nations Volunteers

UNEP United Nations Environment Programme

UNFPA United Nations Population Fund

Functional Commissions

Crime Prevention and Criminal Justice

Narcotic Drugs

Population and Development

Science and Technology for Development

Social Development

Statistics

Status of Women

Sustainable Development

United Nations Forum on Forests

Regional Commissions

ECA Economic Commission for Africa

ECE Economic Commission for Europe

ECLAC Economic Commission for Latin America and the Caribbean

ESCAP Economic and Social Commission for Asia and the Pacific

ESCWA Economic and Social Commission for Western Asia

Departments and Offices

EOSG Executive Office of the Secretary-General

DESA Department of Economic and Social Affairs

DFS Department of Field Support

DGACM Department for General Assembly and Conference Management

DM Department of Management

DPA Department of Political Affairs

DPI Department of Public Information

DPKO Department of Peacekeeping Operations

DSS Department of Safety and Security

OCHA Office for the Coordination of Humanitarian Affairs

OHCHR Office of the United Nations High Commissioner for Human Rights

Notes:

1 The United Nations, its Funds and Programmes, the Specialized Agencies, IAEA and WTO are all members of the United Nations System Chief Executives Board for Coordination (CEB).

2 UNRWA and UNIDIR report only to the General Assembly (GA).

3 IAEA reports to the Security Council and the GA.

4 WTO has no reporting obligation to the GA, but contributes on an ad hoc basis to GA and Economic and Social Council (ECOSOC) work on, inter alia, finance and development issues.

5 Specialized Agencies are autonomous organizations whose work is coordinated through ECOSOC (intergovernmental level) and CEB (inter-secretariat level).

6 The Trusteeship Council suspended operation on 1 November 1994, as on 1 October 1994 Palau, the last United Nations Trust Territory, became independent.

This is not an official document of the United Nations, nor is it intended to be all inclusive.

UN-HABITAT United Nations Human
Settlements Programme

UNHCR Office of the United Nations High Commissioner
for Refugees

UNICEF United Nations Children's Fund

UNODC United Nations Office on Drugs and Crime

UNRWA[2] United Nations Relief and Works Agency
for Palestine Refugees in the Near East

UN-Women United Nations Entity for Gender Equality
and the Empowerment of Women

WFP World Food Programme

Research and Training Institutes

UNICRI United Nations Interregional Crime
and Justice Research Institute

UNIDIR[2] United Nations Institute
for Disarmament Research

Advisory Subsidiary Body
Peacebuilding Commission

UNITAR United Nations Institute for Training
and Research

UNRISD United Nations Research Institute
for Social Development

UNSSC United Nations System Staff College

UNU United Nations University

Other Entities

UNAIDS Joint United Nations Programme on HIV/AIDS

UNISDR United Nations International Strategy
for Disaster Reduction

UNOPS United Nations Office for Project Services

Related Organizations

CTBTO Preparatory Commission Preparatory
Commission for the Comprehensive Nuclear-Test-Ban
Treaty Organization

IAEA[1,3] International Atomic Energy Agency

OPCW Organisation for the Prohibition of Chemical
Weapons

WTO[1,4] World Trade Organization

Specialized Agencies [1,5]

FAO Food and Agriculture Organization
of the United Nations

ICAO International Civil Aviation
Organization

IFAD International Fund for Agricultural
Development

ILO International Labour Organization

IMF International Monetary Fund

IMO International Maritime Organization

ITU International Telecommunication
Union

UNESCO United Nations Educational,
Scientific and Cultural Organization

UNIDO United Nations Industrial
Development Organization

UNWTO World Tourism Organization

UPU Universal Postal Union

WHO World Health Organization

WIPO World Intellectual Property
Organization

WMO World Meteorological
Organization

World Bank Group

* **IBRD** International Bank for
  Reconstruction and
  Development

* **ICSID** International Centre for
  Settlement of Investment
  Disputes

* **IDA** International Development
  Association

* **IFC** International Finance
  Corporation

* **MIGA** Multilateral Investment
  Guarantee Agency

Other Bodies

Committee for Development Policy

Committee of Experts on Public
Administration

Committee on Non-Governmental
Organizations

Permanent Forum on Indigenous Issues

United Nations Group of Experts
on Geographical Names

Other sessional and standing
committees and expert, ad hoc
and related bodies

OIOS Office of Internal Oversight Services

OLA Office of Legal Affairs

OSAA Office of the Special Adviser on Africa

SRSG/CAAC Office of the Special Representative
of the Secretary-General for Children
and Armed Conflict

SRSG/SVC Office of the Special Representative of the
Secretary-General on Sexual Violence in Conflict

UNODA Office for Disarmament Affairs

UNOG United Nations Office at Geneva

UN-OHRLLS Office of the High Representative
for the Least Developed Countries, Landlocked
Developing Countries and Small Island
Developing States

UNON United Nations Office at Nairobi

UNOV United Nations Office at Vienna

Published by the United Nations Department of Public Information   DPI/2470 rev.3—13-38229—August 2013

I. UN CHARTER, STRUCTURE AND SYSTEM

Peacekeepers from the United Nations Stabilization Mission in Haiti and members of the Haitian Department of Civil Protection evacuate residents of Cabaret during a disaster response simulation. (9 July 2012, UN Photo/Victoria Hazou)

The struggle for peace is an enduring one. More than a century ago, in 1899, the first International Peace Conference was held in The Hague to elaborate multilateral instruments for settling crises peacefully, preventing wars and codifying rules of warfare. It adopted the *Convention for the Pacific Settlement of International Disputes* and established the Permanent Court of Arbitration, which began its work in 1902. Subsequently, in 1919, the League of Nations, conceived during the First World War, was established under the *Treaty of Versailles* "to promote international cooperation and to achieve peace and security". While the League of Nations ceased activities after failing to prevent the Second World War, the need for peaceful resolution of conflicts through international collaboration and dialogue continued to grow.

The term 'United Nations' was coined by United States President Franklin D. Roosevelt during the Second World War. It first appeared in the *Declaration by United Nations* of 1 January 1942, which put forth a pledge by 26 nations to fight together against the Axis powers. Following deliberations held in Washington, D.C., in 1944 among representatives from China, the Soviet Union, the United Kingdom and the United States, delegates from 50 countries met in San Francisco in 1945 at the United Nations Conference on International Organization. There, with a firm commitment to end "the scourge of war", they drew up the *Charter of the United Nations*, signed on 26 June 1945.

Headquartered in New York, the United Nations officially came into existence on 24 October 1945 with the ratification of the *Charter* by China, France, the Soviet Union, the United Kingdom, the United States and a majority of other signatories. In commemoration of this historic pledge for world peace, **United Nations Day** is celebrated on 24 October each year. Despite the sharp divisions from which it arose in the Second World War and those of the ensuing cold war that marked many of its deliberations, the UN continues to grow in remaining true to this pledge— one all the more relevant in the face of the tremendous global transformations confronting the world and its peoples at the beginning of the 21st century.

The Charter of the United Nations

The *Charter of the United Nations* (*www.un.org/aboutun/charter*) is the constitutive instrument of the UN, setting out the rights and obligations of member states, and establishing its principal organs and procedures. An international treaty, the *Charter* codifies basic tenets of international relations—from the sovereign equality of states to prohibition of the use of force in any manner inconsistent with the purposes of the United Nations.

The *Charter* consists of a Preamble and 111 articles grouped into 19 chapters. Of these, Chapter 1 sets forth the purposes and principles of the United Nations; Chapter 2 establishes the criteria for UN membership; Chapter 3 names the six principal UN organs; Chapters 4–15 define the functions and powers of these organs; Chapters 16–17 relate the United Nations to existing international law; and Chapters 18–19 define the amendment and ratification of the *Charter*.

The Preamble to the *Charter* expresses the shared ideals and common aims of all the peoples whose governments joined together to form the United Nations:

WE THE PEOPLES OF THE UNITED NATIONS

DETERMINED

> to save succeeding generations from the scourge of war, which twice in our lifetime has brought untold sorrow to mankind, and
>
> to reaffirm faith in fundamental human rights, in the dignity and worth of the human person, in the equal rights of men and women and of nations large and small, and
>
> to establish conditions under which justice and respect for the obligations arising from treaties and other sources of international law can be maintained, and
>
> to promote social progress and better standards of life in larger freedom,

AND FOR THESE ENDS

> to practice tolerance and live together in peace with one another as good neighbours, and
>
> to unite our strength to maintain international peace and security, and
>
> to ensure, by the acceptance of principles and the institution of methods, that armed force shall not be used, save in the common interest, and
>
> to employ international machinery for the promotion of the economic and social advancement of all peoples,

HAVE RESOLVED TO COMBINE OUR EFFORTS

TO ACCOMPLISH THESE AIMS

> Accordingly, our respective Governments, through representatives assembled in the city of San Francisco, who have exhibited their full powers found to be in good and due form, have agreed to the present *Charter of the United Nations* and do hereby establish an international organization to be known as the United Nations.

Purposes and principles

As set forth in the *Charter*, the purposes of the United Nations are to:

- maintain international peace and security;
- develop friendly relations among nations based on respect for the principle of equal rights and self-determination of peoples;
- cooperate in solving international economic, social, cultural and humanitarian problems and in promoting respect for human rights and fundamental freedoms;
- be a centre for harmonizing the actions of nations in attaining these common ends.

In turn, the United Nations acts in accordance with the following principles:

- it is based on the sovereign equality of all its members;
- all members are to fulfil in good faith their *Charter* obligations;
- they are to settle their international disputes by peaceful means and without endangering international peace and security and justice;
- they are to refrain from the threat or use of force against any other state;
- they are to give the United Nations every assistance in any action it takes in accordance with the *Charter*;
- nothing in the *Charter* is to authorize the United Nations to intervene in matters which are essentially within the domestic jurisdiction of any state.

Amendments to the Charter

The *Charter* may be amended by a vote of two thirds of the members of the General Assembly and ratification by two thirds of the members of the United Nations, including the five permanent members of the Security Council. So far, four Articles of the *Charter* have been amended, one of them twice:

- In 1965, the membership of the Security Council was increased from 11 to 15 states (Article 23) and the number of affirmative votes needed for a decision was increased from seven to nine, including the concurring vote of the five permanent members for all matters of substance rather than procedure (Article 27).
- In 1965, the membership of the Economic and Social Council was increased from 18 to 27 states, and again in 1973 to 54 (Article 61).
- In 1968, the number of votes required in the Security Council to convene a General Conference to review the *Charter* was increased from seven to nine (Article 109).

Membership and official languages

Membership in the United Nations is open to all peace-loving nations that accept the obligations of the *Charter* and are willing and able to carry out these obligations. The General Assembly admits new member states on the recommendation of the Security Council. The *Charter* provides for the suspension or expulsion of a member for violation of the principles of the *Charter*, but no such action has ever been taken. Under the *Charter*, the official languages of the United Nations are Chinese, English, French, Russian and Spanish. Arabic was added as an official language in 1973.

UN structure

The *Charter* establishes six principal organs of the United Nations: the General Assembly, the Security Council, the Economic and Social Council, the International Court of Justice, the Trusteeship Council and the Secretariat. The United Nations family, however, is much larger, encompassing 15 specialized agencies and numerous programmes and funds as well as other entities.

General Assembly

The **General Assembly** (*www.un.org/ga*) is the main deliberative organ of the United Nations. It is composed of representatives of all member states, each of which has one vote. Decisions on important questions (such as those on peace and security, admission of new members and budgetary matters) require a two-thirds majority. Decisions on other questions take place by simple majority.

Functions and powers

Under the *Charter*, the functions and powers of the General Assembly include:

- considering and making recommendations on the principles of cooperation in the maintenance of international peace and security, including the principles governing disarmament and arms regulation;

- discussing any question relating to international peace and security and, except where a dispute or situation is being discussed by the Security Council, making recommendations on it;
- discussing and, with the same exception, making recommendations on any question within the scope of the *Charter* or affecting the powers and functions of any organ of the United Nations;
- initiating studies and making recommendations to promote international political cooperation, the development and codification of international law, the realization of human rights and fundamental freedoms for all, and international collaboration in the economic, social, cultural, educational and health fields;
- making recommendations for the peaceful settlement of any situation, regardless of origin, which might impair friendly relations among nations;
- receiving and considering reports from the Security Council and other United Nations organs;
- considering and approving the United Nations budget and apportioning the contributions among members; and
- electing the non-permanent members of the Security Council, the members of the Economic and Social Council and additional members of the Trusteeship Council (when necessary); electing jointly with the Security Council the judges of the International Court of Justice; and, on the recommendation of the Security Council, appointing the Secretary-General.

Under the "Uniting for peace" resolution, adopted by the General Assembly in November 1950, the Assembly may take action if the Security Council, because of lack of unanimity of its permanent members, fails to act where there appears to be a threat to international peace, a breach of the peace or an act of aggression. The Assembly is empowered to consider the matter immediately with a view to making recommendations to members for collective measures, including, in the case of a breach of the peace or an act of aggression, the use of armed forces when necessary to maintain or restore international peace and security.

Sessions

The General Assembly's regular session begins each year on Tuesday in the third week of September, counting from the first week that contains at least one working day. The election of the President of the Assembly, as well as its 21 Vice-Presidents and the Chairpersons of its six Main Committees, takes place at least three months before the start of the regular session. To ensure equitable geographical representation, the presidency of the Assembly rotates each year among five groups of states: African, Asian, Eastern European, Latin American and Caribbean, and Western European and other states. In addition, the Assembly may meet in special sessions at the request of the Security Council, of a majority of member states or of one member, if the majority of members concur. Emergency special sessions may be called within 24 hours of a request by the Security Council on the vote of any nine Council members, or by a majority of the members of the United Nations, or by one member if the majority of members concur. At the beginning of each regular session, the Assembly holds a general debate—often addressed by heads of state and government—in which member states express their views on the most pressing international issues.

Year-round, the work of the United Nations derives largely from the mandates given by the General Assembly—that is to say, the will of the majority of the members as expressed in the resolutions and decisions adopted by the Assembly. That work is carried out by committees and other bodies established by the Assembly to study and report on specific matters such as disarmament, peacekeeping, development and human rights; in international conferences called for by the Assembly; and by the Secretariat of the United Nations—the Secretary-General and his staff of international civil servants.

Most questions are discussed in one of the six **Main Committees** of the Assembly:

*   First Committee (Disarmament and International Security);
*   Second Committee (Economic and Financial);
*   Third Committee (Social, Humanitarian and Cultural);
*   Fourth Committee (Special Political and Decolonization);
*   Fifth Committee (Administrative and Budgetary);
*   Sixth Committee (Legal).

While some issues are considered directly in plenary meetings, most are allocated to one of these committees. Resolutions and decisions, including those recommended by the committees, may be adopted—with or without a vote—in plenary meetings, usually before the recess of the regular session in December.

The Assembly normally adopts its resolutions and decisions by a majority of members present and voting. Important questions—including recommendations on international peace and security, the election of members to some principal organs, and budgetary matters—must be decided by a two-thirds majority. Voting may be conducted as a recorded vote, a show-of-hands or a roll-call vote. While the decisions of the Assembly have no legally binding force for governments, they carry the weight of world opinion and the moral authority of the world community.

Security Council

The **Security Council** (*www.un.org/en/sc*) of the United Nations has primary responsibility, under the *Charter*, for the maintenance of international peace and security. It has 15 members: 5 permanent members (China, France, the Russian Federation, the United Kingdom and the United States) and 10 members elected by the General Assembly for two-year terms. These currently consist of Azerbaijan, Guatemala, Morocco, Pakistan and Togo (with terms ending in 2013); and Argentina, Australia, Luxembourg, Republic of Korea and Rwanda (with terms ending in 2014). Each member has one vote. Decisions on procedural matters are made by an affirmative vote of at least 9 of the 15 members. Decisions on substantive matters require nine votes and the absence of a negative vote (veto) by any of the five permanent members. All five permanent members have exercised the right of veto at one time or another. If a permanent member does not fully agree with a proposed resolution but does not wish to cast a veto, it may choose to abstain, thus allowing the resolution to be adopted if it obtains the required number of nine favourable votes. The presidency of the Council is held by each of the members in turn for one month, following alphabetical order.

The composition of the Council, as well as its procedures, are the subject of a working group of the General Assembly considering Security Council reform, especially the addition of permanent seats or enlargement of non-permanent membership. At issue is the notion of the equitable representation of member states in addressing matters of global consequence. Seventy-three UN member states have never sat on the Council. All members of the United Nations, however, agree to accept and carry out the decisions of the Security Council. While other organs of the United Nations make recommendations to member states, only the Security Council has the power to make decisions that member states are then obligated to implement under the *Charter*.

Functions and powers

The functions and powers of the Security Council include the following:

- maintaining international peace and security in accordance with the principles and purposes of the United Nations;
- formulating plans for establishing a system to regulate armaments;
- calling upon the parties to a dispute to settle it by peaceful means;
- investigating any dispute or situation that might lead to international friction, and recommending methods of adjustment or terms of settlement;
- determining the existence of a threat to the peace or act of aggression and recommending what action should be taken;
- calling upon the parties concerned to comply with such provisional measures as it deems necessary or desirable to prevent an aggravation of the situation;
- calling upon members of the United Nations to apply measures not involving the use of armed force—such as sanctions—to give effect to the Council's decisions;
- resorting to or authorizing the use of force to maintain or restore international peace and security;
- encouraging the peaceful settlement of local disputes through regional arrangements and using such regional arrangements for enforcement under its authority;
- recommending to the General Assembly the appointment of the Secretary-General and, together with the Assembly, electing the judges of the International Court of Justice;
- requesting the International Court of Justice to give an advisory opinion on any legal question; and
- recommending to the General Assembly the admission of new members to the United Nations.

The Security Council is organized in such a way that it can function continuously. A representative of each of its members must be present at all times at UN Headquarters. The Council may meet elsewhere: in 1972 it held a session in Addis Ababa, Ethiopia; in 1973 it met in Panama City, Panama; and in 1990 it met in Geneva.

When a complaint concerning a threat to peace is brought before it, the Council's first action is usually to recommend that the parties try to reach agreement by peaceful means. The Council may set forth principles for such an agreement.

In some cases, the Council itself undertakes investigation and mediation. It may dispatch a mission, appoint special envoys or request the Secretary-General to use his good offices to achieve a pacific settlement of the dispute.

When a dispute leads to hostilities, the Council's primary concern is to bring them to an end as soon as possible. It may issue ceasefire directives that can help prevent an escalation of the conflict. The Council may also dispatch military observers or a peacekeeping force to help reduce tensions, separate opposing forces and establish a calm in which peaceful settlements may be sought. Beyond this, the Council may opt for enforcement measures, including economic sanctions, arms embargoes, financial penalties and restrictions, and travel bans; severance of diplomatic relations; blockade; or even collective military action. A chief concern is to focus action on those responsible for the policies or practices condemned by the international community, while minimizing the impact of the measures taken on other parts of the population and economy.

The Council established the Counter-Terrorism Committee as a subsidiary organ following the terrorist attacks on the United States on 11 September 2001. The Peacebuilding Commission, established by the Council in 2005, supports peace efforts in countries emerging from conflict. The Military Staff Committee helps plan UN military measures and regulate armaments.

Tribunals and courts

Over the past two decades, the Council has established, as subsidiary organs, two ad hoc, territorially specific, international criminal tribunals to prosecute crimes against humanity in the former Yugoslavia and in Rwanda. There are also three 'hybrid' courts established by Cambodia, Lebanon and Sierra Leone, respectively, with substantial help from the United Nations. These are not permanent and will cease to exist once their business draws to a close.

International Criminal Tribunal for the former Yugoslavia (ICTY)

Established by the Security Council in 1993, the International Criminal Tribunal for the former Yugoslavia (*www.icty.org*) is mandated to prosecute persons responsible for genocide, war crimes and crimes against humanity committed in the former Yugoslavia since 1991. Its organizational components are its Chambers, Registry and the Office of the Prosecutor. It has 16 permanent judges, 12 *ad litem* judges (of whom it can call upon up to 12 at any given time) and a staff of 873 representing 77 nationalities. Its 2012–2013 regular budget was $250.8 million. The Tribunal has indicted 161 persons accused of crimes committed against many thousands of victims during the conflicts in Croatia (1991–1995), Bosnia and Herzegovina (1992–1995), Kosovo (1998–1999) and The former Yugoslav Republic of Macedonia (2001). By holding individuals accountable regardless of their position, the Tribunal has substantially contributed to dismantling impunity for war crimes.

President: Judge Theodor Meron (United States)
Prosecutor: Serge Brammertz (Belgium)
Registrar: John Hocking (Australia)
Headquarters: Churchillplein 1, 2517 JW The Hague, The Netherlands
Tel.: (31 70) 512 5000; Fax: (31 70) 512 5355

International Criminal Tribunal for Rwanda (ICTR)

Created by the Security Council in 1994, the International Criminal Tribunal for Rwanda (*www.unictr.org*) has the mandate to prosecute persons responsible for genocide and other serious violations of international humanitarian law committed in Rwanda during 1994, as well as Rwandan citizens responsible for such violations committed in the territory of neighbouring states. Its three Trial Chambers and one Appeals Chamber are composed of 16 independent judges. No two of them may be nationals of the same state. Three judges sit in each of the Trial Chambers and five judges sit in the Appeals Chamber, which is shared with the International Criminal Tribunal for the former Yugoslavia. It also has a pool of 18 *ad litem* judges (of whom it can call upon up to nine at any given time), and 524 staff as of 30 June 2012, among which some 68 nationalities were represented. Its 2012–2013 budget was $171 million. As of 10 May 2013, ICTR had completed trials, at the Trial Chamber level, against all 93 persons accused. Appellate proceedings had been concluded in respect of 46 accused persons. All but one of the remaining appeals would be completed in 2014. Those convicted include Jean Kambanda, Prime Minister of Rwanda during the genocide—the first head of government to be arrested and subsequently convicted for that crime.

President: Judge Vagn Joensen (Denmark)
Prosecutor: Hassan B. Jallow (Gambia)
Registrar: Bongani Majola (South Africa)
Headquarters: Arusha International Conference Centre, P.O. Box 6016, Arusha, Tanzania
Tel.: (255 27) 250 27 4207 4211 or (via New York) (1 212) 963 2850; Fax: (255 27) 250 4000 or (via New York) (1 212) 963 2848

Special Court for Sierra Leone

The Special Court for Sierra Leone (*www.sc-sl.org*) was set up jointly by Sierra Leone and the United Nations in 2002, as requested by the Security Council in 2000. It is mandated to try those who bear the greatest responsibility for serious violations of international humanitarian law and Sierra Leonean law committed in the territory of Sierra Leone since 30 November 1996. The Special Court consists of three organs, including the Chambers (Appeals Chamber, Trial Chamber I and Trial Chamber II), the Registry (including the Defence Office) and the Office of the Prosecutor. The Special Court is the first international criminal tribunal to be funded entirely from voluntary contributions from governments and has received contributions from over 40 states in all world regions. On 26 April 2012, Trial Chamber II unanimously found that Charles Taylor, former president of Liberia, participated in planning the rebel attacks in Sierra Leone between December 1998 and February 1999.

President: Jon M. Kamanda (Sierra Leone)
Prosecutor: Brenda Hollis (United States)
Registrar: Binta Mansaray (Sierra Leone)
Headquarters: Jomo Kenyatta Road, New England, Freetown, Sierra Leone
Tel.: (232 22) 297 000 or (via Italy) (39) 0831 257000; Fax: (232 22) 297 001 or (via Italy) (39) 0831 257001; E-mail: *scsl-mail@un.org*

Extraordinary Chambers in the Courts of Cambodia (ECCC)

The Extraordinary Chambers in the Courts of Cambodia for the Prosecution of Crimes Committed during the Period of Democratic Kampuchea (*www.eccc.gov.kh*), is a national court established in 2006 pursuant to an agreement between Cambodia and the United Nations to try senior members of the Khmer Rouge for serious violations of international humanitarian law and Cambodian law during the period between 17 April 1975 and 6 January 1979, including crimes against humanity, war crimes and genocide. The Pre-Trial and Trial Chambers are each composed of five judges, three of whom are Cambodian and one of these President. The Supreme Court Chamber has seven judges, four of whom are Cambodian and one of these President. International judges are appointed by the Cambodian Supreme Council of Magistracy upon nomination by the Secretary-General of the United Nations. The United Nations Assistance to the Khmer Rouge Trials (UNAKRT) (*www.unakrt-online.org*) provides technical assistance to ECCC.

Pre-Trial Chamber President: Judge Prak Kimsan (Cambodia)
Trial Chamber President: Judge Nil Nonn (Cambodia)
Supreme Court Chamber President: Judge Kong Srim (Cambodia)
Headquarters: National Road 4, Chaom Chau Commune, Porsenchey District, P.O. Box 71, Phnom Penh, Cambodia
Tel.: (855) (0)23 861 500; Fax: (855) (0)23 861 555; E-mail *info@eccc.gov.kh*

Special Tribunal for Lebanon (STL)

In 2005, the Lebanese government requested that the United Nations establish an international tribunal to try persons alleged responsible for the attack of 14 February 2005 in Beirut that killed former Lebanese Prime Minister Rafiq Hariri and 22 other persons. Pursuant to a Security Council resolution, the United Nations and Lebanon negotiated an agreement on the Special Tribunal for Lebanon (*www.stl-tsl.org*). The Special Tribunal, established following a further Security Council resolution in 2007 and officially opened in 2009, sits in Leidschendam-Voorburg, near the Hague. The Chambers of the Special Tribunal consist of one international Pre-Trial Judge; a Trial Chamber (with three judges: one Lebanese and two international, plus two alternate judges: one Lebanese and one international); and an Appeals Chamber (five judges: two Lebanese and three international). The Secretary-General appoints the judges in consultation with the Lebanese government. The Special Tribunal's first indictment was announced in January 2011.

President: Sir David Baragwanath (New Zealand)
Prosecutor: Norman Farrell (Canada)
Registrar: Herman von Hebel (Netherlands)
Headquarters: Dokter van der Stamstraat 1, 2265 BC, Leidschendam, The Netherlands
Tel.: (31 0) 70 800 3400; E-mail *stl-pressoffice@un.org*

Economic and Social Council (ECOSOC)

The *Charter of the United Nations* establishes the **Economic and Social Council** (*www.un.org/ecosoc*) as the principal organ to coordinate the economic, social and related work of the United Nations and the specialized agencies and other bodies. The 54 members of the Council serve for three-year terms. Seats on the Council are allocated based on geographical representation, with 14 allocated to African states, 11 to Asian states, 6 to Eastern European states, 10 to Latin American and Caribbean states, and 13 to Western European and other states. Voting in the Council is by simple majority, with each member having one vote.

Functions and powers

ECOSOC is tasked with:

- serving as the central forum for discussing international economic, social and environmental issues, and for formulating policy recommendations addressed to member states and the United Nations system;
- helping achieve a balanced integration of the three dimensions of sustainable development;
- making or initiating studies and reports and making recommendations on international economic, social, cultural, educational, health and related matters;
- assisting in preparing and organizing major international conferences in the economic, social and related fields and promoting a coordinated follow-up to these conferences; and
- coordinating the activities of the specialized agencies through consultations with and recommendations to them as well as to the General Assembly.

Through its discussion of international economic and social issues and its policy recommendations, ECOSOC plays a key role in fostering international cooperation for development and in setting priorities for action throughout the UN system.

Sessions and subsidiary bodies

The Council normally holds several short sessions and many preparatory meetings, roundtables and panel discussions throughout the year with members of civil society dealing with the organization of its work. It also holds a four-week substantive session in July, alternating annually between New York and Geneva. That session includes a high-level segment, attended by cabinet ministers and other officials, to discuss major economic, social and humanitarian issues. The Council also cooperates with, and to a certain extent coordinates the work of, United Nations programmes (such as UNDP, UNEP, UNFPA, UN-HABITAT and UNICEF) and the specialized agencies (such as FAO, ILO, WHO and UNESCO), all of which report to the Council and make recommendations for its substantive sessions.

The year-round work of the Council is carried out in its subsidiary and related bodies. These include:

- eight functional commissions—deliberative bodies whose role is to consider and make recommendations on issues in their areas of responsibility and expertise: the Statistical Commission, Commission on Population and Development, Commission for Social Development, Commission on the Status of Women, Commission on Narcotic Drugs, Commission on Crime Prevention and Criminal Justice, Commission on Science and Technology for Development, and Commission on Sustainable Development, as well as the United Nations Forum on Forests;
- five regional commissions: Economic Commission for Africa (Addis Ababa, Ethiopia), Economic and Social Commission for Asia and the Pacific (Bangkok, Thailand), Economic Commission for Europe (Geneva), Economic Commission for Latin America and the Caribbean (Santiago, Chile), and Economic and Social Commission for Western Asia (Beirut, Lebanon);

- three standing committees: Committee for Programme and Coordination, Committee on Non-Governmental Organizations, Committee on Negotiations with Intergovernmental Agencies;
- expert bodies on such topics as geographical names, public administration, international cooperation in tax matters, and the transport of dangerous goods;
- other bodies, including the Permanent Forum on Indigenous Issues.

At the United Nations Conference on Sustainable Development (Rio de Janeiro, Brazil, 20–22 June 2012), member states agreed to establish a high-level political forum to replace the Commission on Sustainable Development.

Regional commissions

The regional commissions of the United Nations report to ECOSOC and are funded under the regular UN budget; their secretariats are under the authority of the Secretary-General. Their mandate is to promote the economic development of each region, and strengthen the economic relations of the countries in that region, both among themselves and with other countries of the world.

Economic Commission for Africa (ECA)

Established in 1958, the Economic Commission for Africa (*www.uneca.org*) encourages the growth of the economic and social sectors of the continent. ECA promotes policies and strategies to increase economic cooperation and integration among its 53 member countries, particularly in the production, trade, monetary, infrastructure and institutional fields. It focuses on information and analysis on economic and social issues; food security and sustainable development; development management; the information revolution for development; and regional cooperation and integration. The Commission pays special attention to improving the condition of women, enhancing their involvement and decision-making in development, and ensuring that gender equity is a key element in national development.

Executive Secretary: Dr. Carlos Lopes (Guinea-Bissau)
Address: P.O. Box 3001, Addis Ababa, Ethiopia
Tel.: (251 11) 551 7200; Fax: (251 11) 551-0365; E-mail: *ecainfo@uneca.org*

Economic Commission for Europe (ECE)

Created in 1947, the Economic Commission for Europe (*www.unece.org*) is the forum at which the countries of North America, Europe (including Israel) and Central Asia forge the tools of their economic cooperation. ECE has 56 member countries. Priority areas include economic analysis, environment and human settlements, statistics, sustainable energy, trade, economic cooperation and integration, housing and land management, population, forestry and timber, and transport. It pursues its goals primarily through policy analysis and debates, as well as conventions, regulations, standards and harmonization. Such instruments help facilitate trade in the region and with the rest of the world. Others aim at improving the environment. ECE contributes to their implementation by providing technical assistance, in particular to countries with economies in transition.

Executive Secretary: Sven Alkalaj (Bosnia and Herzegovina)
Address: Palais des Nations, CH-1211 Geneva 10, Switzerland
Tel.: (41 22) 917 4444; Fax: (41 22) 917 0505; E-mail: *info.ece@unece.org*

Economic Commission for Latin America and the Caribbean (ECLAC)

Established in 1948, the Economic Commission for Latin America and the Caribbean (*www.eclac.org*) coordinates policies for promoting sustainable economic and social development in the region. The 33 countries of Latin America and the Caribbean are members of ECLAC, together with 11 North American, Asian and European nations that have historical, economic and cultural ties with the region. Nine non-independent Caribbean territories are associate members of the Commission. It focuses on agricultural development; economic and social planning; industrial, technological and entrepreneurial development; international trade, regional integration and cooperation; investment and financing; social development and equity; integration of women in development; natural resources and infrastructure; environment and human settlements; statistics; administrative management; and demography and population policies.

Executive Secretary: Alicia Bárcena Ibarra (Mexico)
Address: Avenida Dag Hammarskjöld 3477, Casilla 179-D, Santiago de Chile
Tel.: (56 2) 2471 2000; Fax: (56 2) 208 0252; E-mail: *secepal@cepal.org*

Economic and Social Commission for Asia and the Pacific (ESCAP)

Created in 1947, the Economic and Social Commission for Asia and the Pacific (*www.unescap.org*) has a mandate to address the economic and social issues of the region. ESCAP is the only intergovernmental forum for all the countries of Asia and the Pacific. Its 53 member states and 9 associate member states represent some 60 per cent of the world's population. ESCAP gives technical support to governments for social and economic development. This assistance takes the form of advisory services to governments, training, and information-sharing through publications and intercountry networks. The Commission aims to improve socio-economic conditions and help build the foundations of modern society in the region. Four research and training institutions—for agricultural development, agricultural machinery and engineering, statistics, and technology transfer—operate under its auspices. Priority areas are poverty reduction, globalization and emerging social issues.

Executive Secretary: Noeleen Heyzer (Singapore)
Address: United Nations Building, Rajadamnern Nok Avenue, Bangkok 10200, Thailand
Tel.: (66 2) 288 1234; Fax: (66 2) 288 1000; E-mail: *escap-registry@un.org*

Economic and Social Commission for Western Asia (ESCWA)

Established in 1973, the Economic and Social Commission for Western Asia (*www.escwa.un.org*) facilitates concerted action for the economic and social development of the countries of the region by promoting economic cooperation and integration. Comprising 17 member states, ESCWA serves as the main general economic and social development forum for Western Asia in the United Nations system. Its focal areas are sustainable development and productivity; social development; economic development and globalization; information and communication technology; statistics; women's empowerment; and conflict-related issues.

Executive Secretary: Rima Khalaf (Jordan)
Address: P.O. Box 11-8575, Riad el-Solh Square, Beirut, Lebanon
Tel.: (961 1) 98 1301 or (via New York) (1 212) 963 9731; Fax: (961-1) 98-1510

Relations with non-governmental organizations

Non-governmental organizations (NGOs) are regarded by the United Nations as important partners and valuable links to civil society. Consulted regularly on matters of mutual concern in policy and programme, NGOs in growing numbers around the world collaborate daily with the UN community to help achieve its objectives. Indeed, under the *Charter of the United Nations*, the Economic and Social Council may consult not only with member states, but also with NGOs concerned with matters within its competence. As of September 2012, some 3,735 NGOs had consultative status with the Council. The Council recognizes that these organizations should have the opportunity to express their views, and that they possess special experience or technical knowledge valuable for its work.

The Council classifies NGOs into three categories: *general* organizations are those concerned with most of the Council's activities; *special* organizations are those offering competence in particular areas corresponding to the concerns of the Council; and *roster* organizations are those that can contribute to the Council when consulted on an ad hoc basis. NGOs with consultative status may send observers to meetings of the Council and its subsidiary bodies and may submit written statements relevant to its work.

International Court of Justice

The **International Court of Justice** (*www.icj-cij.org*) is the principal judicial organ of the United Nations. Located at The Hague (the Netherlands), it is the only one of the six principal organs not located in New York. It began work in 1946, when it replaced the Permanent Court of International Justice. Also known as the "World Court", ICJ is the only court of a universal character with general jurisdiction. The Statute of the Court is an integral part of the *Charter of the United Nations*.

Mission

The Court has a twofold role: first, to settle, in accordance with international law, legal disputes submitted to it by states (ICJ judgments have binding force and are without appeal for the parties concerned); and, second, to give advisory opinions on legal questions referred to it by duly authorized United Nations organs and agencies of the UN system. Contentious cases have represented 80 per cent of the work of ICJ since its creation, and it has delivered over a hundred judgments on disputes concerning, for example, international boundaries and territorial sovereignty, violations of international humanitarian law, and diplomatic relations. The Court has also rendered nearly 30 advisory opinions.

Jurisdiction

The Court is open to all states that are parties to its Statute, which includes all members of the United Nations. Only states, however, may be parties in contentious cases before the Court and submit disputes to it. The Court's jurisdiction covers all questions referred to it by states and all matters provided for in the *Charter* or in international treaties and conventions. States may bind themselves in advance to accept the jurisdiction of the Court, either by signing a treaty or convention that provides for referral to the Court or by making a declaration to that effect. Such declarations accepting compulsory jurisdiction often contain reservations excluding certain classes of disputes. The Court decides in accordance with international treaties and conventions in force, international custom, the general principles of law and, as subsidiary means, judicial decisions and the teachings of the most highly qualified international law experts.

Judges

The Court is composed of 15 judges elected for a nine-year term by the General Assembly and the Security Council, voting independently. Five posts are renewed every three years and judges can be re-elected for further terms of nine years. The members of the Court must each be from a different country. They do not represent their countries: they are independent magistrates. The composition of the Court has also to reflect the main forms of civilization and the principal legal systems of the world. For a number of years, the composition of the Court has maintained the following geographical balance, corresponding to the current membership of the Security Council: five seats on the bench are occupied by judges from Western Europe and other western countries; three judges are from Africa; three are from Asia; two are from Eastern Europe and two are from Latin America. Although no country is entitled to a seat, there has always been one judge from each of the five permanent members of the Security Council. If, in a particular case, the Court does not have a judge of the nationality of each of the states parties to the case, those States can each appoint what is called an ad hoc judge. Such judges have the same rights and duties as elected judges.

Budget

The annual budget of the ICJ is adopted by the General Assembly. For the biennium 2012–2013, it amounted to some $23.9 million annually.

President: Judge Peter Tomka (Slovakia)
Registrar: Philippe Couvreur (Belgium)
Headquarters: Peace Palace, Carnegieplein 2, 2517 KJ The Hague, The Netherlands
Tel.: (31) 70 302 23 23; Fax: (31) 70 364 99 28

Trusteeship Council

The Trusteeship Council (*www.un.org/en/mainbodies/trusteeship*) was originally established by the *Charter* to provide international supervision for 11 Trust Territories placed under the administration of seven member states, and to ensure that adequate steps were taken to prepare the Territories for self-government or independence. It carried out this work for forty-nine years. By a 1994 resolution, the Council amended its rules of procedure to drop the obligation to meet annually and agreed to meet as occasion required—by its decision or the decision of its President, or at the request of a majority of its members or the General Assembly or the Security Council. Subsequently, on 1 November 1994, the Trusteeship Council suspended operation following the independence of Palau, the last remaining UN Trust Territory, on 1 October of that year.

Secretariat

The **UN Secretariat** (*www.un.org/en/mainbodies/secretariat*)—consisting of staff representing all nationalities working in duty stations around the world—carries out the diverse day-to-day work of the Organization. Calling upon some 42,900 staff members worldwide, the Secretariat services the other principal organs of the United Nations and administers the programmes and policies established by them. At its head is the Secretary-General, who is appointed by the General Assembly on the recommendation of the Security Council for a renewable five-year term.

The United Nations, although headquartered in New York, maintains a significant presence in Addis Ababa, Bangkok, Beirut, Geneva, Nairobi, Santiago de Chile and Vienna, and has other offices around the globe. The United Nations Office at Geneva (UNOG) (*www.unog.ch*) is a centre for conference diplomacy and a forum for disarmament and human rights. The United Nations Office at Vienna (UNOV) (*www. unvienna.org*) is the headquarters for activities in the fields of international drug-abuse control, crime prevention and criminal justice, the peaceful uses of outer space and international trade law. The United Nations Office at Nairobi (UNON) (*www.unon.org*) is the headquarters for activities in the fields of environment and human settlements.

The duties carried out by the Secretariat are as wide-ranging and varied as the manifold concerns and activities of the United Nations itself. These extend from administering peacekeeping operations, mediating international disputes and organizing humanitarian relief programmes to surveying economic and social trends, preparing studies on human rights and sustainable development, and laying the groundwork for international agreements. Secretariat staff also inform the world—the media, governments, NGOs, research and academic networks and the general public—about the work of the United Nations. They organize international conferences on issues of global significance; interpret speeches and translate documents into the Organization's official languages; and establish clearing-houses of information, making possible international collaboration in all areas of science and technology, as well as cultural, economic and social activities.

As international civil servants, staff members and the Secretary-General answer to the United Nations alone for their activities, not to any member state or other organization, even as they serve the community of nations. They pledge not to seek or receive instructions from any government or outside authority. In turn, under the *Charter*, each member state undertakes to respect the exclusively international character of the responsibilities of the Secretary-General and staff members, and to refrain from seeking to influence them improperly.

Secretary-General

The Executive Office of the Secretary-General, comprising the Secretary-General and his senior advisers, establishes general policies and provides overall guidance to the Organization. Equal parts diplomat and advocate, civil servant and chief executive officer, the Secretary-General (*www.un.org/sg*) is a symbol of UN ideals and a spokesperson for the interests of the world's peoples, above all the poor and vulnerable.

Under the *Charter of the United Nations*, the Secretary-General is appointed for a five-year term-of-office by the General Assembly upon the recommendation of the Security Council. The eighth Secretary-General, Ban Ki-moon of the Republic of Korea, first took office in 2007 and began his second five-year term in 2012. Ban Ki-moon's predecessors were: Kofi A. Annan (Ghana), January 1997 to December 2006; Boutros Boutros-Ghali (Egypt), January 1992 to December 1996; Javier Pérez de Cuéllar (Peru), January 1982 to December 1991; Kurt Waldheim (Austria), January 1972 to December 1981; U Thant (Burma, now Myanmar), November 1961, when he was appointed acting Secretary-General (he was formally appointed Secretary-General in November 1962) to December 1971; Dag Hammarskjöld (Sweden), who served from April 1953 until his death in a plane crash on mission in Africa in September 1961—the only Secretary-General to die in office; and Trygve Lie (Norway), the first Secretary-General, who held office from February 1946.

The *Charter* describes the Secretary-General as "chief administrative officer" of the Organization, who acts in that capacity and performs such other functions as are entrusted to him or her by the Security Council, General Assembly, Economic and Social Council and other UN organs. The *Charter* also empowers the Secretary-General to bring to the attention of the Security Council any matter which might threaten the maintenance of international peace and security. These guidelines both define the functions and powers of the office and grant it considerable leeway for action. The Secretary-General must take account of the needs and concerns of individual member states while upholding the values and moral authority of the United Nations, and speaking and acting independently for peace—even at the risk of disagreeing with or challenging those same member states. He maintains this careful balance each day, acknowledging the perspective of individual member states as he searches for solutions to global problems. The Secretary-General's travels allow him to meet citizens of member states and witness first-hand how issues occupying the international agenda concretely affect the lives of people everywhere.

The Secretary-General issues an annual report on the work of the Organization that appraises its activities and outlines future priorities. One of the most vital roles played by the Secretary-General, however, is the use of his good offices—steps taken publicly and in private, drawing upon his independence, impartiality and integrity—to prevent international disputes from arising, escalating or spreading.

Secretary-General Ban Ki-moon visits with Syrian refugees at a camp in the Turkish border town of Islahiye. (7 December 2012, UN Photo/Mark Garten)

Over the years, the good offices of the Secretary-General, including the work of his special and personal representatives and envoys, have proven beneficial in a wide range of situations, including those involving Cyprus, East Timor, Iraq, Libya, the Middle East, Nigeria and Western Sahara.

Each Secretary-General defines his role within the context of his particular time in office. Ban Ki-moon's first-term priorities included climate change; disarmament; combating the global financial crisis and poverty; health; peace and security; women's rights and empowerment; protecting all the world's peoples from genocide, war crimes, ethnic cleansing and crimes against humanity; and UN reform. The priorities for his second term, which he termed "generational imperatives and opportunities", are promoting sustainable development; prevention, as it relates to natural disaster risk, armed conflict, human rights abuses and the effects of economic shocks; building a safer and more secure world; supporting nations in transition; and working with and for women and young people. With demands for UN peacekeeping having grown at an unprecedented rate in recent years, the Secretary-General proposed at the beginning of his first term basic structural reforms to enable the Organization to keep pace. In response, the General Assembly approved the creation of a Department of Field Support to take over the day-to-day management of peacekeeping operations, leaving the Department of Peacekeeping Operations free to focus on overall strategy, planning and deployment. The Secretary-General's UNiTE to End Violence against Women campaign aims to prevent and eliminate violence against women and girls in all parts of the world. He also created the United Nations Office for Disarmament Affairs and appointed a High Representative for Disarmament Affairs.

The Secretary-General's actions build on earlier efforts aimed at helping the UN adapt to a new era in global affairs. For example, the Global Compact, launched in July 2000, is a network-based initiative that brings private corporations together with UN agencies, governments, labour and non-governmental organizations to advance universally recognized principles in the areas of human rights, labour, the struggle against corruption and the environment. Since its establishment, the initiative has grown to over 10,000 participants, including more than 7,000 businesses, as well as international and national labour groups and hundreds of civil society organizations in 145 countries, mostly in the developing world.

Since 1998, distinguished individuals have been appointed by successive Secretaries-General to serve as **United Nations Messengers of Peace** (*www. un.org/sg/mop*) for an initial period of two years. These prominent personalities— carefully selected from the fields of art, literature, music and sports—volunteer their time, talent and passion to help focus worldwide attention on the work of the UN. The 11 current Messengers of Peace are: Princess Haya Bint Al Hussein, Daniel Barenboim, George Clooney, Paolo Coelho, Michael Douglas, Jane Goodall, Midori Goto, Yo-Yo-Ma, Charlize Theron, Elie Wiesel and Stevie Wonder. In 2010, Edward Norton was appointed United Nations Goodwill Ambassador for Biodiversity, the first Goodwill Ambassador appointed by the Secretary-General. Some 200 other Goodwill Ambassadors support the ideals and objectives of UN system agencies, funds, offices and programmes.

Deputy Secretary-General. Louise Fréchette of Canada was appointed as the first Deputy Secretary-General in 1998. She was succeeded in 2006 by Mark Malloch Brown of the United Kingdom; in 2007 by Asha-Rose Migiro of Tanzania; and in 2012 by Jan Eliasson of Sweden.

Departments and Offices

Department of Economic and Social Affairs (DESA)
Under-Secretary-General: Wu Hongbo (China)

- The mission of the Department of Economic and Social Affairs (*www.un.org/en/ development/desa*) is to promote development for all. DESA's work is far-reaching, covering such issues as poverty reduction, population, gender equality and indigenous rights, macroeconomic policy, development finance, public sector innovation, forest policy, climate change and sustainable development.

To this end, DESA

- analyses, generates and compiles a wide range of data and information on development issues;
- brings together the international community at conferences and summits to address economic and social challenges;
- supports the formulation of development policies, global standards and norms;
- monitors and supports the implementation of international agreements; and
- assists states in meeting their development challenges through a variety of capacity-development initiatives.

In carrying out its work, DESA engages with a variety of stakeholders around the world, NGOs, civil society, the private sector, research and academic organizations and intergovernmental organizations, as well as partner organizations in the United Nations system.

Department of Field Support (DFS)
Under-Secretary-General: Ameerah Haq (Bangladesh)

The Department of Field Support (*www.un.org/en/peacekeeping/about/dfs*) deals with matters of finance; logistics; information and communication technology; and human resources and general administration to help missions promote peace and security. Supporting field missions requires the provision of rations to feed troops, air transport to move people around in places where there are often few or no roads or infrastructure, and well-trained staff with the full range of skills required to deliver on Security Council mandates. To do this, DFS liaises with member states and commercial partners. In order to help ensure unity of command in UN peacekeeping, the head of the Department, in a unique structure, reports to and receives direction from the Under-Secretary-General for Peacekeeping Operations.

Department for General Assembly and Conference Management (DGACM)
Acting Head: Jean-Jacques Graisse (Belgium)

The Department for General Assembly and Conference Management (*www. un.org/depts/DGACM*) provides technical and secretariat support services to the General Assembly, the Security Council, the Economic and Social Council, and their committees and other subsidiary bodies, as well as to conferences held away from UN Headquarters. It is responsible for processing and issuing at Headquarters all official documents in the official languages of the Organization, and providing interpretation services for these languages to intergovernmental meetings. In addition, it produces the official records of the United Nations, including summary and verbatim records of meetings. Responsible for UN conference-management policies, the Under-Secretary-General for DGACM advises the President of the General Assembly on all matters relating to the work of the General Assembly.

Department of Management (DM)
Under-Secretary-General: Yukio Takasu (Japan)

The Department of Management (*www.un.org/en/hq/dm*) provides strategic policy guidance and support to all entities of the Secretariat in three management areas: finance, human resources and support services. These fall under the purview of the Offices of Programme Planning, Budget and Accounts; Human Resources Management; and Central Support Services, respectively. DM is responsible for formulating and implementing improved management policies in the Secretariat; the management and training of staff; and programme planning, budgetary, financial and human resources management along with technological innovations. It also provides technical servicing for the General Assembly's Fifth (Administrative and Budgetary) Committee, as well as servicing for the Committee for Programme and Coordination. The head of the Department provides policy guidance, coordination and direction for the preparation of UN budgets; represents the Secretary-General on matters relating to management; monitors emerging management issues; and ensures the efficient implementation of the Organization's internal system of justice.

Department of Political Affairs (DPA)
Under-Secretary-General: Jeffrey Feltman (United States)

The Department of Political Affairs (*www.un.org/depts/dpa*) plays a central role in the efforts of the United Nations to prevent and resolve conflict around the world and to consolidate peace in the aftermath of war. To that end, DPA

- monitors, analyses and assesses political developments throughout the world;
- identifies potential or actual conflicts in whose control and resolution the United Nations could play a useful role;
- recommends to the Secretary-General appropriate action in such cases and executes the approved policy;
- assists the Secretary-General in carrying out political activities decided by him, the General Assembly and the Security Council in the areas of preventive diplomacy, peacemaking, peacekeeping and peacebuilding;
- advises the Secretary-General on requests for electoral assistance received from member states and coordinates programmes established in response to such requests;
- advises and supports the Secretary-General in the political aspects of his relations with member states; and
- services the Security Council and its subsidiary bodies, as well as the Committee on the Exercise of the Inalienable Rights of the Palestinian People and the Special Committee of 24 on Decolonization.

The head of the Department also undertakes consultations and negotiations relating to peaceful settlement of disputes, and is the focal point for UN electoral assistance activities.

Department of Public Information (DPI)
Under-Secretary-General: Peter Launsky-Tieffenthal (Austria)

The Department of Public Information is dedicated to communicating the ideals and work of the United Nations to the world; interacting and partnering with diverse audiences; and building support for peace, development, and human rights. It pursues these ends through news services, radio and television programmes, press releases, publications, informational videos, outreach programmes, and information campaigns. DPI engages prominent personalities as UN Messengers of Peace and organizes exhibits, concerts, seminars and other events to mark occasions of international importance. It also provides library and knowledge-sharing services. In addition to its staff at UN Headquarters, DPI has 63 UN information centres, or UNICs, worldwide (*http://unic.un.org*) and a regional information centre (UNRIC) in Brussels (*www.unric.un.org*).

The Department consists of three divisions. Its Strategic Communications Division develops communication strategies and campaigns to promote United Nations priorities. The News and Media Division produces and distributes UN news and information to the media, including daily press briefings and statements by the Office of the Spokesperson for the Secretary-General, the UN websites, radio broadcasts and live TV feeds. The Outreach Division, which includes the Dag Hammarskjöld Library, publishes books—notably the *Yearbook of the United Nations*—and periodicals such as the *UN Chronicle* and *Africa Renewal*; works with NGOs and educational institutions; organizes special events and exhibitions on priority issues; and offers an annual training programme for journalists from developing countries. It also develops partnerships with the private and public sector to advance UN goals.

Department of Peacekeeping Operations (DPKO)
Under-Secretary-General: Hervé Ladsous (France)

The Department of Peacekeeping Operations (*www.un.org/en/peacekeeping*) is responsible for assisting member states and the Secretary-General in their efforts to maintain, achieve and sustain international peace and security. It does this by planning, preparing and conducting United Nations peacekeeping operations, in accordance with mandates provided by member states.

To this end, DPKO

- undertakes contingency planning for possible new peacekeeping operations;
- secures, through negotiations with member states, the civilian, military and police personnel and equipment and services required to accomplish the mandate;
- provides political and executive guidance, direction and support to peacekeeping operations;
- maintains contact with parties to conflicts and with members of the Security Council on the implementation of Council resolutions;
- manages integrated operational teams to direct and supervise all peacekeeping operations;
- advises the Security Council and member states on key peacekeeping issues, including security sector reform, the rule of law, and the disarmament, demobilization and reintegration of former combatants;

- analyses emerging policy questions and best practices related to peacekeeping, and formulates policies, procedures and general peacekeeping doctrine;
- coordinates all UN activities related to landmines, and develops and supports mine-action programmes in peacekeeping and emergency situations.

The head of the Department directs peacekeeping operations on behalf of the Secretary-General; formulates policies and guidelines for operations; and advises the Secretary-General on all matters relating to peacekeeping and mine action.

Department of Safety and Security (DSS)
Under-Secretary-General: Gregory B. Starr (United States)

The Department of Safety and Security (*http://dss.un.org/public*) provides leadership, operational support and oversight of the security management system for the United Nations, ensuring maximum security for staff and their dependants as well as enabling the safest and most efficient conduct of its programmes and activities throughout the world. Responsible for the safety of UN staff and consultants around the world, DSS was established by the General Assembly in 2005 to meet the need for a unified and strengthened security management system.

Office for the Coordination of Humanitarian Affairs (OCHA)
Under-Secretary-General for Humanitarian Affairs and Emergency Relief Coordinator: Valerie Amos (United Kingdom)

The Office for the Coordination of Humanitarian Affairs (*www.unocha.org*) mobilizes and coordinates humanitarian action in partnership with national and international actors to alleviate human suffering in disasters and emergencies. Through its network of field offices, humanitarian coordinators and country teams, OCHA works to ensure the coherence of relief efforts. It supports the efforts of its humanitarian coordinators and of UN agencies that deliver assistance through needs assessments, contingency planning and the formulation of humanitarian programmes. OCHA also advocates for the rights of people in need (notably with political organs such as the Security Council), promotes preparedness and prevention as well as policy development, and facilitates the implementation of sustainable solutions to humanitarian problems.

The Emergency Relief Coordinator chairs the Inter-Agency Standing Committee, an umbrella organization that comprises all major humanitarian actors— including the Red Cross and Red Crescent Movement and consortia of other NGOs. By developing common policies, guidelines and standards, the Committee ensures a coherent interagency response to complex emergencies and natural and environmental disasters.

Office of the United Nations High Commissioner for Human Rights (OHCHR)
High Commissioner: Navanethem Pillay (South Africa)

The United Nations High Commissioner for Human Rights is the official with principal responsibility for UN human rights activities and is charged with promoting and protecting civil, cultural, economic, political and social rights for all. The Office of the High Commissioner for Human Rights (*www.ohchr.org*) prepares reports and undertakes research at the request of the General Assembly and other policymaking bodies. It cooperates with governments, international and regional organizations, and NGOs. It acts as the secretariat for the meetings of UN human rights bodies. OHCHR's estimated 2012–2013 budget requirement was $448.1 million—$156.5 million from the UN regular budget and $291.6 million from voluntary contributions. OHCHR, with some 1,069 staff as at 31 December 2012, is organized into four divisions:

- The Human Rights Treaties Division supports 10 human rights treaty bodies, the UN Voluntary Fund for Victims of Torture, the UN Voluntary Fund on Contemporary Forms of Slavery, and the Optional Protocol to the Convention against Torture Special Fund. It assists in the preparation and submission of documents and grants for review by these independent expert bodies and funds; processes communications submitted to them under optional procedures; follows up on recommendations and decisions taken at treaty-body meetings; and helps build national capacities to implement recommendations. It also supports field visits by one of the treaty bodies, the Subcommittee on Prevention of Torture.

- The Human Rights Council and Special Procedures Division supports the Human Rights Council, the Council's Universal Periodic Review process and its fact-finding and investigatory mechanisms—including special rapporteurs, and thematic working groups—with a view to documenting human rights violations worldwide, enhancing the protection of victims, and promoting their rights.

- The Research and Right to Development Division is mandated to integrate human rights into the work of the UN system, contribute to the realization of the right to development and increase knowledge and understanding of human rights. It supports certain Human Rights Council mandates, including the Working Group on the Right to Development.

- As the operational division of OHCHR, the Field Operations and Technical Cooperation Division supports the work of human rights field presences and leads OHCHR's dialogue and activities undertaken at the national, regional and subregional levels on human rights issues. Together with the other parts of OHCHR and in close collaboration with UN partners, government actors, national human rights institutions and civil society organizations, the Division supports implementation efforts on the ground.

Office of Internal Oversight Services (OIOS)
Under-Secretary-General: Carman Lapointe-Young (Canada)

The Office of Internal Oversight Services (*www.un.org/depts/oios*) provides independent, professional and timely internal audit, monitoring, inspection, evaluation and investigation services. It promotes responsible administration of resources, a culture of accountability and transparency, and improved programme performance. OIOS assists the Organization and member states in protecting UN assets and ensuring the compliance of programme activities with regulations, rules and policies, as well as the more efficient and effective delivery of UN activities; and detecting fraud, waste, abuse, malfeasance or mismanagement. The Under-Secretary-General is appointed by the Secretary-General and approved by the General Assembly for one five-year term without possibility of renewal.

Office of Legal Affairs (OLA)
Under-Secretary-General: Patricia O'Brien (Ireland)

The Office of Legal Affairs (*http://legal.un.org/ola*) is the central legal service of the Organization. It also contributes to the progressive development and codification of international public and trade law. Among its chief responsbilities, OLA

- provides legal advice to the Secretary-General, Secretariat departments and offices and principal and subsidiary organs of the United Nations in the field of public and private international law;
- performs substantive and secretariat functions for legal organs involved in public international law, the law of the sea and international trade law; and
- carries out the functions conferred on the Secretary-General as depositary of multilateral treaties.

  OLA also
- deals with legal questions relating to international peace and security; the status, privileges and immunities of the United Nations; and the credentials and representations of member states;
- prepares drafts of international conventions, agreements, rules of procedure of United Nations organs and conferences, and other legal instruments; and
- provides legal services and advice on issues of international private and administrative law, and on UN resolutions and regulations.

Office of the Special Adviser on Africa (OSAA)
Under-Secretary-General and Special Adviser: Maged Abdelfatah Abdelaziz (Egypt)

The Office of the Special Adviser on Africa (*www.un.org/africa/osaa*) was established in 2003. OSAA enhances international support for Africa's development and security through its advocacy and analytical work; assists the Secretary-General in improving coherence and coordination of UN system support to Africa; and facilitates intergovernmental deliberations on Africa at the global level, in particular relating to the New Partnership for Africa's Development (NEPAD). OSAA takes the lead in the preparation of Africa-related reports and inputs on NEPAD. The Office also convenes an interdepartmental Task Force on African Affairs to improve coherence in UN support to Africa.

Office of the Special Representative of the Secretary-General for Children and Armed Conflict (SRSG/CAAC)
Special Representative: Leila Zerrougui (Algeria)

The Office of the Special Representative for Children and Armed Conflict (*www.un.org/children/conflict*) promotes and protects the rights of all children affected by armed conflict. The Special Representative serves as a moral voice and independent advocate for the protection and well-being of boys and girls affected by armed conflict; works with partners to propose ideas and approaches that enhance protection; advocates, raises awareness and gives prominence to issues of rights and protection; and undertakes humanitarian and diplomatic initiatives to facilitate the work of those acting on the ground for the sake of children in armed conflict.

Office of the High Representative for the Least Developed Countries, Landlocked Developing Countries and Small Island Developing States (UN-OHRLLS)
Under-Secretary-General and High Representative for the Least Developed Countries, Landlocked Developing Countries and Small Island Developing States:
Gyan Chandra Acharya (Nepal)

UN-OHRLLS (*www.un.org/ohrlls*) was established by the General Assembly in 2001 to help mobilize international support for implementation of the *Brussels Declaration* and Programme of Action for the Least Developed Countries for the Decade 2001–2010. It assists the Secretary-General in coordinating support for implementation of the Brussels Programme of Action and related international commitments. The Office also works to ensure implementation of the 1994 Barbados Programme of Action for the Sustainable Development of Small Island Developing States and the 2005 Mauritius Strategy for carrying out the Barbados Programme. The Office facilitates coordination within the UN system with regard to these programmes and supports the Economic and Social Council and the General Assembly in assessing progress made. It also promotes global awareness of issues affecting these countries in partnership with UN bodies, civil society, the media, academia and foundations.

Office for Disarmament Affairs (UNODA)
High Representative for Disarmament: Angela Kane (Germany)

The Office for Disarmament Affairs (*www.un.org/disarmament*) works towards nuclear disarmament and non-proliferation along with the strengthening of disarmament regimes with respect to other weapons of mass destruction, including chemical and biological weapons. UNODA also promotes disarmament in the area of conventional weapons, especially action against illicit trade in small arms— weapons of choice in many contemporary conflicts. Its purview includes:

• arms collection and stockpile management programmes;
• transparency in military matters, including the UN Register of Conventional Arms and standardized reporting on military expenditures;
• the disarmament and demobilization of former combatants and their reintegration into civil society; and
• restrictions on and eventual disarmament of anti-personnel landmines.

UNODA provides substantive and organizational support for norm-setting in disarmament through the work of the General Assembly and its First Committee, the Disarmament Commission, the Conference on Disarmament and other bodies. It encourages regional disarmament efforts, including nuclear-weapon-free zones and regional and subregional transparency regimes. UNODA also supports educational initiatives on UN disarmament efforts.

Budget

The regular budget of the United Nations is approved by the General Assembly for a two-year period. The budget is initially submitted by the Secretary-General and then reviewed by the Advisory Committee on Administrative and Budgetary Questions. The Advisory Committee consists of 16 experts, nominated by their governments and elected by the General Assembly, who serve in their personal capacity. Programmatic aspects of the budget are reviewed by the Committee for Programme and Coordination, which is made up of 34 experts who are elected by the General Assembly and represent the views of their governments. The budget reflects the main priorities of the Organization, as set out in its strategic framework for each biennium. During the biennium, the approved budget can be adjusted by the General Assembly to reflect changing circumstances.

The main source of funds for the budget lies in the contributions of member states. These are assessed on a scale approved by the General Assembly on the recommendation of the Committee on Contributions, made up of 18 experts serving in their personal capacity and selected by the Assembly on the recommendation of its Fifth (Administrative and Budgetary) Committee. The scale is based on the capacity of countries to pay. This is determined by considering their relative shares of total gross national product, adjusted to take into account a number of factors, including per capita income. The Committee reviews the scale every three years in light of the latest national income statistics in order to ensure that assessments are fair and accurate. There is a fixed maximum of 22 per cent of the budget for any one contributor.

Budget of the United Nations for the biennium 2012–2013

Main categories of expenditure	US dollars
1. Overall policymaking, direction and coordination	721,788,300
2. Political affairs	1,333,849,300
3. International justice and law	93,155,100
4. International cooperation for development	436,635,700
5. Regional cooperation for development	532,892,300
6. Human rights and humanitarian affairs	326,574,200
7. Public information	179,092,100
8. Common support services	600,210,000
9. Internal oversight	38,254,200
10. Jointly financed administrative activities and special expenses	131,219,100
11. Capital expenditures	64,886,900
12. Safety and security	213,412,400
13. Development account	29,243,200
14. Staff assessment	451,086,800
TOTAL	**5,152,299,600**

The regular budget approved for the biennium 2012–2013 amounts to $5.152 billion, including provision for special political missions expected to be extended or approved during the course of the biennium. The budget for such missions—mandated by the Security Council and/or the General Assembly—stood at $499.7 million in 2012–2013. The budget also covers the costs of UN programmes in areas such as development, public information, human rights and humanitarian affairs. The regular budget does not cover peacekeeping operations or international tribunals, which have their own separate budgets. Member states are also separately assessed for the costs of the international tribunals and peacekeeping operations.

The financial position of the regular budget of the Organization on 5 October 2012 was generally sound. Unpaid assessed contributions amounted to $855 million, $12 million lower than in the previous year. The 2012–2103 budget entailed a decrease of .08 per cent against the appropriations for 2010–2011.

Global approved peacekeeping resources stood at $7.3 billion in 2012–2013. The UN mission in the Democratic Republic of the Congo and the hybrid United Nations-African Union mission in Darfur together account for $2.7 billion—nearly 37 per cent—of the 2012–2013 peacekeeping budget. (Noteworthy is the fact that the total amount spent on UN peacekeeping annually represents less than one half of 1 per cent of world military spending, estimated at more than $1.7 trillion in 2012.)

Peacekeeping budgets are approved by the General Assembly for a one-year period beginning on 1 July. The Assembly apportions the costs based on a special scale of assessment applicable to peacekeeping. This scale takes into account the relative economic wealth of member states, with the permanent members of the Security Council paying a larger share because of their special responsibility for the maintenance of international peace and security. Non-payment of assessed contributions delays reimbursements to those member states that contribute troops, equipment and logistical support. Outstanding assessed contributions for peacekeeping operations in October 2012 totalled $1.85 billion. That same month, assessed contributions in the amount of $63 million were outstanding for the international tribunals, as was $4.6 million under the special account for the capital master plan for the renovation of UN Headquarters.

United Nations programmes, funds and offices—among them the United Nations Children's Fund (UNICEF), the United Nations High Commissioner for Refugees (UNHCR) and the United Nations Development Programme (UNDP)—have separate budgets as well. The bulk of their resources is provided by governments on a voluntary basis, but a portion also comes from individuals and institutions. Specialized agencies of the United Nations—like UNESCO and WHO—also have separate budgets supplemented through voluntary state contributions.

UN system

The United Nations system (*www.unsystem.org*) consists of the UN family of organizations. It includes the Secretariat, the United Nations programmes and funds, the specialized agencies and other related organizations. The programmes, funds and offices are subsidiary bodies of the General Assembly. The specialized agencies are linked to the United Nations through individual agreements and report to the Economic and Social Council and/or the Assembly. Related organizations—including IAEA and the World Trade Organization—have their own legislative bodies and budgets. Together, the members of the UN system address all areas of cultural, economic, scientific and social endeavour.

The **United Nations System Chief Executives Board for Coordination (CEB)** (*www.unsystemceb.org*) is the UN system's highest coordinating mechanism. Chaired by the Secretary-General, its members are the leaders of the main parts of the UN system. CEB aims to coordinate UN action in the pursuit of the common goals of member states. It meets twice a year, and is supported in its work by the High-Level Committee on Programmes, the High-Level Committee on Management and the UN Development Group. Its 29 members include the United Nations, FAO, IAEA, ICAO, IFAD, ILO, IMF, IMO, ITU, UNCTAD, UNDP, UNEP, UNESCO, UNFPA, UN-HABITAT, UNHCR, UNICEF, UNIDO, UNODC, UNRWA, UN-Women, UNWTO, UPU, WFP, WHO, WIPO, WMO, World Bank and WTO.

The UN and the Nobel Peace Prize (*www.un.org/aboutun/nobelprize/index.shtml*). The United Nations family and its associates have been awarded the Nobel Peace Prize numerous times in recognition of their contributions to the cause of world peace. UN-related Nobel Peace Prize laureates since the establishment of the Organization include:

- Cordell Hull—United States Secretary of State instrumental in establishing the United Nations (1945);
- John Boyd Orr—founding Director-General of the Food and Agriculture Organization of the United Nations (1949);
- Ralph Bunche—UN Trusteeship Director and principal secretary of the UN Palestine Commission, leader of mediation efforts in the Middle East (1950);
- Léon Jouhaux—a founder of the International Labour Organization (1951);
- Office of the United Nations High Commissioner for Refugees (1954);
- Lester Bowles Pearson—General Assembly President in 1952 honoured for trying to end the Suez conflict and solve the Middle East question through the UN (1957);
- Secretary-General Dag Hammarskjöld—one of only two posthumous awards (1961);
- United Nations Children's Fund (1965);
- International Labour Organization (1969);
- Sean MacBride—UN Commissioner for Namibia and promoter of human rights (1974);
- Office of the United Nations High Commissioner for Refugees (1981);
- United Nations Peacekeeping Forces (1988);
- United Nations and Secretary-General Kofi A. Annan (2001);
- International Atomic Energy Agency and its Director-General Mohamed ElBaradei (2005);
- Intergovernmental Panel on Climate Change and former United States Vice President Albert Arnold (Al) Gore, Jr. (2007).

This list does not include the many Nobel laureates who have worked closely with the United Nations or at common purpose with it in making their contribution to peace.

Programmes and funds, research and training institutes, and other entities

United Nations Conference on Trade and Development (UNCTAD)

Established in 1964 as a permanent intergovernmental body and subsidiary of the General Assembly, the Geneva-based United Nations Conference on Trade and Development (*www.unctad.org*) is the UN focal point for the integrated treatment of trade and development and related issues of finance, investment, technology and sustainable development. UNCTAD's main goal is to help developing countries and transition economies use trade and investment as an engine for development, poverty reduction and integration into the world economy. It works in three main areas: research and analysis; consensus-building through intergovernmental deliberations; and technical cooperation projects carried out with various partners. It also contributes to international debate on emerging issues related to developing countries and the world economy through major reports, policy briefs and contributions to international meetings.

UNCTAD's highest decision-making body is its ministerial conference, at which the organization's 194 member states debate international economic issues and set UNCTAD's mandate. The theme of the thirteenth conference in 2012 (UNCTAD XIII) was "Development-centred globalization: Towards inclusive and sustainable growth and development". UNCTAD has 400 staff members and an annual regular budget of approximately $681 million. Its technical cooperation activities, financed from extra-budgetary resources, amount to more than $39 million, with some 260 technical assistance projects ongoing in more than 100 countries. UNCTAD's main publications are: the *Trade and Development Report, World Investment Report, Economic Development in Africa Report, Least Developed Countries Report, UNCTAD Handbook of Statistics, Information Economy Report,* and *Review of Maritime Transport.*

Secretary-General: Supachai Panitchpakdi (Thailand)
Headquarters: Palais des Nations, CH-1211 Geneva 10, Switzerland
Tel.: (41 22) 917 1234; Fax: (41 22) 917 0057; E-mail: *info@unctad.org*

International Trade Centre (ITC)

The International Trade Centre (*www.intracen.org*) is the joint agency of the World Trade Organization and the United Nations. As the development partner for small business export success, ITC helps developing and transition countries achieve sustainable development through exports. ITC has two mutually reinforcing functions. Affiliation with WTO vests ITC with the role of helping its clients benefit from the opportunities created by the WTO framework. As a UN development organization, ITC's role is to promote the fulfilment of the Millennium Development Goals. The organization's priority is to meet the needs of some 101 countries categorized as least developed countries, landlocked developing countries, and small island developing states, as well as sub-Saharan Africa.

The ITC budget has two parts: the regular budget, which is provided equally by WTO and UNCTAD; and extrabudgetary funds, which are provided by donors as voluntary contributions. At the end of 2012, the ITC regular budget expenditure was about $41.1 million and its gross extrabudgetary expenditure was $39.8 million. ITC has a headquarters staff of around 260, as well as some 700 consultants and individual contractors providing technical expertise.

Executive Director: Arancha González (Spain)
Headquarters: Palais des Nations, CH-1211 Geneva 10, Switzerland
Tel.: (41 22) 730 0111; Fax: (41 22) 733 4439; E-mail: *itcreg@intracen.org*

United Nations Development Programme (UNDP)

The United Nations Development Programme (*www.undp.org*) leads the UN's global development network. With activities in more than 160 countries, UNDP works throughout the developing world helping countries achieve their development goals. Its mandate is to work with countries to reduce poverty, promote democratic governance, prevent and recover from crises, protect the environment and combat climate change. The UNDP network seeks to ensure that developing countries have access to resources and knowledge to meet the Millennium Development Goals.

UNDP is governed by a 36-member Executive Board representing both developing and developed countries. Its flagship publication is the annual *Human Development Report*, which focuses on key development issues and provides measurement tools, innovative analysis and policy proposals. The Programme is funded entirely by voluntary contributions from member states; its annual budget is approximately $5 billion.

Administrator: Helen Clark (New Zealand)
Headquarters: 1 UN Plaza, New York, NY 10017, USA
Tel.: (1 212) 906 5000; Fax: (1 212) 906 5364

United Nations Volunteers (UNV)

The United Nations Volunteers programme (*www.unv.org*) is the UN organization that promotes volunteerism to support peace and development worldwide. To that end, it advocates for volunteerism globally, encouraging partners to integrate volunteerism into development programming. UNV mobilizes some 7,000 volunteers every year in over 130 countries. More than 80 per cent of UN Volunteers come from developing countries, and about 30 per cent volunteer in their own countries. Volunteers assist UN organizations in eradicating poverty and advancing progress towards the Millennium Development Goals. They support the delivery of basic services as well as efforts in the field of sustainable environment and climate change, crisis prevention and recovery, humanitarian assistance and peacebuilding. In addition, more than 10,000 online volunteers provide expertise and services to UN agencies, civil society organizations and local governments via the Internet.

Created by the General Assembly in 1970, UNV is administered by UNDP, reports to the UNDP/United Nations Population Fund (UNFPA) Executive Board and works through UNDP country offices. Its budget increased to $471 million in 2010–2011, compared to $427 million in the previous biennium. UNV funding comes from UNDP, partner agencies and contributions to the UNV Special Voluntary Fund.

Executive Coordinator: Richard Dictus (Netherlands)
Headquarters: Hermann-Ehlers-Str. 10, 53113 Bonn, Germany
Tel.: (49 228) 815 2000; Fax: (49 228) 815 2001; E-mail: *information@unv.org*

United Nations Capital Development Fund (UNCDF)

The United Nations Capital Development Fund (*www.uncdf.org*) is the UN's capital investment agency for the world's 49 least developed countries. It creates new opportunities for poor people and their businesses by increasing access to microfinance and investment capital. UNCDF focuses on Africa, with a special commitment to countries emerging from conflict or crisis. It provides seed capital (grants and loans) and technical support to help microfinance institutions reach more poor households and small businesses. It also helps local governments finance the capital investments—water systems, roads, schools, irrigation schemes—that improve the lives of the poor. Over 65 per cent of the clients of UNCDF-supported microfinance institutions are women. All UNCDF support is provided via national systems, in accordance with the 2005 *Paris Declaration* concerning aid. UNCDF programmes are designed to catalyze larger investment flows from the private sector, development partners and national governments. Established by the General Assembly in 1966 and headquartered in New York, UNCDF is an autonomous UN organization affiliated with UNDP. In 2012, total revenue of the Fund was approximately $57 million. UNCDF employs 150 staff.

Executive Secretary: Marc Bichler (Luxembourg)
Headquarters: 2 UN Plaza, New York, NY 10017, USA
Tel.: (1 212) 906 6565; Fax: (1 212) 906 6479; E-mail: *info@uncdf.org*

United Nations Environment Programme (UNEP)

Founded in 1972, the United Nations Environment Programme (*www.unep.org*) provides leadership and encourages partnerships in caring for the environment, enabling nations and peoples to improve their quality of life without compromising that of future generations. As the principal UN body in the field of the environment, UNEP sets the global environmental agenda, promotes implementation of the environmental dimension of sustainable development in the UN system, and serves as an authoritative advocate of the global environment.

During 2010–2013, UNEP is focused on six priorities:

*   climate change: strengthening the ability of countries—in particular developing countries—to integrate climate change responses into national development processes;
*   ecosystem management: ensuring that countries manage land, water and living resources holistically in a manner conducive to conservation and sustainable use;
*   environmental governance: ensuring that environmental governance and interactions at the country, regional and global levels are strengthened to address environmental priorities;
*   harmful substances and hazardous waste: minimizing their impact on the environment and people;
*   disasters and conflicts: minimizing threats to human well-being from the environmental causes and consequences of natural and man-made disasters; and
*   resource efficiency: ensuring that natural resources are produced, processed and consumed in a more environmentally sustainable way.

UNEP's mandate and focus are determined by its Governing Council, a body of 58 government representatives elected by the General Assembly taking into account equitable regional representation. As a result of a 2012 Assembly resolution, the Council now has universal membership. UNEP's 2012–2013 approved budget is $618.6 million, including $143 million in funding from the Global Environment Facility (GEF). UNEP's main voluntary funding mechanism is the Environment Fund. Additional funds are provided by the UN regular budget as well as those mobilized by UNEP in the form of trust funds and earmarked contributions. UNEP has a global staff of approximately 850.

Executive Director: Achim Steiner (Germany)
Headquarters: United Nations Avenue, Gigiri, P.O. Box 30552, 00100, Nairobi, Kenya
Tel.: (254 20) 762 1234; Fax: (254 20) 762 4489, 4490; E-mail: *unepinfo@unep.org*

United Nations Population Fund (UNFPA)

Established in 1969 at the initiative of the General Assembly, the United Nations Population Fund (*www.unfpa.org*) is the largest internationally funded source of population assistance to developing countries and those with economies in transition. It assists countries in improving reproductive health and family planning services on the basis of individual choice, as well as in formulating population policies for sustainable development. It is a subsidiary organ of the General Assembly and has the same Executive Board as UNDP. With headquarters in New York and a global network of 128 offices, UNFPA supports the development priorities of 156 countries, territories and areas, home to 83 per cent of the world's population. In 2012, the Fund's income totalled $962 million, including $438 million in voluntary contributions from governments and private donors. In 2011, UNFPA provided $158.5 million in assistance for reproductive health—including safe motherhood, family planning and sexual health—to refine approaches to adolescent reproductive health, reduce maternal disabilities such as obstetric fistula, address HIV/AIDS, and give assistance in emergencies. UNFPA also devoted $76 million to population and development strategies, and provided $41.8 million for gender equality and women's empowerment. UNFPA has decentralized its programmes to bring staff closer to the people it serves. At the end of 2012, UNFPA had a global staff of more than 2,300.

Executive Director: Babatunde Osotimehin (Nigeria)
Headquarters: 605 Third Avenue, New York, NY 10158, USA
Tel.: (1 212) 297 5000; Fax: (1 212) 370 0201; E-mail: *hq@unfpa.org*

United Nations Human Settlements Programme (UN-HABITAT)

The United Nations Human Settlements Programme (*www.unhabitat.org*), established in 1978, promotes sustainable human settlements development through advocacy, policy formulation, capacity-building, knowledge creation and the strengthening of partnerships between governments and civil society. UN-HABITAT is responsible for helping the world meet the Millennium Development Goal of improving the lives of at least 100 million slum dwellers by 2020, and reducing by half those without sustainable access to safe drinking water and basic sanitation. The Programme works in partnership with other agencies, governments, local authorities, NGOs and the private sector. Its technical programmes and projects focus on slum upgrading, urban poverty reduction, post-disaster reconstruction, the provision of urban water and sanitation and the mobilization of domestic financial resources for shelter delivery.

UN-HABITAT is governed by a 58-member Governing Council. Expenditures of $393.2 million were approved for 2012–2013, $347.2 million (88 per cent) of which being reserved for programme activities, with the remaining $46 million going for support activities and management functions. The Programme produces two flagship publications: the *Global Report on Human Settlements*, a complete review of human settlements conditions worldwide, and the *State of the World's Cities*.

Executive Director: Joan Clos (Spain)
Headquarters: P.O. Box 30030, GPO, Nairobi, 00100, Kenya
Tel.: (254 20) 762 3120; Fax: (254 20) 762 3477; E-mail: *infohabitat@unhabitat.org*

Office of the United Nations High Commissioner for Refugees (UNHCR)

The Office of the United Nations High Commissioner for Refugees (*www.unhcr. org*)—set up in 1951 to help more than 1 million people still uprooted after the Second World War—was initially given a three-year mandate later prolonged by successive five-year terms until 2003, when the General Assembly extended the mandate "until the refugee problem is solved". UNHCR provides international protection to refugees, guaranteeing respect for their basic human rights, including the ability to seek asylum, and to ensure that no person is returned involuntarily to a country where he or she has reason to fear persecution. It monitors government compliance with international law, and provides emergency and material assistance to those under its care, collaborating with many partners. It seeks long-term solutions for refugees through voluntary repatriation, integration in countries where they first sought asylum, or resettlement in third countries. By the end of 2011, UNHCR was looking after some 25.9 million people, including refugees, returnees, people displaced within their own countries, and stateless people.

At the start of 2012, there were 7,735 UNHCR staff members, including a combined total of 960 working at the Geneva headquarters and the Global Service Centre in Budapest, Hungary. About 85 per cent of UNHCR staff are field-based, working in more than 125 countries. UNHCR works within the UN inter-agency framework and cooperates with a wide range of external partners, including intergovernmental and voluntary organizations, as well as governments. Its Executive Committee is composed of 87 member states. UNHCR is funded almost entirely by voluntary contributions, with 93 per cent coming from governments and 4 per cent from intergovernmental organizations and pooled funding mechanisms, including the UN Central Emergency Response Fund. The remaining 3 per cent comes from the private sector. In addition, the Office receives a limited subsidy from the UN regular budget for administrative costs. UNHCR also accepts 'in-kind' contributions, including relief items such as tents, medicine, trucks and air transport. Its budget for 2012 was $3.59 billion.

High Commissioner: António Guterres (Portugal)
Headquarters: Case Postale 2500, 1211 Geneva 2, Switzerland
Tel.: (41 22) 739 8111; Fax: (41 22) 739 7377

United Nations Children's Fund (UNICEF)

The United Nations Children's Fund (*www.unicef.org*) was created by the General Assembly in 1946 to provide emergency food and health care to children in countries that had been ravaged by World War II. The Fund provides long-term humanitarian and developmental assistance to children and mothers in developing countries. It has evolved from an emergency fund to a development agency, committed to protecting the rights of every child to survival, protection and development. UNICEF works in partnership with governments, civil society and other international organizations to ensure that children are immunized, well nourished, have access to safe drinking water and adequate sanitation, and are protected from HIV and AIDS. It also promotes quality primary education for all girls and boys. UNICEF advocates for a protective environment for children, especially in emergencies, and advances efforts to prevent and respond to violence, exploitation and abuse. UNICEF is guided by the *Convention on the Rights of the Child,* ratified by 193 states parties.

UNICEF is governed by an Executive Board, composed of delegates from 36 UN member states. It has over 10,000 regular employees working in more than 150 countries and territories. The Fund is supported entirely by voluntary contributions; its programme expenditures in 2011 totalled $3.8 billion. Total income was $3.7 billion, coming mostly from governments (60 per cent in 2011).

UNICEF also receives considerable aid from the private sector and NGOs— $1.09 billion, including more than $2.8 million from regular donors who give through and from 36 National Committees. Its flagship publication, *The State of the World's Children*, appears annually.

Executive Director: Anthony Lake (United States)
Headquarters: UNICEF House, 3 United Nations Plaza, New York, NY 10017, USA
Tel.: (1 212) 326 7000; Fax: (1 212) 888 7465

United Nations Office on Drugs and Crime (UNODC)

Established in 1997, the United Nations Office on Drugs and Crime (*www.unodc. org*) is a global leader in the struggle against illicit drugs and transnational organized crime. It is committed to achieving health, security and justice for all, and to delivering legal and technical assistance to prevent terrorism. With its portfolios expanding through the strengthening of concerted international action to further the rule of law, its mission involves: research and analysis to produce authoritative reports; technical assistance to states in ratifying and implementing international treaties on drugs, crime and terrorism; developing domestic legislation consistent with these treaties; and training judicial officials. Other focus areas include prevention, treatment and reintegration, along with the creation of sustainable alternative livelihoods for drug-crop farmers. These measures aim at reducing incentives for illicit activities and addressing drug abuse, the spread of HIV/AIDS and drug-related crime.

UNODC has over 1,500 staff working through a network of more than 50 field and project offices, as well as liaison offices in New York and Brussels. In its two-year budget for 2010–2011, the General Assembly allocated $42.6 million to UNODC, which accounting for 9.1 per cent of total UNODC income. In 2010, voluntary contributions were pledged in the amount of $242.9 million. Overall voluntary funding for the two-year budget period 2010–2011 totalled $468.3 million.

Executive Director: Yury Fedotov (Russian Federation)
Headquarters: Vienna International Centre, Wagramerstrasse 5, P.O. Box 500,
    1400 Vienna, Austria
Tel.: (43 1) 26060; Fax: (43 1) 263 3389; E-mail: *info@unodc.org*

United Nations Relief and Works Agency for Palestine Refugees in the Near East (UNRWA)

The United Nations Relief and Works Agency for Palestine Refugees in the Near East (*www.unrwa.org*) was established by the General Assembly in 1949 to carry out relief work for Palestine refugees. It began operations in May 1950. In the absence of an agreed solution to the refugee problem, its mandate has been periodically renewed; it was most recently extended until 30 June 2014. The Agency is the main provider of basic services—education, health, relief and social welfare—to some 5 million registered Palestine refugees in the Middle East, including some 1.5 million in 58 refugee camps in Jordan, Lebanon and Syria, as well as the Gaza Strip and the West Bank, including East Jerusalem. It manages a microfinance programme and undertakes infrastructure works inside officially designated camp areas. UNRWA has been providing emergency humanitarian assistance to mitigate the effects of the ongoing crisis on the most vulnerable refugees in Gaza and the West Bank since

2000. It has also responded to the emergency needs of conflict-affected refugees in Lebanon since 2006. In response to the situation in Syria, the Agency has been providing emergency and regular services to refugees inside Syria as well as to those who have fled to Lebanon and Jordan.

UNRWA's operations are supported by its two headquarters in Gaza and Amman, Jordan. The Commissioner-General, who reports to the General Assembly, is assisted by a 25-member Advisory Commission composed of Australia, Belgium, Canada, Denmark, Egypt, Finland, France, Germany, Ireland, Italy, Japan, Jordan, Kuwait, Lebanon, Luxembourg, the Netherlands, Norway, Saudi Arabia, Spain, Sweden, Switzerland, Syria, Turkey, the United Kingdom and the United States. The European Union, the League of Arab States and Palestine are observers. UNRWA employs around 33,000 local staff and 146 international staff. UNRWA's 2012–2013 project budget amounted to $2 billion, including $681.2 million for projects. The Agency depends almost entirely on voluntary contributions from donor states; approximately 2.5 per cent of its current biennium budget requirements are met by the UN regular budget. Most voluntary contributions are in cash, but some are in kind—mostly food for needy refugees.

Commissioner-General: Filippo Grandi (Italy)
Headquarters (Gaza): Gamal Abdul Nasser Street, Gaza City
Postal address: P.O. Box 371 Gaza City
Tel.: (972 8) 288 7701; Fax: (972 8) 288 7699
Headquarters (Amman, Jordan): Bayader Wadi Seer, P.O. Box 140157, Amman 11814, Jordan
Tel.: (962 6) 580 8100; Fax: (962 6) 580 8335; E-mail: *HQ-PIO@unrwa.org*

World Food Programme (WFP)

The World Food Programme (*www.wfp.org*) is the world's largest humanitarian organization fighting hunger. Since its founding in 1963, WFP has fed some 2 billion of the world's poorest people, and used food assistance to meet emergency needs and support economic and social development in more than 80 countries. At any given time, WFP has 40 ships at sea, 60 aircraft in the sky and 5,000 trucks on the ground, moving food and other assistance to where it is needed most. Through its global school meals campaign, the Programme supplies daily meals to 24.7 million school children in some 60 countries. In 2012, WFP delivered 3.5 million metric tons of food assistance to 97.2 million people in 80 countries, providing nearly 70 per cent of the world's emergency food aid. During that year, it bought over 2.1 million metric tons of food worth more than $1.1 billion; 86 per cent of the food was purchased in 75 developing countries. The Programme is funded completely by voluntary donations from nations, private donors and individuals. In 2012, it raised $3.9 billion. More than 90 per cent of its 11,799 staff members are field-based. WFP is governed by a 36-member Executive Board. It works closely with its two Rome-based sister organizations, the Food and Agriculture Organization of the United Nations and the International Fund for Agricultural Development. The Programme also partners with more than 2,100 NGOs to distribute food.

Executive Director: Ertharin Cousin (United States)
Headquarters: Via C.G. Viola 68, Parco dei Medici, 00148 Rome, Italy
Tel.: (39 06) 65131; Fax: (39 06) 6590632; E-mail: *wfpinfo@wfp.org*

United Nations Interregional Crime and Justice Research Institute (UNICRI)

The United Nations Interregional Crime and Justice Research Institute (*www. unicri.it*) carries out action-oriented research, training and technical cooperation projects. It supports governments and the international community at large in tackling the threats that crime poses to social peace, development and political stability and in fostering the development of just and efficient criminal justice systems. Established in 1967, UNICRI supports the formulation and implementation of improved policies in the field of crime prevention and justice, the promotion of national self-reliance and the development of institutional capabilities. It works in the fields of crime, justice, security governance and counter-terrorism, providing added value to crime prevention, the advancement of justice and the enhancement of human rights. The Institute also serves as a platform for consultation and cooperation in security governance, crime prevention and criminal justice, bringing together diverse partners, including member states, research institutions, international organizations and civil society to address shared challenges.

UNICRI is funded exclusively through voluntary contributions. It enjoys the support of member states, international and regional organizations, charities and foundations, as well as financial and in-kind contributions from public and private sector organizations. In 2012, programme delivery grew to $24.5 million and was projected to reach $45 million for the 2012–2013 biennium.

Director: Jonathan Lucas (Seychelles)
Headquarters: Viale Maestri del Lavoro 10, 10127 Turin, Italy
Tel.: (39 011) 653 7111; Fax: (39 011) 631 3368; E-mail: *information@unicri.it*

United Nations Institute for Disarmament Research (UNIDIR)

Established in 1980, the United Nations Institute for Disarmament Research (*www. unidir.org*) is an autonomous institute that conducts research on disarmament and security, with the aim of assisting the international community in its disarmament thinking, decisions and efforts. Through its research projects, publications, meetings and expert networks, UNIDIR promotes creative thinking and dialogue on disarmament and security challenges. The Institute explores both current and future security issues, examining topics as varied as tactical nuclear weapons, refugee security, computer warfare, regional confidence-building measures, and small arms. It organizes expert-level meetings and discussions, implements research projects, and publishes books, reports and papers, as well as the quarterly journal *Disarmament Forum*. UNIDIR relies predominantly on voluntary contributions from governments and private funders. It received nearly $4 million in 2012: $2.7 million from governments and $1.3 million in public donations. The Institute's staff of 20 is supplemented by visiting fellows and research interns.

Director: Theresa A. Hitchens (United States)
Headquarters: Palais des Nations, 1211 Geneva 10, Switzerland
Tel.: (41 22) 917 3186; Fax: (41 22) 917 0176; E-mail: *unidir@unog.ch*

United Nations International Strategy for Disaster Risk Reduction (UNISDR)

The United Nations International Strategy for Disaster Risk Reduction (*www.unisdr. org*) was created by the General Assembly in 1999 to provide inter-agency secretariat support for disaster reduction. It is the UN system's focal point for the coordination of disaster risk reduction and the implementation of the international blueprint for disaster risk reduction, the Hyogo Framework for Action. UNISDR campaigns to create global awareness of disaster risk reduction; advocates for greater investments in risk reduction; and informs and connects people by providing practical services and tools. UNISDR publishes the Global Assessment Report and hosts the biennial Global Platform on Disaster Risk Reduction. Currently, UNISDR is facilitating the development of a post-2015 disaster risk reduction framework. Led by the Special Representative of the Secretary-General for Disaster Risk Reduction, UNISDR has around 100 staff members located at its headquarters in Geneva and its regional offices around the world.

Special Representative of the Secretary-General: Margareta Wahlström (Sweden)
Headquarters: Palais des Nations, 1211 Geneva, Switzerland
Tel.: (41 22) 917 8907 8; Fax: (41 22) 917 8964; E-mail: *isdr@un.org*

United Nations Institute for Training and Research (UNITAR)

An autonomous UN body established in 1965, the United Nations Institute for Training and Research (*www.unitar.org*) has the mandate to enhance the effectiveness of the UN through training and research. UNITAR provides training and capacity development to assist mainly developing and in-transition countries in meeting the challenges of the 21st century in the areas of peace, security, diplomacy, environment and governance. It also conducts research on innovative learning approaches, methods, and tools, as well as their practical application in a variety of settings. In 2012, UNITAR delivered close to 400 courses, seminars, workshops and other events benefiting over 23,000 participants—mainly from developing countries and countries in transition. More than 4,000 trainees took part in the Institute's e-Learning courses, which comprise around 35 per cent of all activities. UNITAR is governed by a Board of Trustees. The Institute is fully self-funded and is sponsored by voluntary contributions from governments, intergovernmental organizations, foundations and other non-governmental sources. Its 2012–2013 budget is $44.8 million. UNITAR's activities are conducted from its headquarters in Geneva, as well as through its offices in New York and Hiroshima. Most of its activities take place a the country level. UNITAR has 41 regular staff members and 17 remunerated fellows.

Executive Director: Sally Fegan-Wyles (Ireland)
Headquarters: International Environment House, Chemin des Anémones 11–13, 1219 Châtelaine, Geneva, Switzerland
Tel.: (41 22) 917 8400; Fax: (41 22) 917 8047

United Nations Research Institute for Social Development (UNRISD)

Established in 1963, the United Nations Research Institute for Social Development (*www.unrisd.org*) is an autonomous institution within the UN system that carries out multidisciplinary research and policy analysis on the social dimensions of contemporary development issues such as gender equality, social policy, and sustainable development. UNRISD engages researchers, policymakers and civil society actors from around the world in generating and sharing knowledge. In so doing, it aims to ensure that social equity, inclusion and justice are central to development thinking, policy and practice within the UN system and beyond. UNRISD relies entirely on voluntary contributions for financing its activities and has an average annual operating budget of approximately $4 million. Responsibility for approving the research programme and budget of the Institute is vested in a Board of independent experts nominated by the UN Commission for Social Development and confirmed by ECOSOC.

Director: Sarah Cook (United Kingdom)
Headquarters: Palais des Nations, 1211 Geneva 10, Switzerland
Tel.: (41 22) 917 3020; Fax: (41 22) 917 0650; E-mail: *info@unrisd.org*

United Nations University (UNU)

The United Nations University (*www.unu.edu*), established in 1975 in Tokyo, is an international community of academics engaged in research, policy study, and institutional and individual capacity development, as well as the dissemination of knowledge to further the UN's aims of peace and progress. UNU has a worldwide network of 13 research and training centres and programmes. Its aim is to contribute to solving the pressing global problems of human survival, development and welfare. The University is financed entirely by voluntary contributions from states, agencies, foundations and individual donors. Receiving no funds from the United Nations budget, its annual income for operating expenses comes from investment income derived from its Endowment Fund. UNU's budget for the 2012–2013 biennium was $142.8 million. Its 679 staff members represent both developing and developed countries. The University's governing board—the UNU Council—is composed of 24 members who serve six-year terms; the University Rector; and three ex-officio members: the Secretary-General, the UNESCO Director-General and the UNITAR Executive Director. The United Nations University Press is its publishing division.

Rector: David M. Malone (Canada)
Headquarters: 5-53-70 Jingumae, Shibuya-ku, Tokyo 150-8925, Japan
Tel.: (81 3) 5467 1212; Fax: (81 3) 3499 2828; E-mail: *mbox@hq.unu.edu*

Joint United Nations Programme on HIV/AIDS (UNAIDS)

Active since 1996, UNAIDS (*www.unaids.org*) is the UN entity that spearheads the struggle against HIV worldwide, advocating for accelerated, comprehensive and global action against the epidemic. UNAIDS leads a response that includes preventing transmission, providing care and support to people living with HIV, reducing the vulnerability of persons and communities to HIV, and alleviating the manifold impacts of the epidemic. It promotes a human rights-based approach in responding to HIV and strives to eliminate all forms of discrimination against people living with or affected by the virus. UNAIDS provides information and technical support to guide programming efforts and tracks, monitors and evaluates the epidemic. It leads and inspires the world to achieve its shared vision of zero new HIV infections, zero discrimination and zero AIDS-related deaths. UNAIDS unites the efforts of 11 UN organizations—UNHCR, UNICEF, WFP, UNDP, UNFPA, UNODC, UN-Women, ILO, UNESCO, WHO and the World Bank—and works closely with global and national partners to maximize results for the AIDS response.

Executive Director: Michel Sidibé (Mali)
Headquarters: 20 Avenue Appia, CH-1211 Geneva 27, Switzerland
Tel.: (41 22) 791 3666; Fax: (41 22) 791 4187; E-mail: *communications@unaids.org*

United Nations Office for Project Services (UNOPS)

The mission of the United Nations Office for Project Services (*www.unops.org*) is to expand the capacity of the UN system and its partners to implement peace-building, humanitarian and development operations that matter for people in need. UNOPS supports partners in the implementation of approximately $1 billion worth of projects in three main areas: sustainable infrastructure, sustainable procurement and sustainable project management. Its services range from managing the construction of roads in South Sudan to building shelters in Haiti and procuring educational computers in Argentina. UNOPS customizes its support to individual partner needs, offering everything from stand-alone transactional services to long-term management of development projects. The Office works closely with governments and communities to ensure increased economic, social and environmental sustainability for the projects it supports. With its headquarters in Copenhagen, Denmark, and a network of regional and country offices, UNOPS supports activities in more than 80 countries.

Executive Director: Jan Mattsson (Sweden)
Headquarters: P.O. Box 2695, 2100 Copenhagen, Denmark
Tel.: (45) 4533 7500; Fax: (45) 4533 7501; E-mail: *info@unops.org*

United Nations Entity for Gender Equality and the Empowerment of Women (UN-Women)

The General Assembly created the United Nations Entity for Gender Equality and the Empowerment of Women (*www.unwomen.org*) in 2010 by consolidating the existing mandate and functions of four UN agencies and offices: the United Nations Development Fund for Women, the Division for the Advancement of Women, the Office of the Special Adviser on Gender Issues, and the United Nations International Research and Training Institute for the Advancement of Women. UN-Women aims to accelerate progress in meeting the needs of women and girls worldwide.

The entity supports the Commission on the Status of Women and other inter-governmental bodies in devising policies, and member states in implementing standards relevant to women's issues. It also holds the UN system accountable for its own commitments on gender equality, including regular monitoring of system-wide progress. UN-Women has a targeted budget of $500 million.

Executive Director: Phumzile Mlambo-Ngcuka (South Africa)
Headquarters: 220 East 42nd Street, New York, NY 10017, USA
Tel.: (1 646) 781 4400; Fax: (1 646) 781 4444

Specialized agencies and related organizations

International Labour Organization (ILO)

The International Labour Organization (*www.ilo.org*) promotes social justice and human and labour rights. Established in 1919, it became the first specialized agency of the United Nations in 1946. ILO formulates international policies and programmes to help improve working and living conditions; creates international labour standards to serve as guidelines for national authorities in putting these policies into action; carries out an extensive programme of technical cooperation to help governments in making these policies effective; and engages in training, education and research to help advance these efforts. ILO is unique among world organizations in that workers' and employers' representatives have an equal voice with those of governments in formulating its policies. It is composed of three bodies:

- The International Labour Conference brings together government, employer and worker delegates from member countries every year. It sets international labour standards and acts as a forum where social and labour questions of importance to the entire world are discussed.
- The Governing Body directs ILO operations, prepares the programme and budget and examines cases of non-observance of ILO standards.
- The International Labour Office is the permanent secretariat of ILO.

In addition, opportunities for study and training are offered at the International Training Centre in Turin, Italy. ILO's International Institute for Labour Studies works through research networks; social policy forums; courses and seminars; visiting scholar and internship programmes; and publications. ILO employs 2,983 staff at its Geneva headquarters and in 40 field offices around the world. Its budget for the 2012–2013 biennium amounted to $861.6 million.

Director-General: Guy Ryder (United Kingdom)
Headquarters: 4, route des Morillons, 1211 Geneva 22, Switzerland
Tel.: (41 22) 799 6111; Fax: (41 22) 798 8685; E-mail: *ilo@ilo.org*

Food and Agriculture Organization of the United Nations (FAO)

The Food and Agriculture Organization of the United Nations (*www.fao.org*) is the lead agency for agriculture, forestry, fisheries and rural development in the UN system. World Food Day, observed annually on 16 October, marks the founding of FAO on that date in 1945. FAO works to alleviate poverty and hunger by promoting agricultural development, improved nutrition and the pursuit of food security. Such security exists when all people at all times have physical and economic access to sufficient, safe and nutritious food to meet their dietary needs and food preferences for an active and healthy life. Present in over 130 countries, FAO offers development assistance; provides policy and planning advice to governments; collects, analyses and disseminates information; and acts as an international forum for debate on food and agriculture issues. Special programmes help countries prepare for emergency food crises and provide relief assistance. FAO manages over 2,000 field projects and programmes worth close to $900 million; more than 95 per cent of that amount is funded by voluntary contributions through trust funds.

FAO is governed by its Conference of member nations. Its 49-member elected Council serves as the governing body between sessions of the Conference. FAO has a staff of 3,576 working at headquarters and in the field. Its regular programme budget for 2012–2013 was $1 billion.

Director-General: José Graziano da Silva (Brazil)
Headquarters: Viale delle Terme di Caracalla, 00153 Rome, Italy
Tel.: (39 06) 57051; Fax: (39 06) 570 53152; E-mail: *FAO-HQ@fao.org*

United Nations Educational, Scientific and Cultural Organization (UNESCO)

Created in 1946, UNESCO (*www.unesco.org*) works to create the conditions for dialogue among civilizations, cultures and peoples, based upon respect for commonly shared values and geared towards sustainable development, a culture of peace, observance of human rights and the alleviation of poverty. UNESCO's areas of work are education, natural sciences, social and human sciences, culture, and communication and information. Specific concerns include: achieving education for all; promoting natural and social science research through international and intergovernmental scientific programmes; supporting the expression of cultural identities; protecting and enhancing the world's natural and cultural heritage; and promoting the free flow of information and press freedom, as well as strengthening the communication capacities of developing countries. The Organization also has two global priorities, namely Africa and gender equality.

UNESCO maintains a system of 198 National Commissions and is supported by some 3,800 UNESCO associations, centres and clubs. It enjoys official relations with hundreds of NGOs and a range of foundations and similar institutions. It also works with a network of 9,000 educational institutions in 180 countries. UNESCO's governing body—the General Conference—is made up of its 195 member states. The Executive Board, consisting of 58 members elected by the Conference, is responsible for supervising the programme adopted by the Conference. UNESCO has a staff of more than 2,000 from some 170 countries. Over 870 of those staff work in 65 field offices, institutes and centres worldwide, including four regional bureaux for education in Bangkok, Thailand; Beirut, Lebanon; Dakar, Senegal; and Santiago, Chile. Its approved budget ceiling for 2011–2013 is $653 million.

Director-General: Irina Bokova (Bulgaria)
Headquarters: 7, place de Fontenoy, 75352 Paris 07-SP, France
Tel.: (33) 14568 1000; Fax: (33) 14567 1690; E-mail: *info@unesco.org*

World Health Organization (WHO)

Established in 1948, the World Health Organization (*www.who.int*) is the directing and coordinating authority within the United Nations system for health. WHO is responsible for providing leadership on global health matters; shaping the health research agenda; setting norms and standards; articulating evidence-based policy options; providing technical support to countries; and monitoring and assessing health trends. Its decision-making body is the World Health Assembly, which meets annually and is attended by delegations from all 194 member states. The Executive Board is composed of 34 members technically qualified in the health field. Some 8,000 people from more than 150 countries work for WHO in 150 country offices, its headquarters in Geneva, and its six regional offices in Brazzaville, Congo; Washington, D.C.; Cairo, Egypt; Copenhagen, Denmark; New Delhi, India; and Manila, the Philippines. The programme budget for the biennium 2012–2013 was over $3.9 billion, of which $949 million was financed by the assessed contributions from member states (regular budget), with the remainder coming from voluntary contributions.

Director-General: Margaret Chan (China)
Headquarters: Avenue Appia 20, 1211 Geneva 27, Switzerland
Tel.: (41 22) 791 21 11; Fax: (41 22) 791 31 11; E-mail: *inf@who.int*

World Bank Group

The World Bank Group (*www.worldbankgroup.org*) consists of five institutions:

- the International Bank for Reconstruction and Development (IBRD, founded in 1944);
- the International Finance Corporation (IFC, 1956);
- the International Development Association (IDA,1960);
- the International Centre for Settlement of Investment Disputes (ICSID, 1966);
- the Multilateral Investment Guarantee Agency (MIGA,1988).

The term 'World Bank' refers specifically to two of the five institutions: IBRD and IDA. The goal of the Bank is to reduce poverty around the world by strengthening the economies of poor nations and improving people's living standards by promoting economic growth and development. The Bank orients its lending and capacity-building activities on two pillars for development: building a climate for investment, jobs, and sustainable growth; and investing in poor people and empowering them to participate in development.

The World Bank Group is owned by its 188 member countries, which constitute its Board of Governors. General operations are delegated to a smaller group, the Board of Executive Directors, with the President of the Bank serving as Chairman of the Board. At the end of fiscal year 2012, the institutions of the World Bank Group together had a full-time staff of more than 15,000 professionals and administrative personnel from some 170 countries. About 40 percent of those personnel work in offices in more than 110 developing countries. In fiscal year 2013, the World Bank Group provided $31.5 billion for 276 projects in developing countries, with its financial and/or technical expertise aimed at helping those countries reduce poverty. The Bank is involved in more than 1,330 projects in virtually every sector and developing country. Among its major publications are the annual *World Development Report* and *Doing Business*.

President: Jim Yong Kim (United States)
Headquarters: 1818 H Street NW, Washington, D.C. 20433, USA
Tel.: (1 202) 473 1000; Fax: (1 202) 477 6391; E-mail: *pic@worldbank.org*

International Bank for Reconstruction and Development (IBRD)

The International Bank for Reconstruction and Development (*www.worldbank. org*)—the original institution of the World Bank Group—seeks to reduce poverty in middle-income and creditworthy poorer countries by promoting sustainable development through loans, guarantees, risk management products, and analytical and advisory services. IBRD is structured like a cooperative owned and operated for the benefit of its 188 member countries. It raises most of its funds on the world's financial markets. The income that the Bank has generated over the years has allowed it to fund development activities and ensure its financial strength, which enables it to borrow at low cost and offer good borrowing terms to its clients. The amount paid in by countries when they join the Bank constitutes about 5 per cent of IBRD's subscribed capital, which has been used to fund hundreds of billions of dollars in development loans since the Bank was established. In fiscal 2012, IBRD's new loan commitments amounted to $20.6 billion, covering 93 operations in 38 countries.

International Development Association (IDA)

The International Development Association (*www.worldbank.org/ida*) is the World Bank's fund for the poorest. One of the world's largest sources of aid, IDA, with 172 member states, provides support for health and education, infrastructure and agriculture, and economic and institutional development to 81 of the world's poorest countries. With IDA's help, hundreds of millions of people have escaped abject poverty through the creation of jobs, access to clean water, food security, schools, roads, and electricity. About one fifth of IDA funding is provided as grants; the rest is in the form of interest-free, long-term credits. Since its establishment in 1960, IDA has provided $255 billion in cumulative commitments. Almost fifty per cent of the $14.8 billion in lending in fiscal year 2012 went to Africa, reflecting the fact that half of IDA-eligible countries are situated on that continent. IDA is replenished every three years by both developed and developing country donors, as well as by two other World Bank Group organizations—the International Bank for Reconstruction and Development and the International Finance Corporation. Fifty-two donors contributed to the last IDA replenishment of $49.3 billion.

International Finance Corporation (IFC)

The International Finance Corporation (*www.ifc.org*) is the largest global development institution focused on the private sector in developing countries. It helps developing countries achieve sustainable growth by financing private sector investment, mobilizing capital in international financial markets, and providing advisory services to businesses and services. IFC, which has 184 member countries, joins in an investment only when it can make a special contribution that complements the role of market investors. It also plays a catalytic role by helping introduce innovative solutions to development challenges; helping influence development policies and raise environmental and social standards; demonstrating that investments in challenging markets can be profitable; and improving lives. In fiscal year 2012, IFC invested a record $20.4 billion in developing countries, including nearly $5 billion mobilized from other investors. Since 2007, IFC has invested more than $23 billion in countries eligible to borrow from IDA, and contributed more than $2 billion of its income to IDA replenishments.

Multilateral Investment Guarantee Agency (MIGA)

The mandate of the Multilateral Investment Guarantee Agency (*www.miga.org*) is to promote foreign direct investment in developing countries by providing guarantees (political risk insurance) to investors and lenders. Its subscribed capital comes from its 178 member countries. The agency's strategy focuses on supporting investment in the world's poorest countries, investment in conflict-affected countries, complex deals in infrastructure and the extractive industries, and South-South investments. Since its inception in 1998, MIGA has issued guarantees worth more than $27.2 billion for more than 700 projects in 105 developing countries.

International Centre for Settlement of Investment Disputes (ICSID)

The International Centre for the Settlement of Investment Disputes (*www.worldbank.org/icsid*), which has 147 member countries, aims to foster increased flows of international investment by providing a neutral international forum for the resolution of disputes between governments and foreign investors. ICSID administers procedures for the settlement of such disputes by conciliation and arbitration in cases where both the host and the home country of the investor are ICSID members. ICSID also administers, upon request by the parties or the tribunals involved, other dispute-settlement proceedings between governments and foreign nationals; and it appoints arbitrators and administers proceedings conducted under the Arbitration Rules of the UN Commission on International Trade Law. In addition to its dispute settlement activities, ICSID maintains a publications programme in the area of foreign investment law. Its governing body, the Administrative Council, is composed of one representative of each ICSID member state and is chaired by the President of the World Bank Group.

International Monetary Fund (IMF)

Established at the Bretton Woods Conference in 1944, the International Monetary Fund (*www.imf.org*) facilitates international monetary cooperation; promotes exchange rate stability and orderly exchange arrangements; assists in the establishment of a multilateral system of payments and the elimination of foreign exchange restrictions; and assists members by temporarily providing financial resources to correct maladjustments in their balance of payments. IMF has authority to create and allocate to its members international financial reserves in the form of Special Drawing Rights—IMF's unit of account. The Fund's financial resources consist primarily of the subscriptions ('quotas' determined by a formula based principally on the relative economic size of the members) of its 188 member countries and bilateral arrangements with various members, which totalled about $750 billion as of February 2013. A core responsibility of IMF is to provide loans to countries experiencing balance-of-payment problems. This financial assistance enables such countries to rebuild their international reserves, stabilize their currencies, continue paying for imports, and restore conditions for strong economic growth. In return, members borrowing from the Fund agree to undertake policy reforms to correct the problems that underlie these difficulties. The amounts that IMF members may borrow are limited in proportion to their quotas. The Fund also offers concessional assistance to low-income member countries.

The IMF Board of Governors includes all member states. Its day-to-day work is led by its 24-member Executive Board. IMF has a staff of approximately 2,600 from over 156 countries, headed by a Managing Director selected by the Executive Board. The administrative budget (net of receipts) for the financial year ended 30 April 2013 was $985 million, and the capital budget was about $162 million. IMF publishes the *World Economic Outlook* and the *Global Financial Stability Report*, along with a variety of other studies.

Managing Director: Christine Lagarde (France)
Headquarters: 700 19th Street NW, Washington, D.C. 20431, USA
Tel.: (1 202) 623 7000; Fax: (1 202) 623 6220; E-mail: *publicaffairs@imf.org*

International Civil Aviation Organization (ICAO)

The International Civil Aviation Organization (*www.icao.int*) promotes the safe and orderly development of international civil aviation throughout the world. It sets standards and develops regulations necessary for aviation safety, security, efficiency and regularity, as well as for environmental protection. To achieve safe, secure and sustainable development of civil aviation, it relies on the cooperation of its 191 member states. ICAO has an Assembly—its policymaking body—comprising delegates from all contracting states, and a Council of representatives of 36 nations elected by the Assembly. The Council is the executive body, and carries out Assembly directives.

President of the Council: Roberto Kobeh González (Mexico)
Secretary General: Raymond Benjamin (France)
Headquarters: 999 University Street, Montreal, Quebec H3C 5H7, Canada
Tel.: (1 514) 954 8219; Fax: (1 514) 954 6077; E-mail: *icaohq@icao.int*

International Maritime Organization (IMO)

The International Maritime Organization (*www.imo.org*), which began functioning in 1959, is responsible for the safety and security of shipping in international trade and for preventing marine pollution from ships. IMO helps governments cooperate in formulating regulations and practices relating to technical matters affecting international shipping; facilitates the adoption of the highest practicable standards of maritime safety and efficiency in navigation; and helps protect the marine environment through the prevention and control of pollution from ships. Some 50 conventions and agreements and some 1,000 codes and recommendations have been adopted by IMO. In 1983, it established the World Maritime University in Malmö, Sweden, which provides advanced training for administrators, educators and others involved in shipping at the senior level. The IMO International Maritime Law Institute (Valletta, Malta) was established in 1989 to train lawyers in international maritime law. The Assembly—IMO's governing body—consists of all 170 Member States and three Associate Members. It elects the 40-member Council, IMO's executive organ. The IMO's budget for 2013 stood at £31,686,000. It has a staff of about 300.

Secretary-General: Koji Sekimizu (Japan)
Headquarters: 4 Albert Embankment, London SE1 7SR, United Kingdom
Tel.: (44 207) 735 7611; Fax: (44 207) 587 3210; E-mail: *infor@imo.org*

International Telecommunication Union (ITU)

The International Telecommunication Union (*www.itu.int*) coordinates global telecommunication networks and services for governments and the private sector. The Union is also responsible for the management of the radio-frequency spectrum and satellite orbits. ITU is at the forefront of work to achieve safe and reliable interoperability of networks and equipment amid the rapid advance of information and communication technologies. It puts priority on fostering the deployment of telecommunications in developing countries by advising on policy and regulatory frameworks, and by providing specialized technical assistance and training in such areas as cybersecurity, network installation and maintenance, and early warning and mitigation systems for natural disasters. Founded in Paris in 1865 as the International Telegraph Union, ITU took its present name in 1932 and became a UN specialized agency in 1949. It has a membership of 193 countries and more than 700 sector members and associates, including scientific and industrial bodies, public and private companies, regional and international organizations, and academic institutions. ITU's governing body, the Plenipotentiary Conference, elects its senior officials, as well as the 48-member ITU Council representing all regions of the world. Based in Geneva, ITU has close to 740 staff members of some 93 nationalities. It had a budget of CHF 323.8 million for the biennium 2012–2013.

Secretary-General: Hamadoun I. Touré (Mali)
Headquarters: Place des Nations, 1211 Geneva 20, Switzerland
Tel.: (41 22) 730 5111; Fax: (41 22) 733 7256; E-mail: *itumail@itu.int*

Universal Postal Union (UPU)

Comprising 192 member states, the Universal Postal Union (*www.upu.int*) regulates international postal services. Established in 1874, it became a UN specialized agency in 1948. UPU advises, mediates and renders technical assistance for postal services. Its objectives include the promotion of a universal postal service linking all the nations of the world; growth in mail volume through the provision of up-to-date postal products and services; and improvement in the quality of postal service for customers. The Universal Postal Congress is the supreme authority of UPU, whose annual budget is approximately $37 million. Some 250 staff, drawn from some 50 countries, work at the UPU International Bureau in Berne, Switzerland. UPU has regional coordinators in San José, Costa Rica; Harare, Zimbabwe; Cairo, Egypt; Castries, Saint Lucia; Cotonou, Benin; Bangkok, Thailand; and Berne.

Director-General: Bishar A. Hussein (Kenya)
Headquarters: Weltpoststrasse 4, Case Postale 3000, Berne 15, Switzerland
Tel.: (41 31) 350 3111; Fax: (41 31) 350 3110; E-mail: *info@upu.int*

World Meteorological Organization (WMO)

The World Meteorological Organization (*www.wmo.int*), a United Nations specialized agency since 1951, provides authoritative scientific information on the state and behaviour of the Earth's atmosphere, its interaction with the oceans, the climate it produces and the resulting distribution of water resources, and related environmental issues. WMO operates a global observing system and a network of global, regional and national centres providing weather, climate and hydrological forecasting services. WMO Information System makes possible the rapid exchange of weather, climate and water information, and promotes its application. Its major programmes provide the basis for better preparation and forewarning of most natural hazards. WMO has 191 members, all of which maintain their own meteorological and hydrological services. Its governing body is the World Meteorological Congress. WMO has a staff of around 300. Its budget for 2012–2015 is CHF 276 million.

Secretary-General: Michel Jarraud (France)
Headquarters: 7 bis, avenue de la Paix, Case postale No. 2300, 1211 Geneva 2, Switzerland
Tel.: (41 22) 730 8111; Fax: (41 22) 730 8181; E-mail: *wmo@wmo.int*

Intergovernmental Panel on Climate Change (IPCC)

The Intergovernmental Panel on Climate Change (*www.ipcc.ch*) is the leading body for the assessment of climate change. It was established by the United Nations Environment Programme and WMO to provide a clear scientific view on the state of climate change and its potential environmental and socioeconomic consequences. IPCC reviews and assesses scientific, technical and socioeconomic information produced worldwide that is relevant to the understanding of the global climate. It does not conduct research, nor does it monitor data. The IPCC secretariat is hosted by WMO at its Geneva headquarters and has a staff of 12. IPCC is open to all UN and WMO member countries; 195 countries are IPCC members. Its Bureau and Chair are elected in plenary sessions.

Chair: Rajendra K. Pachauri (India)
Head of Secretariat: Dr. Renate Christ (Austria)
Secretariat: c/o World Meteorological Organization, 7 bis, Avenue de la Paix, C.P. 2300, 1211 Geneva 2, Switzerland
Tel.: (41 22) 730 8208; Fax: (41 22) 730 8025; E-mail: *IPCC-Sec@wmo.int*

World Intellectual Property Organization (WIPO)

The World Intellectual Property Organization (*www.wipo.int*) was established in 1970 and became a UN specialized agency in 1974. Its mandate is to promote the protection of intellectual property (IP) through cooperation among states and in collaboration with other international organizations. It is dedicated to developing a balanced and accessible international IP system that rewards creativity, stimulates innovation and contributes to economic development while safeguarding the public interest. The strategic goals of WIPO include: the balanced evolution of the international normative IP framework; facilitating the use of IP for development; providing global IP services; building respect for IP; developing global IP infrastructure; becoming a world reference source for IP information; and addressing IP in relation to global policy challenges such as climate change, public health and food security. WIPO has 185 member states and administers 25 international treaties on IP and copyright. It is unique among the family of UN organizations in that it is largely self-financing. Over 90 per cent of WIPO's budget of CHF 637.2 million for the 2012–2013 biennium comes from earnings derived from services it provides to industry and the private sector. The remainder of the budget is made up mainly of revenue generated by its Arbitration and Mediation Centre, the sale of publications and contributions from member states.

Director-General: Francis Gurry (Australia)
Headquarters: 34 chemin des Colombettes, P.O. Box 18, 1211 Geneva 20, Switzerland
Tel.: (41 22) 338 9111; Fax: (41 22) 733 5428

International Fund for Agricultural Development (IFAD)

The International Fund for Agricultural Development (*www.ifad.org*) is dedicated to enabling poor rural people to improve their food and nutrition security, increase their incomes and strengthen their resilience. IFAD mobilizes resources from its 172 member countries to provide low-interest loans and grants to finance rural development. It gives grants instead of loans to poor countries unable to sustain debt to ensure that essential financial assistance does not cause undue financial hardship for those most in need. IFAD works in partnership with governments, other UN agencies, bilateral and multilateral development agencies, international agricultural research centres and the private sector. It maintains strong relationships with civil society organizations, particularly those of smallholder farmers and rural people, as well as NGOs, policy research institutes and universities. The Fund is financed by voluntary contributions from governments, special contributions, loan repayments and investment income. From its inception until the end of

2012, IFAD had invested $14.8 billion in some 924 projects and programmes that had reached more than 400 million poor rural people. Governments and other financing sources in recipient countries, including project participants, have contributed $12.3 billion, while approximately $9.6 billion in cofinancing has come from multilateral, bilateral and other donors. IFAD's Governing Council is made up of all member states. The Executive Board, which consists of 18 members and 18 alternates, oversees operations and approves loans and grants.

President: Kanayo F. Nwanze (Nigeria)
Headquarters: Via Paolo di Dono 44, 00142 Rome, Italy
Tel.: (39 06) 54 591; Fax: (39 06) 504 3463; E-mail: *ifad@ifad.org*

United Nations Industrial Development Organization (UNIDO)

The United Nations Industrial Development Organization (*www.unido.org*) promotes equitable wealth creation and global prosperity through sustainable industrial development and international industrial cooperation. Established by the General Assembly in 1966, it became a UN specialized agency in 1985. UNIDO provides developing countries with tailor-made solutions to grow a flourishing productive sector, increase participation in international trade, improve access to energy, and safeguard the environment. It collaborates with governments, the private sector, business associations and other stakeholders to meet complex challenges in industrial development for the benefit of lives and livelihoods. UNIDO's resource pool includes specialist staff in Vienna working in the fields of engineering, industrial and economic policy, technology and the environment, as well as professional staff in its network of Investment and Technology Promotion Offices, International Technology Centres, and National Cleaner Production Centres. Field offices are led by UNIDO regional and country representatives.

UNIDO's 172 member states meet at its General Conference to approve the budget and work programme. The Industrial Development Board, comprising 53 member states, makes recommendations relating to the planning and implementation of the programme and budget. In 2012, UNIDO employed some 700 staff members working at headquarters and worldwide in 30 regional and country offices. The value of technical cooperation delivery amounted to $189.2 million, the highest since UNIDO became a specialized agency.

Director-General: Kandeh K. Yumkella (Sierra Leone)
Headquarters: Vienna International Centre, Wagramerstrasse 5, P.O. Box 300, 1400 Vienna, Austria
Tel.: (43 1) 26026 0; Fax: (43 1) 269 2669; E-mail: *unido@unido.org*

World Tourism Organization (UNWTO)

The World Tourism Organization (*www.unwto.org*) is the leading international organization responsible for promoting the development of responsible, sustainable and universally accessible tourism. Established in 1975, UNWTO became a UN specialized agency in 2003. It serves as a global forum for tourism policy issues and a practical source of tourism know-how. Its membership includes 161 countries and associate members, 2 permanent observers and over 400 affiliate members, including local governments, educational institutions, tourism associations and private sector firms. Through tourism, UNWTO aims to stimulate economic growth, job creation and sustainable development, and promote peace and understanding among nations. UNWTO encourages the implementation of the Global Code of Ethics for Tourism, which sets a frame of reference for the responsible and sustainable development of world tourism. The Code, endorsed by the UN General Assembly in 2001, aims to maximize the socio-economic benefits of tourism while minimizing its possible negative impacts on the environment, cultural heritage and societies.

UNWTO's General Assembly—its supreme body, made up of full, associate and affiliate members—approves the Organization's budget and programme of work, and debates major topics of importance to the tourism sector. The Executive Council is its governing board; it is composed of 31 full members elected by the Assembly, and a permanent member, Spain (the host country of UNWTO headquarters). For the 2012–2013 biennium, UNWTO had a staff of 110 and a budget of €25 million.

Secretary-General: Taleb D. Rifai (Jordan)
Headquarters: Capitán Haya 42, 28020 Madrid, Spain
Tel.: (34 91) 567 8100; Fax: (34 91) 571 3733; E-mail: *omt@unwto.org*

Preparatory Commission for the Comprehensive Nuclear-Test-Ban Treaty Organization (CTBTO)

The *Comprehensive Nuclear-Test-Ban Treaty* was adopted and opened for signature in 1996. It prohibits all nuclear explosions. As of February 2013, 183 States had signed the *Treaty* and 159 had ratified it. Of the 44 nuclear-technology-holding States whose ratification is needed for the *Treaty's* entry into force, eight have yet to ratify: China, the Democratic People's Republic of Korea (DPRK), Egypt, India, Iran, Israel, Pakistan and the United States. India, the DPRK and Pakistan have also yet to sign the *Treaty*. The Vienna-based Preparatory Commission for the Comprehensive Nuclear-Test-Ban Treaty Organization (*www.ctbto.org*) is tasked with building up the CTBT verification regime so that it will be fully operational when the *Treaty* enters into force. Its mandate also includes promoting the signature and ratification of the *Treaty*. The CTBT verification regime consists of a globe-spanning network of 337 facilities monitoring the Earth for signs of a nuclear explosion; an International Data Centre for processing and analysis; and on-site inspections to collect evidence on the ground in the case of a suspicious event. The organization has an annual budget of around $120 million. It employs over 260 staff from 70 countries.

Executive Secretary: Tibor Tóth (Hungary)
Headquarters: Vienna International Centre, P.O. Box 1200, 1400 Vienna, Austria
Tel.: (43 1) 26030 6200; Fax: (43 1) 26030 5823; E-mail: *info@ctbto.org*

International Atomic Energy Agency (IAEA)

The International Atomic Energy Agency (*www.iaea.org*) is the world's centre for cooperation in the nuclear field, working to prevent the spread of nuclear weapons and to help all countries—especially those in the developing world—benefit from the peaceful, safe and secure use of nuclear science and technology. IAEA also serves as the global platform for strengthening nuclear safety and security. As the only organization in the UN system with expertise in nuclear technologies, IAEA helps transfer knowledge and expertise to its 159 member states to ensure greater access to energy, improve human health, increase food production, improve access to clean water and protect the environment. IAEA also verifies states' compliance with their non-proliferation obligations to help prevent the spread of nuclear weapons. IAEA inspectors conduct about 2,000 inspection missions annually to over 1,200 sites in 78 states to verify that nuclear material is not being diverted from peaceful purposes. The Agency was established in 1957 as an autonomous entity under the aegis of the United Nations.

IAEA's governing bodies include the General Conference, which meets annually and consists of all member states, and the 35-member Board of Governors, which meets quarterly and makes major policy decisions. The Director General oversees a secretariat of over 2,400 staff headquartered in Vienna, Austria. IAEA's regular budget, €333 million in 2012, is funded primarily by annual assessments. These are augmented by voluntary contributions, which finance the Technical Cooperation Fund, whose target was $88 million dollars in 2012.

Director General: Yukiya Amano (Japan)
Headquarters: P.O. Box 100, Wagramerstrasse 5, 1400 Vienna, Austria
Tel.: (43 1) 2600 0; Fax: (43 1) 2600 7; E-mail: *Official.Mail@iaea.org*

Organisation for the Prohibition of Chemical Weapons (OPCW)

The Organisation for the Prohibition of Chemical Weapons (*www.opcw.org*) is an independent international organization in close working relationship with the United Nations. It monitors the implementation of the *Convention on the Prohibition of the Development, Production, Stockpiling and Use of Chemical Weapons and on their Destruction*. The *Convention*, which entered into force in 1997, is the first multilateral disarmament and non-proliferation agreement that provides for the global elimination of an entire category of weapons of mass destruction, under stringent international verification and within prescribed timelines.

OPCW is composed of 188 member states. Since 1997, member states have verifiably destroyed more than 55,000 metric tons of chemical agents—78 per cent of the total declared quantity of more than 71,000 metric tons. OPCW inspectors have conducted over 5,000 inspections at military and industrial plants in 84 countries. These missions ensure that chemical weapons production facilities are deactivated and destroyed or verifiably converted to permitted purposes, and prevent the re-emergence of new chemical weapons. Inspectors also verify the destruction of chemical weapons through their presence at destruction facilities. All OPCW member states are obliged to assist one another if they are threatened or attacked with chemical weapons. To handle such a contingency, OPCW regularly tests and enhances its capacity to coordinate a swift and effective international response aimed at protecting lives, as well as to efficiently investigate any alleged use of chemical weapons. OPCW also has a range of international cooperation programmes to facilitate the peaceful uses of chemistry. The OPCW Technical Secretariat, based in The Hague, the Netherlands, has a staff of over 450, representing some 80 nationalities. Its budget for 2012 was just under €70 million.

Director-General: Ahmet Uzümcü (Turkey)
Headquarters: Johan de Wittlaan 32, 2517 JR, The Hague, The Netherlands
Tel.: (31 70) 416 3300; Fax: (31 70) 306 3535; E-mail: *media@opcw.org*

World Trade Organization (WTO)

The World Trade Organization (*www.wto.org*) is the only international organization dealing with global trade rules between nations. Established in 1995, its aim is to help trade flow as smoothly as possible in a system based on multilateral rules agreed to by all its members, settle trade disputes between governments and provide a forum for trade negotiations. At the heart of the WTO system are some 60 agreements and other accords—the legal ground rules for international commerce and trade policy. The principles on which these agreements are based include non-discrimination, more open trade, encouraging competition, and special provisions for less-developed countries.

WTO is the forum for negotiations among its members to achieve reform of the international trading system through lower barriers and revised trade rules. In 2001, WTO launched a new round of multilateral trade negotiations known as the Doha Development Agenda, the fundamental objective of which is to improve the trading prospects of developing countries. The work programme covers about 20 areas of trade. Ministerial discussions have not yet resulted in the necessary breakthroughs to conclude the negotiations. WTO also continues to oversee implementation of the agreements reached in the 1986–1994 Uruguay Round of world trade talks. Over 450 trade disputes have been brought to WTO's dispute settlement mechanism.

WTO has 159 members. Its governing body is the Ministerial Conference; the General Council carries out the day-to-day work. WTO's budget for 2012 was CHF 196 million. WTO employs some 640 staff.

Director-General: Roberto Azevêdo (Brazil)
Headquarters: Centre William Rappard, Rue de Lausanne 154, 1211 Geneva 21, Switzerland
Tel.: (41 22) 739 5111; Fax: (41 22) 731 4206; E-mail: *enquiries@wto.org*

II.   INTERNATIONAL PEACE AND SECURITY

From an observation post near the town of Cheeba, Lebanon, a peacekeeper from the United Nations Interim Force in Lebanon watches over the Blue Line marking Israel's withdrawal from southern Lebanon, as identified by the UN in 2000. (25 April 2012, UN Photo/Pasqual Gorriz)

O   ne of the primary purposes of the United Nations is the maintenance of international peace and security. Since its creation, the United Nations has often been called upon to prevent disputes from escalating into war, to persuade opposing parties to use the conference table rather than the force of arms to settle disputes, or to help restore peace when armed conflict does break out. Over the decades, the UN has helped end numerous conflicts and foster reconciliation, including successful peacekeeping missions in Cambodia, El Salvador, Guatemala, Liberia, Mozambique, Namibia, Sierra Leone, Tajikistan and Timor-Leste. While the Security Council is the primary organ for dealing with issues of international peace and security, the General Assembly and the Secretary-General also play major, complementary roles in fostering peace and security. United Nations activities cover the principal areas of conflict prevention, peacemaking, peacekeeping, enforcement and peacebuilding (see *www.un.org/peace*).

New global threats have emerged with the arrival of the 21st century. Civil conflicts have raised complex issues regarding the adequate response of the international community, including the question of how best to protect civilians in conflicts. The United Nations has reshaped and strengthened its peacekeeping capacity to meet new challenges, increasingly involving regional organizations; enhanced its post-conflict peacebuilding capability; and revived the use of preventive diplomacy. In addressing civil conflicts, which are often characterized by ethnic violence and the lack of internal security, the Security Council has authorized complex and innovative peacekeeping and political missions. These have provided the time and space for building the foundations of sustainable peace, enabled millions of people in dozens of countries to participate in free and fair elections, and helped disarm half a million ex-combatants in the past decade alone.

At the end of the 1990s, continuing crises in the Central African Republic, the DRC, Kosovo, Sierra Leone and Timor-Leste led the Council to establish five new missions. The surge in peacekeeping reached an apex in 2009–2010, when more than 100,000 UN peackeepers—known as 'blue helmets'—were deployed globally. Recurring conflicts over recent years have brought the United Nations to focus increasingly on peacebuilding, with targeted efforts to reduce a country's risk of lapsing or relapsing into conflict by strengthening national capacities for conflict management, and by laying the foundations for sustainable peace and development. Lasting peace depends on pulling together all resources to help countries foster economic development, social justice, respect for human rights and good governance. No other institution has the global legitimacy, multilateral experience, competence, coordinating ability and impartiality that the United Nations brings in support of these tasks. The United Nations has established special political and peacebuilding missions and offices in a number of countries, including Afghanistan, Burundi, the Central African Republic, Guinea-Bissau, Iraq, Lebanon, Libya, Mali, Sierra Leone and Somalia. Regional missions have also been deployed to Central Africa, Central Asia, the Middle East and West Africa.

The UN's efforts to maintain international peace and security are also directed towards the challenges and dangers of international terrorism and weapons of mass destruction. Member states, through the General Assembly and the Security Council, are coordinating counter-terrorism efforts through activities delivered through UN system programmes, offices and agencies. The Organization has placed a high priority on multilateral disarmament, and through sustained efforts the world community has achieved numerous multilateral agreements on disarmament and arms limitation. These include treaties and protocols on reducing and eliminating nuclear weapons, destroying chemical weapons, prohibiting biological weapons and halting the proliferation of small arms and light weapons. The scope of these negotiations continues to change as the international environment evolves, bringing further new security challenges.

Security Council

The *Charter of the United Nations*—an international treaty—obligates member states to settle their disputes by peaceful means, in such a manner that international peace, security and justice are not endangered. They are to refrain from the threat or use of force against any state, and may bring any dispute before the Security Council: the UN organ with primary responsibility for maintaining peace and security. Under the *Charter*, member states are obliged to accept and carry out its decisions. Recommendations of other United Nations bodies do not have the mandatory force of Security Council decisions, but can influence situations by expressing the opinion of the international community.

When a dispute is brought to its attention, the Council usually urges the parties to settle it peacefully. The Security Council may make recommendations to the parties for a peaceful settlement, appoint special representatives, ask the Secretary-General to use his good offices, or undertake investigation and mediation. When a dispute leads to fighting, the Council seeks to bring it to an end as quickly as possible. Often the Security Council has issued ceasefire directives that have been instrumental in preventing wider hostilities. In support of a peace process, the Security Council may deploy military observers or a peacekeeping force to an area of conflict.

Under Chapter VII of the *Charter*, the Security Council is empowered to take measures to enforce its decisions. It can impose embargoes and sanctions, or authorize the use of force to ensure that mandates are fulfilled. In some cases, the Council has authorized the use of military force by a coalition of member states or by a regional organization or arrangement. However, the Security Council takes such action only as a last resort, when peaceful means of settling a dispute have been exhausted, and after determining that a threat to the peace, a breach of the peace or an act of aggression actually exists. Many of the recently established peacekeeping operations have been authorized by the Council in this way, meaning that the peacekeepers may use force if needed to implement their mandates. Also under Chapter VII of the *Charter*, the Security Council has established international tribunals to prosecute those accused of gross violations of human rights and serious breaches of international humanitarian law, including genocide.

General Assembly

Article 11 of the *Charter of the United Nations* empowers the General Assembly to "consider the general principles of cooperation in the maintenance of international peace and security" and "make recommendations … to the Members or to the Security Council or to both". The Assembly offers a means for finding consensus on difficult issues, providing a forum for the airing of grievances and diplomatic exchanges. To foster the maintenance of peace, it has held special sessions or emergency special sessions on such issues as disarmament, the question of Palestine and the situation in Afghanistan. The General Assembly considers peace and security issues in its First Committee (Disarmament and International Security) and in its Fourth Committee (Special Political and Decolonization). Over the years, the Assembly has helped promote peaceful relations among nations by adopting declarations on peace, the peaceful settlement of disputes and international cooperation.

The Assembly in 1980 approved the establishment in San José, Costa Rica, of the **University for Peace**, an international institute for study, research and dissemination of knowledge on peace-related issues. The Assembly has designated 21 September each year as the **International Day of Peace**.

Conflict prevention

The main strategies for preventing disputes from escalating into conflict, and for stopping the recurrence of conflict, are preventive diplomacy and preventive disarmament.

Preventive diplomacy refers to action taken to prevent disputes from arising or from escalating into conflicts, and to limit the spread of conflicts when they occur. It may take the form of mediation, conciliation or negotiation. Early warning is an essential component of prevention, and the United Nations carefully monitors developments around the world to detect threats to international peace and security, thereby enabling the Security Council and the Secretary-General to carry out preventive action. Envoys and special representatives of the Secretary-General are engaged in mediation and preventive diplomacy throughout the world. In some trouble spots, the mere presence of a skilled envoy can prevent the escalation of tension. This work is often undertaken in cooperation with regional organizations.

Complementing preventive diplomacy is preventive disarmament, which seeks to reduce the number of small arms in conflict-prone regions. In Liberia, Sierra Leone, Timor-Leste and elsewhere, this has entailed demobilizing combat forces, as well as collecting and destroying their weapons as part of an overall peace agreement. Destroying yesterday's weapons prevents their being used in tomorrow's wars.

The Secretary-General plays a central role in peacemaking, both personally and by dispatching special envoys or missions for specific tasks, such as negotiation or fact-finding. Under the *Charter*, the Secretary-General may bring to the attention of the Security Council any matter that might threaten the maintenance of international peace and security.

Peacekeeping

United Nations peacekeeping operations (*www.un.org/en/peacekeeping*) are a vital instrument employed by the international community to advance peace and security. While not specifically envisaged in the *Charter of the United Nations*, the UN pioneered peacekeeping in 1948 with the establishment of the United Nations Truce Supervision Organization in the Middle East. Since then, it has established a total of 68 operations, 15 of which were active at the end of May 2013.

Peacekeeping operations are deployed with the authorization of the Security Council and the consent of the host government and/or the main parties to the conflict. Peacekeeping has traditionally involved a primarily military model of observing ceasefires and the separation of forces after inter-state wars. Today, it has evolved into a complex model of many elements—military, police and civilians—working together to help lay the foundations of a sustainable peace.

In recent years, the Council has introduced the practice of invoking the enforcement provisions in Chapter VII of the *Charter* when authorizing the deployment of certain UN peacekeeping operations, or mandating them to perform tasks which may require the use of force, such as the protection of civilians under imminent threat of physical violence. Traditionally, UN peacekeepers could only use their weapons in self-defence, but the more 'robust' mandates under Chapter VII enable them to use force, for example, to protect civilians.

The United Nations has no military force of its own. The military personnel of peacekeeping operations are provided voluntarily and financed by member states. Operations are directed by the Secretary-General, usually through a special representative. Depending on the mission, a Force Commander is responsible for the operation's military aspects, but military contingents answer to their own national defence entities. They wear their country's uniform with a UN blue helmet or beret and a badge. Civilian staff of missions are recruited or volunteer from around the world.

Peacekeeping operations are financed through the peacekeeping budget and include troops from many countries. Member states are assessed under the budget, and troop-contributing states are compensated at a standard rate. The approved peacekeeping budget for 2012–2013 was approximately $7.3 billion—which represents less than 0.5 per cent of global military spending. This worldwide 'burden-sharing' can offer extraordinary efficiency in human, financial and political terms.

Current peacekeeping operations. As of 31 May 2013, 90,241 military and police personnel from 116 countries were serving in the following 15 peacekeeping operations:

- United Nations Truce Supervision Organization (UNTSO, est. 1948), in the Middle East (153 military observers; 234 civilians);
- United Nations Military Observer Group in India and Pakistan (UNMOGIP, est. 1949) (40 military observers; 71 civilians);
- United Nations Peacekeeping Force in Cyprus (UNFICYP, est. 1964) (859 troops; 66 police; 145 civilians);
- United Nations Disengagement Observer Force (UNDOF, est. 1974) in the Syrian Golan Heights (908 troops; 141 civilians);

- United Nations Interim Force in Lebanon (UNIFIL, est. 1978) (10,820 troops; 981 civilians);
- United Nations Mission for the Referendum in Western Sahara (MINURSO, est. 1991) (27 troops; 197 military observers; 6 police; 264 civilians; 12 UN Volunteers);
- United Nations Interim Administration Mission in Kosovo (UNMIK, est. 1999) (9 military observers; 7 police; 340 civilians; 28 UN Volunteers);
- United Nations Mission in Liberia (UNMIL, est. 2003) (6,661 troops; 120 military observers; 1,440 police; 1,365 civilians; 222 UN Volunteers);
- United Nations Operation in Côte d'Ivoire (UNOCI, est. 2004) (8,539 troops; military 185 observers; 1,502 police; 1,192 civilians; 170 UN Volunteers);
- United Nations Stabilization Mission in Haiti (MINUSTAH, est. 2004) (6,179 troops; 2,630 police; 1,758 civilians; 194 UN Volunteers);
- African Union-United Nations Hybrid Operation in Darfur (UNAMID, est. 2007) (14,085 troops; 342 military observers; 4,721 police; 3,997 civilians; 448 UN Volunteers);
- United Nations Organization Stabilization Mission in the Democratic Republic of the Congo (MONUSCO, est. 2010) (17,260 troops; 516 military observers; 1,416 police; 3,960 civilians; 582 UN Volunteers);
- United Nations Interim Security Force for Abyei (UNISFA, est. 2011) (3,829 troops; 113 military observers; 10 police; 156 civilians; 11 UN Volunteers);
- United Nations Mission in the Republic of South Sudan (UNMISS, est. 2011) (6,806 troops; 146 military observers; 649 police; 2,210 civilians; 409 UN Volunteers);
- United Nations Multidimensional Integrated Stabilization Mission in Mali (MINUSMA, est. 2013) (12,640 uniformed personnel authorized).

Since 1948, 3,116 peacekeepers have lost their lives in the line of duty.

MISSIONS DIRECTED BY THE DEPARTMENT OF PEACEKEEPING OPERATIONS

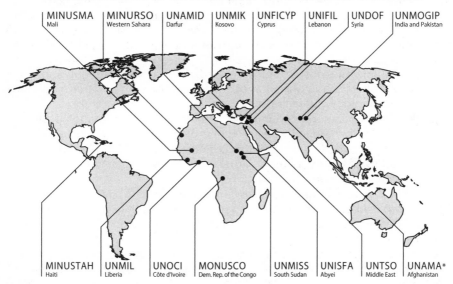

| MINUSMA | MINURSO | UNAMID | UNMIK | UNFICYP | UNIFIL | UNDOF | UNMOGIP |
| Mali | Western Sahara | Darfur | Kosovo | Cyprus | Lebanon | Syria | India and Pakistan |

| MINUSTAH | UNMIL | UNOCI | MONUSCO | UNMISS | UNISFA | UNTSO | UNAMA* |
| Haiti | Liberia | Côte d'Ivoire | Dem. Rep. of the Congo | South Sudan | Abyei | Middle East | Afghanistan |

The roots of today's conflicts may be internal, but they are complicated by cross-border involvement, either by states or by economic interests and other non-state actors. Recent conflicts in Africa, for example, have involved a deadly mix of civil strife and the illegal export of natural resources, such as diamonds, coltan (used in cell phones and electronic devices) and gold, which fuel arms purchases, terrorism, drug trafficking, refugee flows and environmental degradation. The response must be equally multifaceted. The Kimberley Process Certification Scheme (KPCS)—to name one instance—was introduced by the General Assembly in 2000 to prevent diamond sales from financing conflict and human rights violations. KPCS aims at preventing 'blood diamonds' from entering the mainstream market.

United Nations operations, because of their universality, offer unique legitimacy as a means of addressing conflicts. Peacekeepers from outside a conflict can foster discussion among warring parties while focusing global attention on local concerns, opening doors that would otherwise remain closed for collective peace efforts. Prerequisites for the success of an operation include a genuine desire on the part of the opposing forces to resolve their differences peacefully, a clear peacekeeping mandate, strong political support by the international community, and the provision of the financial and human resources necessary to achieve the operation's objectives. Most importantly, peacekeeping must accompany a political process; it cannot substitute for one.

The international community has drawn lessons from past operations and is working to strengthen UN peacekeeping capacity in a number of areas. A blueprint for reform was provided by the 2000 report of the Secretary-General's Panel on Peace Operations, which aimed to make possible the launching of one new multidisciplinary peace mission per year. In effect, the decade ending in 2010 witnessed the start-up or expansion of 11 peacekeeping operations, as well as of a number of special political missions, including in Afghanistan and Iraq.

At the instigation of Secretary-General Ban Ki-moon, a major restructuring of the UN peacekeeping apparatus took place in 2007, through the creation of a **Department of Field Support (DFS)**. While the **Department of Peacekeeping Operations (DPKO)** and the **Department of Political Affairs (DPA)** give political and executive direction, respectively, to peacekeeping operations and special political and peacebuilding missions, DFS provides dedicated support and guidance to all UN field peace operations in the areas of finance, logistics, information, communications and technology, human resources and general administration.

Peacekeeping operations continuously evolve in light of changing circumstances. The tasks discharged by peacekeepers over the years have included:

- maintaining ceasefires and separation of forces: by providing 'breathing space', an operation based on a limited agreement between parties can foster an atmosphere conducive to negotiations;
- protecting humanitarian operations: in many conflicts, civilian populations have been deliberately targeted as a means to gain political ends. In such situations, peacekeepers have been asked to provide protection and support for humanitarian operations;
- implementing a comprehensive peace settlement: complex, multidimensional operations, deployed on the basis of comprehensive peace agreements, can assist in such diverse tasks as providing humanitarian assistance, monitoring human rights, observing elections and coordinating economic reconstruction;

- leading states or territories through a transition to stable government, based on democratic principles, good governance and economic development; and
- protecting civilians: non-combatants, women and children have all too often been the direct or collateral victims of recent conflicts.

Cooperation with regional and collective security organizations. The United Nations has increasingly cooperated with regional organizations and other actors and mechanisms provided for in Chapter VIII of the *Charter*. It has worked closely with the Organization of American States in Haiti; the European Union in the former Yugoslavia and the Democratic Republic of the Congo; the Economic Community of West African States in Liberia and Sierra Leone; and the African Union in Western Sahara, the Great Lakes region and Darfur—to name just a few. United Nations military observers have cooperated with peacekeeping forces of regional organizations in Georgia, Liberia, Sierra Leone and Tajikistan; the North Atlantic Treaty Organization works alongside UN personnel in Afghanistan and Kosovo. This is a welcome development, insofar as the global demand for peace operations now outstrips the capacity of any single actor, including the UN. Efforts by regional actors to develop their own abilities to plan, manage and sustain peace operations give a greater depth to response options, thus spawning a more flexible and responsive system that is better able to face the complex challenges posed by internal conflict.

Enforcement

Under Chapter VII of the *Charter*, the Security Council can take enforcement measures to maintain or restore international peace and security. Such measures range from economic sanctions to international military action.

Sanctions

The Security Council has resorted to mandatory sanctions as an enforcement tool when peace was threatened and diplomatic efforts had failed. Sanctions have been imposed in recent years on Afghanistan, the Democratic People's Republic of Korea, Eritrea, Ethiopia, Haiti, Iran, Iraq, Liberia, Libya, Rwanda, Sierra Leone, Somalia, the Sudan, the forces of the National Union for the Total Independence of Angola, and the former Yugoslavia. The range of sanctions has included comprehensive economic and trade sanctions, or more specific measures such as arms embargoes, travel and sport bans, as well as financial or diplomatic restrictions.

The point of sanctions is to apply pressure on a state or entity to comply with the objectives set by the Council without resorting to the use of force. Sanctions offer the Council an important tool to enforce its decisions. The universal character of the UN makes it an appropriate body to establish and monitor sanctions. Yet many states and humanitarian organizations have expressed concerns at the possible adverse impact of sanctions on the most vulnerable segments of the civilian population, such as the elderly, the disabled, refugees or mothers with children. Concerns also exist about the negative economic, social and even political impact sanctions can have on the economies of third or neighbouring countries, where trade and economic relations with the sanctioned state are interrupted.

It is increasingly accepted that the design and application of sanctions need to be improved. The negative effects of sanctions can be reduced either by incorporating humanitarian exceptions into Security Council resolutions, or by better targeting them. So-called 'smart sanctions', which seek to pressure those in power rather than the population at large, thus reducing humanitarian costs, have been gaining support. Smart sanctions may, for instance, involve freezing assets and blocking the financial transactions of elites or other political entities whose illicit activities triggered action in the first place.

Authorizing military action

When peacemaking efforts fail, stronger action by member states may be authorized under Chapter VII of the *Charter*. The Security Council has authorized coalitions of member states to use "all necessary means", including military action, to deal with a conflict—as it did to restore the sovereignty of Kuwait after its invasion by Iraq (1991); to establish a secure environment for humanitarian relief operations in Somalia (1992); to contribute to the protection of civilians at risk in Rwanda (1994); to restore the democratically elected government in Haiti (1994); to protect humanitarian operations in Albania (1997); to restore peace and security in East Timor (1999 and 2006); and to protect civilians in Libya (2011). These actions, though authorized by the Security Council, were entirely under the control of the participating states. They were not UN peacekeeping operations, which are established by the Council and directed by the Secretary-General.

Peacebuilding

For the United Nations, peacebuilding refers to assisting countries and regions in their transitions from war to peace. A peacebuilding process normally begins with the signing of a peace agreement by former warring parties and a UN role in facilitating its implementation. This may include a continued diplomatic role for the UN, to ensure that difficulties are overcome through negotiation rather than a resort to arms. It may also include the deployment of peacekeepers; the repatriation and reintegration of refugees; the monitoring of elections; and the disarmament, demobilization and reintegration of combatants. At the heart of peacebuilding is the attempt to build a new and legitimate state that will have the capacity to peacefully manage disputes, protect its civilians and ensure respect for human rights.

Peacebuilding involves action by a wide array of organizations of the UN system, including the World Bank, regional economic commissions, NGOs and local citizens' groups. Peacebuilding has played a prominent role in UN operations in Bosnia and Herzegovina, Cambodia, El Salvador, Guatemala, Kosovo, Liberia and Mozambique, as well as more recently in Afghanistan, Iraq, Libya and Sierra Leone. Inter-state peacebuilding was guided by the UN Mission in Ethiopia and Eritrea.

Peacebuilding architecture

The UN peacebuilding architecture comprises the Peacebuilding Commission, the Peacebuilding Fund and the Peacebuilding Support Office.

The **Peacebuilding Commission** (*www.un.org/en/peacebuilding*) is a 31-member intergovernmental advisory body of the United Nations dedicated to helping countries in transition from war to lasting peace. It brings together all relevant peacebuilding actors, including international donors and financial institutions, governments, troop-contributing countries and representatives of civil society; proposes integrated strategies for post-conflict peacebuilding and recovery; helps ensure predictable financing for early recovery activities and sustained financial investment; extends the period of attention by the international community to post-conflict recovery; and develops best practices on issues that require collaboration among political, military, humanitarian and development actors.

The **Peacebuilding Fund** (*www.unpbf.org*) is a multi-year standing fund for post-conflict peacebuilding supported by voluntary contributions. It aims to ensure the immediate release of resources needed to launch peacebuilding activities, as well as the availability of appropriate financing for recovery. The Fund had more than $527 million in commitments by the end of 2012. At a high-level stakeholders meeting held in November 2012, $77 million in contributions were confirmed for that year, the highest annual level since 2008.

The **Peacebuilding Support Office** (*www.un.org/peace/peacebuilding*) assists and supports the Peacebuilding Commission, administers the Peacebuilding Fund, and serves the Secretary-General in coordinating UN agencies in their peacebuilding efforts.

Current political and peacebuilding missions. As of 31 May 2013, 3,825 personnel were serving in the following 13 political and peacebuilding missions:

- Office of the United Nations Special Coordinator for the Middle East (UNSCO, est. 1999) (58 civilians);
- Office of the Special Representative of the Secretary-General for West Africa (UNOWA, est. 2001) (39 civilians; 3 military advisers);
- United Nations Assistance Mission in Afghanistan (UNAMA, est. 2002) (1,734 civilians; 20 military advisers; 5 police; 66 UN Volunteers);
- United Nations Assistance Mission for Iraq (UNAMI, 2003) (staff based in Iraq, Jordan and Kuwait: 816 civilians; 272 troops; 5 military advisers; 4 police);
- Office of the United Nations Special Coordinator for Lebanon (UNSCOL, est. 2007) (81 civilians);
- United Nations Regional Centre for Preventive Diplomacy for Central Asia (UNRCCA, est. 2007) (29 civilians);
- United Nations Integrated Peacebuilding Office in Sierra Leone (UNIPSIL, est. 2008) (55 civilians; 6 police; 7 UN Volunteers);
- United Nations Integrated Peacebuilding Office in the Central African Republic (BINUCA, est. 2010) (144 civilians; 2 military advisers; 2 police; 2 UN Volunteers);
- United Nations Integrated Peacebuilding Office in Guinea-Bissau (UNIOGBIS, est. 2010) (98 civilians; 2 military advisers; 12 police; 6 UN Volunteers);
- United Nations Office in Burundi (BNUB, est. 2011) (105 civilians; 1 military adviser; 1 police; 4 UN Volunteers);
- United Nations Regional Office for Central Africa (UNOCA, est. 2011) (25 civilians; 1 military adviser);
- United Nations Support Mission in Libya (UNSMIL, est. 2011) (210 civilians; 7 police; 3 UN Volunteers);
- United Nations Assistance Mission in Somalia (UNSOM, est. 2013).

ONGOING POLITICAL AND PEACEBUILDING MISSIONS

UNOWA	BINUCA	UNSMIL	UNSCOL	UNSCO	UNRCCA	UNAMA*
West Africa	Central African Republic	Libya	Lebanon	Middle East	Central Asia	Afghanistan

UNIOGBIS	UNIPSIL	UNOCA	BNUB	UNSOM	UNAMI
Guinea-Bissau	Sierra Leone	Gabon	Burundi	Somalia	Iraq

Map No. 4147 Rev. 40(E)   UNITED NATIONS   * Mission directed by the Department of Peacekeeping Operations   Department of Field Support
June 2013   Cartographic Section

Electoral assistance

The UN has played a variety of roles in electoral processes, ranging from techni-cal assistance to the actual conducting of the process. In some cases, the UN coordinates the activities of international observers. Typically, such observers follow the registration of voters, the electoral campaign and the organization of the polls. The degree and type of involvement depends on such factors as the requests received from governments, provisions of peace agreements, or mandates from the General Assembly or the Security Council. When requested to step in after a conflict, the Organization has carried out wide-ranging tasks— on occasion taking up the full range of government powers while working with local political and civil leaders to build a self-sustaining government.

The United Nations has provided electoral assistance to more than 100 countries, including advisory services, logistics, training, civic education, com-puter applications and short-term observation. The **Electoral Assistance Division in the Department of Political Affairs** (*www.un.org/depts/dpa/ead*) is the focal point for electoral affairs within the UN system. The Division has increas-ingly been called upon to provide support and guidance for electoral processes as key elements of UN-brokered peace negotiations, or in the context of peace-keeping and peacebuilding efforts. UNDP provides technical support to the elec-tion process, helps countries establish electoral structures, and often coordinates UN electoral assistance in the field. OHCHR helps train election officials, establish guidelines for drafting electoral laws and procedures, and sets up information activities on human rights and elections.

The United Nations broke new ground in 1989, when it supervised the entire election process that led to the independence of Namibia. Since then, the UN, at the request of governments, has assisted with elections in a number of countries, including Nicaragua (1990), Angola (1992), Cambodia (1993), El Salvador, South Africa and Mozambique (1994), Eastern Slavonia (Croatia) (1997), the Central African Republic (1998, 1999), Afghanistan (2004, 2005, 2010), Iraq (2005, 2010), Liberia (2005, 2011), Haiti (2006, 2010), the Democratic Republic of the Congo (2006) and Côte d'Ivoire (2010, 2011). It observed the 1993 referendum in Eritrea. The UN organized and conducted the 2001 and 2002 elections in East Timor, which led to its independence as Timor-Leste, as well as its elections in 2007. In 2010, the United Nations Mission in Sudan (UNMIS) assisted in the first multiparty elections in that country in 20 years. In 2011, the UNMIS Electoral Assistance Division and UNDP supported the referendum for the self-determination of South Sudan, which led to that country's independence.

Building peace through development

Healthy and balanced development is the best form of conflict prevention. The United Nations aims to consolidate peace through development assistance. Organizations including UNDP, UNICEF, WFP, and UNHCR play key roles in the recovery stage, which is crucial for providing opportunities for displaced persons and restoring confidence in national and local institutions. The United Nations can help repatriate refugees, clear landmines, repair infrastructure, mobilize resources and stimulate economic recovery.

Action for peace

United Nations peacekeeping and peacebuilding missions are underway throughout the world—in Africa, Asia and the Pacific (including the Middle East), the Americas and Europe. Current operations are described below in their historical context. For a full list of past and present peacekeeping missions, see p. 245.

Africa

Africa is an area of major focus and action for the United Nations (see *www.un.org/africa/osaa*). The Organization has addressed the challenges posed by protracted conflicts and longstanding disputes on the continent in innovative ways and at the highest level. In their *Millennium Declaration* of September 2000, world leaders resolved to give full support, including special measures to help Africa tackle its peace and development issues.

Great Lakes region

Burundi. A decade of civil strife in Burundi (1993–2003) had left between 250,000 and 300,000 people dead and several hundred thousand displaced. By mid-2003, ceasefire agreements had been signed with three major factional groups. The African Union (AU) had authorized deployment of the African Mission in Burundi (AMIB), comprising up to 3,500 troops. By the end of April, midway through the transitional period, a Hutu President and Tutsi Vice-President were sworn in. However, deadly attacks continued to take place in Bujumbura, Burundi's capital, and the UN was forced to withdraw its nonessential staff from the city.

Sustained efforts by South Africa and other countries in the region resulted in a ceasefire agreement in November 2003. There was real hope that peace would emerge, and the presence of AMIB had played a key role in making it possible. The Mission suffered from a serious lack of funds and logistics support, however, and the AU requested that AMIB be taken over by the United Nations. In May 2004, acting under the enforcement provisions of the *Charter*, the Security Council authorized the deployment of the United Nations Operation in Burundi (ONUB)— to be composed, initially, of more than 2,000 AMIB troops re-branded as UN forces. In 2005, a referendum on Burundi's post-transitional constitution was held, followed by communal elections in June, and the election of the country's first post-transitional president in August. A ceasefire agreement was signed in September, and the UN helped implement it.

In January 2007, ONUB was replaced by the United Nations Integrated Office in Burundi (BINUB), to support the peace consolidation process and assist the government in strengthening national institutions, training the police, professionalizing the national defence force, completing demobilization and reintegration of former combatants, protecting human rights, reforming the justice and legal sector, and promoting economic growth and poverty reduction. In January 2011, the **United Nations Office in Burundi (BNUB)** replaced BINUB. In February 2013, the Security Council extended the BNUB mandate until 15 February 2014 and asked it to support the government in facilitating dialogue between national actors; strengthening national institutions; fighting impunity; promoting and protecting human rights; supporting the socioeconomic development of women and youth, as well as the reintegration of conflict-affected populations; and increasing Burundi's regional integration.

Democratic Republic of the Congo (DRC). Following the 1994 genocide in Rwanda and the establishment of a new government there, some 1.2 million Rwandan Hutus—including elements that had taken part in the genocide—fled to the neighbouring Kivu provinces of the DRC, formerly Zaïre. A rebellion began in those provinces in 1996. Forces led by Laurent Désiré Kabila, aided by Rwanda and Uganda, took the capital city of Kinshasa in 1997 and renamed the country the Democratic Republic of the Congo. In 1998, a rebellion against the Kabila government, led by the Congolese Rally for Democracy (RCD), started in the Kivu regions. The rebels, supported by Rwanda and Uganda, seized large areas of the country. Angola, Chad, Namibia and Zimbabwe promised President Kabila military support, but the rebels maintained their grip on the eastern regions. The Security Council called for a ceasefire and the withdrawal of foreign forces. In early 1999, the DRC, along with Angola, Namibia, Rwanda, Uganda and Zimbabwe, signed the Lusaka Ceasefire Agreement, which provided for the holding of an inter-Congolese dialogue. The RCD and the Mouvement de Libération du Congo signed it in August. The Council subsequently established the United Nations Mission in the Democratic Republic of the Congo (MONUC) to assist in implementing the agreement.

In January 2001, President Kabila was assassinated. He was succeeded by his son Joseph. In October, the long-awaited inter-Congolese dialogue began in Addis Ababa, Ethiopia. In July 2002, an agreement was signed by the DRC and Rwanda on the withdrawal of Rwandan combatants from the DRC. In September, a similar agreement was reached between the DRC and Uganda. By October, however, renewed fighting in the eastern part of the DRC threatened to destabilize the entire country. By the end of the year, the parties to the conflict, under UN and South African mediation, agreed to form a transitional government. The Security Council enlarged MONUC to 8,700 military personnel and expanded its presence eastward, but fighting erupted again in South Kivu, generating massive refugee flows. Finally, in May 2003, the parties signed a ceasefire agreement for the Ituri region. Following the ceasefire, the Security Council authorized deployment of an Interim Emergency Multinational Force (IEMF) to Bunia, the capital city of the Ituri province, to help stabilize the situation. In June of that year, the government and the country's main opposition factions signed an agreement on military and security arrangements, and subsequently, a power-sharing government of national unity and transition was installed—led by President Kabila. The Council increased MONUC's military strength to 10,800. Acting under Chapter VII of the *Charter of the United Nations*, it authorized the mission to use force to fulfil its mandate in Ituri and North and South Kivu. In September, IEMF handed over its security responsibilities to MONUC.

The country's first free and fair elections in 46 years were held in July 2006, with voters electing a 500-seat National Assembly. Joseph Kabila won a run-off election for the presidency in October. The electoral process represented one of the most complex votes the UN had ever helped organize.

Through MONUC, the UN remained actively involved in trying to resolve the conflict in North Kivu between the army and dissident forces. In October 2008, UN armoured vehicles were used to halt the advance of the RCD on the city of Goma after the national army retreated under pressure from the rebels. Peacekeepers were deployed from Goma to North Kivu. In November, the Security Council sent an additional 3,085 peacekeepers to the area, citing "extreme concern at the deteriorating humanitarian situation and in particular the targeted attacks against the civilian population, sexual violence, recruitment of child soldiers and summary executions".

In July 2010, MONUC became the **United Nations Organization Stabilization Mission in the Democratic Republic of the Congo (MONUSCO)**, reflecting the new phase reached in the country. The Council decided that MONUSCO would comprise, in addition to its civilian and judiciary components, a maximum of 19,815 military personnel, 760 military observers, 391 police personnel and 1,050 members of formed police units. Future reconfigurations of MONUSCO would be determined as the situation evolved, including: the completion of military operations in North and South Kivu as well as the Orientale provinces; improved government capacity to protect the population; and the consolidation of state authority throughout the DRC. In June 2012, the Council decided that the Mission would provide technical and logistical support for the organization and holding of provincial and local elections.

On 20 November 2012, after intense fighting involving the DRC armed forces and MONUSCO, the former National Congress for the Defence of the People (CNDP)—later known as the Mouvement du 23 mars (M23)—occupied Goma; it withdrew from the city on 2 December. The situation in the eastern DRC remained fragile, as M23 elements further consolidated their control over a significant portion of North Kivu.

In February 2013, the Peace, Security and Cooperation Framework for the DRC and the region was signed in Addis Ababa, Ethiopia, by representatives of 11 countries in the region, the AU, the International Conference on the Great Lakes Region, the Southern African Development Community and the UN Secretary-General. In March, the Security Council extended MONUSCO's mandate until 31 March 2014 and created an 'intervention brigade' to strengthen the peacekeeping operation. The brigade would be set up for an initial period of one year within the Mission's authorized troop ceiling.

Central African Republic. The conflict in the Central African Republic began when soldiers staged a series of mutinies in the mid-1990s. In 1998, the UN established the United Nations Mission in the Central African Republic (MINURCA) to help improve security in the capital, Bangui. The UN also provided support for the 1999 presidential elections. The United Nations Peacebuilding Support Office in the Central African Republic (BONUCA) succeeded MINURCA in February 2000.

In March 2003, a rebel military group seized power, ousting the elected president. The Security Council condemned the coup, stressing that the Bangui authorities had to elaborate a plan for national dialogue, including a timeframe for the holding of elections. A process of national dialogue led to two rounds of legislative and presidential elections in 2005. In the final runoff, François Bozizé, who had led the coup, was elected President. The newly elected National Assembly held its first regular session in mid-2006.

BONUCA played a significant role in encouraging the signing in 2008 of the Global Peace Agreement between the government and three main rebel groups. It also facilitated the holding in December 2008 of the Inclusive Political Dialogue between the government, leaders of rebel groups, exiled political opponents, civil society and other stakeholders. The Dialogue called for the creation of a government of national unity; the holding of municipal, legislative and presidential elections; the creation of a truth and reconciliation commission; and the launch of a programme for the disarmament, demobilization and reintegration of former combatants.

In 2009, the **United Nations Integrated Peacebuilding Office in the Central African Republic (BINUCA)** succeeded BONUCA. The Peacebuilding Office operates under a mandate from the Security Council to help consolidate peace and national reconciliation, strengthen democratic institutions to promote the rule of law, and mobilize international political support and resources for national reconstruction and economic recovery. It also promotes public awareness of human rights issues.

In late 2012, a rebel coalition known as Séléka seized large parts of the country. Agreements to resolve the crisis were signed in January 2013 in the Gabonese capital Libreville, under the aegis of the Economic Community of Central African States. BINUCA provided logistical and technical support to the talks among the warring parties. On 24 January, the Security Council extended BINUCA's mandate until 31 January 2014.

West Africa

In 2001, the Secretary-General decided to establish the **Office of the Special Representative of the Secretary-General for West Africa (UNOWA)** (*www.un.org/unowa*) to promote an integrated, subregional strategy involving the UN and its partners to address the interlinked political, economic and social problems faced by West African countries. Based in Dakar, Senegal, UNOWA became operational in 2002.

UNOWA is the first UN regional peacebuilding office. It carries out good offices roles and special assignments in West African countries, liaising with subregional organizations and reporting to UN Headquarters on key development issues. The special representative has been closely involved in international efforts aimed at resolving conflicts in Côte d'Ivoire and Liberia. UNOWA is involved in addressing such cross-border challenges as mercenaries; child soldiers; small arms proliferation; security sector reform; democratization; economic integration; youth unemployment; and transborder cooperation. It has organized regional meetings aimed at harmonizing programmes for the disarmament, demobilization and reintegration of former combatants.

The special representative is also chairperson of the Cameroon-Nigeria Mixed Commission, established by the Secretary-General at the request of the Presidents of Nigeria and Cameroon, to consider all aspects of the implementation of an October 2002 ruling by the International Court of Justice on the boundary between the two countries. Relations between Cameroon and Nigeria have been strained over issues relating to their 1,600-kilometre land boundary, extending from Lake Chad to the Bakassi peninsula, with a maritime boundary in the Gulf of Guinea. In 2006, the Presidents of both countries signed an agreement to end the border dispute over the Bakassi peninsula, following intense mediation by the Secretary-General. By mid-August, Nigeria had completely withdrawn its troops and formally transferred authority over the region to Cameroon. In 2007, the parties agreed on the delineation of the maritime boundary line between the two countries, and thereby resolved the four sections addressed by the Court's ruling. Progress continues to be made in marking their common land boundary, under the supervision of the Mixed Commission.

Côte d'Ivoire. In September 2002, military personnel attempted a coup in Côte d'Ivoire and occupied the northern part of the country. The attempted coup resulted in a de facto partition of the country, with the government of President Laurent Gbagbo controlling only the south. The fighting caused massive displacements. The Economic Community of West African States (ECOWAS) established a peacekeeping force in Côte d'Ivoire to monitor a ceasefire agreement between the government and one of the country's rebel groups. In January 2003, the government and the remaining rebel groups agreed to a ceasefire. A peace agreement was reached, and President Gbagbo established a national reconciliation government in March. Two months later, the army and the Forces nouvelles—comprising three rebel groups—signed a ceasefire agreement. Subsequently, the Security Council established the United Nations Mission in Côte d'Ivoire (MINUCI) to facilitate implementation of the agreement. In September, however, the Forces nouvelles rejected President Gbagbo's appointment of defence and internal security ministers and pulled out of the government. It also protested that President Gbagbo had not delegated enough power to the Prime Minister and national reconciliation government.

Responding to this situation, the Security Council, in early 2004, established the United Nations Operation in Côte d'Ivoire (UNOCI), asking the Secretary-General to transfer authority from MINUCI and the ECOWAS forces to UNOCI, and authorizing the French troops in the country to use all necessary means to support the new Mission, which had an authorized maximum strength of 6,240 military personnel and a wide-ranging mandate.

In April 2005, the government and the rebel Forces nouvelles began a withdrawal of weapons from the frontline—an area held by peacekeepers of UNOCI and the UN-authorized French forces. In June, the Security Council expanded UNOCI to prevent the situation from deteriorating. President Gbagbo and Forces nouvelles secretary-general Guillaume Soro signed the 'Ouagadougou Agreement' in March 2007. It called for the creation of a new transitional government; free and fair presidential elections; merging the Forces nouvelles with the national forces; dismantling the militias; and replacing the so-called zone of confidence separating the government-controlled south and rebel-controlled north with a 'green line' to be monitored by UNOCI.

Presidential elections were held in November 2010; the Independent Electoral Commission declared Alassane Ouattara the winner. The President of the Constitutional Council, however, stated that the results were invalid, and declared Mr. Gbagbo the winner. Both Gbagbo and Ouattara claimed victory and took the presidential oath of office. The UN, AU, ECOWAS, EU and most states recognized Mr. Ouattara as President-elect and called for Mr. Gbagbo to step down. Mr. Gbagbo refused, and ordered UN peacekeepers to leave the country. The Security Council extended UNOCI's mandate until the end of June 2011, and decided to send 2,000 supplementary peacekeepers. The World Bank halted loans to the country and travel restrictions were placed on Mr. Gbagbo and his allies.

In April 2011, following military operations conducted by forces loyal to President Ouattara, UNOCI and French troops, Mr. Gbagbo was arrested and placed in government custody. The Constitutional Council ratified the results of the presidential election showing that Mr. Ouattara had won, reversing its 2010 decision to reject the results. In May 2011, Mr. Ouattara was sworn in as President. In November, the International Criminal Court (ICC) issued an arrest warrant against Mr. Gbagbo for crimes against humanity, and he was transferred by Ivorian authorities to the ICC detention centre at The Hague.

In June 2012, UNOCI peacekeepers were attacked by a group of unidentified armed elements while on reconnaissance patrol in south-western Côte d'Ivoire and seven military personnel from the Niger contingent were killed. In July, the Security Council extended UNOCI's mandate until 31 July 2013 and adjusted the Operation's military component to 8,837 personnel.

Liberia. After eight years of civil strife, a democratically elected government was installed in Liberia in 1997, and the United Nations Peacebuilding Support Office in Liberia (UNOL) was established. In 1999, however, fighting broke out between government forces and the Liberians United for Reconciliation and Democracy (LURD). In early 2003, a new armed group emerged—the Movement for Democracy in Liberia (MODEL). By May, rebel forces controlled 60 per cent of the country. As the parties gathered in June in Accra, Ghana, for peace talks sponsored by ECOWAS, the UN-backed Special Court for Sierra Leone announced its indictment of Liberian President Charles Taylor for war crimes in Sierra Leone during its 10-year civil war. The President offered to remove himself from the peace process. Two weeks later, the government, LURD and MODEL signed a ceasefire accord, aiming to reach a comprehensive peace agreement within 30 days and the formation of a transitional government without President Taylor. Despite that promising development, the fighting escalated, and ECOWAS deployed a vanguard force of over 1,000 troops.

President Taylor resigned in mid-August; Vice-President Moses Blah succeeded him, heading an interim government. A few days later, the Secretary-General's special representative secured an agreement by the parties to ensure unimpeded access of humanitarian aid to all territories under their control, and to guarantee the security of aid workers. The parties also signed a comprehensive peace agreement.

In September 2003, the Security Council established the **United Nations Mission in Liberia (UNMIL)**—with up to 15,000 military personnel and over 1,000 civilian police officers—to take over from the ECOWAS force, and replace UNOL. Its mandate included: monitoring the ceasefire; assisting in the disarmament, demobilization, reintegration and repatriation of all armed parties; providing security at key government installations and vital infrastructure; protecting UN staff, facilities and civilians; and assisting in humanitarian aid and human rights. UNMIL was also mandated to help the transitional government develop a strategy to consolidate its institutions, with a view to holding free and fair elections by October 2005. As scheduled, 3,500 ECOWAS soldiers were 'rehatted' with the UN blue helmet. In October, the national transitional government was installed, led by Chairman Gyude Bryant, and former President Blah turned over a large quantity of arms to UN peacekeepers.

In late 2004, Liberia's warring militias formally disbanded in a ceremony at UNMIL headquarters in Monrovia. In October 2005, after 15 years of conflict, the people of Liberia, with UN assistance, held their first post-war elections, electing Ellen Johnson-Sirleaf as President. By the end of February 2006, more than 300,000 internally displaced Liberians had returned to their home villages.

In 2007, Liberia became eligible to receive assistance from the UN Peacebuilding Fund. The funding was allocated to projects that consolidated peace, addressed insecurity and catalyzed the nation's broader development. Work on these projects began in 2009.

In September 2012, the Security Council extended the UNMIL mandate until 30 September 2013. It endorsed the Secretary-General's recommendation to decrease UNIMIL's military strength to approximately 3,750 personnel by July 2015. The Council also increased UNMIL's authorized formed police units by three additional units for a new ceiling of 1,795 personnel. Future reconfigurations of the Mission should be based on the evolution of the situation on the ground and on the improved capacity of the government to protect the population, with a view to government forces progressively taking over UNMIL's security role.

Guinea-Bissau. In June 2009, the **United Nations Integrated Peacebuilding Office in Guinea-Bissau (UNIOGBIS)** was established for an initial 12-month period from 1 January to 31 December 2010. UNIOGBIS succeeded the Peacebuilding Support Office in Guinea-Bissau, which was launched in March 1999 following a period of conflict in the country. Unrest occurred again in April 2010, when Prime Minister Carlos Gomes Júnior was briefly detained by soldiers, along with the Army Chief of Staff. In this critical context, UNIOGBIS assists the UN Peacebuilding Commission in its multidimensional engagement with Guinea-Bissau; works to strengthen the capacity of national institutions to maintain constitutional order and respect for the rule of law; supports the establishment of effective and efficient law enforcement and criminal justice systems; provides support in developing and coordinating the implementation of the security sector reform strategy; and promotes human rights in general and women's rights in particular. In doing so, UNIOGBIS cooperates with the AU, the Community of Portuguese Language Countries (CPLP), ECOWAS, the EU, and other partners.

On 12 April 2012, elements of the Guinea-Bissau armed forces carried out a coup d'état, in which Interim President Raimundo Pereira, the Prime Minister and Armed Forces Chief of General Staff General Antonio Indjai were arrested and detained. The coup took place against the backdrop of tensions arising from the rejection by five of nine presidential candidates of the outcome of the first round of elections held in March. The Security Council condemned the coup and demanded the unconditional release of all detained officials. Following discussions held between the military junta and ECOWAS on 27 April, the junta agreed to the deployment of an ECOWAS force to Guinea-Bissau and released the Interim President Pereira and the Prime Minister, who then travelled with the ECOWAS delegation to Abidjan, Côte d'Ivoire.

In February 2013, the Security Council extended the UNIOGBIS mandate until 31 May 2013.

Sierra Leone. In 1991, the Revolutionary United Front (RUF) launched a war to overthrow the government of Sierra Leone, but in 1992, the country's own army overthrew the government. In 1995, the Secretary-General appointed a special envoy who, working with the Organization of African Unity and ECOWAS, negotiated a return to civilian rule. Following presidential elections in 1996, in which the RUF did not participate, the army relinquished power to the winner, Ahmad Tejan Kabbah. The special envoy then helped negotiate the 1996 Abidjan Peace Accord between the government and the RUF. Following a military coup in 1997, the army joined with the RUF to form a ruling junta. President Kabbah went into exile, and the Security Council imposed an oil and arms embargo—authorizing ECOWAS to ensure its implementation by using the troops of the Economic Community of West African States Monitoring Group (ECOMOG).

In February 1998, in response to an attack by rebel and junta forces, ECOMOG conducted military operations that led to the fall of the junta. President Kabbah returned to office, and the Council ended the embargo. In June, the Council established the United Nations Observer Mission in Sierra Leone (UNOMSIL) to monitor the security situation, the disarmament of combatants, and the restructuring of the security forces. Unarmed UNOMSIL teams, under ECOMOG protection, documented atrocities and human rights abuses.

The rebel alliance, however, soon gained control of more than half of the country, and in January 1999 overran the capital, Freetown. Later that month, ECOMOG troops retook Freetown and reinstalled the government. The fighting resulted in 700,000 internally displaced persons (IDPs) and 450,000 refugees. The special representative, in consultation with West African states, began diplomatic efforts to open up a dialogue with the rebels. The negotiations led in July to the Lomé Peace Agreement to end the war and form a government of national unity.

The Security Council replaced UNOMSIL in October 1999 with the larger United Nations Mission in Sierra Leone (UNAMSIL), to help the parties put the agreement into effect and assist in disarming, demobilizing and reintegrating some 45,000 combatants. In February 2000, following the announced withdrawal of ECOMOG, UNAMSIL's strength was increased to 11,000 troops. In April, however, RUF attacked UN forces, killing four peacekeepers and taking hostage nearly 500 UN personnel. In May, British troops serving under a bilateral arrangement secured the capital and its airport, and assisted in capturing RUF leader Foday Sankoh. By the end of the month, around half of the UN hostages had been released. The Council increased UNAMSIL's strength to 13,000 troops to help restore peace, and in July UNAMSIL rescued the remaining hostages. In August, the Council began the process of setting up a special court to try those responsible for war crimes.

UNAMSIL completed its deployment to all areas of the country in November 2001, and the disarmament process was completed in January 2002. Following presidential and parliamentary elections in May 2002, the Mission focused on extending state authority throughout the country, reintegrating ex-combatants, and resettling IDPs and returnees. IDP resettlement was completed in December and the repatriation of some 280,000 Sierra Leonean refugees in July 2004. A Truth and Reconciliation Commission and the Special Court for Sierra Leone began to function in mid-2002.

When UNAMSIL was withdrawn in December 2005, it left the country with a growing sense of stability and an improvement in basic services. It was replaced in January 2006 by the UN Integrated Office in Sierra Leone (UNIOSIL), the first integrated UN office established to support a peace-consolidation process.

Sierra Leone's development efforts took a significant leap forward when the UN Peacebuilding Commission singled it out, along with Burundi, for its first activities. In March 2007, on the Commission's recommendation, Secretary-General Ban Ki-moon made $35 million available for Sierra Leone from the UN Peacebuilding Fund, set up the previous October to assist countries emerging from conflict to rebuild and avert a relapse into bloodshed.

In July 2007, campaigning began for Sierra Leone's presidential and parliamentary elections. UNIOSIL's participation included training 49 district officers on polling and counting procedures, to be passed on to 37,000 polling staff. The elections were held in August with high voter turnout. In a run-off election, Ernest Bai Koroma was elected President. He was inaugurated in November 2007.

In August 2008, the Security Council established the **United Nations Integrated Peacebuilding Office in Sierra Leone (UNIPSIL)**, which took over from UNIOSIL. With some 70 staff, UNIPSIL provides advice to foster peace, offering support and training to the national police and security forces. The Office also helps build democratic institutions in furtherance of good governance and the promotion of human rights.

UNIPSIL assisted in the preparations for the presidential, parliamentary and local elections held on 17 November 2012. The elections—the third since the end of the civil war—were considered a success for the people of Sierra Leone and its institutions. President Koroma won the election and was inaugurated in February 2013. In March, the Security Council extended the UNIPSIL mandate until 31 March 2014 and decided that, in accordance with the views of the government and conditions on the ground, UNIPSIL should be fully drawn down by that date.

Mali. In 2012, Mali became a significant source of international concern. In mid-January, the Tuareg Mouvement national pour la libération de l'Azawad (MNLA), along with Islamic armed groups including Ansar Dine, Al-Qaida in the Islamic Maghreb (AQIM) and the Mouvement pour l'unicité et le jihad en Afrique de l'Ouest (MUJAO), as well as deserters from the Malian armed forces, attacked government forces in the north of the country. In March, a mutiny by disaffected soldiers from defeated units resulted in a military coup d'état. A military junta took power, suspended the constitution and dissolved government institutions. On 27 March, ECOWAS appointed President Blaise Compaoré of Burkina Faso to mediate in the crisis. On 6 April, the military junta and ECOWAS signed a framework agreement that led to the resignation of President Amadou Toumani Touré on 8 April, and the appointment of Dioncounda Traoré as interim President on 12 April. On 17 April, Cheick Modibo Diarra was appointed interim Prime Minister.

MNLA overran government forces in the Kidal, Gao and Timbuktu regions and proclaimed an independent State of Azawad in April. Ideological tensions later emerged among the armed groups in the north and, by 18 November, Ansar Dine and MUJAO had driven MNLA out of the main towns of Kidal, Gao, and Timbuktu. Those groups then controlled two thirds of Malian territory. Some 430,000 people were displaced as a result of the crisis.

The United Nations has been working with national authorities and regional partners to help Mali return to constitutional order and territorial integrity. In December 2012, the Security Council authorized the deployment of an African-led International Support Mission in Mali (AFISMA) for an initial period of one year. The Mission would, among other tasks, contribute to the rebuilding of the capacity of the Malian Defence and Security Forces and support Malian authorities in recovering territory under the control of terrorist, extremist and armed groups; maintaining security and consolidating state authority; protecting the population; and creating a secure environment for the delivery of humanitarian assistance and the return of IDPs and refugees. The Secretary-General was asked to establish a multidisciplinary UN presence in Mali to support the political and security processes underway.

In early January 2013, Ansar Dine, AQIM and MUJAO elements advanced southwards. The capture of the town of Konna led the transitional authorities to request the assistance of France to defend Mali's sovereignty and restore its territorial integrity. Military operations led by France began on 11 January, and the deployment of African forces with AFISMA was accelerated. By the end of the month, state control had been restored in most major northern towns, and most terrorist and associated forces had withdrawn. On 29 January, the Malian Parliament approved a road map for the transition. A Dialogue and Reconciliation Commission was established in March. The transitional authorities committed to organizing presidential elections on 7 July and legislative elections on 21 July.

The **United Nations Office in Mali (UNOM)** began its deployment to the Malian capital, Bamako, on 21 January. The Office was assisting Malians to achieve a broad-based, national dialogue leading to national elections, and to negotiate with armed groups that cut off ties with terrorist organizations and respected Mali's territorial integrity. The Security Council established the **United Nations Multidimensional Integrated Stabilization Mission in Mali (MINUSMA)** in April. UNOM was subsumed into MINUSMA, and the Mission took over authority from AFISMA on 1 July. MINUSMA would comprise up to 11,200 military personnel and 1,440 police. Its mandate included the stabilization of population centres; protection of civilians and UN personnel; and promotion and protection of human rights. It would also support the re-establishment of State authority throughout the country; the implementation of the transitional road map; cultural preservation; national and international justice; and humanitarian assistance.

Central and East Africa

The **United Nations Regional Office for Central Africa (UNOCA)** (*http://unoca. unmissions.org*) was launched in March 2011 in Libreville, Gabon, with an initial two-year mandate to assist member states and subregional organizations in consolidating peace and preventing potential conflicts. Key missions of UNOCA included undertaking, on behalf of the Secretary-General, good offices and other tasks in countries of the subregion, particularly in the areas of conflict prevention and peacebuilding; cooperating with and assisting the Economic Community of Central Africa States (ECCAS) and other regional organizations in promoting peace and stability; strengthening DPA's capacity to advise the Secretary-General on matters relating to peace and security in the region; and enhancing linkages in the work of the United Nations and other partners, with a view to promoting an integrated, subregional approach. UNOCA is headed by the Special Representative of the Secretary-General for Central Africa, Abou Moussa (Chad), who has identified six main priorities for the Office:

- provide technical assistance to regional organizations, particularly ECCAS, to help build their capacity in early warning and other areas;
- support mediation efforts to foster the peaceful management of crises and the use of good offices for the prevention of conflicts in the subregion;
- coordinate UN and regional efforts to fight against the Lord's Resistance Army;
- help address youth unemployment, which is considered a threat to stability in the subregion;
- promote a regional and integrated, strategic approach to resolve border disputes in the subregion and fight against piracy and maritime insecurity in the Gulf of Guinea; and
- provide support to the United Nations Standing Advisory Committee on Security Questons in Central Africa (UNSAC). UNOCA has been serving as the Secretariat of UNSAC since May 2011.

In August 2012, the Security Council renewed UNOCA's mandate until 28 February 2014.

The Sudan and South Sudan. The Sudan has endured years of civil conflict since it became independent on 1 January 1956. In the phase that began in 1983, the government and the Sudan People's Liberation Movement/Army (SPLM/A), the main rebel movement in the south, fought over resources, power, the role of religion in the state, and self-determination. Over 2 million people died, 4 million were uprooted and some 600,000 others fled the country until the signing of the Comprehensive Peace Agreement (CPA) in January 2005. Under the Agreement, interim institutions would govern for six-and-a-half years, following which the people would vote for Sudanese unity or secession in an internationally monitored referendum.

In March 2005, the Security Council established the United Nations Mission in the Sudan (UNMIS) to support implementation of the CPA; facilitate and coordinate humanitarian assistance and the voluntary return of refugees and internally displaced persons; and assist the parties in mine action. It was also mandated to protect and promote human rights, and coordinate international efforts to protect civilians—with particular attention to vulnerable groups. In September 2005, a Government of National Unity was established.

In January 2011 a referendum took place in Southern Sudan on whether the region should remain a part of Sudan or become independent. The Southern Sudan Referendum Commission organized the referendum process, while the United Nations provided technical and logistical assistance in preparation for the referendum. An overwhelming majority of participants—98.8 per cent—voted for independence. The AU and the Intergovernmental Authority on Development observer missions declared the process free and fair. On 9 July, with the expiration of the interim period under the CPA, the Republic of South Sudan was formally declared an independent state. The President of South Sudan, Salva Kiir, took the oath of office and signed the country's Transitional Constitution.

The UNMIS mandate also ended on 9 July; as of that date, the Security Council established the **United Nations Mission in the Republic of South Sudan (UNMISS)**. The new Mission's mandate was to help establish the conditions for development in South Sudan, with a view to strengthening the government's capacity to govern effectively and democratically and establish good relations with its neighbours. UNMISS would consist of up to 7,000 military personnel, up to 900 civilian police and an appropriate civilian component.

On 14 July 2011, the General Assembly admitted South Sudan as the 193rd member state of the United Nations.

Negotiations between South Sudan and the Sudan on outstanding issues continued under the auspices of the AU High-level Implementation Panel. The relationship took a turn for the worse in March 2012, however, when violence along the border increased substantially. The conflict escalated on 10 April, when SPLA captured and occupied oil-rich Heglig, effectively shutting down more than 50 per cent of the Sudan's oil production. Responding to international pressure, including from the UN, South Sudan announced the unconditional withdrawal of SPLA from Heglig on 20 April.

In July 2012, the Security Council extended the UNMISS mandate through 15 July 2013.

Abyei. At the end of 2010, tensions increased in the Abyei Area of the Sudan in the lead-up to the referendum on the self-determination of Southern Sudan. Those tensions led to a series of violent incidents in early January 2011 and a build-up of armed forces from the North and the South. A simultaneous referendum to be held in Abyei on whether the Area should become part of South Sudan was postponed due to demarcation and residency issues. Temporary security arrangements were agreed on by the parties to the 2005 Comprehensive Peace Agreement (CPA), in the Kadugli Agreements of January 2011 and the Abyei Agreement of March. The Agreements, however, were not fully implemented and a number of incidents occurred between the parties and/or their proxies in April and May. The security situation deteriorated further when, on 19 May, an UNMIS convoy transporting a Sudanese Armed Forces (SAF) Joint Integrated Unit was attacked in Dokura, an area controlled by Southern police. On 21 May, following the SAF takeover of Abyei town, the government of the Sudan unilaterally dissolved the Abyei Administration. As the violence unfolded, more than 100,000 civilians fled southward.

In June, the government of the Sudan and SPLM signed the Agreement on Temporary Arrangements for the Administration and Security of the Abyei Area. The Agreement provided for: the establishment of an Abyei Area Administration, led jointly by a Chief Administrator nominated by SPLM and a Deputy nominated by the government of the Sudan, and the Abyei Joint Oversight Committee; the total withdrawal of all armed elements from the Area and full demilitarization, to be observed by the new Joint Military Observer Committee; and the establishment of an Abyei Police Service. The UN was asked to deploy an interim security force to support the arrangements and provide security in the Area.

Children at Abu Shouk camp for internally displaced persons, North Darfur, celebrate the opening of ten new classrooms built by UNAMID in the camp's three primary schools. (18 April 2012, UN Photo/Albert González Farran)

On 27 June 2011, the Security Council established the **United Nations Interim Security Force for Abyei (UNISFA)** for an initial period of 6 months, with a mandate to monitor and verify the redeployment of SAF and SPLA from the Abyei Area; participate in relevant Abyei Area bodies; provide demining assistance and technical advice; facilitate the delivery of humanitarian aid; strengthen the capacity of the Abyei Police Service; and provide security for oil infrastructure, in cooperation with the police. On 29 June, the parties signed an Agreement on Border Security and the Joint Political and Security Mechanism, which provided for the establishment of a safe demilitarized border zone, and requested UNISFA to provide protection for an international border monitoring verification mission. In December, the Security Council broadened the UNISFA mandate to include, among other tasks, assistance in the process of border normalization.

In May 2012, the Council demanded that the Sudan redeploy all remaining military and police personnel from the Abyei Area, and that both the Sudan and South Sudan finalize the establishment of the Abyei Area Administration and the Police Service. In November, the Council extended the UNISFA mandate until 31 May 2013.

Darfur. Ethnic, economic and political tensions had long combined with competition over scarce resources to fuel violence in the Darfur region of the Sudan. After three years of intense conflict involving the government, SLM/A, the Justice and Equality Movement (JEM), and the Janjaweed and other militias, AU efforts led, in May 2006, to the signing of the Darfur Peace Agreement. The Agreement addressed power-sharing, wealth-sharing, a comprehensive ceasefire and security arrangements. All parties to the conflict were present, but only the government and the SLM/A signed the Agreement. In August 2006, the Security Council authorized an expansion of the UNMIS mandate to enable its deployment to Darfur. The Sudanese government, however, objected to the deployment of UN peacekeepers in the region. After months of negotiations, in July 2007, the Council established the **African Union-United Nations Hybrid Operation in Darfur (UNAMID)** to deal with the situation in Darfur in a comprehensive manner—the first hybrid force involving the United Nations, and the largest UN peacekeeping operation ever.

In April 2007, the ICC issued arrest warrants against a former Minister of State for the Interior and a Janjaweed militia leader for crimes against humanity and war crimes. The Sudanese government's stance has been that the ICC has no jurisdiction to try Sudanese citizens and that it will not hand the two over to authorities in The Hague. In 2008, the ICC Prosecutor filed charges of war crimes and crimes against humanity against the Sudan's President, and an arrest warrant was issued in March 2009. In July 2010, the President was further charged on three counts of genocide.

Full deployment of UNAMID was marred by a lack of cooperation from the government and delays in the readiness of troop and police contributors, together with the immense logistical challenges inherent to the area. Despite its limited resources, however, the mission has provided protection to civilians, facilitated the humanitarian aid operation, and helped provide an environment in which peace can take root. The humanitarian situation worsened due to resumed clashes between government forces and rebels, as well as tribal fighting. It was further aggravated by attacks on UN-AU peacekeepers and abductions and mistreatment of UN staff and aid workers.

On 14 July 2011, the government of the Sudan and the Liberation and Justice Movement signed a protocol agreement committing themselves to the *Doha Document for Peace in Darfur*. The *Document*—now the framework for the comprehensive peace process in Darfur—addressed the root causes of the conflict and its consequences, including those related to power-sharing, wealth-sharing, human rights, justice and reconciliation. UNAMID lent technical expertise to the process, and it continues to support the dissemination of the *Document* and urge non-signatory movements to sign on. It chairs the Cease Fire Commission called for by the *Document*, and participates in the Implementation Follow-on Commission in Doha, Qatar. The Secretary-General welcomed the *Doha Peace Document* as the basis to end the eight-year conflict in western Sudan.

In July 2012, the Security Council extended the UNAMID mandate until 31 July 2013 and approved the Secretary-General's recommendation that the Mission's strength be reconfigured to focus on the areas of Darfur with the highest security threats.

Somalia. The people of Somalia have been living with anarchy since 1991, when the government was overthrown and civil war broke out, dividing the country into fiefdoms controlled by rival warlords. Arms, ammunition and explosives flowed freely across Somalia's borders in breach of a UN embargo. When talks organized by the Secretary-General led to a ceasefire in the capital, Mogadishu, the Security Council in April 1992 established the United Nations Operation in Somalia (UNOSOM I) to monitor the ceasefire; provide protection and security for UN personnel, equipment and supplies; and escort deliveries of humanitarian supplies. The deteriorating security situation, however, led the Council in December to authorize member states to form a Unified Task Force (UNITAF) to ensure the safe delivery of humanitarian assistance. In March 1993, the Council established UNOSOM II to complete UNITAF's efforts to restore peace, but the escalation of inter-clan fighting led to the withdrawal of the Operation in March 1995.

In April 1995, the Secretary-General established the United Nations Political Office for Somalia (UNPOS) (*www.un-somalia.org*) to help him advance peace and reconciliation through contacts with Somali leaders, civic organizations, and concerned states and organizations. UNPOS supported a Djibouti initiative that led, in 2000, to the formation of a Transitional National Government, but its authority was subsequently challenged by Somali leaders in the south, and by regional administrations in 'Puntland' in the north-east, and 'Somaliland' in the north-west.

In 2002, a national reconciliation conference sponsored by the Intergovernmental Authority on Development (IGAD) led to agreement on a cessation of hostilities and on structures and principles to govern the national reconciliation process. In 2004, Somali leaders agreed on the establishment of two Transitional Federal Institutions (TFIs): a Transitional Federal Government (TFG)—the internationally recognized federal government of Somalia—and a Transitional Federal Parliament (TFP). The TFG and TFP were defined in the *Transitional Federal Charter*, also adopted in 2004. The *Charter* outlined a five-year mandate leading to the establishment of a new constitution and a transition to a representative government after the holding of national elections. The President of 'Puntland', Abdullahi Yusuf Ahmed, was elected President of the TFG in October 2004, and all 25 presidential candidates promised to support him and to demobilize their militias. By May 2006, however, militias of the Alliance for the Restoration of Peace and Counter-Terrorism and of the Sharia Courts were battling each other in Mogadishu. In July, forces loyal to the Islamic Courts advanced towards the city of Baidoa.

In December 2006, the Security Council authorized IGAD and AU member states to establish a protection and training mission in Somalia. With hundreds of thousands fleeing heavy fighting in Mogadishu, the Council, in February 2007, authorized the AU to establish a wider operation—the African Union Mission in Somalia (AMISOM)—to replace the IGAD mission. AMISOM was authorized to take all necessary measures to fulfil its mandate to create a secure environment. The Council extended AMISOM several times and approved contingency planning for a possible UN operation. In 2009, the United Nations Support Office for AMISOM (UNSOA) was established in Nairobi to provide logistical and technical support to the AU operation. Up to late 2010, Secretary-General Ban Ki-moon maintained that deploying a UN mission was not viable given the security situation. The UN focused, therefore, on encouraging dialogue between the TFG and opposition groups and on strengthening AMISOM.

In 2006, the Islamic Courts Union (ICU) had taken over much of the south. The TFG, with the assistance of Ethiopian troops and AU peacekeepers, managed to drive out the ICU, which then splintered into factions. Radical elements, including Al-Shabab, regrouped to resume the insurgency against the TFG and oppose the Ethiopian military presence. By 2008, Al-Shabab had gained control of key areas, including Baidoa. In December 2008, President Abdullahi Yusuf Ahmed resigned. In January 2009, Sharif Ahmad was elected President, and Omar Abdirashid Ali Sharmarke was selected as Prime Minister. During that same month, the Ethiopian troops withdrew. The TFG, backed by AU troops, began a counteroffensive in February 2009 to retake control of the south. Fighting continued throughout 2010.

A consequence of the conflict was an upsurge in piracy off the coast of Somalia. The Security Council adopted resolutions to combat the problem and, in 2008, a multinational coalition established a Maritime Security Patrol Area within the Gulf of Aden. Acts of piracy reached unprecedented levels in 2011 but declined sharply in 2012, thanks to the joint efforts of the international community and the private sector.

A major military offensive against Al-Shabaab began in February 2011, and TFG forces, supported by AMISOM, made significant territorial gains in Mogadishu. By mid-August, the TFG had influence over 90 per cent of the capital. As a result of those gains, the Secretary-General's Special Representative for Somalia was able to relocate his office to Mogadishu on 24 January 2012.

Somalia's eight-year political transition ended successfully with the establishment of a new Federal Parliament on 20 August 2012. The Parliament selected the President, Hassan Sheikh Mohamud. UNPOS provided good offices and political support to facilitate the end of the transition. Despite reports of intimidation and interference, the process yielded the most transparent and representative election in Somalia's 20-year crisis, and the first to be held inside the country. Nevertheless, the security situation in Mogadishu, though improved, remained unpredictable. Somali National Security Forces and AMISOM maintained their hold on the city, but Al-Shabaab attacks occurred frequently.

In March 2013, the Security Council authorized AU member states to maintain AMISOM until 28 February 2014. The Mission was to assist the Federal Government in: reducing the threat posed by Al-Shabaab and other armed opposition groups, and extending state authority in areas recovered from Al-Shabaab; providing protection to the Federal Government and those involved with the peace and reconciliation process; and creating security conditions for the provision of humanitarian assistance. The Council agreed with the Secretary-General's assessment that UNPOS had fulfilled its mandate and should be dissolved; the Office should be replaced by a new, expanded political mission as soon as possible. In May, the Security Council decided to establish, for an initial period of 12 months, the **United Nations Assistance Mission in Somalia (UNSOM)** by 3 June 2013, following the end of the UNPOS mandate on 2 June. The Mission was mandated to provide good offices supporting the Federal Government's peace and reconciliation process, and provide strategic policy advice to the Federal Government and AMISOM. UNSOM would assist the Federal Government in coordinating international donor support; and help build the Federal Government's capacity in the areas of human rights and women's empowerment, child protection, conflict-related sexual and gender-based violence, and justice. It would also monitor, help investigate and prevent, and report to the Council on abuses or violations of human rights or international humanitarian law committed in Somalia, as well as abuses committed against children or women.

The Americas

The United Nations has been instrumental in bringing peace to the Central American region—including the countries of Costa Rica, El Salvador, Guatemala, Honduras and Nicaragua—where it conducted some of its most complex and successful operations. Its support of peace and security in Haiti is ongoing.

Haiti. As Haiti celebrated its bicentennial in January 2004, a severe political deadlock threatened the country's stability. Clashes between pro- and anti-government militias led to a spiral of increasing violence, which forced President Jean-Bertrand Aristide, who had been serving a second term since 2001, to resign and leave the country. The Security Council authorized the immediate deployment of a Multinational Interim Force, following a request for assistance by the new President, Boniface Alexandre. A United States-led force was quickly deployed. In April 2004, the Council established the **United Nations Stabilization Mission in Haiti (MINUSTAH)** to support the continuation of a peaceful and constitutional political process in a secure and stable environment. In the following years, the mandate of MINUSTAH, its concept of operations and the authorized strength were adjusted by the Council on several occasions to adapt to the changing circumstances on the ground and to the evolving requirements as dictated by the prevailing political, security and socio-economic situation.

Following the devastating January 2010 earthquake, the Council increased the overall force levels of MINUSTAH to support recovery, reconstruction and stability efforts. MINUSTAH, together with the UN Office for the Coordination of Humanitarian Affairs and the United Nations Country Team, provided humanitarian and recovery assistance. It supported the government in its resettlement strategy for displaced persons. The UN also coordinated international electoral assistance to Haiti in cooperation with other international stakeholders.

The run-off round of the presidential election was won by Michel Martelly on 20 March 2011. For the first time in Haiti's history, power was transferred peacefully from one democratically elected president to another from the opposition. In October 2012, the Security Council, recognizing that the situation in Haiti had improved considerably over the previous two years, extended the MINUSTAH mandate until 15 October 2013 and reduced its force levels to 6,270 troops and a police component of 2,601 personnel.

Asia and the Pacific

The Middle East

From its earliest days, the United Nations has been concerned with the question of the Middle East. It has formulated principles for a peaceful settlement and dispatched various peacekeeping operations. It continues to support efforts towards a just, lasting and comprehensive solution to the underlying political problems.

The question has its origin in the issue of the status of Palestine, one among former Ottoman territories placed under United Kingdom administration by the League of Nations in 1922. All of these territories eventually became fully independent states, except Palestine, where in addition to "the rendering of administrative assistance and advice" the British Mandate incorporated the "Balfour Declaration" of 1917, expressing support for "the establishment in Palestine of a national home for the Jewish people". During the Mandate, from 1922 to 1947, large-scale Jewish immigration, mainly from Eastern Europe took place. Arab demands for independence and resistance to immigration led to a rebellion in 1937, followed by continuing violence from both sides.

In 1947, the United Kingdom turned the question of Palestine over to the UN. Palestine had a population of some 2 million—two thirds Arabs and one third

Jews. The 57-member General Assembly, on 29 November 1947, endorsed a plan prepared by the United Nations Special Committee on Palestine for the partition of the territory in May 1948 when the British mandate ended. The plan provided for creating an Arab and a Jewish state, with Jerusalem under a special international regime administered by the Trusteeship Council on behalf of the United Nations. The plan was rejected by the Palestinian Arabs, the Arab states and other states. The Palestine problem quickly widened into a Middle East dispute between those states and Israel. On 14 May 1948, the United Kingdom relinquished its mandate, and the Jewish Agency for Israel proclaimed the state of Israel. The following day, the Palestinian Arabs, assisted by Arab states, opened hostilities against the new state. The military confrontation was halted through a truce called for by the Security Council and supervised by a mediator appointed by the General Assembly, who was assisted by a group of military observers that came to be known as the **United Nations Truce Supervision Organization (UNTSO)**—the first United Nations observer mission.

As a result of the conflict, some 750,000 Palestinian Arabs lost their homes and livelihoods and became refugees. To assist them, the General Assembly in 1949 established the **United Nations Relief and Works Agency for Palestine Refugees in the Near East (UNRWA)**, which has since been a major provider of assistance and a force for stability in the region. Today, 5 million Palestine refugees benefit from UNRWA services in Jordan, Lebanon, the Gaza Strip, the Syrian Arab Republic and the West Bank, including East Jerusalem.

The conflict remaining unresolved, Arab-Israeli warfare erupted again in 1956, 1967 and 1973, each time leading member states to call for United Nations mediation and peacekeeping missions. The 1956 conflict saw the deployment of the first full-fledged peacekeeping force—the United Nations Emergency Force (UNEF I)—which oversaw troop withdrawals and contributed to peace and stability.

The 1967 war involved fighting between Israel and the Arab states Jordan and Syria, during which Israel occupied the Sinai Peninsula, the Gaza Strip, the West Bank of the Jordan River, including East Jerusalem, and part of Syria's Golan Heights. The Security Council called for a ceasefire, and subsequently dispatched observers to supervise the ceasefire in the Egypt-Israel sector.

The Council, by resolution 242(1967), defined principles for a just and lasting peace, namely: "withdrawal of Israel armed forces from territories occupied in the recent conflict"; and "termination of all claims or states of belligerency and respect for and acknowledgement of the sovereignty, territorial integrity and political independence of every state in the area and their right to live in peace within secure and recognized boundaries, free from threats or acts of force". The resolution also affirmed the need for "a just settlement of the refugee problem".

After the 1973 war between Israel and Egypt and Syria, the Security Council adopted resolution 338(1973), which reaffirmed the principles of resolution 242(1967) and called for negotiations aimed at "a just and durable peace". These resolutions remain the basis for an overall settlement in the Middle East.

To monitor the 1973 ceasefire, the Security Council established two peacekeeping forces. One of them, the **United Nations Disengagement Observer Force (UNDOF)**, established to supervise the disengagement agreement between Israel and Syria, is still in place on the Golan Heights. The other operation was UNEF II, which was deployed to supervise the ceasefire between Egypt ans Israel.

In the following years, the General Assembly called for an international peace conference on the Middle East, under United Nations auspices. In 1974, the Assembly invited the Palestine Liberation Organization (PLO) to participate in its work as an observer. The following year, it established the **Committee on the Exercise of the Inalienable Rights of the Palestinian People**, which continues to work as the General Assembly's subsidiary organ supporting the rights of the Palestinian people and a peaceful settlement of the question of Palestine.

Bilateral negotiations between Egypt and Israel, mediated by the United States, led to the Camp David accords (1978) and the Egypt-Israel peace treaty (1979). Israel withdrew from the Sinai, which was returned to Egypt. Israel and Jordan concluded a peace treaty in 1994.

The Middle East peace process (1987–2013). In 1987, the Palestinian uprising (intifada) began in the occupied territories of the West Bank and Gaza Strip with a call for Palestinian independence and statehood. In 1988, the Palestine National Council proclaimed the state of Palestine, which the General Assembly acknowledged. The Assembly also decided to employ the designation 'Palestine' when referring to the PLO within the UN system, without prejudice to its observer status. In September 1993, following talks in Madrid and subsequent Norwegian-mediated negotiations, Israel and the PLO established mutual recognition and signed the *Declaration of Principles on Interim Self-Government Arrangements*. The UN created a task force on the social and economic development of Gaza and Jericho. It also appointed a special coordinator for UN assistance, whose mandate was expanded in 1999 to include good offices assistance to the Middle East peace process.

The transfer of powers from Israel to the Palestinian Authority (PA) in the Gaza Strip and Jericho began in 1994. One year later, Israel and the PLO signed an agreement on Palestinian self-rule in the West Bank, providing for the withdrawal of Israeli troops and the handover of civil authority to an elected Palestinian Council. In 1996, Yasser Arafat was elected President of the PA. An interim agreement in 1999 led to further redeployment of Israeli troops from the West Bank, agreements on prisoners, the opening of safe passage between the West Bank and Gaza, and resumption of negotiations on permanent status issues. High-level peace talks held under United States mediation, however, ended inconclusively in the middle of 2000. Unresolved issues included the status of Jerusalem, the Palestinian refugee question, security, borders and Israeli settlements.

Road Map. In September 2000, a new wave of violence flared up. The Security Council repeatedly called for an end to the violence and affirmed the vision of two states, Israel and Palestine, living side by side within secure and recognized borders. International efforts to bring the two parties back to the negotiating table were increasingly carried out through the mechanism of the Middle East 'Quartet'— composed of the European Union, the Russian Federation, the United States and the United Nations.

In April 2003, the Quartet presented its 'road map' to a permanent two-state solution—a plan with distinct phases and benchmarks, calling for parallel and reciprocal steps by the two parties, to resolve the conflict by 2005. It also envisaged a comprehensive settlement of the Middle East conflict, including the Syrian-Israeli and Lebanese-Israeli tracks. The Security Council endorsed the road map in resolution 1515(2003) and both parties accepted it. Nevertheless, the last half of 2003 saw a sharp escalation of violence. The UN special coordinator for the Middle East peace process said neither side had addressed the other's concerns: for Israel, security and freedom from terrorist attack; for Palestinians, a viable and independent state based on pre-1967-war borders. Palestinian suicide bombings continued, and Israel constructed a 'separation barrier' in the West Bank—later held to be contrary to international law under an advisory opinion of the International Court of Justice requested by the General Assembly.

In 2005, Israel unilaterally withdrew its military and settlements from the Gaza Strip. In November, PA President Yasser Arafat died, and was replaced in January 2005 by Mahmoud Abbas in elections conducted with UN technical and logistic support. In February, Israeli Prime Minister Ariel Sharon and President Abbas met in Egypt and announced steps to halt the violence. They met again in June, and by September Israel's withdrawal was complete. Despite these positive developments, two significant events took place in January 2006 that changed the political landscape: Prime Minister Sharon suffered a stroke and fell into a coma; and in legislative elections, the Palestinians voted the militant Hamas faction into power.

Despite appeals from the Quartet and others, Hamas did not formally recognize Israel's right to exist. The Israeli government, now led by Ehud Olmert, took the position that the entire PA had become a terrorist entity, and imposed a freeze on Palestinian tax revenues. Violence escalated, including the launching of rockets from Gaza into Israel, along with major Israeli counter-operations. International aid donors balked at funding the Hamas-led government as long as it did not renounce violence, recognize Israel's right to exist, and abide by signed agreements. The humanitarian situation in the West Bank and Gaza deteriorated.

In May 2007, intra-Palestinian clashes left 68 dead and more than 200 wounded, as Hamas and PA security forces clashed. As a result, the PA ended up governing the West Bank and Hamas governing the Gaza strip. Rocket attacks from Gaza into southern Israel escalated, followed by Israeli strikes aimed at militants and their facilities. Towards the end of 2008, following a spate of rocket attacks from Gaza, Israel launched a military operation against the territory, which culminated in a ground invasion. The operation worsened the humanitarian situation in Gaza and strengthened the three-year blockade of Gaza; led to massive damage to infrastructure, including to United Nations facilities; and hundreds of civilians died, mostly Palestinians.

In early 2009, the Security Council adopted resolution 1860(2009), calling for an immediate ceasefire leading to the withdrawal of Israeli forces from Gaza and condemning violence and acts of terrorism. The Secretary-General began a mission to the Middle East to obtain a ceasefire. Following intense diplomatic efforts, Israel announced a unilateral ceasefire in mid-January, followed by a unilateral ceasefire declaration by Hamas.

That same month, the UN Human Rights Council approved an investigation into the conflict and, shortly afterwards, appointed South African former judge Richard Goldstone as the head of the investigative team. A September report recommended, among other things, that the Security Council monitor investigations by both Israel and Gaza authorities. The report concluded that both sides had committed violations amounting to crimes against humanity. Two months later, the General Assembly in resolution 64/10 endorsed the Goldstone report and requested the Secretary-General to report on implementation of the resolution "with a view to considering further action ... including [by] the Security Council". Meeting in June and September 2009, the Middle East Quartet called on the Israelis and the Palestinians to implement their obligations under the road map.

In March 2010, the Quartet urged Israel to freeze all settlement activity and reaffirmed that unilateral action would not be recognized by the international community. It underscored that the status of Jerusalem was an issue that remained to be resolved. In September, the United States launched direct Israeli-Palestinian negotiations in Washington, D.C., with a one-year time limit. The talks ended, however, when an Israeli partial moratorium on settlement construction in the West Bank expired. The Palestinians refused to negotiate if Israel did not extend the freeze.

In September 2011, the Quartet urged resumption of direct bilateral Israeli-Palestinian negotiations without delay or preconditions and proposed concrete steps to re-establish the trust necessary for such a negotiation to succeed.

In October 2011, the UNESCO General Conference admitted Palestine as a member. In April 2012, the Quartet supported the exploratory Israeli-Palestinian talks held in early 2012 in Amman. In November, however, a fresh cycle of violence erupted between Israel and Gaza, which concluded with an Egyptian-brokered ceasefire.

On 29 November 2012, the 193-member UN General Assembly, by a vote of 138 in favour to nine against with 41 abstentions, accepted Palestine as a non-member with observer status in the UN, without prejudice to the acquired rights, privileges and role of the PLO in the United Nations as the representative of the Palestinian people.

Lebanon. From April 1975 through October 1990, Lebanon was torn by civil war. Early on, southern Lebanon became a theatre of hostilities between Palestinian groups on one hand and, on the other, Israeli forces and their local Lebanese auxiliary. After Israeli forces invaded southern Lebanon in 1978, following a Palestinian commando raid in Israel, the Security Council adopted resolutions 425(1978) and 426(1978), calling on Israel to withdraw and establishing the **United Nations Interim Force in Lebanon (UNIFIL)**. The Force was set up to confirm the Israeli withdrawal, restore international peace and security, and assist Lebanon in re-establishing its authority in the area. In 1982, after intense exchanges of fire in southern Lebanon and across the Israel-Lebanon border, Israeli forces moved into Lebanon, reaching and surrounding Beirut. Israel withdrew from most of the country in 1985, but kept control of a strip of land in southern Lebanon, where Israeli forces and their local Lebanese auxiliary remained, and which partly overlapped UNIFIL's area of deployment. Hostilities between Lebanese groups and Israeli forces continued. In May 2000, Israeli forces withdrew in accordance with the 1978 Security Council resolutions. The Council endorsed the Secretary-General's plan to assist Lebanon in re-establishing its authority. Nevertheless, the situation along the 'Blue Line' marking Israel's withdrawal from southern Lebanon remained precarious.

Tensions escalated in February 2005, when former Lebanese Prime Minister Rafiq Hariri was assassinated. In November, the Security Council supported establishment of a special tribunal to try those allegedly responsible for the assassination. In April, the UN verified the withdrawal of Syrian troops, military assets and intelligence operations from Lebanon. In May and June, parliamentary elections were held with UN assistance. Violations of the Blue Line continued through 2005 and 2006 with intermittent clashes between Israel and Hizbullah. When two Israeli soldiers were seized by Hizbullah in July 2006, Israel responded with air attacks, and Hizbullah retaliated with rocket attacks. The 34-day conflict ended in August, by the terms of Security Council resolution 1701(2006), which called for an immediate cessation of hostilities, to be followed by deployment of Lebanese troops; a significantly expanded UNIFIL peacekeeping presence across southern Lebanon (from 2,000 troops in August 2006 to a maximum of 15,000); and the withdrawal of Israeli forces from the area. Since 1978, UNIFIL has had 296 fatalities. A significant problem facing UNIFIL was the risk posed by up to 1 million pieces of unexploded ordnance left from the conflict.

In 2009, Israel handed over to UNIFIL technical strike data for the cluster bombs used in Lebanon, which the UN had requested repeatedly since the cessation of hostilities in August 2006.

Between 2009 and the close of 2012, violations of the Blue Line were reported by Israel and Lebanon. In November 2012, the Secretary-General reported that while the parties continued to affirm their commitment to resolution 1701(2006), there was no substantive progress in implementation of their respective obligations outstanding under the resolution.

Lebanon and Syria established diplomatic relations in October 2008. The Secretary-General welcomed the peaceful conduct of parliamentary elections in June 2009, when the alliance led by Saad Hariri won majority in Parliament against the Hizbullah's coalition. Newly elected Prime Minister Hariri formed a national unity government in November. In 2011, the unity government collapsed after Hizbullah and its allies resigned from the cabinet over arguments stemming from the investigation into the assassination of Rafiq Hariri and others in 2005. Five days later the prosecutor of the Special Tribunal for Lebanon filed a confidential indictment in connection with the attack on Mr. Hariri. The indictment was filed with the Tribunal's registrar, to be submitted to the pre-trial judge. In 2012 and early 2013, the Tribunal heard and dismissed challenges to its legality. The pre-trial judge set 13 January 2014 as a tentative date for the start of trial.

Syria. A civil war in Syria between government forces and armed rebels erupted in March 2011. The ongoing conflict has so far resulted in close to 100,000 people dead and more than 2 million having fled to neighbouring countries. In April 2012, the United Nations established the **UN Supervision Mission in Syria (UNSMIS)** to monitor a cessation of armed violence by all parties and to support implementation of the six-point plan to end the conflict, put forth by the United Nations/League of Arab States Joint Special Envoy, former UN Secretary-General Kofi Annan. Intensified armed violence across the country forced UNSMIS to suspend its activities in June 2012. A month later, the Security Council decided to extend the Mission for a final 30 days, and that any further extension would be possible only "in the event that the Secretary-General reports and the Security Council confirms the cessation of the use of heavy weapons and a reduction in the level of violence sufficient by all sides" to allow the UNSMIS monitors to implement their mandate. As those conditions were not met, the Mission's mandate ended on 19 August 2012.

On 25 March 2012, the Syrian Government committed to the six-point plan proposed by Joint Special Envoy Annan, which was endorsed by the Security Council. The plan included provisions for immediate steps by the Syrian Government, and a cessation of armed violence in all its forms by all parties to protect civilians and stabilize the country. To this end, it required the Syrian government immediately to cease troop movements towards, and the use of heavy weapons in, population centres and to begin to pull back military concentrations in and around such centres. It also required a range of other steps by the Syrian government to alleviate the crisis, including humanitarian access, access to and release of detainees, access and freedom of movement for journalists, and freedom of association and the right to demonstrate peacefully. The plan embodied the need for an inclusive Syrian-led political process to address the legitimate aspirations and concerns of the Syrian people.

In August 2012, Joint Special Envoy Annan said that he did not intend to continue his work when his mandate expired. The same month Secretary-General Ban Ki-moon, along with Arab League Secretary-General Nabil El Araby, announced the appointment of Lakhdar Brahimi as their Joint Special Representative for Syria, who continues his efforts to bring the warring parties to an agreed solution.

Afghanistan

In September 1995, the Taliban faction in Afghanistan's civil war took Kabul, its capital, after having seized most of the country. President Burhannudin Rabbani fled and joined the 'Northern Alliance', which held territory in the northern part of the country. In August 1998, following the terrorist bomb attacks on United States embassies in Nairobi, Kenya, and Dar-es-Salaam, Tanzania, the Council repeated its concern at the continuing presence of terrorists in Afghanistan. In December, it demanded that the Taliban, which was never recognized as Afghanistan's legitimate government, stop providing sanctuary and training for international terrorists and their organizations. The Taliban failed to respond.

In October 1999, the Council applied broad sanctions under the enforcement provisions of the UN *Charter*. It then demanded that the Taliban turn over to the appropriate authorities Osama bin Laden, who had been indicted by the United States for the embassy bombings.

On 11 September 2001, members of bin Laden's Al-Qaida organization hijacked four commercial jets in the United States, crashing two into the World Trade Center in New York City, one into the Pentagon in the US capital, and the fourth into a field in Pennsylvania when passengers tried to stop the hijacking. Nearly 3,000 people were killed in the attacks. In the days that followed, the US administration issued an ultimatum to the Taliban: turn over bin Laden and close the terrorist operations in Afghanistan or risk a massive military assault. The Taliban refused. In October, forces of the United States and United Kingdom unleashed missile attacks against Taliban military targets and bin Laden's training camps in Afghanistan. Two weeks of bombings were followed by the deployment of US ground forces. The Security Council supported efforts of the Afghan people to replace the Taliban regime, as the United Nations promoted dialogue among Afghan parties aimed at establishing a broad-based, inclusive government. A UN-organized meeting of Afghan political leaders in Bonn, Germany, concluded in December with agreement on a provisional arrangement, pending re-establishment of permanent government institutions. As a first step, the Afghan Interim Authority was established. The Security Council authorized the establishment of the International Security Assistance Force (ISAF) to help the Authority maintain security in Kabul and its surrounding areas. Later that month, the internationally recognized administration of President Rabbani handed power over to the new Afghan Interim Authority, headed by Chairman Hamid Karzai, and the first ISAF troops were deployed.

In January 2002, an International Conference on Reconstruction Assistance to Afghanistan garnered pledges of over $4.5 billion. The Security Council, welcoming the positive changes in Afghanistan as a result of the collapse of the Taliban, adjusted its sanctions to target Al-Qaida and its supporters. In March, the Council established the **United Nations Assistance Mission in Afghanistan (UNAMA)** to fulfill the tasks entrusted to the UN under the Bonn Agreement in such areas as human rights, the rule of law and gender issues. Headed by the Secretary-General's special representative, UNAMA would also promote national reconciliation, while managing all UN humanitarian activities in coordination with the Interim Authority and its successors. UNAMA's mandate has been extended every year since then.

In June, a nine-day Emergency Loya Jirga ('Grand Council', a traditional forum in which tribal elders come together and settle affairs) was opened by Zahir Shah, the former King of Afghanistan, who nominated Hamid Karzai to lead the nation. Subsequently, Mr. Karzai was elected as Afghanistan's head of state to lead the transitional government for the following two years. In January 2004, the Constitutional Loya Jirga reached agreement on a text that was adopted as Afghanistan's Constitution. In October of that year, more than 8 million Afghans went to the polls, choosing Hamid Karzai as the country's first-ever elected President. In September 2005, the Afghan people voted for the members of their National Assembly and Provisional Councils, despite a series of deadly attacks during the campaign. Parliament was inaugurated at the end of December.

In January 2006, a high-level group meeting in London launched the Afghanistan Compact—a five-year agenda to consolidate democratic institutions, curb insecurity, control the illegal drug trade, stimulate the economy, enforce the law, provide basic services to the Afghan people, and protect their human rights. The next month, the Security Council endorsed the Compact as providing a framework for partnership between the Afghan government and the international community. In June 2008, the International Conference in support of Afghanistan, co-chaired by Afghanistan, France and the United Nations, brought together delegations from 67 countries and 17 international organizations. About $20 billion was pledged to finance the Compact's implementation, including support for the preparation of elections in 2009 and 2010, which saw the re-election of President Karzai.

Violence escalated throughout 2008 and 2009. In a Taliban attack on a UN guesthouse in Kabul in October 2009, five foreign UN employees and three Afghans were killed. In January 2010, the Secretary-General, the Afghan President and the British Prime Minister co-hosted an international conference on Afghanistan that highlighted the need to transfer responsibility for security matters to the Afghan authorities by 2011. In July, a conference co-hosted by the UN and the Afghan government discussed the transition of Afghan provinces from ISAF control to the National Security Forces by 2014. The conference also considered issues of good governance, fairness of the judicial system and human rights, as well as the continuing problem posed by drug trafficking.

On 20 September 2011, former President Rabbani was killed by a suicide bomber. Mr. Rabbani's death—the culmination of a series of high-profile assassinations of figures formerly part of or close to the Northern Alliance—intensified internal political manoeuvring and weakened trust between factions and ethnic groups.

At a meeting of defence ministers of the North Atlantic Treaty Organization held in Brussels in October 2012, ISAF was directed to begin planning a post-2014 training mission. On 15 November, Afghanistan and the United States launched negotiations on a bilateral security agreement in line with their strategic partnership agreement. In March 2013, the Security Council called on the United Nations to support Afghanistan's National Priority Programmes covering the issues of security, governance, justice and economic and social development, as well as implementation of the National Drug Control Strategy.

Iraq

The United Nations' response to Iraq's invasion of Kuwait in 1990, and the situation following the collapse of Saddam Hussein's regime in 2003, illustrate the scope of the challenges the UN faces in seeking to restore international peace and security. In August 1990, the Security Council demanded Iraq's withdrawal from Kuwait and imposed sanctions, including a trade and oil embargo. On 16 January 1991, multinational forces authorized by the Council, but not under UN direction or control, launched military operations against Iraq. Hostilities were suspended in February after the Iraqi forces withdrew from Kuwait.

The Council decided that Iraq's weapons of mass destruction should be eliminated and established the United Nations Special Commission (UNSCOM) on the disarmament of Iraq, with powers of no-notice inspection, and entrusted the International Atomic Energy Agency (IAEA) with similar verification tasks in the nuclear sphere. The Council also established a United Nations Compensation Commission to process claims and compensate governments, nationals or corporations for any loss or damage resulting from Iraq's invasion of Kuwait, out of a percentage of the proceeds from sales of Iraqi oil.

UNSCOM and the IAEA uncovered and eliminated large quantities of Iraq's banned weapons programmes and capabilities in the nuclear, chemical and biological field. In 1998, Iraq called on the Council to lift its oil embargo, declaring that there were no more proscribed weapons. In October, Iraq suspended cooperation with UNSCOM, which conducted its final mission in December. In the same month, the United States and the United Kingdom launched air strikes on Iraq.

In December 1999, the Security Council established the United Nations Monitoring, Verification and Inspection Commission (UNMOVIC) to replace UNSCOM. In November 2002, the Council adopted resolution 1441(2002), providing for an enhanced inspection regime and offering Iraq a final opportunity to comply with its resolutions. UN inspectors returned to Iraq, and the Council was repeatedly briefed by the UNMOVIC Executive Chairman and the IAEA Director-General. In the midst of negotiations, and outside the framework of the Security Council, Spain, the United Kingdom and the United States presented Iraq with a 17 March 2003 deadline to disarm completely. With military action imminent, the Secretary-General ordered the withdrawal of UN international staff on 17 March and the suspension of all operations. Military action by a coalition headed by the United Kingdom and the United States began three days later. Following the collapse of Saddam Hussein's regime, the Security Council, in May, adopted resolution 1483(2003), stressing the right of the Iraqi people to freely determine their political future. It recognized the authorities, responsibilities and obligations of the Coalition (the 'Authority') until the swearing-in of an internationally recognized government.

It also lifted international sanctions and provided a legal basis for the UN to resume operations in Iraq.

In August 2003, the Security Council established the **United Nations Assistance Mission for Iraq (UNAMI)** with a mandate to coordinate humanitarian and reconstruction aid and assist with the establishment of an internationally recognized, sovereign Iraqi government. On 19 August, the UN headquarters in Baghdad was the target of a terrorist attack that resulted in 22 deaths, and more than 150 injured. Fifteen of the dead were UN staff, including the head of the mission, Sergio Vieira de Mello. The Secretary-General withdrew most UN international personnel from Baghdad, maintaining only a small team, principally Iraqis, to provide essential humanitarian assistance, including the delivery of food, water and health care. In October, the Council authorized a multinational force under unified command to take all necessary measures to contribute to the maintenance of security and stability in Iraq, and to the security of UNAMI and institutions of the Iraqi Interim Administration. In November, the Iraqi Governing Council and the Coalition Provisional Authority (CPA) reached agreement on the restoration of sovereignty by the end of June 2004.

Following requests from the Iraqi Governing Council and the CPA for UN help with the transition to sovereignty, the Secretary-General sent an electoral assistance team to assess what was needed to hold credible elections in January 2005. He also asked his special adviser on Iraq, who arrived there in April 2004, to work with the Iraqis on such arrangements. In May, the Iraqi Governing Council named Iyad Allawi as Iraq's Prime Minister-designate. The following month, the Security Council endorsed the formation of the new interim government. On 28 June 2004, sovereignty was officially transferred from the CPA to the new Iraqi interim government.

The Independent Electoral Commission of Iraq, established in June 2004, conducted in just over 18 months, with UN support, two national elections and a constitutional referendum, despite a serious security situation on the ground. At the beginning of 2005, millions participated in elections for a provisional national assembly responsible for the drafting of a constitution. The Transitional National Assembly held its first meeting in March. Its President requested UN support in drafting and building consensus around the country's new constitution. In October, Iraq's draft constitution was adopted in a nation-wide referendum. Parliamentary elections were held in December. By June 2006, the new government had been formed. Despite the successful political transition, however, the security situation worsened, as waves of sectarian violence and revenge swept the country. By late 2007, some 2.2 million Iraqis had fled the country, and there were nearly 2.4 million IDPs. The United Nations took on a lead role in addressing the refugee and IDP situation.

Nonetheless, there were some positive developments. In March 2007, the International Compact with Iraq was launched, with world leaders pledging billions of dollars to Iraq's five-year plan for peace and development. In June, the Security Council formally terminated the UNMOVIC and IAEA mandates in Iraq. In August 2008, the United Nations and the Iraqi government signed the United Nations Assistance Strategy for Iraq 2008–2010, which defined UN support for Iraq's reconstruction, development and humanitarian needs over three years.

Parliamentary elections, assisted by UNAMI, were held in March 2010. Iraq's Supreme Court validated the results in June, and the Security Council called on all political actors to engage in an inclusive process to form a representative govern-ment. In December, the parliament unanimously approved Nouri al-Maliki's new government, which includes Kurds, Shias and Sunnis. In May 2010, Iraq and UNAMI launched a UN Development Assistance Framework for 2011–2014 to support the country's five-year National Development Plan.

In accordance with the 2008 status-of-forces agreement between the United States and Iraq, United States forces completed their withdrawal from Iraq on 18 December 2011. In July 2012, the Security Council extended the UNAMI man-date until 31 July 2013.

India–Pakistan

Relations between India and Pakistan have been troubled by a decades-old dis-pute over Kashmir. The issue dates back to the 1940s, when the princely state of Jammu and Kashmir became free to accede to India or Pakistan under a par-tition plan and the India Independence Act of 1947. The Hindu Maharaja of mostly Muslim Jammu and Kashmir signed the state's instrument of accession to India.

The Security Council first discussed the issue of Jammu and Kashmir in 1948, following India's complaint that tribesmen and others, with Pakistan's support and participation, were invading the state, and fighting was taking place. Paki-stan denied the charges and declared Jammu and Kashmir's accession to India illegal. Since 1949, based on a ceasefire signed by the parties, the **United Nations Military Observer Group in India and Pakistan (UNMOGIP)** has monitored the ceasefire line in Jammu and Kashmir, and the UN is committed to promoting harmonious relations between the two countries.

In 2003, India's Prime Minister and the President of Pakistan began a series of reciprocal steps to improve bilateral relations. In November, Pakistan offered to implement a unilateral ceasefire along the Line of Control in Jammu and Kashmir. India responded positively. Those efforts led to a summit meeting in 2004 in Islam-abad, Pakistan, between Prime Minister Atal Bihari Vajpayee of India and Pakistan's President Pervez Musharraf and its Prime Minister Zafarullah Khan Jamali. A bus service across the ceasefire line was inaugurated in 2005 as a powerful gesture of peace and an opportunity to reunite families divided for nearly 60 years. An attack on the Delhi-Lahore 'Friendship Express' in February 2007, however, left 67 people dead and nearly 20 injured. The Secretary-General, in a statement echoed by the Security Council, strongly condemned the terrorist bombing and called for the perpetrators to be brought to justice.

A wave of coordinated terrorist attacks took place in November 2008 across Mumbai, India's financial hub, by Lashkar-e-Taiba extremists, a terrorist group based in Pakistan. The attacks, which drew global condemnation, lasted three days, killing at least 173 people and wounding more than 300. An operation by India's armed forces resulted in the death of the attackers at the Taj Mahal hotel, with one captured alive. Pakistan condemned the attacks, but the atrocities committed by the terrorists sharply strained relations between the two neighbours once again. The Security Council and the Secretary-General condemned the attacks and urged all states to cooperate with India to bring the perpetrators, organizers, financiers and sponsors of these acts of terrorism to justice.

Central Asia

The **United Nations Regional Centre for Preventive Diplomacy for Central Asia** (*http://unrcca.unmissions.org*) was inaugurated in December 2007. Based in Ashgabat, Turkmenistan, the Centre was established to help the governments of the region peacefully and cooperatively manage an array of common challenges and threats—including terrorism, drug trafficking, organized crime and environmental degradation. The Centre offers governments assistance in a number of areas, including: building capacity to prevent conflict; facilitating dialogue; and catalysing international support for specific projects and initiatives. The Centre cooperates closely with the UN programmes and agencies in Central Asia, as well as with regional organizations. Among its priorities in 2012–2014 were cross-border threats, including terrorism, extremism and organized crime, especially drug trafficking; the implications of national developments on regional stability; and the management of common natural resources and environmental degradation.

Cambodia

Following Cambodia's emergence from French colonialism in the 1950s, the country suffered the spillover of the Viet Nam war in the 1960s and 1970s, as well as devastating civil conflicts and the genocidal totalitarian rule of Pol Pot. Under his 'Khmer Rouge' regime, from 1975 to 1979, nearly 2 million people perished of murder, disease or starvation, many in Cambodia's infamous 'killing fields'. In 1993, with help from the United Nations Transitional Authority in Cambodia, the country held its first democratic elections. Since then, UN agencies and programmes have assisted the government in strengthening reconciliation and development.

In 2003, agreement was reached with the government for the UN to help it set up and run a special court to prosecute crimes committed under the Khmer Rouge. The **Extraordinary Chambers in the Courts of Cambodia (ECCC)** was established in 2005 and issued its first charges for crimes against humanity in July 2007, taking several persons into provisional detention. In 2008, the Cambodians who suffered under the Khmer Rouge participated for the first time in the court through their lawyers.

In July 2010, Kaing Guek Eav, the first person to stand trial before the ECCC, was found guilty of crimes against humanity and grave breaches of the 1949 *Geneva Conventions*. In February 2012, the Supreme Court Chamber sentenced him to life imprisonment, the maximum sentence available under the law.

The four most senior members of the Democratic Kampuchea regime—Ieng Sary, Ieng Thirith, Khieu Samphan and Nuon Chea—were indicted in 2010 on charges of crimes against humanity; the genocide of the Cham and Vietnamese ethnic groups; grave breaches of the *Geneva Conventions*; and violations of the 1956 Cambodian criminal code, including murder, torture and religious persecution. In September 2012, the Trial Chamber affirmed that Ieng Thirith was unfit to stand trial, and she was released from provisional detention.

Myanmar

Since Myanmar's military leadership voided the results of democratic elections in 1990, the UN has sought to help bring about a return to democracy and improvements in the human rights situation there through an all-inclusive process of national reconciliation. In 1993, the General Assembly urged an accelerated return to democracy, asking the Secretary-General to assist the government in that process. Using his good offices to that end, the Secretary-General designated successive special envoys to engage in dialogue with all parties.

The Assembly has renewed the Secretary-General's good offices mandate annually since 1993. Through the mandate, the UN seeks to promote progress in four key areas: the release of political prisoners, a more inclusive political process, a halt to hostilities in the border areas, and a more enabling environment for the provision of humanitarian assistance.

The Secretary-General visited the country in 2009, at the invitation of the government. He argued for the release of all political prisoners, including the detained opposition leader Aung San Suu Kyi of the National League for Democracy (NLD) party; the resumption of substantive dialogue between the government and the opposition; and the creation of conditions conducive to credible and legitimate elections. In August of that year, however, Aung San Suu Kyi was sentenced to three years of hard labour, which was commuted to 18 months of house arrest—a verdict criticized by the Secretary-General.

In March 2010, the government approved new laws relating to elections. The political-parties registration law prohibited persons serving a prison term from voting or being a member of a political party, which effectively prevented Aung San Suu Kyi from participating in the elections. The Secretary-General said that the new election laws did not meet "international expectations of what is required for an inclusive political process".

In May, Cyclone Nargis devastated the Irrawaddy delta and left tens of thousands dead and missing. It was estimated that between 1.2 million and 1.9 million people were affected, left homeless, and exposed to the risk of disease and possible starvation. UN agencies offered assistance, but the government only allowed in limited aid and restricted the access of foreign aid workers. The Secretary-General expressed his concern and frustration at the unacceptably slow response to the crisis, and travelled to Myanmar to persuade the government to accept international aid. Subsequently, the government accepted humanitarian personnel, who began to arrive in early June. It was also agreed that the aid effort should be led by the Association of Southeast Asian Nations (ASEAN), which resulted in the formation of an ASEAN-UN-Myanmar tripartite mechanism.

In November 2010, the Secretary-General described the elections held that month—Myanmar's first in 20 years and only the third multiparty poll in more than 60 years since independence—as "insufficiently inclusive, participatory and transparent", and called for the release of all political prisoners. On 13 November, Aung San Suu Kyi was released from house arrest.

On 19 August 2011, the new President, U Thein Sein, met with Aung San Suu Kyi in talks aimed at finding common ground. In October, the Secretary-General welcomed the release of a number of political prisoners by the government as part of amnesty granted by the President.

In April 2012, candidates from various political parties, including NLD, participated freely in parliamentary by-elections, in which Aung San Suu Kyi won a seat in Parliament. A UN team witnessed the voting in a number of constituencies. On 30 April, the United Nations and the government signed an agreement on UN assistance in the census to be held in Myanmar in 2014—the first in 30 years. Despite these positive developments, the Secretary-General, in October, saw a need to call on the Myanmar authorities to bring lawlessness under control in the country, characterizing the recent outbreak of communal violence in the northern Rakhine region as "deeply troubling".

In January 2013, the Secretary-General noted reports of air strikes against targets in Kachin State and called on the authorities to desist from any action that could endanger the lives of civilians living in the area or further intensify the conflict in the region. In March, he welcomed the agreement between the Union Peace Working Committee and the Kachin Independence Organization to work towards ceasefire, and encouraged the parties to redouble their efforts toward a fair, genuine and durable solution.

Timor-Leste

In 2002, the formerly dependent Territory of East Timor, following engagement by the United Nations over many years in its struggle for self-determination, declared its independence as Timor-Leste. Its constituent assembly was subsequently transformed into a national parliament, and in September of that year, Timor-Leste became the 191st member state of the UN. Following the declaration of independence, the Security Council established a United Nations Mission of Support in East Timor (UNMISET) to assist the nascent state in developing core administrative structures, providing interim law enforcement and security, developing a police service, and contributing to the maintenance of internal and external security.

In 2005, UNMISET was replaced by the United Nations Office in Timor-Leste (UNOTIL), which worked to support the development of critical state institutions, the police and the border patrol unit, and to provide training in democratic governance and the observance of human rights.

In 2006, the dismissal of nearly 600 members of the armed forces triggered a violent crisis that peaked in May. The government requested the deployment of international police and military assistance to secure critical locations and facilities. The Secretary-General sent his special envoy to help diffuse the crisis and find a political solution. Following extensive negotiations among the political actors, a new government was formed in July. The next month, the Council established a new and expanded operation, the **United Nations Integrated Mission in Timor-Leste (UNMIT)**, to support the government in "consolidating stability, enhancing a culture of democratic governance, and facilitating dialogue among Timorese stakeholders". Since then, stability in the country has been largely maintained, and presidential and parliamentary elections were held in a generally calm security environment in 2007. Nevertheless, in early 2008, a group led by a former military officer attacked both the President and the Prime Minister of Timor-Leste. The Security Council condemned the attacks and urged full cooperation of all parties to bring to justice those responsible.

In February 2011, the Security Council requested UNMIT to support, within its current mandate, the preparation of parliamentary and presidential elections planned for 2012, as requested by Timorese authorities.

The National Electoral Commission supervised two rounds of the presidential election on 17 March and 16 April 2012, and parliamentary elections on 7 July. The elections were characterized by high voter turnout, a calm security environment and acceptance of the results by all candidates. Taur Matan Ruak was sworn in as President on 20 May, and the new Parliament was inaugurated on 30 July. UNMIT ended its mandate as scheduled on 31 December 2012.

Europe

Cyprus

The **United Nations Peacekeeping Force in Cyprus (UNFICYP)** was established in 1964 to prevent a recurrence of fighting between the Greek Cypriot and Turkish Cypriot communities and to contribute to the maintenance and restoration of law and order and a return to normal conditions. In 1974, a coup d'état by Greek Cypriot and Greek elements favouring union of the country with Greece was followed by military intervention by Turkey and the de facto division of the island.

Since that year, UNFICYP has supervised a de facto ceasefire that came into effect on 16 August 1974, and maintained a buffer zone between the lines of the Cyprus National Guard and of the Turkish and Turkish Cypriot forces. In the absence of a political settlement, UNFICYP continues its presence on the island.

The Secretary-General used his good offices in search of a comprehensive settlement, hosting proximity talks between the two Cyprus leaders in 1999 and 2000, followed by intensive direct talks beginning in 2002. He also submitted a comprehensive proposal aimed at bridging the gaps between them, but agreement could not be reached on submitting it to referendums on each side in time to allow a reunited Cyprus to sign the *Treaty of Accession* to the EU. The talks were suspended in 2003. In April of that year, the Turkish Cypriot authorities began to open crossing points for public travel by Greek Cypriots to the north and Turkish Cypriots to the south for the first time in nearly three decades. As UN engineers worked to improve the roads, the Security Council authorized an increase in UNFICYP's police component to ensure the safe and orderly passage of people and vehicles. Seven months later, there had been some 2 million crossings.

The Secretary-General welcomed the new initiative, but stressed that it could not substitute for a comprehensive settlement. In 2004, the Greek Cypriot and Turkish Cypriot leaders—along with the guarantor nations of Greece, Turkey and the United Kingdom—resumed negotiations in New York on the basis of the Secretary-General's detailed proposals. After six weeks of negotiations, with agreement just out of reach, the Secretary-General stepped in to complete the "Comprehensive Settlement of the Cyprus Problem", calling for creation of a United Cyprus Republic composed of a Greek Cypriot constituent state and a Turkish Cypriot constituent state linked by a federal government. Seventy-six per cent of voters in the Greek Cypriot referendum opposed the plan, while 65 per cent of voters in the Turkish Cypriot referendum supported it. Without the approval of both communities, the plan was defeated, and so Cyprus entered the European Union as a divided and militarized island.

In 2006, the Greek Cypriot and Turkish Cypriot leaders met face-to-face, together with the UN Under-Secretary-General for Political Affairs. They committed to the unification of Cyprus based on a bi-zonal, bi-communal federation and political equality, as set out in Security Council resolutions, and to a process to achieve that end. They also met in 2007 at the official residence of the Secretary-General's special representative in Cyprus, where they agreed on the need for the earliest start of that process.

The last round of negotiations was initiated following the agreement in 2008 between the Greek Cypriot and the Turkish Cypriot leaders, who also decided to open a crossing at Ledra Street in the centre of old town Nicosia, which had for many years been a symbol of the division of Cyprus. Negotiations began later that year, and joint papers were produced by the leaders, their representatives and experts, setting out the positions of the two sides on different issues and indicating areas of convergence and divergence.

In January 2012, Greek and Turkish Cypriot leaders met with the Secretary-General in New York to address issues related to the election of the executive, property and citizenship. The Secretary-General reported that despite "robust and intensive" discussions, limited progress was achieved. He urged the leaders to make decisive steps toward a final settlement.

The Balkans

Kosovo. In 1989, the Federal Republic of Yugoslavia revoked local autonomy in Kosovo, a province in southern Yugoslavia historically important to Serbs that was more than 90 per cent ethnically Albanian. Kosovo Albanians dissented, boycotting Serbian state institutions and authority in a quest for self-rule. Tensions increased, and the Kosovo Liberation Army (KLA) surfaced in 1996, seeking independence through armed rebellion. It launched attacks against Serb officials and Albanians who collaborated with them, and Serb authorities responded with mass arrests. Fighting erupted in March 1998 as Serbian police swept the Drenica region, ostensibly looking for KLA members. The Security Council imposed an arms embargo against Yugoslavia, including Kosovo, but the situation deteriorated into open warfare.

In 1999, following warnings to Yugoslavia, and against the backdrop of a Serbian offensive in Kosovo, NATO began air strikes against Yugoslavia. Yugoslavia launched a major offensive against the KLA and began mass deportations of ethnic Albanians from Kosovo, causing an unprecedented outflow of 850,000 refugees. UNHCR and other humanitarian agencies rushed to assist them in Albania and The former Yugoslav Republic of Macedonia. Yugoslavia accepted a peace plan proposed by the Group of Eight (seven Western industrialized nations and Russia). The Security Council endorsed it and authorized member states to establish a security presence to deter hostilities, demilitarize the KLA and facilitate the return of refugees. It also asked the Secretary-General to establish an interim international civilian administration, under which the people could enjoy substantial autonomy and self-government. Yugoslav forces withdrew, NATO suspended its bombings, and a 50,000-strong multinational Kosovo Force (KFOR) arrived to provide security.

The **United Nations Interim Administration Mission in Kosovo (UNMIK)** (*www.unmikonline.org*) immediately established a presence on the ground. Its task was unprecedented in complexity and scope. The Security Council vested UNMIK with authority over the territory and people of Kosovo, including all legislative and executive powers and administration of the judiciary. At least 841,000 refugees of the approximately 850,000 who fled during the war returned. UNMIK made significant progress towards re-establishing normal life and ensuring long-term economic reconstruction. The KLA was completely demilitarized before the end of 1999 and its members reintegrated in civil society. In the following months, as some 210,000 non-Albanian Kosovars left Kosovo for Serbia and Montenegro. Remaining non-Albanian minorities lived in isolated enclaves guarded by KFOR.

In 2001, the International Criminal Tribunal for the former Yugoslavia indicted former Yugoslav President Slobodan Milosevic and four others for crimes against humanity during a "systematic attack directed against the Kosovo Albanian civilian population of Kosovo". Milosevic died in 2006 of natural causes while in detention. He was facing 66 counts of genocide, crimes against humanity and war crimes in Bosnia and Herzegovina, Croatia, and Kosovo.

Also in 2001, the Security Council lifted its arms embargo. In November, a 120-member Kosovo Assembly was elected which, in 2002, elected the province's first President and Prime Minister. In December, UNMIK completed the transfer of responsibilities to local provisional institutions, though it retained control over security, foreign relations, protection of minority rights, and energy—pending determination of the province's final status.

During 2006, the Secretary-General's special envoy conducted four rounds of direct negotiations between the parties and the first high-level meeting between top Serbian and Kosovar leaders, but Kosovo's ethnic Albanian government and Serbia remained at odds. In February 2007, he presented his final status plan as "a compromise proposal", but the parties were unmoved. He subsequently reported that the only viable option for Kosovo was independence—which has been consistently opposed by Serbia. Later that year, the Secretary-General welcomed an agreement to have a troika composed of the European Union, Russia and the United States lead further negotiations on Kosovo's future status; however, the parties have not been able to reach an agreement.

In 2008, the Assembly of Kosovo adopted a declaration of independence. In 2010, the International Court of Justice issued an advisory opinion on the declaration that stated it did not violate international law. By September, Kosovo had been recognized as an independent state by 70 of the 192 UN member states, while Serbia considers it as part of its territory. At the same time, the Secretary-General reaffirmed the readiness of the UN to contribute to the process of dialogue between Belgrade and Pristina in close coordination with the EU. The dialogue began in 2011, with meetings held in Brussels in March and April. Further meetings continued into 2012, despite some disruptions related to renewed tensions between the parties in northern Kosovo.

On 19 October 2012, the first high-level meeting in Brussels between Prime Ministers Ivica Dačić of Serbia and Hashim Thaçi of Kosovo was held under the auspices of the EU. As of 22 March 2013, the two Prime Ministers had met for seven rounds of dialogue.

Disarmament

Since the birth of the United Nations, the goals of multilateral disarmament and arms limitation have been central to its efforts to maintain international peace and security (*www.un.org/disarmament*). The UN has given highest priority to reducing and eventually eliminating nuclear weapons, destroying chemical weapons and strengthening the prohibition of biological weapons—all of which pose the most dire threats to humankind. While these objectives have remained constant over the years, the scope of deliberations and negotiations has changed as political realities and the international situation evolved. The international community is now considering more closely the excessive and destabilizing proliferation of small arms and light weapons and has mobilized to combat the massive deployment of landmines—phenomena that threaten the economic and social fabric of societies and kill and maim civilians, all too many of whom are women and children. Consideration is also being given to the need for multilaterally negotiated norms against the spread of ballistic missile technology, the explosive remnants of war, and the impact of new information and telecommunications technologies on international security.

The tragic events of 11 September 2001 in the United States, and subsequent terrorist attacks in a number of countries, have underlined the potential danger of weapons of mass destruction falling into the hands of non-state actors. Such attacks could have had even more devastating consequences had the terrorists been able to acquire and use chemical, biological or nuclear weapons. Reflecting these concerns, the General Assembly adopted in 2002, for the first time, a resolution (57/83) on measures to prevent terrorists from acquiring weapons of mass destruction and their means of delivery.

In 2004, the Security Council took its first formal decision on the danger of the proliferation of weapons of mass destruction, particularly among non-state actors. Acting under the enforcement provisions of the *Charter of the United Nations*, the Council unanimously adopted resolution 1540(2004), obliging states to refrain from any support for non-state actors in the development, acquisition, manufacture, possession, transport, transfer or use of nuclear, chemical and biological weapons and their means of delivery. The resolution imposes far-reaching obligations on states to establish domestic measures to prevent the proliferation of such weapons including the establishment of appropriate controls over related materials. Subsequently, the General Assembly adopted the *International Convention for the Suppression of Acts of Nuclear Terrorism*, which entered into force in 2007.

In addition to its role in disarmament and in verifying compliance, the UN assists member states in establishing new norms in multilateral disarmament and in strengthening and consolidating existing agreements. One of the most effective means of deterring the use or threatened use of weapons of mass destruction by terrorists is to strengthen multilateral regimes already developed to ban those weapons and prevent their proliferation.

Disarmament machinery

The *Charter* gives the General Assembly chief responsibility for considering "the general principles of cooperation in the maintenance of international peace and security, including the principles governing disarmament and the regulation of armaments" (Article 11). The Assembly has two subsidiary bodies dealing with disarmament issues: the First (Disarmament and International Security) Committee, which meets during the Assembly's regular session and deals with all disarmament issues on its agenda; and the Disarmament Commission, a specialized deliberative body that focuses on specific issues and meets for three weeks every year.

The **Conference on Disarmament** is the international community's sole multilateral negotiating forum for disarmament agreements. The Conference has negotiated the *Biological Weapons Convention,* the *Chemical Weapons Convention,* the *Comprehensive Nuclear-Test-Ban Treaty* and the *Treaty on the Non-Proliferation of Nuclear Weapons.* Since 1997, however, the Conference has been unable to adopt and carry out a programme of work due to lack of consensus among its members on disarmament priorities. Since the Conference addresses matters that touch upon the national security interests of states, it works strictly on the basis of consensus. It has a limited membership of 65 states and a unique relationship with the General Assembly. While the Conference defines its own rules and develops its own agenda, it takes into account the recommendations of the Assembly and reports to it annually.

The **United Nations Office for Disarmament Affairs (UNODA)** implements the decisions of the Assembly on disarmament matters. The **United Nations Institute for Disarmament Research (UNIDIR)** undertakes independent research on disarmament and related problems, particularly international security issues. The **Advisory Board on Disarmament Matters** advises the Secretary-General on matters relating to arms limitation and disarmament, and serves as the Board of Trustees of UNIDIR. It also advises on implementation of the recommendations of the **United Nations Disarmament Information Programme**.

Multilateral agreements

Important international disarmament and arms regulation measures concluded through negotiations in multilateral and regional forums include:

- 1925 *Geneva Protocol*: prohibits the first use of chemical and biological weapons.
- 1959 *Antarctic Treaty*: demilitarizes the continent and bans the testing of any kind of weapon on the continent.
- 1963 *Treaty Banning Nuclear Weapon Tests in the Atmosphere, in Outer Space and under Water (Partial Test-Ban Treaty)*: restricts nuclear testing to underground sites only.
- 1967 *Treaty for the Prohibition of Nuclear Weapons in Latin America and the Caribbean (Treaty of Tlatelolco)*: prohibits testing, use, manufacture, storage, or acquisition of nuclear weapons by the countries of the region.
- 1967 *Treaty on Principles Governing the Activities of States in the Exploration and Use of Outer Space, including the Moon and Other Celestial Bodies (Outer Space Treaty)*: mandates that outer space be used for peaceful purposes only and that nuclear weapons not be placed or tested in outer space.
- 1968 *Treaty on the Non-Proliferation of Nuclear Weapons (NPT)*: establishes that the non-nuclear-weapon states agree never to acquire nuclear weapons and, in exchange, are promised access to and assistance in the peaceful uses of nuclear energy. Nuclear-weapon states pledge to carry out negotiations relating to the cessation of the nuclear arms race and to nuclear disarmament, and not to assist in any way in the transfer of nuclear weapons to non-nuclear-weapon states.
- 1971 *Treaty on the Prohibition of the Emplacement of Nuclear Weapons on the Sea-bed and the Ocean Floor and in the Subsoil Thereof (Sea-bed Treaty)*: bans the emplacement of nuclear weapons, or any weapon of mass destruction, on the sea-bed or ocean floor.
- 1972 *Convention on Bacteriological (Biological) Weapons (BWC)*: bans the development, production and stockpiling of biological and toxin agents, and provides for the destruction of such weapons and their means of delivery.
- 1980 *Convention on Certain Conventional Weapons (CCW)*: prohibits certain conventional weapons deemed excessively injurious or having indiscriminate effects. Protocol I bans weapons which explode fragments that are undetectable by X-ray within the human body. Amended Protocol II (1995) limits the use of certain types of mines, booby-traps and other devices. Protocol III bans incendiary weapons. Protocol IV bans the use of blinding laser weapons.

- 1985 *South Pacific Nuclear Free Zone Treaty (Treaty of Rarotonga)*: bans the stationing, acquisition or testing of nuclear explosive devices and the dumping of nuclear waste within the zone.
- 1990 *Treaty on Conventional Armed Forces in Europe (CFE Treaty)*: limits the numbers of various conventional armaments in a zone stretching from the Atlantic Ocean to the Urals.
- 1992 *Open Skies Treaty*: enables states parties to overfly and observe the territory of one another, based on principles of cooperation and openness. Has been used for the verification of several arms control agreements and for other monitoring mechanisms.
- 1993 *Chemical Weapons Convention (CWC)*: prohibits the development, production, stockpiling and use of chemical weapons and requires their destruction.
- 1995 *Southeast Asia Nuclear-Weapon-Free Zone Treaty (Treaty of Bangkok)*: bans the development or stationing of nuclear weapons on the territories of the states parties.
- 1996 *African Nuclear-Weapon-Free Zone Treaty (Treaty of Pelindaba)*: bans the development or stationing of nuclear weapons on the African continent.
- 1996 *Comprehensive Nuclear-Test-Ban Treaty (CTBT)*: places a worldwide ban on nuclear test explosions of any kind and in any environment.
- 1997 *Mine-Ban Convention*: prohibits the use, stockpiling, production and transfer of antipersonnel mines and provides for their destruction.
- 2005 *International Convention for the Suppression of Acts of Nuclear Terrorism (Nuclear Terrorism Convention)*: outlines specific acts of nuclear terrorism, aims to protect a broad range of possible targets, bring perpetrators to justice and promote cooperation among countries.
- 2006 *Central Asia Nuclear-Weapon-Free Zone Treaty*: establishes zone comprising the five central Asian states—Kazakhstan, Kyrgyzstan, Tajikistan, Turkmenistan and Uzbekistan.
- 2008 *Convention on Cluster Munitions (CCM)*: prohibits the use, development, production, acquisition, stockpiling, retention or transfer of such munitions.
- 2010 *Central African Convention for the Control of Small Arms and Light Weapons (Kinshasha Convention)*: restricts the manufacture, transfer between states, and possession by civilians of small arms and light weapons; requires arms to be marked, brokering activities and brokers to be regulated and states to limit the number of entry points of weapons on their national territory.
- 2013 *Arms Trade Treaty (ATT)*: regulates international trade in conventional weapons.

(For status of ratification of these agreements, see *http://disarmament.un.org/treaties/* and *http://treaties.un.org/Pages/Treaties.aspx?id=26&subid=A&lang=en*)

Weapons of mass destruction

Nuclear weapons

Through sustained efforts, the world community has achieved numerous multilateral agreements aimed at reducing nuclear arsenals; excluding their deployment from certain regions and environments (such as outer space and the ocean floor); limiting their proliferation; and ending testing. Despite these achievements, the world stockpile of 19,000 nuclear weapons and their proliferation remain major threats to peace and a major challenge to the international community. Issues of concern in this area include the need for reductions in nuclear weapons, upholding the viability of the nuclear non-proliferation regime, and preventing the development and proliferation of ballistic missiles and missile defence systems.

Bilateral agreements on nuclear weapons. While international efforts to contain nuclear weapons continue in different forums, it has been generally understood that the nuclear-weapon powers hold special responsibility for maintaining a stable international security environment. During and after the cold war, the two major powers arrived at agreements that have significantly reduced the threat of nuclear war.

Multilateral agreements on nuclear weapons and non-proliferation. The *Treaty on the Non-Proliferation of Nuclear Weapons* (NPT), the most universal of all multilateral disarmament treaties, was opened for signature in 1968 and came into force in 1970. A total of 190 states have joined. The NPT is the cornerstone of the global nuclear non-proliferation regime and the foundation for the pursuit of nuclear disarmament. The decision by the Democratic People's Republic of Korea (DPRK) to withdraw from the *Treaty* in January 2003—the first such decision since the *Treaty's* entry into force 33 years earlier—was of great concern to the international community.

Participants in the 2005 Review Conference of the Parties to the NPT were unable to reach agreement on a substantive outcome. Five years later, however, the 2010 Review Conference adopted a 22-point Action Plan on Nuclear Disarmament, outlining concrete steps in the areas of nuclear disarmament, security assurances, nuclear testing and fissile materials. The Conference also endorsed the convening of a conference in 2012, attended by all Middle Eastern states, on the establishment of a zone free of nuclear weapons in the region. The meeting, however, was not held due to the political turmoil in the Middle East. In November 2012, Secretary-General Ban Ki-moon reaffirmed his support to convene a Conference in early 2013.

To verify obligations assumed under the NPT, states parties are required to accept the nuclear safeguards of the International Atomic Energy Agency. At the end of 2012, there were safeguards agreements in force with 179 states. In addition to the NPT, the *Treaties of Bangkok, Pelindaba, Rarotonga, Tlatelolco* and on a *Nuclear-Weapon-Free Zone in Central Asia* require non-nuclear-weapon states to apply IAEA safeguards.

In 1996, an overwhelming majority of General Assembly members adopted the *Comprehensive Nuclear-Test-Ban Treaty* (CTBT), proscribing any nuclear-test explosions anywhere. Originally proposed in 1954, it took four decades to adopt the *Treaty*, which extended the 1963 partial test ban to all environments. Over 2000 nuclear explosions were recorded between July 1945 when the first nuclear bomb was tested by the United States and 1996 when the CTBT banning such explosions was opened for signature. The CTBT has not yet entered into force. As at January 2013, 183 states had signed the CTBT, with 159 states ratifying. The *Treaty* will enter into force 180 days after the 44 states listed in its Annex 2 have ratified it. These 'Annex 2' states are countries that participated in the negotiations for the CTBT between 1994 and 1996 and possessed nuclear power reactors or research reactors at that time. As of January 2013, eight Annex 2 states remained outside of the treaty: China, DPRK, Egypt, India, Iran, Israel, Pakistan and the United States. The UN Secretary-General, in his capacity as the Depositary of the *Treaty*, has convened a series of Conferences on Facilitating the Entry into Force of the CTBT—in 1999, 2001, 2003, 2005, 2007, 2009 and 2011. At the latest conference, states unanimously adopted the Final Declaration that outlined 10 practical measures for early entry into force and universalization of the *Treaty*. Work continues in the Provisional Technical Secretariat, established in 1997, to ensure that an international monitoring system is operational by the time the *Treaty* enters into force. When complete, the monitoring system will consist of 337 monitoring facilities, complemented by an intrusive on-site inspection regime applicable once the *Treaty* has entered into force.

Nuclear-weapon-free zones. In a development that was to herald a new movement in regional arms control, the signing of the 1967 *Treaty for the Prohibition of Nuclear Weapons in Latin America and the Caribbean (Treaty of Tlatelolco)* established for the first time a nuclear-weapon-free zone in a populated area of the world. With the deposit of Cuba's instrument of ratification in 2002, the nuclear-weapon-free zone in Latin America and the Caribbean was consolidated to include all states in the region. Subsequently, four additional zones were established—in the South Pacific *(Treaty of Rarotonga,* 1985), South-East Asia *(Treaty of Bangkok,* 1995), Africa *(Treaty of Pelindaba,* 1996), and Central Asia (*Central Asia Nuclear-Weapon-Free Zone Treaty*, 2006). Proposals have been made for establishing nuclear-weapon-free zones in Central Europe and South Asia, as well as for a zone free of weapons of mass destruction in the Middle East. The concept of an individual country as a nuclear-weapon-free zone was acknowledged by the international community in 1998, when the General Assembly supported Mongolia's self-declaration of its nuclear-weapon-free status.

Preventing nuclear proliferation. The **International Atomic Energy Agency (IAEA)** (*www.iaea.org*) serves as the world's inspectorate, advisor and facilitator for the application of nuclear safeguards and verification measures covering civilian nuclear programmes. Under agreements concluded with states, IAEA inspectors regularly visit nuclear facilities to verify records on the whereabouts of nuclear material, check IAEA-installed instruments and surveillance equipment and confirm inventories of nuclear material. Taken together, these and other safeguards provide independent, international verification that governments are abiding by their commitment to peaceful uses of nuclear energy.

IAEA experts conduct hundreds of inspections every year to verify the implementation of the safeguards agreements in force in 179 states. Their aim is to ensure that the nuclear material held in some 900 installations in dozens of countries is not diverted away from legitimate, peaceful uses to military purposes. Through such annual inspections, IAEA contributes to international security, and reinforces efforts to halt the spread of arms and move towards a world free of nuclear weapons.

Various types of safeguards agreements can be concluded with IAEA. Those in connection with the NPT, the *Model Protocol Additional to Existing Safeguards Agreements,* as well as those relating to the nuclear-weapon-free zones treaties of *Tlatelolco, Rarotonga, Bangkok, Pelindaba* and *Central Asia,* require non-nuclear-weapon states to submit their entire nuclear-fuel-cycle activities to IAEA safeguards. Other agreements cover safeguards at single facilities. IAEA safeguards under the NPT are an integral part of the international regime for non-proliferation and play an indispensable role in ensuring the implementation of the NPT.

In 2010, the Security Council imposed yet more sanctions on Iran for failing to comply with its previous resolutions on ensuring the peaceful nature of its nuclear programme. The Council expanded an arms embargo and tightened restrictions on financial and shipping enterprises related to "proliferation-sensitive activities". The Council also requested the Secretary-General to create a panel of experts to monitor implementation of the sanctions. In March 2013, the Security Council further tightened sanctions on the DPRK's trade and banking, as well as travel by targeted officials for having conducted an underground nuclear test. Sanctions were first imposed on the DPRK by the Council following nuclear tests in 2006 and 2009, including a ban on the import of nuclear and missile technology. The sanctions were tightened in January 2013 after the country reportedly launched a long-range Unha-3 rocket from its west coast. Two sanctions committees have been established to oversee the sanctions on Iran and the DPRK.

Chemical and biological weapons

The entry into force of the *Chemical Weapons Convention* (CWC) in 1997 completed a process that began in 1925, when the *Geneva Protocol* prohibited the use of poison gas weapons. The *Convention* created, for the first time in the history of international arms control, a stringent international verification regime involving the collection of information on chemical facilities and routine global inspections to oversee compliance with treaty obligations by states parties to the *Convention*. Established for that purpose at The Hague, the **Organisation for the Prohibition of Chemical Weapons (OPCW)** (*www.opcw.org*) is very active. As at March 2013, 188 nations, representing 98 per cent of the global population, had joined OPCW.

Unlike the CWC, the 1972 *Biological and Toxin Weapons Convention* (BTWC or BWC) (*www.opbw.org*), which entered into force in 1975, does not provide for a verification mechanism. States parties exchange, as a confidence-building measure, detailed information each year on such items as their high-risk biological research facilities. In 2006, the Sixth Review Conference of the States Parties to the Biological and Toxin Weapons Convention decided to establish an Implementation Support Unit to help states parties bolster implementation of the *Convention*. Unlike the nuclear non-proliferation and chemical weapons treaties, which are supported by IAEA and OPCW, respectively, there was no institutional support with respect to biological weapons. Meetings of the states parties to the *Convention* take place at the UN on a regular basis, with the Seventh Review Conference held in 2011.

Conventional weapons, confidence-building and transparency

Small arms, light weapons and practical disarmament. Following the end of the cold war, the international community was confronted with the eruption of intra-state conflicts in many parts of the world in which small arms and light weapons were the weapons of choice. Though not the root cause of conflict, these weapons exacerbate violence, facilitate the use of child combatants, hinder humanitarian assistance and delay post-conflict reconstruction and development.

There are hundreds of millions of licensed firearms in the world. Of these, roughly two thirds are in the hands of civil society, while the rest belong to state militaries and law enforcement agencies. Estimates of most other types of small arms and light weapons remain elusive. The legal trade in these arms and weapons exceeds several billion dollars a year, while the illicit trade is believed to be worth over $1 billion annually. Controlling the proliferation of illicit weapons is a necessary step towards better international, regional or national control over all aspects of the issue of small arms.

In 2001, an international Conference on the Illicit Trade in Small Arms and Light Weapons in All Its Aspects was held at the United Nations. Under its resulting programme of action, member states agreed to: ensure that licensed manufacturers apply a reliable marking on each small arm and light weapon in the production process; keep comprehensive and accurate records on the manufacture, holding and transfer of such weapons; improve their ability to cooperate in identifying and tracing the illicit trade of such weapons; and guarantee that all small arms and light weapons thus confiscated, seized or collected are destroyed. The result was a huge increase in government anti-trafficking activities. In the five years following adoption of the programme, nearly 140 countries had reported on illegal gun trafficking, while a third of all states had made efforts to collect weapons from those not legally entitled to hold them. There was also increased cooperation among and within regions to stem the flow of illicit weapons across borders. In 2006, more than 2,000 representatives from governments, international and regional organizations and civil society took part in a two-week event at UN Headquarters to review implementation of the programme of action. Another review conference of the programme of action took place in 2012 at the United Nations.

Since the uncontrolled spread of illicit small arms impacts many aspects of UN work—from children to health to refugees to development—a mechanism called Coordinating Action on Small Arms (CASA) was put in place in 1998 to guarantee coherence within the UN system on a range of arms-related topics such as small arms, armed violence, the arms trade and ammunition stockpile management. A comprehensive global effort to address the small arms scourge was also

A team contracted by the United Nations Mine Action Coordinating Centre in the Democratic Republic of the Congo is dispatched to destroy an unexploded grenade in a residential area of Goma. (26 February 2013, UN Photo/Sylvain Liechti)

launched and sustained by civil society through research, the promotion of coordinated national action, and global lobbying for an international convention on the arms trade.

Arms Trade Treaty. Virtually all areas of world trade are covered by regulations that bind countries to agreed conduct, but there is no global set of rules governing the trade in conventional weapons. Governments are expected to show responsibility in their decisions regarding arms transfers. This means that before approving any international transfer of weapons, they should assess the risk of the transfer exacerbating conflict or facilitating violations of international humanitarian law and human rights law.

Countries have discussed the matter within the UN since 2006, and in 2012 they gathered at UN Headquarters for a historical initiative in the area of conventional arms: to negotiate an arms trade treaty (ATT). The Conference, however, could not reach agreement on a treaty text. The UN General Assembly then convened a Final Conference on the ATT in March 2013 to conclude the work begun in 2012. The General Assembly adopted the *Arms Trade Treaty* on 2 April 2013. It was opened for signature on 3 June 2013.

Anti-personnel mines. The growing proliferation and indiscriminate use of anti-personnel landmines around the world has been a particular focus of the UN's attention. In 1995, a review of the *Convention on Certain Conventional Weapons (CCW)*—also known as the *Inhumane Weapons Convention*—produced the *Amended Protocol II*, which entered into force in 1998, strengthening restrictions on certain uses, transfers and types (self-destroying and detectable) of landmines. As of March 2013, 98 states were bound by this *Protocol*. The *Convention* has five protocols that, besides banning landmines and booby-traps, also ban non-detectable fragments, incendiary weapons, blinding lasers and explosive remnants of war.

Not satisfied with what they considered an inadequate response to a serious humanitarian crisis, a group of like-minded states negotiated an agreement on a total ban on all anti-personnel landmines—the *Convention on the Prohibition of the Use, Stockpiling, Production and Transfer of Anti-personnel Mines and on Their Destruction (Mine-Ban Convention)*, which was opened for signature in 1997 and entered into force in 1999. As of March 2013, 161 states had become parties to it.

Implementation of both instruments has led to the destruction of stockpiles, mine clearance in affected countries, and fewer victims. A total of 4,286 new casualties from landmines and explosive remnants of war were recorded in 2011, which is similar to the number of casualties identified in 2009 and 2010 (see *www.icbl.org*). On the ground, 14 UN agencies, programmes, departments and funds are active in mine-related service.

The **United Nations Mine Action Service (UNMAS)** (*www.mineaction.org*) coordinates all mine-related activities of the UN system. It develops policies and standards; conducts assessment and monitoring of the threat posed by mines and unexploded ordnance; teaches people how to remain safe in mine-affected areas; mobilizes resources; assists victims; destroys stockpiles; and advocates the global ban on antipersonnel landmines and promotes the *Mine-Ban Convention*. While much of the work in demining and mine-risk education is carried out by NGOs, commercial contractors and, in some situations, militaries, also provide humanitarian mine-action services.

Explosive remnants of war (ERW) and mines other than anti-personnel mines (MOTAPM). While significant steps have been taken to address anti-personnel landmines, many civilians are killed or injured by other explosive munitions. They pose a potential hazard to populations through inadvertent contact or deliberate tampering, especially if the danger is not well understood. They can cause severe damage even in small numbers; when placed in strategic locations, a single mine can cause entire roads to be closed and can disrupt normal activities. Combined with other possible characteristics of MOTAPM, such as anti-handling devices and minimum metal content, their humanitarian impact can be quite serious.

Under *Protocol V* to the CCW, states parties to armed conflict are required to take action to clear, remove or destroy ERW, and record, retain and transmit information related to the use or abandonment of explosive ordnance. They are also obligated to take all feasible precautions for the protection of civilians and humanitarian missions and organizations. States parties in a position to do so should provide co-operation and assistance for marking, clearance, removal, destruction, and victim assistance. *Protocol V* entered into force in 2006.

Register of Conventional Arms. In order to contribute to building confidence and security among states, the General Assembly in 1991 established the *United Nations Register of Conventional Arms* (*www.un.org/disarmament/convarms/Register*). The *Register* is maintained by the United Nations Office for Disarmament Affairs (UNODA). This voluntary reporting arrangement enables participating governments to provide information on the export and import of seven categories of major conventional weapons systems: warships, including submarines; battle tanks; armoured combat vehicles; combat aircraft; attack helicopters; large-calibre artillery; and missiles and missile-launchers, including short-range man-portable, air-defence systems. Member states are also invited to provide data on transfers of small arms and light weapons, procurement through national production, and military holdings. Such data are compiled and published annually by the UN as official documents available to the general public, as well as through the United Nations website. By 2012, 173 states had reported to the *Register* one or more times since 1991. As of January 2013, UNODA had received 51 national reports. It is estimated that the *Register* captures more than 95 per cent of the global trade in major conventional weapons.

Transparency of military expenditures. Another global mechanism designed to promote transparency in military matters is the United Nations Report on Military Expenditures (*www.un.org/disarmament/convarms/Milex*), introduced in 1980. This voluntary instrument covers national expenditures on military personnel, operations and maintenance, procurement and construction, and research and development. The UN collects this information and makes it public. As of July 2012, 30 countries had reported to this instrument at least once since its inception.

Prevention of an arms race in outer space. Matters related to outer space have been pursued in international forums along two separate lines: those related to peaceful applications of space technology, and those related to the prevention of an arms race in that environment. These issues have been discussed in the General Assembly, the Committee on the Peaceful Uses of Outer Space and its subsidiary bodies, and the Conference on Disarmament. The discussions have contributed to the conclusion of a number of international agreements concerning both peaceful and military aspects of the use of outer space. Reflecting the importance of preventing the militarization of outer space, the General Assembly's first special session on disarmament (1978) called for international negotiations on the issue. Since 1982, the Conference on Disarmament has had on its agenda an item entitled "Prevention of an arms race in outer space", but little progress has been made to date in negotiating a multilateral agreement, owing to continuing differences among its members.

Relationship between disarmament and development. The question of promoting economic and social progress, especially for less developed nations, by using the resources released through general disarmament under a system of effective international control has long been debated among member states. An international conference on the relationship between disarmament and development was held in 1987. The General Assembly has urged the international community to devote part of the resources made available through disarmament and arms limitation agreements to economic and social development, with a view to reducing the gap between developed and developing countries.

Regional approaches to disarmament. The United Nations supports both regional and subregional initiatives towards disarmament, promoting security and confidence-building measures among states within a region. It also assists them in implementing the guidelines and recommendations for regional approaches to disarmament adopted by the Disarmament Commission in 1993. To foster regional disarmament, the UN works with governmental organizations and arrangements—such as the African Union, the European Union, the Euro-Atlantic Partnership Council, the League of Arab States, the Organization of American States, the Organisation of Islamic Cooperation, the Organisation for Security and Co-operation in Europe, and the Stability Pact for South Eastern Europe—as well as with international, regional and local NGOs.

Disarmament information and education activities. The UN undertakes information and education activities on multilateral disarmament in the framework of its Disarmament Information Programme—through publications, special events, meetings, seminars, panel discussions, exhibits and a comprehensive website on disarmament issues. Since its inception in 1979, the United Nations Programme of Fellowship on Disarmament has trained nearly 860 public officials from over 160 countries—many of whom are now in positions of responsibility in the field of disarmament within their own governments. (For further information on UN involvement in disarmament and educational resources, see *www.un.org/ disarmament/education.*)

Gender perspective in disarmament. The face of warfare has changed in recent years as women and girls have increasingly been affected by conflicts, both as victims and perpetrators. The UN promotes understanding of the importance of gender perspectives in all aspects of disarmament, including collecting and destroying weapons, demining, conducting fact-finding missions, and participating in decision-making and peace processes. A gender perspective on small arms, for example, would consider how their spread affects women in particular and what might be done about their negative effects. In October 2000, the Security Council, in its landmark resolution 1325(2000), encouraged "all those involved in the planning for disarmament, demobilization and reintegration to consider the different needs of female and male ex-combatants and to take into account the needs of their dependants".

Peaceful uses of outer space

The United Nations works to ensure that outer space is used for peaceful purposes and that the benefits from space activities are shared by all nations. This concern with the peaceful uses of outer space began soon after the launch of Sputnik—the first artificial satellite—by the Soviet Union in 1957, and has kept pace with advances in space technology. The UN has played an important role by developing international space law and by promoting international cooperation in space science and technology.

The main intergovernmental body in this field is the **United Nations Committee on the Peaceful Uses of Outer Space** (*www.unoosa.org*). Established by the General Assembly in 1959, the Committee reviews the scope of international cooperation in peaceful uses of outer space, devises programmes and directs UN technical cooperation, encourages research and dissemination of information, and contributes to the development of international space law. The Committee comprises 74 member states, and a number of international organizations, both intergovernmental and non-governmental, have observer status. It has two subcommittees: the Scientific and Technical Subcommittee is the focal point of international cooperation in space technology and research, and the Legal Subcommittee works to develop a legal framework concomitant with the rapid technological advances of space activities. The Committee and its subcommittees meet annually to consider questions put forth by the General Assembly, reports submitted to them and issues raised by member states. Working on the basis of consensus, the Committee makes recommendations to the General Assembly.

Legal instruments

The work of the Committee and its Legal Subcommittee has resulted in the adoption by the General Assembly of five legal instruments, all of which are in force:

- The 1966 *Treaty on Principles Governing the Activities of States in the Exploration and Use of Outer Space, including the Moon and Other Celestial Bodies (Outer Space Treaty)* provides that space exploration shall be carried out for the benefit of all countries, irrespective of their degree of development. It seeks to maintain outer space as the province of all humankind, free for exploration and use by all states, solely for peaceful purposes, and not subject to national appropriation.
- The 1967 *Agreement on the Rescue of Astronauts, the Return of Astronauts and the Return of Objects Launched into Outer Space (Rescue Agreement)* provides for aiding the crews of spacecraft in case of accident or emergency landing, and establishes procedures for returning to the launching authority a space object found beyond the territory of that authority.
- The 1971 *Convention on International Liability for Damage Caused by Space Objects (Liability Convention)* provides that the launching state is liable for damage caused by its space objects on the earth's surface, to aircraft in flight, and to space objects of another state or persons or property on board such objects.
- The 1974 *Convention on Registration of Objects Launched into Outer Space (Registration Convention)* provides that launching states maintain registries of space objects and share that information with the United Nations. Under the *Convention*, the Office for Outer Space Affairs maintains a register of such objects. Information has been provided by all launching states and organizations. A searchable index of launched objects is available at *www.unoosa.org*.

- The 1979 *Agreement Governing Activities of States on the Moon and Other Celestial Bodies (Moon Agreement)* elaborates the principles relating to the moon and other celestial bodies set out in the 1966 *Treaty*, and sets up the basis to regulate the future exploration and exploitation of natural resources on those bodies.

On the basis of the work of the Committee and its Legal Subcommittee, the General Assembly has adopted sets of principles, including the following, on the conduct of space activities:

- The *Principles Governing the Use by States of Artificial Earth Satellites for International Direct Television Broadcasting* (1982) recognize that such use has international political, economic, social and cultural implications. Such activities should promote the dissemination and exchange of information and knowledge, foster development, and respect the sovereign rights of states, including the principle of non-intervention.
- The *Principles Relating to Remote Sensing of the Earth from Outer Space* (1986) state that such activities are to be conducted for the benefit of all countries, respecting the sovereignty of all states and peoples over their natural resources, and for the rights and interests of other states. Remote sensing is to be used to preserve the environment and to reduce the impact of natural disasters.
- The *Principles Relevant to the Use of Nuclear Power Sources in Outer Space* (1992) recognize that such sources are essential for some space missions, but that their use should be based on a thorough safety assessment. The *Principles* provide guidelines for the safe use of nuclear power sources and for notification of a malfunction of a space object where there is a risk of re-entry of radioactive material to the earth.
- The *Declaration on International Cooperation in the Exploration and Use of Outer Space for the Benefit and in the Interest of All States, Taking into Particular Account the Needs of Developing Countries* (1996) provides that states are free to determine all aspects of their participation in international space cooperation on an equitable and mutually acceptable basis, and that such cooperation should be conducted in ways that are considered most effective and appropriate by the countries concerned.

Office for Outer Space Affairs

The Vienna-based **United Nations Office for Outer Space Affairs** (*www.unoosa.org*) serves as the secretariat for the Committee on the Peaceful Uses of Outer Space and its subcommittees, and assists developing countries in using space technology for development. The Office disseminates space-related information to member states through its International Space Information System, and maintains the United Nations register on objects launched into outer space. Through its United Nations Programme on Space Applications, the Office works to improve the use of space science and technology for the economic and social development of all nations, in particular developing countries. Under this programme, it also provides technical advisory services to member states in conducting pilot projects, and undertakes training and fellowship programmes in such areas as remote sensing, satellite communication, satellite meteorology, satellite navigation, basic space science and space law.

The Office is a cooperating body of the *International Charter 'Space and Major Disasters'*—a mechanism through which UN agencies can request satellite imagery to support their response to disasters. The Office also serves as secretariat to the International Committee on Global Navigation Satellite Systems—an informal body that promotes cooperation on civil satellite-based positioning, navigation, timing and value-added services, as well as on the compatibility and interoperability of global navigation satellite systems, while increasing their use to support sustainable development, particularly in developing countries.

The Office for Outer Space Affairs manages the **United Nations Platform for Space-based Information for Disaster Management and Emergency Response (UN-SPIDER).** Established by the General Assembly in December 2006, UN-SPIDER (*www.un-spider.org*) aims to provide all countries and relevant international and regional organizations with universal access to all types of space-based information and services supporting the full disaster-management cycle. It helps increase the number of countries that receive assistance with respect to disaster-management planning, risk reduction and emergency response using space-based information, and devises policies on the use of space-based technologies.

The Office provides technical assistance to the regional centres for space science and technology education and to the network of space science and technology education affiliated with the United Nations. The centres work with member states to enhance their capability in space science and technology. They also help scientists and researchers develop skills and knowledge in using space science and technology for sustainable development. There are four regional centres: two African regional centres in Morocco and Nigeria; the Asia and the Pacific regional centre in India; the Western Asia regional centre in Jordan; and the joint Latin America and Caribbean centre in Mexico and Brazil.

The Office for Outer Space Affairs also serves as secretariat to the Inter-Agency Meeting on Outer Space Activities, which has met annually since 1975 to increase space-related cooperation among UN bodies, coordinate activities, build synergies, and consider new initiatives. The Meeting produces the Secretary-General's report on the coordination of space-related activities of the UN system.

Conferences. The United Nations has organized three major conferences on the exploration and peaceful uses of outer space, all held in Vienna. The first, held in 1968, examined the practical benefits deriving from space research and exploration, and the extent to which non-spacefaring countries might enjoy them. The second conference (UNISPACE '82) assessed the state of space science and technology; considered the applications of space technology for development; and discussed international space cooperation. UNISPACE III, held in 1999, outlined actions to: protect the global environment and manage natural resources; increase use of space applications for human security, development and welfare; protect the space environment; increase developing countries' access to space science and its benefits; and enhance training and education opportunities, especially for young people. UNISPACE III also called for a global system to manage natural disaster mitigation, relief and prevention; the improvement of educational programmes and satellite-related infrastructure to promote literacy; and international coordination of activities related to near-earth objects.

In 2004, the General Assembly conducted a five-year review of progress made in implementing the UNISPACE III recommendations. A plan of action endorsed by the

Assembly calls for further action in the use of space to support global agendas for sustainable development. Implementation of the UNISPACE III recommendations has resulted in the establishment of UN-SPIDER and the International Committee on Global Navigation Satellite Systems.

Decolonization

Nearly 100 nations whose peoples were formerly under colonial rule or a trusteeship arrangement have joined the United Nations as sovereign, independent states since the Organization was founded in 1945. Additionally, many other Territories have achieved self-determination through political association or integration with an independent state. The United Nations has played a crucial role in that historic change by encouraging the aspirations of people in dependent territories and by setting goals and standards to accelerate their attainment of independence. United Nations missions have supervised elections leading to independence in Togoland (1956 and 1968), Western Samoa (1961), Namibia (1989) and, most recently, in Timor-Leste (2002). Despite the great progress made against colonialism, nearly 2 million people still live under colonial rule, and the United Nations continues its efforts to help achieve self-determination in the remaining Non-Self-Governing Territories (see *www.un.org/en/decolonization*).

The decolonization efforts of the United Nations derive from the *Charter* principle of "equal rights and self-determination of peoples", as well as from three specific chapters in the *Charter*—Chapters XI, XII and XIII—which are devoted to the interests of dependent peoples. Since 1960, the United Nations has also been guided by the General Assembly's *Declaration on the Granting of Independence to Colonial Countries and Peoples*, also known as the *Declaration on Decolonization*, by which member states proclaimed the necessity of bringing colonialism to a speedy end. General Assembly resolution 1541(XV) of 1960 defined three options offering full self-government for Non-Self-Governing Territories:

• free association with the administering power or another independent state as a result of a free and voluntary choice by the people of the Territory expressed through an informed and democratic process;

• integration with the administering power or another independent state on the basis of complete equality between the peoples of the Non-Self-Governing Territory and those of the independent state; and

• becoming independent.

International Trusteeship System

Under Chapter XII of the *Charter*, the United Nations established the International Trusteeship System for the supervision of Trust Territories placed under it by individual agreements with the states administering them. The System applied to: Territories held under mandates established by the League of Nations after the First World War; Territories detached from "enemy states" as a result of the Second World War; and Territories voluntarily placed under the system by states responsible for their administration. The goal of the Trusteeship System was to promote the political, economic and social advancement of the Territories and their development towards self-government and self-determination.

The **Trusteeship Council** was established under Chapter XIII of the *Charter* to supervise the administration of Trust Territories and to ensure that governments responsible for their administration took adequate steps to prepare them for the achievement of the *Charter* goals.

In the early years of the United Nations, 11 Territories were placed under the trusteeship system. Over the years, all 11 Territories either became independent states or voluntarily associated themselves with a state. The last one to do so was the Trust Territory of the Pacific Islands (Palau), administered by the United States. The Security Council in 1994 terminated the United Nations Trusteeship Agreement for that Territory after it chose free association with the United States in a 1993 plebiscite. Palau became independent in 1994, joining the United Nations as its 185th member state. With no Territories left on its agenda, the Trusteeship System had completed its historic task.

Non-Self-Governing Territories

The *Charter of the United Nations* also addresses the issue of other Non-Self-Governing Territories not brought into the Trusteeship System. Chapter XI of the *Charter*—the *Declaration regarding Non-Self-Governing Territories*—provides that member states administering such Territories recognize "that the interests of the inhabitants of these Territories is paramount" and accept the obligation to promote their well-being as a "sacred trust". To this end, administering powers, in addition to ensuring the political, economic, social and educational advancement of those peoples, undertake to assist them in developing self-government and democratic political institutions. Administering powers have an obligation to transmit regularly to the Secretary-General information on the economic, social and educational conditions in the Territories under their administration.

In 1946, eight member states—Australia, Belgium, Denmark, France, the Netherlands, New Zealand, the United Kingdom and the United States—identified the Non-Self-Governing Territories under their administration. There were 72 such Territories in all, of which eight became independent before 1959. In 1963, the Assembly approved a revised list of 64 Territories to which the 1960 *Declaration on Decolonization* applied. Today, 16 such Non-Self-Governing Territories remain, with France, New Zealand, the United Kingdom and the United States as administering powers.

In 2005, Tokelau's national representative body, the General Fono, approved a draft treaty of free association between Tokelau and New Zealand, and then a draft constitution. In a 2006 referendum, 60 per cent of registered Tokelauans voted in favour of free association, falling short of the required two-thirds majority. A second referendum, held in 2007, fell just 16 votes short of the required majority, with 446 votes in favour out of 692 votes cast. As of June 2012, the UN General Assembly acknowledged the 2008 decision of the General Fono that consideration of any future act of self-determination by Tokelau would be deferred; and that New Zealand and Tokelau would enhance essential services and infrastructure on the atolls of Tokelau, thereby ensuring better quality of life for the people of those islands.

Declaration on the Granting of Independence to Colonial Countries and Peoples

The desire of the peoples of dependent Territories to achieve self-determination, and the international community's perception that principles of the *Charter of the United Nations* were being too slowly applied, led the General Assembly to proclaim in 1960 the *Declaration on the Granting of Independence to Colonial Countries and Peoples* (resolution 1514(XV)). The *Declaration* states that subjecting peoples to alien subjugation, domination and exploitation constitutes a denial of fundamental human rights; is contrary to the *Charter*; and is an impediment to the promotion of world peace and cooperation. It adds that "immediate steps shall be taken, in Trust and Non-Self-Governing Territories or all other Territories which have not yet attained independence, to transfer all powers to the peoples of those Territories, without any conditions or reservations, in accordance with their freely expressed will and desire, without any distinction as to race, creed or colour in order to enable them to enjoy complete independence and freedom". In resolution 1541(XV), the Assembly also defined the three legitimate political status options offering full self-government—free association with an independent state, integration into an independent state, or independence.

Territories to which the Declaration on the Granting of Independence to Colonial Countries and Peoples continues to apply

Territory	Administering authority
Africa	
Western Sahara	—
Asia and the Pacific	
American Samoa	United States
Guam	United States
New Caledonia	France
Pitcairn	United Kingdom
Tokelau	New Zealand
Atlantic Ocean, Caribbean and Mediterranean	
Anguilla	United Kingdom
Bermuda	United Kingdom
British Virgin Islands	United Kingdom
Cayman Islands	United Kingdom
Falkland Islands (Malvinas)	United Kingdom
Gibraltar	United Kingdom
Montserrat	United Kingdom
Saint Helena	United Kingdom
Turks and Caicos Islands	United Kingdom
United States Virgin Islands	United States

In 1961, the Assembly established a special committee to examine the application of the *Declaration* and make recommendations on its implementation. Commonly referred to as the Special Committee on Decolonization, its full title is the **Special Committee on the Situation with Regard to the Implementation of the Declaration on the Granting of Independence to Colonial**

Countries and Peoples. It meets annually, hears petitioners and representatives of the Territories, dispatches visiting missions to the Territories, and organizes annual seminars on the political, social, economic and educational situations in the Territories.

Western Sahara. On 26 February 1976, Spain informed the Secretary-General that as of that date it had terminated its presence in the Territory of the Sahara, and deemed it necessary to place on record that Spain considered itself thenceforth exempt from any international responsibility in connection with its administration, in view of the cessation of its participation in the temporary administration established for the Territory. In 1990, the General Assembly reaffirmed that the question of Western Sahara was a question of decolonization that remained to be completed by the people of Western Sahara.

New Caledonia. On 2 December 1986, the General Assembly determined that New Caledonia was a Non-Self-Governing Territory.

In the years following the adoption of the *Declaration*, some 60 colonial Territories, inhabited by more than 80 million people, attained self-determination through independence, and joined the United Nations as sovereign members. The Assembly has called upon the administering powers to take all necessary steps to enable the peoples of the Non-Self-Governing Territories to exercise fully their right to self-determination and independence. It has also called upon the administering powers to complete the withdrawal of remaining military bases from those Territories, and to ensure that no activity of foreign economic and other interests hinders the implementation of the *Declaration*.

In this respect, New Zealand has extended continuous cooperation to the Special Committee regarding Tokelau. France began cooperating with the Committee in 1999, following the signing of an agreement on the future of New Caledonia. In recent years, two administering powers have not participated formally in the Committee's work. The United States has maintained that it remains conscious of its role as an administering power and will continue to meet its responsibilities under the *Charter of the United Nations*. The United Kingdom has repeatedly stated that while most of the Territories under its administration chose independence, a small number have preferred to remain associated with it.

At the end of the first International Decade for the Eradication of Colonialism (1991–2000), the General Assembly declared a Second International Decade for the Eradication of Colonialism (2001–2010), calling on member states to redouble their efforts to achieve complete decolonization. In the case of certain Territories, such as Western Sahara, the Assembly has entrusted the Secretary-General with specific tasks to facilitate the process of decolonization, in accordance with the *Charter of the United Nations* and the objectives of the *Declaration*. By resolution 65/119 of 10 December 2010, the Assembly declared a Third International Decade (2011–2020).

Namibia

The United Nations helped bring about the independence of Namibia in 1990—a case revealing the complexity of the efforts needed to ensure the peaceful transition of a Territory to independence. Formerly known as South West Africa, Namibia was an African Territory under the League of Nations mandate system.

In 1946, the General Assembly asked South Africa to administer the Territory under the trusteeship system. South Africa refused, and in 1949 informed the United Nations that it would no longer transmit information on the Territory, maintaining that the mandate had ended with the demise of the League. The General Assembly, stating that South Africa had not fulfilled its obligations, terminated that mandate in 1966 and placed the Territory under the responsibility of the United Nations Council for South West Africa, which was renamed the Council for Namibia in 1968. In 1976, the Security Council demanded that South Africa accept elections for the Territory under UN supervision. The General Assembly stated that independence talks would have to involve the South West Africa People's Organization (SWAPO)—the sole representative of the Namibian people.

In 1978, Canada, France, the Federal Republic of Germany, the United Kingdom and the United States submitted to the Security Council a settlement proposal providing for elections for a constituent assembly under UN auspices. The Council endorsed the Secretary-General's recommendations for implementing the proposal, asked him to appoint a special representative for Namibia, and established the United Nations Transition Assistance Group (UNTAG). Years of negotiations by the Secretary-General and his special representative, as well as United States mediation, led in 1988 to agreements for the achievement of peace in southern Africa, by which South Africa agreed to cooperate with the Secretary-General to ensure Namibia's independence through elections.

The operation that led to Namibia's independence started in 1989. UNTAG supervised and controlled the entire electoral process, which was conducted by the Namibian authorities. It monitored the ceasefire between SWAPO and South Africa and the demobilization of all military forces, and ensured a smooth electoral process, including the monitoring of local police.

The elections for the constituent assembly were won by SWAPO and were declared "free and fair" by the Secretary-General's special representative. Following the elections, South Africa withdrew its remaining troops. The constituent assembly drafted a new constitution, approved in February 1990, and elected SWAPO leader Sam Nujoma as President for a five-year term. In March, Namibia became independent, with the Secretary-General administering the oath of office to Namibia's first President. In April of the same year, it joined the United Nations.

Timor-Leste

Another United Nations success story is the process that led to the independence of Timor-Leste—formerly known as East Timor. A major UN operation oversaw its transition towards independence, after the East Timorese people voted in favour of independence in a popular consultation conducted by the UN in 1999.

The island of Timor lies to the north of Australia, in the south-central part of the chain of islands forming Indonesia. Its western part had been a Dutch colony, and became part of Indonesia when that country attained independence. East Timor was a Portuguese colony.

In 1960, the General Assembly placed East Timor on the list of Non-Self-Governing Territories. In 1974, recognizing its right to self-determination, Portugal sought to establish a provisional government and popular assembly to determine East Timor's status. In 1975, however, civil war broke out between the Territory's newly formed political parties. Portugal withdrew, stating it could not control the situation. One East Timorese side declared independence as a separate country, while another proclaimed independence and integration with Indonesia.

In December, Indonesian troops landed in East Timor, and a provisional government was formed. Portugal broke off relations with Indonesia and brought the matter before the Security Council, which called on Indonesia to withdraw its forces and urged all states to respect the right of the East Timorese people to self-determination. In 1976, the provisional government held elections for an assembly, which then called for integration with Indonesia. When Indonesia issued a law supporting that decision, the pro-independence movement began an armed resistance. In 1983, the Secretary-General started talks with Indonesia and Portugal, but it was only in 1999, through the good offices of the Secretary-General, that agreements were reached, paving the way for a popular consultation.

On the basis of those agreements, the United Nations Mission in East Timor (UNAMET) organized and conducted voter registration and an official ballot. In August 1999, however, when 78.5 per cent of 450,000 registered voters rejected autonomy within Indonesia, militias opposing independence unleashed a campaign of systematic destruction and violence, killing many and forcing more than 200,000 East Timorese to flee their homes. After intensive talks, Indonesia accepted the deployment of a UN-authorized multinational force. In September, acting under Chapter VII of the *Charter*, the Security Council authorized the dispatch of the International Force in East Timor (INTERFET), which helped restore peace and security. Immediately following that action, the Council, in October, established the United Nations Transitional Administration in East Timor (UNTAET), giving it full executive and legislative authority during the country's transition to independence.

In August 2001, more than 91 per cent of East Timor's eligible voters went to the polls to elect an 88-member constituent assembly, tasked with writing and adopting a new constitution and establishing the framework for future elections and the transition to full independence. In March 2002, the constituent assembly signed into force the Territory's first constitution. The following month, after winning 82.7 per cent of the vote, Xanana Gusmão was appointed president-elect. On 20 May 2002, the Territory attained independence. The constituent assembly was transformed into the national parliament, and the new country adopted the name Timor-Leste. In September of that year, it became the 191st member state of the United Nations.

Following the successful decolonization of East Timor, the UN has remained committed to supporting the independent country of Timor-Leste in consolidating democratic institutions and advancing socio-economic development.

Western Sahara

The United Nations has been dealing with an ongoing dispute concerning Western Sahara—a Territory on the north-west coast of Africa bordering Algeria, Mauritania and Morocco—since 1963.

Western Sahara became a Spanish colony in 1884. In 1963, both Mauritania and Morocco laid claim to it. The International Court of Justice, in a 1975 opinion requested by the General Assembly, rejected the claims of territorial sovereignty by Mauritania and Morocco.

The United Nations has been seeking a settlement in Western Sahara since the withdrawal of Spain in 1976 and the ensuing fighting between Morocco—which had 'reintegrated' the Territory—and the Popular Front for the Liberation of Saguia el-Hamra and Río de Oro (Frente Polisario), supported by Algeria. In 1979, the Organization of African Unity (OAU) called for a referendum to enable the people of the Territory to exercise their right to self-determination. By 1982, 26 OAU member states had recognized the "Saharawi Arab Democratic Republic" (SADR) proclaimed by Polisario in 1976. When SADR was seated at the 1984 OAU summit, Morocco withdrew from the OAU.

A joint good offices mission by the Secretary-General and the OAU Chairman led to settlement proposals in 1988 calling for a ceasefire and referendum to choose between independence and integration with Morocco, to which the parties agreed in principle. By resolution 690(1991), the Security Council created the **United Nations Mission for the Referendum in Western Sahara (MINURSO)** in 1991 to assist the Secretary-General's special representative in all matters related to the organization and conduct of a referendum of self-determination for the people of Western Sahara. All Western Saharans aged 18 and over counted in the 1974 Spanish census would have the right to vote, whether living in the Territory or outside. An identification commission would update the census list and identify voters. Refugees living outside the Territory would be identified with the assistance of the Office of the United Nations High Commissioner for Refugees (UNHCR).

In September 1991, the ceasefire came into effect. It has been observed ever since by MINURSO's military observers, with no major violations. However, the parties have continued to differ on implementation of the settlement plan—particularly with respect to voter eligibility for the referendum. In 1997, a compromise was brokered by the Secretary-General's personal envoy for Western Sahara, and the identification process was completed at the end of 1999. Nevertheless, despite continuing consultations and negotiations, disagreements persisted over implementation of the plan.

In 2004, Morocco rejected a proposal put forward by the personal envoy as well as the settlement plan itself. Despite the continuing stalemate, there were some positive developments over the ensuing years, including the Frente Polisario's release of all remaining Moroccan prisoners of war in August 2005, and the 2004 establishment of a UNHCR-sponsored 'family visits' programme between Western Saharan refugees living in the camps in Tindouf, Algeria, and their relatives in Western Sahara Territory—some of whom had not seen each other for 30 years.

In 2007, the Secretary-General's personal envoy observed that there were two options left: indefinite prolongation of the impasse, or direct negotiations. The Security Council called for good faith negotiations without preconditions. The envoy then facilitated meetings with the parties in New York, also attended by Algeria and Mauritania. At the second meeting, the parties acknowledged that the status quo was unacceptable and committed themselves to continuing the negotiations in good faith.

Despite the continued divergence in positions, this renewed dialogue marked the first direct negotiations between the parties in more than seven years. A third round was held in 2008, and the parties came together for five more informal meetings in 2009, 2010, 2011 and 2012. However, no progress was registered on the core issues of the future status of Western Sahara and the means by which the self-determination of the people of Western Sahara is to occur. The Secretary-General observed that at a time of protest and contestation throughout the Middle East/North Africa region, the sentiments of the population of Western Sahara, both inside and outside the Territory, with regard to its final status were more central than ever to the search for a just and lasting settlement. Meanwhile, MINURSO continues to support a range of assistance programmes for the displaced and separated Sahrawi families. It has assisted both parties in maintaining the ceasefire across the buffer strip, which stretches along the entire length of the disputed territory and separates the Moroccan-administered portion in the west from the area that is controlled by the Frente Polisario in the east.

III. ECONOMIC AND SOCIAL DEVELOPMENT

A young woman helps build a community centre in El Fasher, North Darfur, Sudan, as part of a project sponsored by the African Union-United Nations Hybrid Operation in Darfur. (15 August 2012, UN Photo/Abert González Farran)

Many people associate the United Nations with the issues of peace and security, but most of Organization's resources are in fact devoted to advancing the *Charter's* pledge to "promote higher standards of living, full employment, and conditions of economic and social progress and development". United Nations development efforts have profoundly affected the lives and well-being of millions of people throughout the world. UN endeavours are guided by the conviction that lasting international peace and security are possible only if the economic and social well-being of people everywhere is assured.

Many of the economic and social transformations that have taken place globally since 1945 have been significantly affected in their direction and shape by the work of the United Nations. As the global centre for consensus-building, the UN has set priorities and goals for international cooperation to assist countries in their development efforts and foster a supportive global economic environment.

The UN provides a platform for formulating and promoting new developmental objectives on the international agenda through global conferences. It articulates the need for incorporating issues such as the advancement of women, human rights, sustainable development, environmental protection and good governance into the development paradigm. This global consensus has also been expressed through a series of international development decades, the first beginning in 1961. These broad statements of policy and goals emphasized certain issues of particular concern in each decade, and stressed the need for progress in all aspects of development and the importance of narrowing the disparities between industrialized and developing countries.

At the **Millennium Summit** in 2000, member states adopted the *Millennium Declaration*, which contained a set of wide-ranging goals for the future course of the Organization. The *Declaration* was translated into a road map that included eight time-bound and measurable goals to be reached by 2015, known as the **Millennium Development Goals (MDGs)**. The MDGs aim to eradicate extreme poverty and hunger; achieve universal primary education; promote gender equality and the empowerment of women; reduce child mortality; improve maternal health; combat HIV/AIDS, malaria and other diseases; ensure environmental sustainability; and develop a global partnership for development. The international community recommitted itself to the Goals during the World Summit in 2005.

In 2010, the UN Summit on the MDGs—formally known as the High-level Plenary Meeting on the Millennium Development Goals—concluded with the adoption of a global action plan to achieve the eight anti-poverty goals by their 2015 target date and the announcement of major new commitments for the health of women and children and other initiatives against poverty, hunger and disease.

International debate on economic and social issues has increasingly reflected the commonality of interests among rich and poor countries in solving the many problems that transcend national boundaries. Issues related to refugee populations, organized crime, drug trafficking, HIV and AIDS and climate change are seen as global challenges requiring coordinated action. The impact of persistent poverty and unemployment in one region can be quickly felt in others, not least through migration, social disruption and conflict. Similarly, in the age of a global economy, financial instability in one country can at once affect the markets of others.

There is also growing consensus on the role played by democracy, human rights, popular participation, good governance and the empowerment of women in fostering economic and social development.

Coordinating development activities

Despite advances on many fronts, gross disparities in wealth and well-being continue to characterize the world's economic and social structure. Reducing poverty and redressing inequalities, both within and between countries, remain fundamental goals of the United Nations.

The UN system works in a variety of ways to promote common economic and social goals: by providing policy analysis and addressing ongoing and emerging global challenges; advising governments on their development plans and strategies; setting international norms and standards; and mobilizing funds for development programmes. Through the work of its various funds and programmes, and its family of specialized agencies, the UN touches the lives of people everywhere, in fields as diverse as education, air safety, environmental protection and labour conditions.

The **Economic and Social Council (ECOSOC)** (*www.un.org/en/ecosoc*) is the principal body coordinating the economic and social work of the United Nations and its operational arms. It is also the central forum for discussing international economic and social issues and for formulating policy recommendations. The Council's responsibilities include: promoting higher standards of living, full employment, and economic and social progress; identifying solutions to economic, social and health problems; facilitating cultural and educational cooperation; and encouraging universal respect for human rights and fundamental freedoms.

Under ECOSOC, the **Committee for Development Policy**, made up of 24 experts working in their personal capacity, acts as an advisory body on emerging economic, social and environmental issues. It also sets the criteria for the designation of least developed countries (LDCs) and reviews the list of those countries.

At the 2005 World Summit, ECOSOC was mandated to hold Annual Ministerial Reviews (AMRs) and a biennial Development Cooperation Forum (DCF). The AMR assesses progress in achieving the internationally agreed development goals arising out of major conferences and summits. It consists of an annual thematic review and national voluntary presentations on progress and challenges towards achieving those goals.

The objective of the DCF is to enhance the coherence and effectiveness of development partners' activities. It is tasked with providing policy guidance and recommendations to improve development cooperation.

The **United Nations Development Group** (*www.undg.org*) unites the 32 UN funds, programmes, agencies, departments and offices that play a role in the management and coordination of development work within the Organization. This executive body works to enhance cooperation between policymaking entities and the distinct operational programmes.

The **Executive Committee on Economic and Social Affairs** (*www.un.org/en/development/other/ecesa.shtml*), composed of Secretariat bodies and including the regional commissions, is also an instrument for policy development and management. It aims to bring coherence among UN entities engaged in normative, analytical and technical work in the economic and social field.

Within the United Nations Secretariat, the **Department of Economic and Social Affairs (DESA)** (*www.un.org/esa/desa*) helps countries address their economic, social and environmental challenges. It operates within a framework of internationally agreed goals known as the UN development agenda. Within this framework, DESA provides analytical support, as well as substantive and technical support to member states in the social, economic and environmental spheres, and carries out policy analysis and coordination. It also provides support in setting norms and standards, and in agreeing on common courses of action in response to global challenges. DESA serves as a crucial interface between global policies and national action, and among research, policy and operational activities.

The five regional commissions facilitate similar exchanges of economic and social information and policy analysis in the regions of Africa (ECA) (*www.uneca.org*), Asia and the Pacific (ESCAP) (*www.unescap.org*), Europe (ECE) (*www.unece.org*), Latin America and the Caribbean (ECLAC) (*www.eclac.org*), and Western Asia (ESCWA) (*www.escwa.org*). Many United Nations funds and programmes deal with operational activities for development in programme countries, and several UN specialized agencies provide support and assistance for countries' development efforts. In a time of increasingly limited resources, both human and financial, enhanced coordination and cooperation among the various arms of the UN system are vital if development goals are to be realized.

Economic development

The world has witnessed enormous economic development in recent decades, but the generation of wealth and prosperity has been uneven. Economic imbalances exacerbate social problems and political instability in virtually every region of the world. The end of the cold war and the accelerating integration of the global economy have not solved persistent problems of extreme poverty, indebtedness, underdevelopment and trade imbalance.

One of the founding principles of the United Nations is the conviction that economic development for all peoples is the surest way to achieve political, economic and social security. It is a central concern of the Organization that almost half the world's population—mostly in Africa, Asia, and Latin America and the Caribbean—must live on less than $2 per day. It was estimated that more than 197 million workers were unemployed worldwide in 2011, and more than 868 million earned less than $2 a day. The number of undernourished people in developing countries was estimated at approximately 850 million in 2012.

The UN continues to be the sole institution dedicated to ensuring that economic expansion and globalization are guided by policies promoting human welfare, sustainable development, the eradication of poverty, fair trade and the reduction of immobilizing foreign debt. It urges the adoption of macroeconomic policies that address current imbalances—particularly the growing gap between the North and South—as well as the persistent problems of the LDCs and the unprecedented needs of countries in transition from centralized to market economies.

UN programmes of assistance promote poverty reduction, child survival, environmental protection, women's progress and human rights. For millions of people in poor countries, these programmes *are* the United Nations.

Official development assistance

Through their policies and loans, the lending institutions of the UN system have, collectively, a strong influence on the economies of developing countries. This is especially true for the LDCs—49 nations whose extreme poverty and indebtedness have marginalized them from global growth and development (*www.unohrlls.org/en/ldc/25*). These nations, 34 of which are in Africa, are given priority attention in several UN assistance programmes.

Small island developing states, landlocked developing countries and countries with economies in transition also suffer from critical problems requiring special attention from the international community. These, too, are given priority in the assistance programmes of the UN system, as well as through official development assistance (ODA) from member states. Of the world's 31 landlocked developing countries, 16 are LDCs. Of the 38 small island developing states, 12 are LDCs.

In 1970, the General Assembly set an ODA target of 0.7 per cent of gross national product (GNP)—now referred to as gross national income (GNI). (GDP is the market value of all final goods and services made within the borders of a nation annually; GNI is GDP plus net receipts of primary income from other countries.) For years, the collective effort of members of the Development Assistance Committee (DAC) of the Organization for Economic Co-operation and Development (OECD), now comprising 34 industrialized countries, hovered at around half the target level. The UN-hosted International Conference on Financing for Development, held in Monterrey, Mexico, in 2002, stimulated commitments from major donors to increase ODA. It also sought to shift the focus of such assistance towards poverty reduction, education and health.

Among DAC members, total ODA stood at 0.31 per cent of combined GNI in 2011, at $134 billion. Five countries—Denmark, Luxembourg, the Netherlands, Norway and Sweden—exceeded the 0.7 per cent target for ODA. The United Kingdom was on track to meet the target in 2013. The largest donor nations by volume were France, Germany, Japan, the United Kingdom and the United States.

United Nations ODA is derived from two sources: grant assistance from UN specialized agencies, funds and programmes; and support from lending institutions of the UN system, such as the World Bank and IFAD. It is widely distributed among the many countries in need.

The World Bank Group committed $52.6 billion in loans, grants, equity investments and guarantees to help promote economic growth and overcome poverty in developing countries in fiscal year 2012. Between 1978 and 2011, IFAD invested $12.9 billion in projects and programmes, reaching some 400 million rural people. Governments and other financing sources in recipient countries contributed $11.7 billion, and multilateral, bilateral and other donors provided approximately $9.2 billion in co-financing.

In 2011, the UN system spent $24.5 billion on operational activities for development. Total contributions towards such activities amounted to $22.9 billion.

Some 67 per cent of the contributions were development-related, with 33 per cent having a humanitarian assistance focus.

Promoting development worldwide

The **United Nations Development Programme (UNDP)** (*www.undp.org*) is committed to making a pivotal contribution to halving world poverty by 2015. UNDP provides sound policy advice and helps build institutional capacity that generates equitable economic growth.

UNDP works on the ground in more than 177 countries to help people help themselves. It focuses on assisting countries in building and sharing solutions to challenges such as poverty reduction and the achievement of the MDGs; democratic governance, including the governance of HIV/AIDS responses; crisis prevention and recovery; and environment and sustainable development. In each of these areas, UNDP advocates for the protection of human rights and the empowerment of women.

Most of UNDP's core programme funds go to those countries that are home to the world's extreme poor. Globally, the number of people living below the international poverty line fell from 1.9 billion in 1990 to 1.2 billion in 2010, representing 20.6 per cent of the population of the developing world. However, progress was uneven across regions. With 1.18 billion people living on $1.25–$2 per day in 2010, many people remained vulnerable and poor by the standards of middle-income developing countries. Almost 870 million people were chronically undernourished in the 2010–2012 period, a vast majority of them living in developing countries.

In 2011, UNDP spent some $4.7 billion on development activities. Contributions to UNDP are voluntary and come from nearly every government in the world. Countries that receive UNDP-administered assistance contribute to project costs through personnel, facilities, equipment and supplies.

To ensure maximum impact from global development resources, UNDP coordinates its activities with other UN funds and programmes and international financial institutions, including the World Bank and the International Monetary Fund (IMF). In addition, UNDP's country and regional programmes draw on the expertise of developing country nationals and NGOs. Seventy-five per cent of all UNDP-supported projects are implemented by local organizations.

At the country level, UNDP promotes an integrated approach to the provision of UN development assistance. In several developing countries, it has established a **United Nations Development Assistance Framework (UNDAF)** made up of UN teams under the leadership of the local United Nations resident coordinator, who is in many instances the resident representative of UNDP. The frameworks articulate a coordinated response to the main development challenges identified for the United Nations by governments. Resident coordinators serve as coordinators of humanitarian assistance in cases of human disasters, natural disasters and complex emergency situations.

In addition to its regular programmes, UNDP administers various special-purpose funds. The **UN Capital Development Fund (UNCDF)** offers a combination of investment capital, capacity-building and technical advisory services to promote microfinance and local development in the least developed countries.

The **United Nations Volunteers (UNV) programme** (*www.unv.org*) is the UN focal point for promoting and harnessing volunteerism for effective development. More than 6,800 UNVs from 159 countries were deployed worldwide in 2011.

UNDP, together with the World Bank and the United Nations Environment Programme (UNEP), is one of the managing partners of the Global Environment Facility. UNDP is also one of the sponsors of the Joint United Nations Programme on HIV/AIDS (UNAIDS).

Lending for development

The **World Bank** (*www.worldbank.org*) comprises two unique institutions—the International Bank for Reconstruction and Development and the International Development Association—and works in more than 100 developing countries, bringing finance and/or technical expertise to help them reduce poverty. Its portfolio of projects covers Latin America and the Caribbean, the Middle East and North Africa, Europe and Central Asia, East Asia and the Pacific, Africa, and South Asia.

The Bank is currently involved in more than 1,330 projects in virtually every sector and developing country. One of the world's largest sources of development assistance, the Bank supports the efforts of developing country governments to build schools and health centres, provide water and electricity, fight disease and protect the environment. It does this through the provision of loans, which are repaid. In fiscal year 2013, the Bank provided $31.5 billion for 276 projects in developing countries worldwide.

There are two types of World Bank lending. The first type is for higher-income developing countries that are able to pay near-market interest rates or can borrow from commercial sources. These countries receive loans from the **International Bank for Reconstruction and Development (IBRD)**, which aims to reduce poverty in middle-income and creditworthy poorer countries by promoting sustainable development through loans, guarantees, risk management products, and analytical and advisory services. IBRD loans allow countries more time to repay than if they borrowed from a commercial bank: 15 to 20 years with a three-to-five-year grace period before the repayment of principal begins. Funds are borrowed for specific programmes in support of poverty reduction, delivery of social services, environmental protection and economic growth. In fiscal 2012, lending commitments by IBRD totalled $20.6 billion for 93 operations—significantly higher than the historical average of $13.5 billion but less than the record $44.2 billion in fiscal 2010, when the economic and financial crisis peaked. IBRD, with its AAA credit rating, raises nearly all its money through the sale of its bonds in the world's financial markets.

The second type of loan goes to the poorest countries, which are usually not creditworthy in the international financial markets and are unable to pay near market interest rates on the money they borrow. The **International Development Association (IDA)** makes loans to the world's poorest countries and aims to reduce poverty by providing grant financing and credits for programmes that boost economic growth, reduce inequalities and improve people's living conditions. The 'credits' are actually interest-free loans with a 10-year grace period and maturities of 35 to 40 years. IDA assistance is largely funded by contributions from its richer member countries. In 2012, IDA commitments amounted to $14.8 billion for development activities in 81 countries.

Under its regulations, the Bank can lend only to governments, but it works closely with local communities, NGOs and private enterprise. Its projects are designed to assist the poorest sectors of the population. Successful development requires that governments and communities have ownership of their development projects. The Bank encourages governments to work closely with NGOs and civil society to strengthen participation by people benefiting from Bank-financed projects. NGOs based in borrowing countries collaborate in about half of these projects.

The Bank advocates stable economic policies, sound government finances, and open, honest and accountable governance. It supports many areas in which private-sector development is making rapid inroads—finance, power, telecommunications, information technology, oil and gas, and industry. The Bank's regulations prohibit it from lending directly to the private sector, but a Bank affiliate—the **International Finance Corporation (IFC)**—exists expressly to promote private sector investment by supporting high-risk sectors and countries. Another affiliate, the **Multilateral Investment Guarantee Agency (MIGA)**, provides political risk insurance (guarantees) to those who invest in or lend to developing countries.

The World Bank does much more than lend money. It also routinely includes technical assistance in the projects it finances. This may include advice on such issues as the overall size of a country's budget and where the money should be allocated, or how to set up village health clinics, or what sort of equipment is needed to build a road. The Bank funds a few projects each year devoted exclusively to providing expert advice and training. It also trains people from borrowing countries on how to create and carry out development programmes.

IBRD supports sustainable development projects in such areas as reforestation, pollution control and land management; water, sanitation and agriculture; and conservation of natural resources. It is the main funder of the **Global Environment Facility (GEF)**, which is itself the largest funder of projects to improve the global environment. IBRD and IDA also support the **Heavily Indebted Poor Countries (HIPC)** Initiative, which aims to reduce the external debt of the world's poorest, most heavily indebted countries. In fiscal year 2012, $5 million of development credits and $2 million of charges were written off as debt relief under the partial forgiveness of the IDA debt service as it came due. At their July 2005 summit, the leaders of the 'Group of Eight' developed nations proposed 100 per cent cancellation of debt owed to IDA, IMF and the African Development Fund by some of the world's poorest countries, mostly in Africa and Latin America. Debt relief under the resulting **Multilateral Debt Relief Initiative (MDRI)** amounted to $1.6 billion of development credits being written as of July 2012 as one country—Cote d'Ivoire—reached its HIPC completion point. On a cumulative basis, nearly $37 billion of development credits had been written off under MDRI as of June 2012.

Lending for stability

Many countries turn to the **International Monetary Fund (IMF)** (*www.imf.org*), a UN specialized agency, when internal or external factors seriously undermine their balance-of-payments position, fiscal stability or capacity to meet debt service commitments. IMF offers advice and policy recommendations to overcome these problems, and often makes financial resources available to member countries in support of economic reform programmes.

Members with balance-of-payments problems generally avail themselves of IMF's financial resources by purchasing reserve assets—in the form of other members' currencies and Special Drawing Rights (SDRs)—with an equivalent amount of their own currencies. IMF levies charges on these loans and requires that members repay the loans by repurchasing their own currencies from IMF over a specified time.

In 2010, IMF upgraded its support for low-income countries (LICs) to reflect the changing nature of economic conditions in those countries and their increased vulnerability due to the effects of the global economic crisis. It would more than double the resources available to LICs to up to $17 billion in 2014. As part of a broader reform to make the Fund's financial support more flexible and better tailored to the needs of LICs, IMF established the **Poverty Reduction and Growth Trust** with three concessional lending windows: extended, standby and rapid credit facilities, which became effective in January 2010. In April 2013, these instruments were refined to improve the flexibility of Fund support.

The main IMF financing facilities are:

- Stand-By Arrangements, designed to provide medium-term balance-of-payments assistance for temporary, short-term or cyclical nature deficits;
- Flexible Credit Line, designed to address all potential or actual balance-of-payments needs;
- Precautionary and Liquidity Line, designed to meet the crisis prevention and resolution needs of countries that have sound economic fundamentals and institutional policy frameworks, but have some remaining vulnerabilities that preclude them from using the Flexible Credit Line;
- Extended Fund Facility, designed to provide assistance for balance-of-payments difficulties of a long-term character or stemming from macroeconomic and structural problems;
- Extended Credit Facility, designed to provide longer-term assistance to LICs with deep-seated balance-of-payments difficulties of a structural nature, with the goal of sustained poverty reduction;
- Standby Credit Facility, providing flexible support to LICs with short-term financing and adjustment needs caused by domestic or external shocks or policy slippages;
- Rapid Credit Facility, a concessional facility that provides rapid financial support with limited conditionality in a single, up-front payout for LICs facing urgent balance of payment needs arising from such shocks as natural disasters, commodity price changes or crises in neighbouring countries;
- Rapid Financing Instrument, providing rapid financial assistance with limited conditionality to all members facing an urgent balance of payments need.

To provide debt relief to heavily indebted poor countries following sound policies, IMF and the World Bank jointly provide, under the Heavily Indebted Poor Countries (HIPC) Initiative, exceptional assistance to eligible countries to reduce their external debt burdens to sustainable levels. They have now also joined in supporting the Multilateral Debt Relief Initiative developed to supplement the HIPC Initiative.

Surveillance is the process by which IMF appraises its members' exchange rate policies through a comprehensive analysis of the general economic situation and policies of each member. IMF carries out surveillance through annual consultations with individual countries; multilateral surveillance twice a year; regional surveillance through discussion with regional groupings; and precautionary arrangements, enhanced surveillance, and programme monitoring, which provide a member with close IMF monitoring in the absence of the use of the IMF resources.

IMF provides technical assistance to its members in several broad areas: the design and implementation of fiscal and monetary policy; institution-building; and the collection and refinement of statistical data. IMF also provides training to member country officials at its principal training locations: IMF Headquarters in Washington, D.C., and its regional centres in Abu Dhabi (United Arab Emirates), Brasilia, Dalian (China), Pune (India), Singapore, Tunis and Vienna.

Investment and development

As foreign direct investment (FDI) has continued to expand dramatically, developing countries have increasingly opened up their economies to such investment. At the same time, they also are investing more in other developing countries. Various parts of the UN system, such as the Food and Agriculture Organization of the United Nations (FAO), UNDP and the United Nations Industrial Development Organization (UNIDO), monitor and assess developments and assist developing country governments in attracting investment.

Two affiliates of the World Bank—the International Finance Corporation and the Multilateral Investment Guarantee Agency—help promote investment in developing countries. Through its advisory work, the **International Finance Corporation (IFC)** (*www.ifc.org*) helps governments create conditions that stimulate the flow of both domestic and foreign private savings and investment. It also mobilizes private investment in the developing world by demonstrating that investments there can be profitable. In fiscal year 2012, IFC invested a record $20.4 billion—including nearly $5 billion mobilized from other investors—in 576 projects in 103 countries. Since its establishment in 1956, IFC has committed more than $126 billion of its own funds for private sector investments in developing countries and mobilized billions more from others.

The **Multilateral Investment Guarantee Agency (MIGA)** is an investment insurance affiliate of the Bank. Its goal is to facilitate the flow of private investment for productive purposes to developing member countries, by offering investors long term political risk insurance—coverage against the risks of expropriation, currency transfer, war and civil disturbance—and by providing advisory services. MIGA carries out promotional programmes, disseminates information on investment opportunities, and provides technical assistance that enhances the investment promotion capabilities of countries. In fiscal year 2012, MIGA issued $2.7 billion in investment guarantees (insurance) for 50 projects in developing countries. Since its inception in 1988, MIGA has issued 1,096 guarantees amounting to $27.2 billion for 701 projects in 105 countries.

Trade and development

The **United Nations Conference on Trade and Development (UNCTAD)** (*www. unctad.org*) is tasked with ensuring the integration of all countries in global trade. As the UN focal point for dealing with development-related issues in the areas of trade, finance, technology, investment and sustainable development, UNCTAD works to maximize the trade, investment and development opportunities of developing countries. It helps them face the challenges arising from globalization and integrate into the world economy on an equitable basis. UNCTAD pursues these goals through research and policy analysis, intergovernmental deliberations, technical cooperation and interaction with civil society and the business sector. In particular, UNCTAD:

- examines trends in the global economy and evaluates their impact on development;
- helps developing countries—particularly the least developed ones— to become part of the international trading system and actively involved in international trade negotiations;
- examines global trends in FDI flows and their impact on trade, technology and development;
- helps developing countries attract investment;
- assists developing countries in establishing enterprises and entrepreneurship; and
- helps developing countries and countries with economies in transition improve the efficiency of their trade-supporting services.

UNCTAD assists developing countries and economies in transition to promote FDI and improve their investment climate. It also helps governments understand the policy implications of FDI and formulate and implement policies accordingly. It promotes understanding of the linkages between investment, trade, enterprise development and technological capacity-building. Global trends in FDI are presented in UNCTAD's annual *World Investment Report, Investment Policy Reviews, World Investment Directory* and other studies.

UNCTAD's work helps clarify trends and shape thinking and policies on the trade development nexus in the context of globalization. UNCTAD was one of the main authors of the notion of special and differential treatment for developing countries, and a key actor in its incorporation into the General Agreement on Tariffs and Trade and the World Trade Organization. It is also the UN system focal point on trade logistics. By providing institutional, legal and operational solutions to reduce transaction costs and increase transport connectivity, it improves developing countries' access to world markets.

UNCTAD promotes enterprise development, particularly for small and medium-sized enterprises, through regular intergovernmental discussions and technical cooperation. Its technical cooperation activities include:

- The Automated System for Customs Data (*www.asycuda.org*), using state-of-the-art technology, helps governments modernize customs procedures and management. Used by over 90 countries, the System is fast becoming the internationally accepted standard for customs automation. It is also an instrument for improving economic governance.
- The EMPRETEC Programme (*www.unctadxi.org/templates/Startpage_7428.aspx*) promotes small and medium-sized enterprise development. An information network provides entrepreneurs with access to business databases.

The **International Trade Centre UNCTAD/WTO (ITC)** (*www.intracen.org*) is the focal point in the UN system for technical cooperation with developing countries in trade promotion. It works with developing countries and countries with economies in transition in setting up trade promotion programmes to expand their exports and improve their import operations.

ITC's mission is to foster sustainable economic development and contribute to achieving the MDGs in developing countries and countries with economies in transition through trade and international business development. The MDGs serve as critical benchmarks for ITC in its efforts to reduce poverty and enhance the competitiveness of enterprises in poor communities by promoting their integration into the global value chain.

The Centre's objectives are to build awareness and improve the availability and use of trade intelligence; strengthen trade support institutions; enhance policies for the benefit of exporting enterprises; build the export capacity of exporting enterprises; and mainstream inclusiveness and sustainability into trade promotion and export development policies. Technical cooperation projects in trade promotion are carried out by ITC specialists working closely with local trade officials. National projects often take the form of a broad-based package of services to expand country exports and improve import operations.

Agricultural development

The majority of the world's people continue to live in rural areas and mostly derive their livelihood, directly or indirectly, from agriculture. In recent decades, rural poverty has spread and deepened and, in the rush to industrialization, insufficient investment has been made in the agricultural sector. The UN has addressed this imbalance in a variety of ways.

The **Food and Agriculture Organization of the United Nations (FAO)** (*www.fao. org*) is the lead agency for agriculture, forestry, fisheries and rural development. It gives practical help to developing countries through a wide range of technical assistance projects. A specific priority is to encourage rural development and sustainable agriculture—a long-term strategy for increasing food production and food security while conserving and managing natural resources. FAO is active in land and water development; plant and animal production; forestry; fisheries; economic, social and food security policy; investment; nutrition; food standards and food safety; and commodities and trade.

In promoting sustainable agricultural development, FAO encourages an integrated approach, with environmental, social and economic considerations included in the formulation of development projects. In some areas, for example, particular combinations of crops can improve agricultural productivity, provide a source of fuel wood for local villagers, improve soil fertility and reduce the impact of erosion.

FAO has more than 1,000 field projects operating worldwide at any given time, ranging from integrated land management projects and emergency response to policy and planning advice to governments in areas as diverse as forestry and marketing strategies. FAO usually takes one of three roles: implementing its own programme; executing programmes on behalf of other agencies and donors; or providing advice and management assistance to national projects.

The FAO Investment Centre assists developing and in-transition countries in formulating investment operations in agricultural and rural development, in partnership with international financing institutions (IFIs). Since 1964, the Centre and its IFI partners have facilitated more than $105.2 billion in agriculture and rural development investment for 1,952 projects. Of that amount, IFIs have financed over $65.4 billion.

The **International Fund for Agricultural Development (IFAD)** (*www.ifad.org*) finances agricultural development programmes and projects that enable rural people to overcome poverty. It provides loans and grants for programmes and projects that promote economic advancement and food security. IFAD-supported initiatives enable poor rural people to access the land, water, financial resources, and agricultural technologies and services they need to farm productively; and to access markets and opportunities for enterprise to help them increase their incomes. It also works to build the knowledge, skills and organizations of the rural poor.

IFAD-supported programmes and projects benefit the poorest of the world's people: small farmers, landless labourers, nomadic pastoralists, artisanal fishing communities, indigenous peoples and, across all groups, poor rural women. Most of IFAD's resources are made available to poor countries on highly concessional terms, repayable over 40 years, including a grace period of 10 years, and a 0.75 per cent service charge per annum. The Fund is particularly committed to achieving the Millennium Development Goal of halving the proportion of hungry and extremely poor people by 2015.

Since starting operations in 1978, IFAD has invested $14.8 billion in 924 projects and programmes, reaching some 400 million people in 119 countries. Governments and other financing sources in recipient countries, including project participants, have contributed $12.3 billion, while multilateral, bilateral and other donors have provided an additional $9.6 billion in co-financing.

Industrial development

The globalization of industry has created unprecedented industrial challenges and opportunities for developing countries and countries with economies in transition. The **United Nations Industrial Development Organization (UNIDO)** (*www.unido.org*) is the specialized agency helping these countries pursue sustainable industrial development in the new global environment. UNIDO has assumed an enhanced role in the global development agenda by focusing its activities on poverty reduction, inclusive globalization and environmental sustainability. Its services are based on two core functions: as a global forum, it generates and disseminates industry-related knowledge; and as a technical cooperation agency, it provides technical support and implements projects. UNIDO's technical cooperation programmes focus on the following three thematic priorities, which directly respond to global development priorities:

- Poverty reduction through productive activities—by providing a range of services, from industrial policy advice to entrepreneurship and small and medium enterprise development, and from technology diffusion to sustainable production and the provision of rural energy for productive uses;

- Trade capacity-building—by providing trade-related development services and advice and integrated technical assistance in the areas of competitiveness, trade policies, industrial modernization and upgrading, and compliance with trade standards, testing methods and metrology; and

- Environment and energy—by promoting sustainable patterns of industrial consumption and production and assisting clients in implementing multilateral environmental agreements, while simultaneously reaching their economic and environmental goals.

UNIDO assists governments, business associations and the private industrial sector with services that translate its core functions and thematic priorities into action. UNIDO's 13 investment and technology promotion offices, financed by the countries in which they are located, promote business contacts between industrialized countries and developing countries and countries with economies in transition.

Labour

Concerned with both the economic and social aspects of development, the **International Labour Organization (ILO)** (*www.ilo.org*) is responsible for drawing up and overseeing international labour standards and is the only tripartite UN agency that brings together representatives of governments, employers and workers to shape policies and programmes promoting decent work for all. The main goals of ILO are to promote rights at work, encourage decent employment opportunities, enhance social protection and strengthen dialogue on work-related issues. ILO has provided a framework of labour standards and guidelines which have been adopted in national legislation by virtually all countries.

ILO is guided by the principle that social stability and integration can be sustained only if they are based on social justice—particularly the right to employment with fair compensation in a healthy workplace. Over the decades, ILO has helped create such hallmarks as the eight-hour work day, maternity protection, child-labour laws, and a wide range of policies that promote safety in the workplace and peaceful industrial relations. Specifically, ILO engages in:

- the formulation of international policies and programmes to promote basic human rights, improve working and living conditions and enhance employment opportunities;
- the creation of international labour standards to serve as guidelines for national authorities in putting sound labour policies into practice;
- an extensive programme of technical cooperation, formulated and carried out in partnership with beneficiaries, to help countries make these policies effective; and
- training, education, research and information activities to help advance all these efforts.

The central purpose of ILO is to promote opportunities for decent work for all people. The organization has four strategic objectives that converge on that primary goal:

- to promote and realize standards and fundamental principles and rights at work;
- to create greater opportunities for women and men to secure decent employment and income;
- to enhance the coverage and effectiveness of social protection for all; and
- to strengthen dialogue among governments, labour and business.

To implement those objectives, ILO focuses on areas such as the progressive abolition of child labour; safety and health at work; socio-economic security; promoting small and medium-sized enterprises; developing skills, knowledge and employability; eliminating discrimination and gender inequality; and promoting the *ILO Declaration on Fundamental Principles and Rights at Work,* adopted by the International Labour Conference in 1998.

ILO's technical cooperation focuses on support for democratization, poverty alleviation through employment creation, and the protection of workers. It helps countries develop their legislation and take practical steps towards putting ILO standards into effect—for instance, by developing occupational health and safety departments, social security systems and worker education programmes. Projects are carried out through close cooperation between recipient countries, donors and ILO, which maintains a network of area and regional offices worldwide. ILO conducts more than 1,000 technical cooperation programmes in over 80 countries. In the last decade, ILO spent an average of $130 million annually on technical cooperation projects.

The ILO **International Training Centre** (*www.itcilo.org/en*), located in Turin, Italy, carries out training for senior and mid-level managers in private and public enterprises, leaders of workers' and employers' organizations, government officials and policymakers. It runs more than 450 programmes and projects each year for some 11,000 people from over 180 countries.

The ILO **International Institute for Labour Studies** (*www.ilo.org/inst*), located in Geneva, promotes policy research and public discussion of emerging issues of concern to ILO. The organizing theme is the relationship between labour institutions, economic growth and social equity. The Institute acts as a global forum on social policy, maintains international research networks and carries out educational programmes.

International civil aviation

In 2012, an estimated 2.9 billion passengers flew via civil aviation, 51 million tonnes of freight were shipped by air, and the number of aircraft departures reached a record 31 million. The **International Civil Aviation Organization (ICAO)** (*www.icao. int*) is a UN specialized agency that serves as the global forum for cooperation among its member states and with the world aviation community. ICAO's ongoing mission is to foster a global civil aviation system that consistently and uniformly operates at peak efficiency and provides optimum safety, security and sustainability. ICAO activities are guided by its strategic objectives, which focus on three main areas, namely safety, security, and environmental protection and sustainable development of air transport.

To meet those objectives, ICAO:

- adopts international standards and recommendations applied to the design and performance of aircraft and much of their equipment; the performance of airline pilots, flight crews, air traffic controllers and ground and maintenance crews; and the security requirements and procedures at international airports;
- formulates visual and instrument flight rules, as well as the aeronautical charts used for international navigation, and is responsible for aircraft telecommunications systems, radio frequencies and security procedures;

- works towards minimizing the impact of aviation on the environment through reductions in aircraft emissions and through noise limits; and
- facilitates the movement of aircraft, passengers, crews, baggage, cargo and mail across borders by standardizing customs, immigration, public health and other formalities.

ICAO pursues policies and programmes designed to prevent acts of unlawful interference, which pose a serious threat to the safety and security of international civil aviation. In response to the terrorist attacks of 11 September 2001 in the United States, ICAO developed an aviation security plan of action, including a universal audit programme to evaluate the implementation of security standards and recommend remedial action where necessary.

During its thirty-seventh Assembly in 2010, ICAO produced new agreements and declarations on air transport's challenges and priorities. Meeting participants endorsed ICAO's approach for addressing runway safety and adopted a historic resolution on reducing the impact of aviation emissions on climate change that will guide the activities of its 190 member states on that issue through 2050. The thirty-eighth Assembly session would take place in September and October 2013.

ICAO meets requests from developing countries for assistance in improving air transport systems and training for aviation personnel. It has helped to establish regional training centres in several developing countries. The criteria for ICAO assistance are based on what countries need to make civil aviation safe and efficient, in accordance with ICAO's Standards and Recommended Practices.

ICAO works in close cooperation with other UN specialized agencies such as IMO, ITU and WMO. The International Air Transport Association, the Airports Council International, the International Federation of Air Line Pilots' Associations and other organizations also participate in ICAO meetings.

International shipping

When the **International Maritime Organization (IMO)** (*www.imo.org*) held its first Assembly in 1959, it had less than 40 member states. Today it has 170 members (169 UN member states plus the Cook Islands) and three associate members. Over 98 per cent of the world's merchant fleets (by tonnage) adhere to the key international shipping conventions developed by IMO.

The adoption of maritime legislation is IMO's best-known responsibility. IMO has adopted some 50 conventions and protocols—mostly related to changes in world shipping—and more than 1,000 codes and recommendations concerning maritime safety, the prevention of pollution and related matters. Maritime security has been added to IMO's objectives of improving the safety of international shipping and preventing marine pollution from ships. Key environmental concerns being addressed include the transfer of harmful aquatic organisms in ballast water and sediments, the emission of greenhouse gases from ships, and ship recycling.

Initially, IMO focused on the safety of life at sea. Later, environmental concerns became a part of its mandate—originally oil pollution, then expanding to such issues as the carriage of chemicals, sewage, garbage, air pollution, anti-fouling paint, ballast water and ship recycling. Liability and compensation treaties have been adopted and, more recently, security matters have forced their way to the forefront of IMO's concerns, particularly the problem of piracy off the coast of

Somalia. Technical assistance, implementation and capacity-building have become key elements in the adoption of new or amended regulations. IMO is now transitioning its member state audit scheme from a voluntary to a mandatory measure, putting more emphasis on the performance of maritime administrations of member states.

The main IMO treaties on maritime safety and prevention of marine pollution by ships that are in force worldwide include: the *International Convention on Load Lines*, 1966; the *International Regulations for Preventing Collisions at Sea*, 1972; the *International Convention for Safe Containers*, 1972; the *International Convention for the Prevention of Pollution from Ships, 1973 as modified by the Protocol of 1978 relating thereto*; the *International Convention for the Safety of Life at Sea* (SOLAS), 1974; the *International Convention on Standards of Training, Certification and Watchkeeping for Seafarers* (STCW), 1978; and the *International Convention on Maritime Search and Rescue*, 1979.

Numerous codes, some of which have been made mandatory, address specific issues, such as carriage of dangerous goods and high-speed craft. The International Safety Management Code, made mandatory by means of SOLAS amendments adopted in 1994, pertains to the people who operate and run ships. Special attention has been paid to crew standards, including the complete revision in 1995 of the 1978 STCW, which for the first time gave IMO the task of monitoring compliance with the *Convention*.

Safety of life at sea remains one of IMO's key priorities. In 1999, the Global Maritime Distress and Safety System became fully operational, guaranteeing assistance to a ship in distress virtually anywhere in the world. Even if a ship's crew does not have time to radio for help, the System allows a message to be transmitted automatically.

Various IMO conventions address liability and compensation issues. The most significant include the 1992 *Protocol of the International Convention on Civil Liability for Oil Pollution Damage* (1969) and the 1992 *Protocol of the International Convention on the Establishment of an International Fund for Compensation for Oil Pollution Damage* (IOPC Fund, 1971), which together provide compensation to victims of oil pollution damage. The *Athens Convention relating to the Carriage of Passengers and their Luggage by Sea* (1974) sets compensation limits for passengers on ships.

In 2002, IMO adopted the International Ship and Port Facility Security Code, which requires compliance with new measures aimed at protecting shipping against terrorist attacks. Adopted under amendments to SOLAS, the Code became mandatory in 2004. The next year, IMO adopted amendments to the *Convention for the Suppression of Unlawful Acts Against the Safety of Maritime Navigation*, 1988 and its related *Protocol* introducing the right of a state party to board a ship flying the flag of another state party when the requesting party has reasonable grounds to suspect that the ship or a person on board the ship is, has been, or is about to be involved in the commission of an offence under the *Convention*.

IMO's technical cooperation programme aims to support the implementation of its international standards and regulations, particularly in developing countries, and to assist governments in operating a shipping industry successfully. The emphasis is on training, and IMO has under its auspices the World Maritime University in Malmö, Sweden, the International Maritime Law Institute in Malta, and the International Maritime Academy in Trieste, Italy.

Telecommunications

Telecommunications have become a key to the global delivery of services. Banking, tourism, transportation and the information industry all depend on quick and reliable global telecommunications. The sector is being revolutionized by powerful trends, including globalization, deregulation, restructuring, value-added network services, intelligent networks and regional arrangements.

The **International Telecommunication Union (ITU)** (*www.itu.int*) serves as a global forum through which government and industry work towards consensus on issues affecting the future of this increasingly important industry. ITU's mission is to enable the growth and sustained development of telecommunications and information networks, and to facilitate universal access so that people everywhere can participate in, and benefit from, the information society and global economy. A key priority lies in bridging the digital divide—the gap between people with effective access to digital and information technology and those with very limited or no access. ITU also concentrates on strengthening emergency communications for disaster prevention and mitigation. In order to achieve its goals, ITU coordinates the public and private sectors to provide global telecommunications networks and services. Specifically, ITU:

- develops standards that foster the interconnection of national communications infrastructures into global networks, allowing the seamless exchange of information around the world;

- works to integrate new technologies into the global telecommunications network, allowing for the development of new applications;

- adopts international regulations and treaties governing the sharing of the radio frequency spectrum and satellite orbital positions—finite resources that are used by a wide range of equipment, including television and radio broadcasting, mobile telephones, satellite-based communications systems, aircraft and maritime navigation and safety systems, and wireless computer systems; and

- strives to expand and improve telecommunications in the developing world by providing policy advice, technical assistance, project management and training, and by fostering partnerships between telecommunications administrations, funding agencies and private organizations.

In addition to its 193 member states, ITU has over 700 sector members and associates, representing scientific and industrial companies, public and private operators and broadcasters, and regional and international organizations. ITU membership gives governments and private organizations a unique opportunity to contribute to the technological developments rapidly reshaping the world.

As the UN specialized agency for information and communication technology (ICT), ITU had the leading managerial role for the World Summit on the Information Society (WSIS) held in Geneva in 2003 and in Tunis, Tunisia, in 2005. The Summit adopted a *Declaration of Principles* and *Plan of Action* aimed at building a people-centred, inclusive and development-oriented information society, where everyone can create, access, use and share information and knowledge.

Taking the lead in implementing the Summit goals, ITU organized the Connect Africa Summit in Kigali, Rwanda, in 2007, bringing together governments, the private sector and funding agencies to invest in the ICT infrastructure in Africa. Participants committed $55 billion towards the goal of connecting all African cities.

ITU also maintains the WSIS Stocktaking Database, a publicly accessible system providing information on ICT-related initiatives and projects with reference to the 11 WSIS action lines.

International postal service

More than 5 million postal employees worldwide process and deliver 380 billion letter-posts each year, as well as 6.1 billion parcels, international and domestic, and offer a range of electronic and financial services. Some 670,000 post offices are in operation throughout the world. The **Universal Postal Union (UPU)** (*www.upu.int*) is the UN specialized agency regulating the international postal service.

UPU forms a single postal territory of countries for the reciprocal exchange of letter-post items. Every member state agrees to transmit the mail of all other members by the best means used for its own mail. As the primary vehicle of cooperation between national postal services, UPU works to improve international postal services, provide postal customers in every country with harmonized and simplified procedures for their international mail, and make available a universal network of up-to-date products and services.

UPU sets indicative rates, maximum and minimum weight and size limits, and the conditions of acceptance of letter-post items, including priority and non-priority items, letters, aerogrammes, postcards, printed matter and small packets. It prescribes the methods for calculating and collecting transit charges for letter-post items passing through one or more countries and terminal dues for imbalance of mails. It also establishes regulations for registered and air mail, and for items requiring special precautions, such as infectious and radioactive substances.

Thanks to UPU, new products and services are integrated into the international postal network. In this way, such services as registered letters, postal money orders, international reply coupons, small packets, postal parcels and expedited mail services have been made available to most of the world's inhabitants. The agency has taken a leadership role in certain activities, such as the application of electronic data interchange technology by the postal administrations of member countries and the monitoring of the quality of postal services worldwide.

UPU provides technical assistance through multi-year projects aimed at optimizing national postal services. It also conducts short-term projects, which may include study cycles, training fellowships, and the expertise of development consultants who carry out on-the-spot studies on training, management or postal operations. UPU has made international financial institutions increasingly aware of the need for investment in the postal sector.

Around the world, postal services are making a determined effort to revitalize the postal business. As part of a communications market that is experiencing explosive growth, they have to adapt to a rapidly changing environment, becoming more independent, self-financing enterprises and providing a wider range of services. UPU takes the lead in promoting this revitalization.

Intellectual property

Intellectual property in various forms—books, feature films, artistic performance media and computer software—has become a central issue in international trade relations. Millions of patent, trademark and industrial design registrations are currently in force worldwide. In today's knowledge-based economy, intellectual property is a tool for promoting wealth creation as well as economic, social and cultural development.

A UN specialized agency, the **World Intellectual Property Organization (WIPO)** (*www.wipo.int*), is responsible for promoting the protection of intellectual property (IP) all over the world through cooperation among states, and for administering various international treaties dealing with the legal and administrative aspects of intellectual property. IP comprises two main branches: industrial property, which primarily consists of inventions, trademarks, industrial designs and appellations of origin; and copyright, covering chiefly literary, musical, artistic, photographic and audiovisual works.

WIPO administers 25 treaties covering all aspects of intellectual property, some dating back to the 1880s. The two pillars of the international IP system are the *Paris Convention for the Protection of Industrial Property* (1883) and the *Berne Convention for the Protection of Literary and Artistic Works* (1886). WIPO member states concluded the *Singapore Treaty on the Law of Trademarks* (2006). WIPO's policy of adopting recommendations on such themes as the protection of well-known marks (1999), trademark licenses (2000) and marks on the Internet (2001) complements the treaty-based approach to international legal standard-setting.

Its **Arbitration and Media Centre** helps individuals and companies from around the world resolve their disputes, particularly those relating to technology, entertainment and other issues involving intellectual property. It is also the leading dispute resolution service for challenges relating to abuses in the registration and use of Internet domain names, known as 'cybersquatting'. It provides this service both for the generic top-level domains, such as .com, .net, .org, and .info, and for certain country-code domains. WIPO's dispute resolution mechanism is much faster and cheaper than litigation in the courts; a domain name case is normally concluded within two months using online procedures.

WIPO helps countries strengthen their intellectual property infrastructure, institutions and human resources while promoting the development of international IP law. It provides a forum for formulating policies, and hosts international discussions on IP with respect to traditional knowledge, folklore, biodiversity and biotechnology.

In addition, WIPO offers expert advice to developing countries to strengthen their capacity for the strategic use of intellectual property to promote economic, social and cultural development. It provides legal and technical advice and expertise in drafting and revising national legislation. Training programmes are organized for policymakers, officials and students. The organization's focal point for training is the WIPO Worldwide Academy (*www.wipo.int/academy/en*).

WIPO also provides services to industry and the private sector to facilitate the process of obtaining IP rights in multiple countries in a simple, efficient and cost-effective manner. These include services offered under the *Patent Cooperation Treaty*, the *Madrid System for the International Registration of Trademarks*, the *Hague System for the International Registration of Industrial Designs*, the *Lisbon Agreement for the Protection of Appellations of Origin and their International Registration* and the *Budapest Treaty on the International Recognition of the Deposit of Microorganisms for the Purposes of Patent Procedure*. The revenues from these services generate some 95 per cent of WIPO's income.

Global statistics

Governments, public institutions and the private sector rely heavily on relevant, accurate, comparable and timely statistics at national and global levels, and the United Nations has served as a global focal point for statistics since its founding.

The United Nations **Statistical Commission**, an intergovernmental body composed of 24 member states, is the highest decision-making body for international statistical activities. It oversees the work of the **UN Statistics Division** (*http:// unstats.un.org/unsd*), which compiles and disseminates global statistical information, develops standards and norms for statistical activities, and supports countries' efforts to strengthen their national statistical systems. The Division also facilitates the coordination of international statistical activities and supports the functioning of the Commission.

The Statistics Division offers a broad range of services for producers and users of statistics, including the following: the UN-data portal (*http://data.un.org*), the *Statistical Yearbook*, the *Monthly Bulletin of Statistics*, the *World Statistics Pocketbook*, the official *Millennium Development Goals Indicators* database, the *Demographic Yearbook* and *UN Comtrade*. Its specialized publications cover such matters as demographic, social and housing statistics, national accounts, economic and social classifications, energy, international trade, the environment and geospatial information.

The Division aims to strengthen national capabilities in developing countries by providing technical advisory services, training programmes and workshops organized throughout the world on various topics.

Public administration

A country's public sector is arguably the most important component in the successful implementation of its national development programmes. The new opportunities created by globalization, the information revolution and democratization have dramatically affected the state and how it functions. Managing the public sector in an environment of unremitting change has become a demanding challenge for national decision makers, policy developers and public administrators.

The UN, through its **Programme on Public Administration and Finance** (*www. unpan.org/dpadm*), assists governments in their efforts to strengthen and improve their governance systems and administrative institutions, and to address emerging issues of a globalized world. Managed by DESA's Division for Public Administration and Development Management, the Programme helps governments function in an effective, responsive, pro-poor and democratic manner. Assistance is provided to governments in three focus areas: institutional and human resource capacity development; e-government and mobile-government development; and development management through citizen engagement.

The Programme carries out analytical research; advisory services and technical assistance; training and tools such as the UNPAN Training Centre; and advocacy, including such stakeholder dialogue and knowledge-sharing platforms as the UN Public Service Day Awards and Forum and the UN Public Administration Network (UNPAN) (*www.unpan.org*).

Science and technology for development

The United Nations has been promoting the application of science and technology for the development of its member states since the 1960s. The 43-member **Commission on Science and Technology for Development** (*www.unctad.org/cstd*) was established in 1992 to examine science and technology questions and their implications for development; promote the understanding of science and technology policies in respect of developing countries; and formulate recommendations on science and technology matters within the UN system.

The Commission also serves as a focal point for the Economic and Social Council, its parent body, in the system-wide follow-up to the World Summit on the Information Society (WSIS). At its 2013 session, the Commission reviewed progress made in the implementation of WSIS outcomes. It considered two priority themes: "Science, technology and innovation for sustainable cities and peri-urban communities" and "Internet broadband for an inclusive digital society". Substantive and secretariat support for the Commission is provided by UNCTAD.

UNCTAD also promotes policies favouring technological capacity-building, innovation and technology flows to developing countries. It helps these countries review their science and technology policies, promotes South-South scientific networking, and provides technical assistance on information technologies.

FAO, IAEA, ILO, UNDP, UNIDO and WMO all address scientific and technological issues within their specific mandates. Science for development is also an important element in the work of UNESCO.

Social development

Inextricably linked to economic development, social development has been a cornerstone of UN work from its inception. Over the decades, the United Nations has emphasized the social aspects of development to ensure that the aim of better lives for all people remains at the centre of development efforts.

In its early years, the United Nations arranged for groundbreaking research and data collection in the areas of demographics, education and health, compiling—often for the first time—reliable data on global social indicators. In addition, the UN undertook efforts to protect cultural heritage, from architectural monuments to languages, reflecting concern for those societies particularly vulnerable to the rapid processes of change.

The Organization has been in the forefront of supporting government efforts to extend social services relating to health, education, family planning, housing and sanitation to all people. In addition to developing models for social programmes, the UN has helped integrate economic and social aspects of development. Its evolving policies and programmes have always stressed that the components of development—social, economic, environmental and cultural—are interconnected and cannot be pursued in isolation.

Globalization and liberalization are posing new challenges to social development. There is a growing desire to see a more equitable sharing of the benefits of globalization. The UN takes a people-centred approach to social issues, placing individuals, families and communities at the centre of development strategies. It emphasizes social development and addresses such issues as health, education and population, and the situation of vulnerable groups, including women, children and older persons.

The UN strives to strengthen international cooperation for social development, particularly in the areas of poverty eradication, full and productive employment, and the social inclusion of older persons, youth, families, persons with disabilities, indigenous peoples and others marginalized from society and development. Many UN global conferences have focused on these issues, including the 1995 World Summit for Social Development, which marked the first time the international community came together to advance the struggle against poverty, unemployment and social disintegration. The resulting *Copenhagen Declaration for Social Development* and its 10 commitments represent a social contract at the global level.

The diverse issues of social development represent a challenge for developing and developed countries alike. To differing degrees, all societies are confronted by the problems of unemployment, social fragmentation and persistent poverty. A growing number of social problems—from forced migration to drug abuse, organized crime and the spread of diseases—can be successfully tackled only through concerted international action.

The United Nations addresses social development issues through the General Assembly and the Economic and Social Council (ECOSOC), where system-wide policies and priorities are set and programmes endorsed. One of the Assembly's six main committees—the **Social, Humanitarian and Cultural Committee**—takes up agenda items relating to the social sector. Under ECOSOC, the main intergovernmental body dealing with social development concerns is the **Commission for Social Development** (*www.un.org/esa/socdev/csd*). Composed of 46 member states, the Commission advises ECOSOC and governments on social policies and on the social aspects of development. The priority theme for the Commission's 2013 session was "Promoting empowerment of people in achieving poverty eradication, social integration and full employment and decent work for all".

Within the Secretariat, the **Division for Social Policy and Development** (*www.un.org/esa/socdev*) of the Department of Economic and Social Affairs services these intergovernmental bodies, providing research, analysis and expert guidance. Throughout the UN system, there are also many specialized agencies, funds, programmes and offices that address different aspects of social development.

The Millennium Development Goals

At the UN Millennium Summit held in September 2000 in New York, 189 world leaders endorsed the *Millennium Declaration*, a commitment to a new global partnership to reduce extreme poverty and build a safer, more prosperous and equitable world. The *Declaration* was translated into a road map setting out eight time-bound goals to be reached by 2015, known as the **Millennium Development Goals (MDGs)** (*www.un.org/millenniumgoals*). The 2010 Summit on the MDGs concluded with the adoption of a global action plan, entitled "Keeping the promise:

united to achieve the Millennium Development Goals", to achieve the eight anti-poverty goals by their 2015 target date. New commitments for women's and children's health and other initiatives against poverty, hunger and disease were also announced. The MDGs and their related targets for poverty, disease, the environment and development are as follows:

Goal 1: Eradicate extreme poverty and hunger

Reduce by half, between 1990 and 2015, the proportion of people whose income is léss than $1 a day—later recalibrated to $1.25 a day—and the proportion of people who suffer from hunger; achieve full and productive employment and decent work for all, including women and young people.

Goal 2: Achieve universal primary education

Ensure that by 2015, children everywhere—boys and girls alike—will be able to complete a full course of primary schooling.

Goal 3: Promote gender equality and empower women

Eliminate gender disparity in primary and secondary education, preferably by 2005, and in all levels of education no later than 2015.

Goal 4: Reduce child mortality

Reduce by two thirds, between 1990 and 2015, the under-five mortality rate.

Goal 5: Improve maternal health

Reduce by three quarters, between 1990 and 2015, the maternal mortality ratio; achieve universal access to reproductive health by 2015.

Goal 6: Combat HIV/AIDS, malaria and other diseases

Halt and reverse the spread of HIV/AIDS by 2015; achieve universal access to treatment for HIV/AIDS for all those who need it by 2010; halt and reverse the incidence of malaria and other major diseases by 2015.

Goal 7: Ensure environmental sustainability

Integrate sustainable development principles into country policies and programmes and reverse the loss of environmental resources; reduce biodiversity loss, achieving a significant reduction in the rate of loss by 2010; reduce by half, by 2015, the proportion of the population without sustainable access to safe drinking water and basic sanitation; achieve, by 2020, a significant improvement in the lives of at least 100 million slum dwellers.

Goal 8: Develop a global partnership for development

Develop further an open, rule-based, predictable, non-discriminatory trading and financial system; address the special needs of LDCs, landlocked countries and small island developing states; deal with developing countries' debt problems; in cooperation with pharmaceutical companies, provide access to affordable essential drugs in developing countries; in cooperation with the private sector, make available the benefits of new technologies, especially in information and communications.

Progress in achieving the MDGs

Extreme poverty and hunger. According to *The Millennium Development Goals Report, 2013*, the MDG target to halve the proportion of people whose income is less than $1.25 a day was reached five years ahead of the 2015 deadline. In 2010, the proportion of people living in extreme poverty decreased in every developing region, from 47 per cent in 1990 to 22 per cent. Nonetheless, about 1.2 billion people continue to live in extreme poverty, and it is estimated that 970 million people will still be living on less than a $1.25 a day in 2015. Progress among regions has been uneven. While extreme poverty in China dropped from 60 per cent in 1990 to 12 per cent in 2010, it remains widespread in sub-Saharan Africa and Southern Asia. These regions will each be home to about 40 per cent of the developing world population living in extreme poverty by 2015.

Some progress has been made towards the MDG target to halve, between 1990 and 2015, the proportion of people suffering from hunger. The number of undernourished people in developing regions has decreased from 23.2 per cent in 1990–1992 to 14.9 per cent in 2010–2012. However, about 870 million people, one in eight worldwide, did not consume enough food to meet the minimum dietary energy requirements between 2010 and 2012.

Universal primary education. Developing regions have made significant progress in expanding access to primary education, with enrolment growing from 83 per cent in 2000 to 90 per cent in 2011. Over the same period, the number of primary school age children out of school worldwide declined by almost half, from 102 million to 57 million. Sub-Saharan Africa is home to more than half of the world's out-of-school children. While primary school enrolment in the region increased from 60 to 77 per cent between 2000 and 2011, its rapidly growing population meant 32 million more children were of primary school age by 2011. Considerable progress has been made in Southern Asia, where primary school enrolment increased to 93 per cent in 2011.

Gender equality and empowering women. Steady progress has been made towards equal access of boys and girls to education. In developing regions overall, the gender parity index (the ratio between the school enrolment rate of girls and that of boys) at each level of education is close to or in the range of the accepted measure for parity. Significant gender disparities, however, remain among regions at all levels of education. While gender parity is closest to being achieved at the primary level, only 2 out of 130 countries have achieved that target across education levels. Girls continue to face barriers to primary and secondary schooling in Northern Africa, sub-Saharan Africa, Western Asia and Southern Asia. Women are gaining ground globally in the labour market, with 40 out of every 100 wage-earning jobs in the non-agricultural sector held by women in 2011. Parity in the number of women and men holding wage-earning jobs has been nearly achieved in Eastern Asia, the Caucasus and Central Asia, and Latin America and the Caribbean.

Reduce child mortality. Worldwide, the under-five child mortality rate has dropped by 41 per cent since 1990. Improvements in child survival are evident in all regions, led by Eastern Asia and Northern Africa—the only regions that have met the 2015 target of a two-thirds reduction in child deaths. Latin America and the Caribbean, South-Eastern Asia and Western Asia have reduced their under-five mortality rate by more than 50 per cent. While sub-Saharan Africa and Southern Asia have achieved reductions of 39 per cent and 47 per cent, respectively, the pace of change must accelerate even further, particularly in these regions, to meet the MDG target.

Improve maternal health. Maternal mortality has declined by 47 per cent since 1990. All regions have made progress, with the highest reductions in Eastern Asia (69 per cent), Northern Africa (66 per cent) and Southern Asia (64 per cent).

In developing regions, between 1990 and 2011, the proportion of deliveries attended by skilled personnel rose from 55 to 66 per cent, and antenatal care increased from 63 to 81 per cent. Meeting the MDG target of reducing the maternal mortality ratio by three quarters, however, will require accelerated efforts. It is estimated that nearly 50 million babies worldwide are delivered without skilled care. Women who give birth in rural areas still remain at a disadvantage in receiving care. Although progress has been made in reducing the birth rate among adolescents, particularly in Southern Asia, more than 15 million out of 135 million live births worldwide are among women between the ages of 15 and 19.

HIV/AIDS, malaria and other diseases. Globally, the number of people newly infected with HIV continues to fall, dropping 21 per cent from 2001 to 2011. New infections fell by 25 per cent in sub-Saharan Africa and 43 per cent in the Caribbean. An estimated 2.5 million people were infected with HIV in 2011. The scaling up of antiretroviral therapy and a decline in new infections means that fewer people are dying from AIDS-related causes. In 2011, an estimated 1.7 million people died from AIDS — a decline of 25 per cent since 2005. Furthermore, at the end of 2011, 8 million people in developing regions were receiving antiretroviral medicines for HIV or AIDS. At the current rate of increase, almost 15 million people may be receiving life-sustaining treatment by the end of 2015.

Between 2000 and 2010, malaria mortality rates fell by more than 25 per cent worldwide, with an estimated 1.1 million malaria deaths averted. By 2011, 50 of 99 countries with ongoing malaria transmission were on track to reduce incidence rates by 75 per cent by 2015. Over the past decade, substantial progress has been made across sub-Saharan Africa in scaling up use of insecticide-treated mosquito nets. By 2011, over a third of children under five slept under such nets.

In 2011, an estimated 8.7 million people worldwide were newly diagnosed with tuberculosis. While the rate of decline is slow, it is estimated that the world will achieve the MDG target to halt and reverse the spread of tuberculosis by 2015. Between 1995 and 2011, a cumulative total of 51 million patients were successfully treated, saving 20 million lives.

Environmental sustainability. At the 2012 United Nations Climate Change Conference in Doha, Qatar, consensus was forged on a second commitment period under the *Kyoto Protocol*, from 2013 to 2020.

More than 2.1 billion people have gained access to improved drinking water sources since 1990, exceeding the MDG target to halve by 2015 the proportion of people without sustainable access to safe drinking water. Access for the rural poor remains a serious concern, with 83 per cent of those without access to an improved drinking water source living in rural areas. From 1990 to 2011, 1.9 billion people gained access to a latrine, flush toilet or other improved sanitation facility. Strong efforts are needed to ensure this number increases by another 1 billion by 2015 to meet the MDG target.

Between 2000 and 2012, over 200 million slum dwellers gained access to improved water sources, sanitation facilities, durable housing or sufficient living space, exceeding the MDG target to achieve significant improvement in the lives of at least 100 million slum dwellers. Nonetheless, the number of slum dwellers in the developing world continues to grow, with an estimated 863 million people living in slums in 2012, compared to 650 million in 1990.

Global partnership for development. Duty-free market access to developed countries by developing countries and LDCs improved in 2011, reaching 83 and 80 per cent of their exports, respectively. Debt service payments for developing regions as a proportion of export revenues declined to 3.1 per cent in 2011, compared to 11.9 per cent in 2000.

While the global financial crisis continues to affect official development assistance (ODA), some countries have maintained or increased their aid budgets in pursuit of set targets. In 2012, net ODA increased in nine countries belonging to the Development Assistance Committee.

By the end of 2013, it is projected that there will be 6.8 million mobile cellular subscriptions worldwide, a global penetration rate of 96 per cent. By the end of 2013, an estimated 2.7 billion people will be using the Internet. Major regional differences remain, however, with 31 per cent of the population online in the developing world, compared to 77 per cent in the developed world.

Reducing poverty

The UN system put poverty reduction at the top of the international agenda when it proclaimed 1997–2006 as the International Decade for the Eradication of Poverty. In December 2007, the General Assembly proclaimed 2008–2017 as the Second UN Decade for the Eradication of Poverty, reiterating that eradicating poverty was the greatest global challenge facing the world and a core requirement for sustainable development, especially for developing countries. The theme for the UN system-wide plan of action for the Second Decade is "Full Employment and Decent Work for All".

The **United Nations Development Programme (UNDP)** has made poverty alleviation its chief priority. It works to strengthen the capacity of governments and civil society organizations to address the whole range of factors that contribute to poverty. These include increasing food security; generating employment opportunities; increasing people's access to land, credit, technology, training and markets; improving the availability of shelter and basic services; and enabling people to participate in the political processes that shape their lives. The heart of UNDP's anti-poverty work lies in empowering the poor.

Fighting hunger

Food production has increased at an unprecedented rate since the United Nations was founded in 1945, and during the period 1970–1997, the number of hungry people worldwide fell dramatically, from 959 million to 791 million. However, that number has risen again, and today approximately 870 million people do not have enough to eat. This is despite the fact that there is currently enough food in the world for every man, woman and child to lead a healthy and productive life.

Most of the UN bodies fighting hunger have important social programmes to advance food security for the poorer sectors of the population, particularly in rural areas. Since its establishment, the Food and Agriculture Organization of the **United Nations (FAO)** (*www.fao.org*) has been working to alleviate poverty and hunger by promoting agricultural development, improved nutrition and the pursuit of food security—physical and economic access by all people at all times to sufficient, safe and nutritious food to meet their dietary needs and food preferences for an active and healthy life.

FAO's Committee on World Food Security is responsible for monitoring, evaluating and consulting on the international food security situation. It analyses the underlying causes of hunger and food shortages, assesses availability and stock levels, and monitors policies aimed at food security. FAO, through its Global Information and Early Warning System, uses meteorological and other satellites to monitor conditions affecting food production and alert governments and donors to any potential threat to food supplies.

FAO's Special Programme for Food Security is its flagship initiative for reaching the MDG target to reduce by half the proportion of hungry people in the world by 2015. Through projects in over 100 countries, it has promoted effective solutions for the elimination of hunger, undernourishment and poverty. It seeks to achieve food security by assisting governments to run focused national food security programmes, and by working with regional economic organizations to optimize regional conditions for attaining food security in such areas as trade policy.

At the 1996 World Food Summit, hosted by FAO, 186 countries approved a *Declaration and Plan of Action on World Food Security*, which aims to halve hunger by 2015 and outlines ways to achieve universal food security. Participants at the 2002 World Food Summit renewed their commitment to reduce the number of hungry by half—to about 400 million—by 2015. The Summit asked FAO to elaborate guidelines in support of the progressive realization of the right to adequate food in the context of national food security. Those voluntary guidelines, also known as the "Right to Food Guidelines", were adopted by the FAO Council in 2004.

In 2009, the World Summit on Food Security adopted a declaration committing all nations to eradicate hunger at the earliest possible date. It pledged to substantially increase aid for agriculture in developing countries, confirmed the target of 2015 for reducing hunger by half, and agreed to face up to the challenges that climate change poses to food security.

The **International Fund for Agricultural Development (IFAD)** (*www.ifad.org*) provides development funding to combat rural poverty and hunger in the poorest regions of the world. The majority of the world's poorest people—those living on less than $1 a day—live in rural areas of developing countries and depend on agriculture and related activities for their livelihoods. To ensure that development aid reaches those who need it most, IFAD involves poor rural men and women in their own development, working with them and their organizations to develop opportunities that enable them to thrive economically in their own communities.

IFAD-supported initiatives enable the rural poor to access the land, water, financial resources and agricultural technologies and services needed to farm productively. These initiatives also allow them to access markets and enterprise opportunities. In addition, IFAD helps them advance their knowledge, skills and organization so they can take the lead in their own development and influence the decisions and policies that affect their lives.

Since starting operations in 1978, IFAD has invested $14.7 billion in 924 projects and programmes, reaching some 400 million people in over 119 countries, with its partners contributing $21.9 billion in co-financing.

The **World Food Programme (WFP)** (*www.wfp.org*), founded in 1961, is the UN front-line agency in the fight against global hunger. In 2012, WFP food assistance reached more than 97 million people in 80 countries. With around half of its received donations in cash, the agency is able to purchase three quarters of that food in developing countries. With the aim of reinforcing local economies, WFP buys more goods and services from developing countries than any other UN agency or programme. WFP also provides passenger air transport to the entire humanitarian community through the UN Humanitarian Air Service, which flies to more than 200 locations worldwide.

WFP's efforts to combat hunger focus on emergency assistance, relief and reha-bilitation, development aid and special operations. In emergencies, WFP is often first on the scene, delivering food aid to the victims of war, civil conflict, drought, floods, earthquakes, hurricanes, crop failures and natural disasters. When the emergency subsides, WFP uses food aid to help communities rebuild shattered lives and livelihoods.

Food and food-related assistance are among the most effective weapons in the struggle to break the cycle of hunger and poverty that entraps so many in the developing world. WFP development projects focus on nutrition, especially for mothers and children, through programmes such as school feeding. In 2012, 17.5 million children were fed under the school feeding programme. WFP builds in-country capacity and infrastructure to help governments and their people in a number of areas, including disaster mitigation.

Breaking the hunger cycle requires that humanitarian responses include long-lasting measures that address the root causes of crises. To meet these challenges, WFP has developed programmes that focus on selected vulnerable sectors of so-ciety. These include food and nutrition programmes, including school feeding; livelihood support programmes such as food-for-training and food-for-work; programmes to address the generational hunger cycle such as mother-and-child nutrition; and nutritional support to HIV/AIDS victims.

WFP works with the Government of Bangladesh to provide schoolchildren with a daily nutritious snack at school. For families who cannot afford enough nutritious food every day, school feeding is a powerful incentive to enrol their children and ensure they attend class every day.
(8 May 2013, WFP/GMB Akash)

WFP relies entirely on voluntary contributions to finance its humanitarian and development projects. Governments are its principal source of funding, but WFP's corporate partners are making an increasingly vital contribution to its mission. In 2012, WFP raised $3.9 billion from some 98 funding sources, including 90 government donors. Despite global financial challenges, more than 50 donor governments increased their contributions above the 2011 levels, demonstrating continued support and increased commitment to WFP operations. WFP also works with around 2,000 NGOs, whose grass-roots and technical knowledge are invaluable in assessing how to deliver its food aid.

Health

In most parts of the world, people are living longer, infant mortality is decreasing and illnesses are being kept in check as more people have access to basic health services, immunization, clean water and sanitation. The United Nations has been deeply involved in many of these advances, particularly in developing countries, by supporting health services, delivering essential drugs, making cities healthier, providing health assistance in emergencies and fighting infectious diseases. The *Millennium Declaration* includes measurable targets to be achieved by countries in nutrition, access to safe water, maternal and child health, infectious disease control, and access to essential medicines by 2015.

Illness, disability and death caused by infectious diseases have a massive social and economic impact. New diseases, including avian influenza and SARS (severe acute respiratory syndrome), add to the urgency of the need to control epidemics. The causes and the solutions for most infectious diseases are known, however, and illness and death can in most cases be avoided at an affordable cost. The major infectious diseases are HIV/AIDS, malaria and tuberculosis. Stopping and reversing their transmission is a key Millennium Development Goal. The **Global Fund to Fight AIDS, Tuberculosis and Malaria** (*www.theglobalfund.org*) is a major contributor to these efforts.

Considerable progress has been made in the fight against HIV/AIDS. The **Joint United Nations Programme on HIV/AIDS (UNAIDS)** (*www.unaids.org*) estimated that, at the end of 2011, 34 million people worldwide were living with the HIV virus. The number of newly infected stood at 2.5 million worldwide—20 per cent lower than in 2001—and the rate of new infection had decreased by 50 per cent or more in 25 countries, 13 of them in sub-Saharan Africa. More than 8 million people living with HIV had access to antiretroviral therapy, and the number of people accessing treatment increased by 63 per cent from 2009. Despite that progress, however, an estimated 7 million people eligible for HIV treatment still did not have access to it, including 72 per cent of children living with the virus. In 2011, 1.7 million people died from AIDS-related causes worldwide, 24 per cent fewer than in 2005.

UNAIDS leads the world to achieve the vision of zero new HIV infections, zero discrimination and zero AIDS-related deaths. It unites the efforts of 11 UN organizations—UNHCR, UNICEF, WFP, UNDP, UNFPA, UNODC, UN-Women, ILO, UNESCO, WHO and the World Bank—and works closely with global and national partners to maximize results for the AIDS response.

The General Assembly, at its High-Level Meeting on AIDS (New York, 8–10 June 2011) adopted the *United Nations Political Declaration on HIV and AIDS: Intensifying Our Efforts to Eliminate HIV and AIDS*, in which countries pledged to take steps to achieve ambitious goals by 2015. Drawing from the *Declaration*, UNAIDS has articulated 10 specific targets for 2015 to guide collective action:

- reduce sexual transmission by 50 per cent;
- reduce HIV transmission among people who inject drugs by 50 per cent;
- eliminate new infections among children and substantially reduce the number of mothers dying from AIDS-related causes;
- provide antiretroviral therapy to 15 million people;
- reduce the number of people living with HIV who die from tuberculosis by 50 per cent;
- close the global AIDS resource gap and reach an annual global investment of $22 to $24 billion in low- and middle-income countries;
- eliminate gender inequalities and gender-based abuse and violence, and increase the capacity of women and girls to protect themselves from HIV;
- eliminate stigma and discrimination against people living with and affected by HIV by promoting laws and policies that ensure the full realization of all human rights and fundamental freedoms;
- eliminate restrictions for people living with HIV on entry, stay and residence; and
- eliminate parallel systems for HIV-related services to strengthen the integration of the AIDS response in global health and development efforts.

For decades, the UN system has been at the forefront of the fight against disease through the creation of policies and systems that address the social dimensions of health problems. The **United Nations Children's Fund (UNICEF)** focuses on child and maternal health, and the **United Nations Population Fund (UNFPA)** deals with reproductive health and family planning. The specialized agency coordinating global action against disease is the **World Health Organization (WHO)** (*www.who.int*). WHO has set ambitious goals for achieving health for all, making reproductive health available, building partnerships and promoting healthy lifestyles and environments.

WHO was the driving force behind various historic accomplishments, including the global eradication of smallpox in 1979, achieved after a 10-year campaign. Another UN entity, FAO, led the way in the eradication of rinderpest, achieved in 2010. The disease, which has remained undetected in the field since 2001, is the first animal disease ever to be eliminated. This achievement marks only the second time that a disease has been eradicated worldwide, after smallpox in humans.

The **Roll Back Malaria (RBM) Partnership** (*www.rollbackmalaria.org*) was launched in 1998 by WHO, UNICEF, UNDP and the World Bank to provide a co-ordinated global response to the disease. It includes malaria endemic countries, their bilateral and multilateral development partners, the private sector, NGOs, community-based organizations, foundations, and academic institutions, working together to bring about a world in which malaria is no longer a major cause of mortality or a barrier to economic and social development.

The global **Stop TB Partnership** (*stoptb.org*) is a WHO initiative comprising some 1,000 partners, including governments, NGOs and international organizations, and public and private-sector donors. It aims to halve tuberculosis (TB) deaths and prevalence, relative to 1990 levels, by 2015, and eliminate TB as a global health problem by 2050.

Together with its partners, WHO helped eliminate poliomyelitis from the Americas in 1994, the Western Pacific region in 2000 and the European region in 2002. It remains engaged in a global effort to eliminate this disease entirely. Since the launch of the **Global Polio Eradication Initiative** (*www.polioeradication.org*) in 1988, polio cases have decreased by over 99 per cent, from an estimated 350,000 cases that year to 223 reported cases in 2012. In 2013, only three countries— Afghanistan, Nigeria and Pakistan—remain polio-endemic, down from more than 125 in 1988. Through the Initiative, more than 2.5 billion children have been immunized against the disease worldwide. The public health savings resulting from polio eradication, once immunization stops, are estimated to be $1.5 billion a year.

The adoption of a ground-breaking public health treaty to control tobacco supply and consumption was another major achievement. The *WHO Framework Convention on Tobacco Control* covers tobacco taxation, smoking prevention and treatment, illicit trade, advertising, sponsorship and promotion, and product regulation. It was adopted unanimously by WHO's member states in 2003 and became binding international law in 2005. The *Convention* is a key part of the global strategy to reduce the worldwide epidemic of tobacco use, which kills nearly 5 million people every year. WHO also takes a leading role in action to combat obesity, a worldwide health concern affecting an increasing number of people every year. WHO projects that by 2015, approximately 2.3 billion adults will be overweight and more than 700 million will be obese.

Between 1980 and 1995, a joint UNICEF-WHO effort raised global immunization coverage against six killer diseases—polio, tetanus, measles, whooping cough, diphtheria and tuberculosis—from 5 to 80 per cent, saving the lives of some 2.5 million children a year. A similar initiative—the **Global Alliance for Vaccines and Immunization (GAVI)** (*www.gavialliance.org*)—was launched in 1999 with initial funds from the Bill and Melinda Gates Foundation. Since 2000, GAVI has helped prevent 5.5 million future deaths through routine immunization against hepatitis B, *Haemophilus influenzae* type 'b' (Hib) and pertussis (whooping cough), and through one-off investments in immunization against measles, polio and yellow fever. The Alliance incorporates WHO, UNICEF, the World Bank and private sector partners.

WHO priorities in the area of communicable diseases are: to reduce the impact of malaria and tuberculosis through global partnership; to strengthen surveillance, monitoring and response to communicable diseases; to reduce the impact of diseases through intensified and routine prevention and control; and to generate new knowledge, intervention methods, implementation strategies and research capabilities for use in developing countries. WHO is also a key player in promoting primary health care, delivering essential drugs, making cities healthier, promoting healthy lifestyles and environments, and in tackling health emergencies.

The WHO-UNICEF Global Immunization Vision and Strategy, 2006–2015, aims to reduce global measles deaths by 95 per cent by the end of 2015. In 2012, the WHO Measles and Rubella Initiative launched the Global Measles and Rubella Strategic Plan, which included new global goals for 2015 and 2020. WHO has been fighting malaria for decades. It estimated that $5.1 billion was needed every year between 2011 and 2020 to achieve universal access to malaria interventions; only $2.3 billion was available in 2011.

A motor for health research. Working with its partners in health research, WHO gathers data on current conditions and needs, particularly in developing countries. These range from epidemiological research in remote tropical forests to monitoring the progress of genetic research. The WHO tropical disease research programme has focused on the resistance of the malaria parasite to the most commonly used drugs, and on fostering the development of new drugs and diagnostics against tropical infectious diseases. Its research also helps to improve national and international surveillance of epidemics, and to develop preventive strategies for new and emerging diseases.

Standard-setting. WHO establishes international standards on biological and pharmaceutical substances. It developed the concept of 'essential drugs' as a basic element of primary health care. WHO works with countries to ensure the equitable supply of safe and effective drugs at the lowest possible cost and with the most effective use. To this end, it has developed a 'model list' of several hundred drugs and vaccines considered essential to help prevent or treat over 80 per cent of all health problems. The list is updated every two years. WHO also cooperates with member states, civil society and the pharmaceutical industry to develop new essential drugs for priority health problems in poor and middle-income countries, and to continue production of established essential drugs.

Through the international access afforded to the United Nations, WHO oversees the global collection of information on communicable diseases, compiles comparable health and disease statistics, and sets international standards for safe food as well as for biological and pharmaceutical products. It also provides unmatched evaluation of the cancer-producing risks of pollutants, and has put into place the universally accepted guidance for global control of HIV/AIDS.

Human settlements

In 2012, more than half of the world's population of 7.1 billion lived in towns and cities. Nearly 1 billion people lived in slums; in developing countries, about one third of the urban population lived in slums. The **United Nations Human Settlements Programme (UN-HABITAT)** (*www.unhabitat.org*) is the lead agency within the UN system for addressing urban issues. It is mandated by the General Assembly to promote socially and environmentally sustainable towns and cities, with the goal of providing adequate shelter for all. To that end, it implements dozens of technical programmes and projects in a wide range of countries, most of them in the least developed world. In 1996 the Second United Nations Conference on Human Settlements, known as Habitat II, adopted the *Habitat Agenda*, a global plan of action in which governments committed themselves to the goals of adequate shelter for all and sustainable urban development. UN-HABITAT is the focal point for implementing the Agenda, assessing its implementation, and monitoring global trends and conditions.

UN-HABITAT coordinates the World Urban Campaign (*www.worldurbancampaign.org*), a global advocacy platform to promote a positive vision of cities in the twenty first century. The Campaign's goals are to: demonstrate to the public, private and social sectors that investing in creative, resilient and sustainable communities is essential to our future; provide the means to achieve such communities; create linkages among 'city changers' and help coordinate partners; and establish benchmarks, monitor progress and share knowledge worldwide.

Through various means, UN-HABITAT focuses on a range of issues and special projects that it helps implement. Together with the World Bank, it began a slum upgrading initiative called the **Cities Alliance** (*www.citiesalliance.org*). Other initiatives over the years have addressed post-conflict land management and reconstruction in countries devastated by war or natural disasters, and ensured that women's rights and gender issues are brought into urban development and management policies. The agency also helps strengthen rural-urban linkages, as well as infrastructure development and public service delivery.

UN-HABITAT programmes include:

- Best Practices and Local Leadership Programme—a global network of government agencies, local authorities and civil society organizations dedicated to identifying and disseminating best practices to improve the living environment and apply lessons learned to policy development and capacity building.
- Housing Rights Programme—a joint UN-HABITAT/Office of the United Nations High Commissioner for Human Rights initiative to assist states and other stakeholders to implement their commitments in the Habitat Agenda to ensure the full and progressive realization of the right to adequate housing, as provided for in international instruments.
- Global Urban Observatory—monitors global progress in implementing the Habitat Agenda, and monitors and evaluates urban conditions and trends. The programme aims to improve the worldwide urban knowledge base by supporting governments, local authorities and civil society in the development and application of policy-oriented urban indicators, statistics and other urban information.
- Sustainable Cities Programme—a joint UN-HABITAT/UNEP initiative that builds capacities in urban environmental planning and management. With its sister programme, Localizing Agenda 21, it operates in over 30 cities worldwide.
- Localizing Agenda 21 Programme—promotes the global plan of action for sustainable development adopted at the 1992 'Earth Summit' (*Agenda 21*) by translating its human settlements components into action at the local level and stimulating joint initiatives in selected medium-sized cities;
- Safer Cities Programme—launched in 1996 at the request of African mayors, it promotes the development of strategies at the city level to adequately address and ultimately prevent urban crime and violence.
- Urban Management Programme—a joint effort by UN-HABITAT, UNDP and external support agencies. This network of over 40 anchor and partner institutions, covering 140 cities in 58 countries, works to strengthen the contribution made by cities and towns in developing countries towards economic growth, social development and poverty alleviation;
- Water and Sanitation Programme—aims to improve access to safe water, help provide adequate sanitation to millions of low-income urban dwellers, and measure the impact of those efforts. It supports the MDG target to halve, by 2015, the proportion of people without sustainable access to safe drinking water and basic sanitation, as well as the related target of the 2002 World Summit on Sustainable Development.

Education

Great strides have been made in education in recent years, marked by a significant increase in the number of children in schools. Nevertheless, some 59 million primary school-aged children were out of school in 2010. In some countries, civil strife, acts of terrorism and insurgency prevent school attendance. Despite enormous efforts to increase literacy, 775 million adults—two thirds of them women—lacked minimum literacy skills.

Research has shown that access to education is closely related to improved social indicators. Schooling has a multiplier effect for women. An educated woman will typically be healthier, and have fewer children and more opportunities to increase household income. Her children, in turn, will experience lower mortality rates, better nutrition and better overall health. For this reason, girls and women are the focus of the education programmes of numerous UN agencies. Because of the multiplicity of factors involved in education, many parts of the UN system are involved in the funding and development of a variety of education and training programmes. These range from traditional basic schooling, to technical training for human resources development in areas such as public administration, agriculture and health services, to public awareness campaigns to educate people about HIV/AIDS, drug abuse, human rights, family planning, and other issues. UNICEF, for example, devotes more than 20 per cent of its annual programme expenditure to education, paying special attention to girls' education.

The lead agency in the area of education is the **United Nations Educational, Scientific and Cultural Organization (UNESCO)** (*www.unesco.org*). Together with other partners, it works to ensure that all children are enrolled in child-friendly schools with trained teachers providing quality education. UNESCO provides the secretariat for the campaign to achieve universal, quality primary education by 2015, the most ambitious UN inter-agency campaign ever launched. The campaign's goal was based on a framework for action adopted by more than 160 nations at the World Education Forum in Dakar, Senegal, in 2000, and was reconfirmed by world leaders in their *Millennium Declaration*, adopted in September of that year.

UNESCO's education sector focuses on: providing educational access to all, at all levels; the success of special-needs and marginalized populations; teacher training; developing competencies for work forces; success through education; ensuring opportunities for non-formal and lifelong learning; and using technology to enhance teaching and learning, and to expand educational opportunities. UNESCO undertakes these actions in the context of the *Dakar Framework for Action*; the UN Decade of Education for Sustainable Development, 2005–2014; and the Global Initiative on Education and HIV/AIDS. It is also working towards the MDG targets to ensure that all boys and girls complete primary school, and to eliminate disparities in primary and secondary education at all levels by 2015.

In addition to declaring universal primary education the second MDG, the UN has launched numerous education initiatives. The **UN Cyberschoolbus** (*cyberschoolbus.un.org*) is an award-winning UN website where primary and secondary school students can learn about the origins, purpose and structure of the United Nations; gain information about member states; and find out about issues on the UN agenda. Teachers can find lesson plans on agenda issues. The Cyberschoolbus reaches over 200 countries and territories around the world and is available in English, Spanish, French and Russian.

Every year, hundreds of Model UN conferences are held at all educational levels and a variety of configurations, including the **Global Model United Nations Conference** (*un.org/gmun*). Through these programmes, students act as diplomats and participate in simulated sessions of the General Assembly and other UN system bodies.

United Nations Academic Impact (UNAI) (*academicimpact.org*) is a global initiative that aligns institutions of higher education with the UN in supporting 10 universally accepted principles in the areas of human rights, literacy, sustainability and conflict resolution. It recognizes the potential of higher education to foster world peace, along with economic and social development. Participating colleges and universities formally endorse the principles of the Academic Impact Programme, and UNAI asks those institutions to demonstrate support for at least one of the principles each year.

Research and training

A number of specialized UN organizations conduct academic work in the form of research and training. This work is aimed at enhancing understanding of global problems, as well as fostering the human resources required for the more technical aspects of economic and social development and the maintenance of peace and security.

The **United Nations University (UNU)** (*www.unu.edu*) contributes, through research and capacity-building, to efforts to resolve the pressing global problems that are the concern of the United Nations, its peoples and member states. UNU is a bridge between the United Nations and the international academic community, acting as a think-tank for the UN system; a builder of capacities, particularly in developing countries; and a platform for dialogue and new creative ideas. UNU partners with over 40 UN entities and hundreds of cooperating research institutions around the world.

UNU's academic activities are conducted within five interdependent thematic clusters under the overarching theme of sustainability. These include population and health; development governance; peace, security and human rights; global change and sustainable development; and science, technology and society. The University encompasses 15 research and training institutes and programmes in 13 countries around the world. The global UNU system is coordinated by the UNU Centre in Tokyo and includes the following:

- Institute on Globalization, Culture and Mobility (UNU-GCM), Barcelona, Spain;
- Institute on Comparative Regional Integration Studies (UNU-CRIS), Bruges, Belgium;
- Institute for Environment and Human Security (UNU-EHS), Bonn, Germany;
- Fisheries Training Programme (UNU-FTP), Reykjavík, Iceland;
- Geothermal Training Programme (UNU-GTP), Reykjavík, Iceland;
- Institute of Advanced Studies (UNU-IAS), Yokohama, Japan;
- Institute for Sustainability and Peace (UNU-ISP), Tokyo, Japan;
- International Institute for Global Health (UNU-IIGH), Kuala Lumpur, Malaysia;
- International Institute for Software Technology (UNU-IIST), Macau, China;

- Institute for Natural Resources in Africa (UNU-INRA), Accra, Ghana;
- International Network on Water, Environment and Health (UNU-INWEH), Hamilton, Ontario, Canada;
- Land Restoration Training Programme (UNU-LRT), Reykjavík, Iceland;
- Maastricht Economic and Social Research and Training Centre on Innovation and Technology (UNU-MERIT), Maastricht, The Netherlands;
- Water Decade Programme on Capacity Development (UN-WDPC), Bonn, Germany;
- World Institute for Development Economics Research (UNU-WIDER), Helsinki, Finland.

The Geneva-based **United Nations Institute for Training and Research (UNITAR)** (*www.unitar.org*) works to enhance the effectiveness of the United Nations through training and research. It conducts training and capacity development programmes in multilateral diplomacy and international cooperation for diplomats accredited to the UN, as well as for national officials working on international issues. UNITAR also carries out a wide range of training programmes in the fields of social and economic development, and the maintenance of peace and security. UNITAR conducts research on training methodologies and knowledge systems, encompassing capacity development, e-learning and adult training. It also develops pedagogical materials, including distance learning training packages, workbooks, software and video training packs. UNITAR is supported entirely from voluntary contributions, principally from governments, intergovernmental organizations and foundations.

The **United Nations System Staff College (UNSSC)** (*www.unssc.org*), located in Turin, Italy, assists the staff of UN organizations in developing the skills and competencies needed to meet the global challenges faced by the United Nations. It does so by strengthening inter-agency collaboration; promoting a cohesive management culture; supporting continuous learning and staff development; and fostering strategic leadership. Thematic areas of its work include: leadership; UN coherence at the country level; monitoring and evaluation; social and economic development; conflict prevention and peacebuilding; staff safety and security; staff orientation; learning methods and knowledge management; and communities of practice.

The **United Nations Research Institute for Social Development (UNRISD)** (*www.unrisd.org*), located in Geneva, engages in multidisciplinary research on the social dimensions of contemporary development issues. Working through a global network of researchers and institutes, UNRISD provides governments, development agencies, civil society organizations and scholars with a better understanding of how development policies and processes affect different social groups. Recent research themes have included gender equality, social policy, poverty reduction, governance and politics, and corporate social responsibility.

Population and development

The United Nations estimates that despite reductions in fertility as contraceptive use has increased in most countries, world population increased globally by about 1.16 per cent per year over the 2005–2010 period. More significantly, world population, which reached 7 billion in 2011, is expected to increase to over 9 billion by

2050, with most of the additional people enlarging the population of developing countries. Rapid population growth weighs heavily on the earth's resources and environment, often outstripping development efforts. The UN has addressed the relationship between population and development in many ways, placing special emphasis on advancing the rights and status of women, which is seen as key to social and economic progress.

Shifting demographic patterns are creating new needs. For example, the global number of persons aged 60 or over—the fastest growing segment of the population—is expected to increase from 784 million in 2011 to over 2 billion in 2050, when the number of older persons will exceed the number of children for the first time in history. Hence, whereas in the more developed regions the population in the main working ages of 25 to 59 is expected to peak over the next decade and decline thereafter, reaching 531 million in 2050, in the less developed regions it will continue to rise, reaching 3.6 billion in 2050. Already, and again for the first time in history, more than half of the world's people are now living in cities.

The United Nations has been at work in many developing countries in response to population trends. Various parts of the Organization have worked together to build national statistical offices, take censuses, make projections and disseminate reliable data. The pioneering quantitative and methodological work of the United Nations, particularly its authoritative estimates and projections of population size and change, has led to a significant increase in the capacities of nations to plan ahead, incorporate population policies into development planning, and take sound economic and social decisions.

The **Commission on Population and Development**, composed of 47 member states, is charged with studying and advising ECOSOC on population changes and their effects on economic and social conditions. It holds primary responsibility for reviewing the implementation of the programme of action of the 1994 International Conference on Population and Development.

The **Population Division of the United Nations Department of Economic and Social Affairs** (*www.un.org/esa/population*) serves as the secretariat of the Commission. It also provides the international community with up-to-date, scientifically objective information on population and development. It undertakes studies on population levels, trends, estimates and projections, as well as on population policies and the link between population and development. The Division maintains major databases, among them the *Population, Resources, Environment and Development Databank; World Population Prospects; World Population Policies;* and *World Urbanization Prospects*. In addition, it coordinates the Population Information Network (POPIN), which promotes the use of the Internet to facilitate global sharing of population information.

The **United Nations Population Fund (UNFPA)** (*www.unfpa.org*) leads the operational activities of the UN system in this field, helping developing countries and those with economies in transition find solutions to their population problems. It assists states in improving reproductive health and family planning services on the basis of individual choice, and in formulating population policies in support of sustainable development. It also promotes awareness of population problems, and helps governments deal with them in ways best suited to each country's needs. In line with its mission statement, UNFPA "promotes the right of every woman, man and child to enjoy a life of health and equal opportunity. UNFPA supports countries in using population data for policies and programmes to reduce poverty and to ensure that every pregnancy is wanted, every birth is safe, every young person is free of HIV/AIDS, and every girl and woman is treated with dignity and respect". Its primary role in fulfilling this mission is as a funding organization for population projects and programmes carried out by governments, UN agencies and NGOs.

Its core programme areas are:

- reproductive health, assisting governments in delivering sexual and reproductive health care throughout the life cycle of women, with a particular focus on improving maternal health;
- gender equality, which is intimately linked to improving maternal and newborn health and reducing the spread of HIV; critical factors include girls' education, women's economic empowerment, women's political participation and the balancing of reproductive and productive roles;
- population and development strategies, which help countries gather adequate information about population dynamics and trends in order to create and manage sound policies and generate the political will to address both current and future needs, especially with regard to migration, ageing, climate change and urbanization.

UNFPA does not provide support for abortion services. Rather, it seeks to prevent abortion by helping to increase access to family planning. It also addresses the reproductive health needs of adolescents with programmes to prevent teenage pregnancy, prevent and treat fistulas, prevent HIV/AIDS and other sexually transmitted infections, reduce recourse to abortion, and improve access to reproductive health services and information.

The ability of parents to choose the number and spacing of their children is an essential component of reproductive health and an internationally recognized basic human right. It is estimated that at least 200 million women want to use safe and effective family planning methods, but are unable to do so because they lack access to information and services or the support of their husbands and communities. UNFPA works with governments, the private sector and NGOs to meet family planning needs.

Gender equality and empowerment of women

Promotion of equality between women and men and the empowerment of women are central to the work of the United Nations. Gender equality is not only a goal in its own right, but is also recognized as a critical means for achieving all other development goals, including the MDGs. Eradicating poverty and hunger, achieving universal primary education and health for all, combating HIV/AIDS and facilitating sustainable development all require systematic attention to the needs, priorities and contributions of women as well as men. The Organization actively promotes women's human rights and works to eradicate the scourge of violence against women, including in armed conflict and through trafficking. The UN also adopts global norms and standards and supports follow-up and implementation at the national level, including through its development assistance activities.

United Nations conferences in Mexico City (1975), Copenhagen (1980), Nairobi (1985) and Beijing (1995) galvanized commitment and action towards gender equality and the empowerment of women around the world. At the Fourth (1995) World Conference on Women, 189 governments adopted the *Beijing Declaration* and *Platform for Action* to address inequality and discrimination and ensure women's empowerment in all spheres of life. In 2010, the Beijing+15 review welcomed progress made towards achieving gender equality and emphasized the necessity of the implementation of the *Declaration* and *Platform for Action* for achieving internationally agreed development goals, including the MDGs.

UN-Women (*www.unwomen.org*) is the **United Nations Entity for Gender Equality and the Empowerment of Women**, which resulted from the 2010 merger of the Office of the Special Adviser on Gender Issues and Advancement of Women, the Division for the Advancement of Women in the Department of Economic and Social Affairs, the International Research and Training Institute for the Advancement of Women, and the United Nations Development Fund for Women. UN-Women works towards eliminating discrimination against women and girls, empowering women and achieving equality between women and men as partners and beneficiaries of development, human rights, humanitarian action, and peace and security. UN-Women supports intergovernmental bodies, such as the Commission on the Status of Women, in formulating policies, global standards and norms; helps member states implement these standards by providing suitable technical and financial support and forging effective partnerships with civil society; and holds the UN system itself accountable for its commitments on gender equality, including regular monitoring of system-wide progress.

Under the Economic and Social Council (ECOSOC), the **Commission on the Status of Women** (*www.un.org/womenwatch/daw/csw*) monitors progress towards gender equality throughout the world by reviewing implementation of the platform for action that emerged from the Fourth World Conference on Women. The Commission makes recommendations for further action to promote women's rights, and to address discrimination and inequality in all fields. Major accomplishments of the 45-member Commission over its more than 60 years of activity include the preparation of, and follow-up to, four world conferences on women and development of the treaty on women's human rights: the 1979 *Convention on the Elimination of All Forms of Discrimination against Women*.

The **Committee on the Elimination of Discrimination against Women (CEDAW)** monitors adherence to the *Convention*. The 23-member Committee holds constructive dialogue with states parties on their implementation of the *Convention*, based on reports they submit. Its recommendations have contributed to a better understanding of women's rights, and of the means to ensure the enjoyment of those rights and the elimination of discrimination against women.

Beyond the Secretariat, all the organizations of the UN family address issues relating to women and gender in their policies and programmes; and empowering women is central to the MDGs.

Promoting the rights and well-being of children

The child mortality rate has dropped sharply in recent years, but more needs to be done to achieve the Millennium Development Goal of reducing, by 2015, the 1990 rate by two thirds. In 2011, 6.9 million children died before their fifth birthday, down from 12 million in 1990. Almost two thirds of all child deaths are the result of infectious diseases—malaria, pneumonia, diarrhoea, sepsis, measles, and AIDS—that could be prevented through cost-effective, available interventions. Poor nutrition increases a child's susceptibility to death from disease. It can also result in long-lasting cognitive and physical problems, including intellectual impairment. This represents a terrible loss to families, communities, nations and the world. Beyond infancy, the young still confront forces that threaten their lives and well-being. They are made more vulnerable because their rights are often denied them, including their right to education, participation and protection from harm.

The **United Nations Children's Fund (UNICEF)** (*www.unicef.org*) acts to ensure children's rights to survival, development and protection. It advocates for full implementation of the *Convention on the Rights of the Child* along with the *Convention on the Elimination of All Forms of Discrimination against Women*. In 191 countries, UNICEF works in partnership with governments, international organizations, civil society and young people to overcome obstacles faced by children, including poverty, violence, disease and discrimination. UNICEF's major areas of focus are child survival and development; basic education and gender equality; HIV/AIDS and children; child protection; and policy advocacy and partnerships. These aims are congruent with the MDGs and with the objectives expressed in *A World Fit for Children*, the outcome document of the 2002 special session of the General Assembly on children.

The Fund is widely engaged in every facet of child health, from before birth through adolescence. It acts to ensure that pregnant women have access to proper prenatal and delivery care, strengthens the ability of families to manage childhood illnesses at home, and offers guidance to communities in achieving the best health care possible. UNICEF works to reduce the risks of HIV/AIDS to young people by sharing information that will keep them safe. It makes special efforts to see that children who lose their parents to HIV/AIDS receive the same kind of care as their peers. It also helps women and children afflicted with AIDS to live their lives with dignity.

UNICEF is also involved in worldwide immunization efforts, from the purchase and distribution of vaccines to safe inoculation. It is a global leader in vaccine supply, reaching 36 per cent of the world's children. Together with WHO, UNICEF has worked to achieve Universal Childhood Immunization with the six vaccines of the Expanded Programme on Immunization: BCG, OPV, diphtheria, tetanus, pertussis and measles. In 2011, 107 million children were vaccinated and global immunization coverage reached 83 per cent. The Fund uses the opportunity of immunization to deliver other life-saving services, including providing regular vitamin A supplements and insecticide-treated mosquito nets to help protect families from malaria.

In its support of various initiatives that educate children from pre-school age through adolescence, UNICEF mobilizes teachers, registers children, prepares school facilities and organizes curricula, sometimes rebuilding educational systems from the ground up. It makes sure that children have the chance to play and learn, even in times of conflict, because sports and recreation are equally important to a child's progress. It encourages proper nutrition for pregnant mothers and breastfeeding after birth. It improves water and sanitation facilities at kindergartens and child-care centres. The Fund also helps create protective environments for the young. It encourages legislation that bans child labour, condemns female genital mutilation, and acts to make it more difficult to exploit children for sexual and economic ends. UNICEF also designs landmine awareness campaigns and helps demobilize child soldiers.

Social integration

The United Nations has come to recognize several social groups as deserving special attention, including youth, older persons, the impoverished, persons with disabilities, minorities and indigenous populations. Their concerns are addressed by the General Assembly, ECOSOC and the Commission for Social Development. Specific programmes for these groups are carried out within the UN Department of Economic and Social Affairs (*http://undesadspd.org*). The UN has been instrumental in defining and defending the human rights of such vulnerable groups. It has helped formulate international norms, standards and recommendations for policies and practices regarding these groups, and strives to highlight their concerns through research and data gathering, as well as through the declaration of special years and decades aimed at encouraging awareness and international action.

Families

The United Nations recognizes the family as the basic unit of society. Families have been substantially transformed over the past 60 years as a result of changes in their structure (smaller-sized households, delayed marriage and childbearing, increased divorce rates and single parenthood); global trends in migration; the phenomenon of demographic ageing; the HIV/AIDS pandemic; and the impact of globalization. These dynamic social forces have had a manifest impact on the capacities of families to perform such functions as socializing children and caregiving for younger and older family members. The **International Day of Families,** commemorated each year on 15 May, aims at increasing awareness of issues relating to the family and encouraging appropriate action.

The **UN Focal Point on the Family** (*http://undesadspd.org/Family.aspx*) provides substantive servicing to UN intergovernmental bodies in the areas of family and family policy; promotes the realization of the objectives of the International Year of the Family (1994), along with the integration of a family perspective into national, regional and international policymaking; acts as an exchange for expertise and experiences, disseminating information and supporting networking on family issues; supports family research and diagnostic studies; encourages and supports coordination on family policies and programmes within governments and the UN system; provides technical assistance and capacity-building support to developing country governments; and liaises with governments, civil society and the private sector on family issues.

Youth

The General Assembly has adopted several resolutions and campaigns specific to youth—defined as those between 15 and 24 years of age—and the Secretariat has overseen related programmes and information campaigns. The **UN Programme on Youth** (*http://undesadspd.org/Youth.aspx*) is the focal point on youth within the United Nations. It aims to build an awareness of the global situation of young people; promote their rights and aspirations; and increase participation of young people in decision-making as a means of achieving peace and development. Governments regularly include youth delegates in their official delegations to the Assembly and other UN meetings.

At the outset of his second term in January 2012, Secretary-General Ban Ki-moon set out his five-year action agenda, in which he identified working with and for women and young people as one of his priorities. In that context, he appointed his **Envoy on Youth** in January 2013. The Envoy on Youth works to increase youth accessibility to the United Nations; promote stronger youth participation in setting, implementing and evaluating development frameworks, and increase international awareness of, and attention to, youth issues; engage member states, the private sector, academic institutions, media and civil society, and facilitate partnerships on youth issues; and work to enhance the coordination and harmonization of youth programming among UN agencies.

In 1999, the General Assembly declared that **International Youth Day** be commemorated each year on 12 August. It also recommended that public information activities be organized to support the Day as a way to enhance awareness of the *World Programme of Action for Youth*, adopted in 1995 as a policy framework and set of practical guidelines for national action and international support to improve the situation of young people around the world.

The **Youth Employment Network** (*www.ilo.org/yen*) is a joint initiative of the United Nations, the ILO and the World Bank to translate into action the commitments of the 2000 Millennium Summit to "develop and implement strategies that give young people everywhere a real chance to find decent and productive work".

Older persons

The world is in the midst of a historically unique and irreversible process of demographic transition due to falling birth and death rates, which will result in older populations everywhere. By 2050, one out of five persons will be 60 years or older. The world community has come to recognize the need to integrate the process of global ageing into the larger context of development, and to design policies within a broader 'life-course' and a society-wide perspective. Creating a new 'architecture' for ageing and transmitting it to the world stage and into policy is the focus of the **UN Programme on Ageing** (*http://undesadspd.org/Ageing.aspx*).

The United Nations has taken several initiatives in response to the challenges and opportunities of global ageing:

- The first World Assembly on Ageing (Vienna, 1982) adopted the *Vienna International Plan of Action on Ageing*, which recommended measures in such areas as employment and income security, health and nutrition, housing, education and social welfare. It saw older persons as a diverse and active population group with wide-ranging capabilities and particular health-care needs.
- The *United Nations Principles for Older Persons,* adopted by the General Assembly in 1991, established universal standards pertaining to the status of older persons in five areas: independence, participation, care, self-fulfilment and dignity.
- The Second World Assembly on Ageing (Madrid, 2002) designed international policy on ageing for the 21st century. It adopted the *Madrid International Plan of Action on Ageing*, by which member states committed themselves to action in three priority areas: older persons and development; advancing health and well-being into old age; and ensuring the existence of enabling and supportive environments.

Indigenous issues

There are more than 370 million indigenous people living in some 90 countries worldwide, where they often face discrimination and exclusion from political and economic power. Indigenous people are overrepresented among the poorest, the illiterate and the destitute of the world. They have often been displaced by wars and environmental disasters, removed from their ancestral lands, and deprived of resources needed for physical and cultural survival. Indigenous people have also seen their traditional knowledge marketed and patented without their consent or participation. The **International Day of the World's Indigenous Peoples** is commemorated on 9 August each year to promote and endorse the rights of the world's indigenous population.

The **Permanent Forum on Indigenous Issues** (*http://undesadspd.org IndigenousPeoples.aspx*), established by the Economic and Social Council in 2000, considers indigenous issues relating to economic and social development, culture, education, environment, health and human rights. It provides expert advice and recommendations to the Council and, through it, to the programmes, funds and agencies of the United Nations. The aim is to raise awareness, promote the integration and coordination of activities relating to indigenous issues within the UN system, and disseminate information on indigenous issues. The Forum also addresses ways in which indigenous issues may best be pursued in meeting the MDGs, given the fact that, in many countries, attention to indigenous communities will directly contribute to the goal of halving extreme poverty by 2015.

Indigenous delegates in the General Assembly Hall at the opening of the twelfth (2013) session of the Permanent Forum on Indigenous Issues. (20 May 2013, UN Photo/Rick Bajornas)

The General Assembly declared the 2005–2015 period as the **Second International Decade on the World's Indigenous People**. Its main objectives are to:

- promote non-discrimination and the inclusion of indigenous people in the design, implementation and evaluation of laws, policies, resources, programmes and projects;
- promote the full and effective participation of indigenous people in decisions that affect their lifestyles, traditional lands and territories, cultural integrity, collective rights, and any other aspect of their lives;
- re-evaluate development policies that depart from a vision of equity, including respect for the cultural and linguistic diversity of indigenous people;
- adopt targeted policies, programmes, projects and budgets for the development of indigenous people, including concrete benchmarks, with particular emphasis on indigenous women, children and youth; and
- develop strong monitoring mechanisms and enhance accountability at all levels in the implementation of legal, policy and operational frameworks for the protection of indigenous people and the improvement of their lives.

In 2007, the General Assembly adopted the *United Nations Declaration on the Rights of Indigenous Peoples*, setting out the individual and collective rights of indigenous people, including their rights to culture, identity, language, employment, health and education. The *Declaration* emphasizes the rights of indigenous people to maintain and strengthen their own institutions, cultures and traditions, and to pursue their development in keeping with their own needs and aspirations. It prohibits discrimination against them, and promotes their full and effective participation in all matters that concern them, as well as their right to remain distinct and to pursue their own visions of economic and social development.

Persons with disabilities

Persons with disabilities are often excluded from the mainstream of society. Discrimination takes various forms, ranging from invidious discrimination, such as the denial of educational opportunities, to more subtle forms of discrimination, such as segregation and isolation because of the imposition of physical and social barriers. Society also suffers, since the loss of the enormous potential of persons with disabilities impoverishes humankind. Changes in the perception and concepts of disability involve both changes in values and increased understanding at all levels of society. Since its inception, the United Nations has sought to advance the status of persons with disabilities and improve their lives. The Organization's concern for the well-being and rights of such persons is rooted in its founding principles, which are based on human rights, fundamental freedoms and the equality of all human beings.

Following three decades of advocacy and standard-setting for equal treatment and access to services for disabled persons, the General Assembly, in 2006, adopted the *Convention on the Rights of Persons with Disabilities* and its *Optional Protocol*. The *Convention*, which entered into force in 2008, codified all categories of human rights and fundamental freedoms to be applied to all persons with disabilities. It is based on the following principles: respect for inherent dignity and individual autonomy; non-discrimination; full and effective participation and inclusion in society; respect for differences and acceptance of persons with disabilities as part of human diversity; equal opportunity; accessibility; equality of men and women; and respect for the evolving capacities of children with disabilities and their right to preserve their identities. The *Convention* focuses particularly on areas where rights have been violated, where protections must be reinforced, and where adaptations are needed to enable such persons to exercise their rights. It requires states to monitor its implementation through national focal points, as well as independent monitoring mechanisms. Within the UN system, the focal point on persons with disabilities (*http:// undesadspd.org/Disability.aspx*) serves as the *Convention's* secretariat.

The Committee on the Rights of Persons with Disabilities, composed of 18 expert members, monitors implementation of the *Convention*. Under the *Convention's Optional Protocol*, states parties recognize the Committee's competence to examine individual complaints with regard to alleged violations of the *Convention* by parties to the *Protocol*.

Uncivil society: crime, illicit drugs and terrorism

Transnational organized crime, illicit drug trafficking and terrorism have become social, political and economic forces capable of altering the destinies of entire countries and regions. Such practices as the large-scale bribery of public officials, the growth of 'criminal multinationals', trafficking in human beings, and the use of terrorism to intimidate communities large and small and to sabotage economic development are threats that require effective international cooperation. The United Nations is addressing these threats to good governance, social equity and justice for all, and is orchestrating a global response.

The Vienna-based **United Nations Office on Drugs and Crime (UNODC)** (*www. unodc.org*) leads the international effort to combat drug trafficking and abuse, organized crime and international terrorism—what have been called the 'uncivil' elements of society. The Office is composed of a crime programme, which also addresses terrorism and its prevention, and a drug programme. It has 21 field offices, and liaison offices in New York.

Drug control

Up to 272 million people a year worldwide use illicit drugs, and between 15 and 39 million persons are addicts or 'problem users'. Drug abuse is responsible for lost wages, soaring health-care costs, broken families and deteriorating communities. In particular, drug use by injection is fuelling the spread of HIV/AIDS and hepatitis in many parts of the world. There is a direct link between drugs and an increase in crime and violence. Drug cartels undermine governments and corrupt legitimate businesses. Revenues from illicit drugs fund some of the deadliest armed conflicts. The financial toll is staggering. Enormous sums are spent to strengthen police forces, judicial systems and treatment and rehabilitation programmes. The social costs are equally high: street violence, gang warfare and urban decay.

The United Nations is tackling the global drug problem on many levels. The **Commission on Narcotic Drugs**, a functional commission of ECOSOC, is the main intergovernmental policymaking and coordination body on international drug control. Made up of 53 member states, it analyses the world drug abuse and trafficking problem and develops proposals to strengthen drug control. It monitors implementation of international drug control treaties, as well as the guiding principles and measures adopted by the General Assembly.

The **International Narcotics Control Board (INCB)** (*www.incb.org*) is a 13-member, independent, quasi-judicial body that monitors and assists in governments' compliance with international drug control treaties. It strives to ensure that drugs are available for medical and scientific purposes and to prevent their diversion into illegal channels. The Board sends investigative missions and makes technical visits to drug-affected countries. It also conducts training programmes for drug control administrators, particularly those from developing countries.

A series of treaties, adopted under UN auspices, require that governments exercise control over the production and distribution of narcotic and psychotropic substances; combat drug abuse and illicit trafficking; and report to international organs on their actions.

- The *Single Convention on Narcotic Drugs* (1961) seeks to limit the production, distribution, possession, use and trade in drugs exclusively to medical and scientific purposes, and obliges states parties to take special measures for particular drugs, such as heroin. Its 1972 *Protocol* stresses the need for treatment and rehabilitation of drug addicts.
- The *Convention on Psychotropic Substances* (1971) establishes an international control system for psychotropic substances. It stands as a response to the diversification and expansion of the drug spectrum, and introduces controls over a number of synthetic drugs.
- The *United Nations Convention against Illicit Traffic in Narcotic Drugs and Psychotropic Substances* (1988) provides comprehensive measures against drug trafficking, including provisions against money laundering and the diversion of precursor chemicals. States parties commit themselves to eliminating or reducing drug demand.

UNODC provides leadership for all UN drug control activities, working with NGOs and civil society, including through community-based programmes in prevention, treatment and rehabilitation, as well as the provision of new economic opportunities to economies dependent on illicit crops.

Crime prevention

Crime threatens the safety of people around the world and hampers the social and economic development of countries. Globalization has opened up new forms of transnational crime. Multinational criminal syndicates have expanded the range of their operations from drug and arms trafficking to money laundering. Traffickers move millions of illegal migrants each year, generating billions in profits. A country plagued by corruption is likely to attract less investment than a relatively uncorrupt country, and lose economic growth as a result.

The **Commission on Crime Prevention and Criminal Justice**, made up of 40 member states, is a functional body of ECOSOC. It formulates international policies and coordinates activities in crime prevention and criminal justice. UNODC carries out the mandates established by the Commission, and is the UN office responsible for crime prevention, criminal justice and criminal law reform. It pays special attention to combating transnational organized crime, corruption, terrorism and trafficking in human beings. The UNODC strategy is based on international cooperation and the provision of assistance for those efforts. It fosters a culture based on integrity and respect for the law, and promotes the participation of civil society in combating crime and corruption.

UNODC supports the development of international legal instruments on global crime, including the *United Nations Convention against Transnational Organized Crime* and its three *Protocols*, which entered into force in 2003; and the *United Nations Convention against Corruption*, which entered into force in 2005. It also helps states put those instruments into effect. The Office provides technical co-operation to strengthen the capacity of governments to modernize their criminal justice systems. Its Anti-Organized Crime and Law Enforcement Unit assists states in taking effective, practical steps, in line with the *Convention against Corruption*, to fight organized crime.

UNODC advances the application of UN standards and norms in crime prevention and criminal justice as cornerstones of humane and effective criminal justice systems—basic requisites for fighting national and international crime. More than 100 countries have relied on these standards for elaborating national legislation and policies. The Office also analyses emerging trends in crime and justice; develops databases; issues global surveys; gathers and disseminates information; and undertakes country-specific needs assessments and early warning measures with regard to such issues as the escalation of terrorism.

In 2003, UNODC expanded its technical cooperation activities to strengthen the legal regime against terrorism, providing legal technical assistance to countries for becoming party to and implementing the universal anti-terrorism instruments.

UNODC also collaborates with the **Counter-Terrorism Implementation Task Force**, established by the Secretary-General in 2005 to enhance coordination and coherence of the UN system's counter-terrorism efforts. The working groups of this task force consist of 31 international entities that, by virtue of their work, have a stake in such efforts. They deal with preventing and resolving conflict; supporting victims of terrorism; preventing and responding to terrorist attacks involving weapons of mass destruction; tackling the financing of terrorism; countering the use of the Internet for terrorist purposes; strengthening the protection of vulnerable targets; and protecting human rights while countering terrorism.

The **Global Programme against Money Laundering** assists governments in confronting criminals who launder the proceeds of crime through the international financial system. In close cooperation with international anti-money laundering organizations, the Programme provides governments, law enforcement and financial intelligence units with anti-money laundering schemes; advises on improved banking and financial policies; and assists national financial investigation services.

In 2007, UNODC launched the **Global Initiative to Fight Human Trafficking (UN.GIFT)** (*www.ungift.org*), aimed at advancing the worldwide movement against this crime.

The **United Nations Interregional Crime and Justice Research Institute (UNICRI)** (*www.unicri.it*), the interregional research body that works in close association with UNODC's crime programme, undertakes and promotes research aimed at preventing crime, treating offenders and formulating improved policies. As decided by the General Assembly, a United Nations Congress on the Prevention of Crime and the Treatment of Offenders is held every five years as a forum to exchange policies and stimulate progress in the fight against crime. Participants include criminologists, penologists and senior police officers, as well as experts in criminal law, human rights and rehabilitation. The Twelfth Crime Congress met in

Salvador, Brazil, in April 2010 on the theme "Comprehensive strategies for global challenges: crime prevention and criminal justice systems and their development in a changing world".

Science, culture and communication

The United Nations sees cultural and scientific exchanges, as well as communication, as instrumental in the advancement of international peace and development. Several UN entities concern themselves with activities in these areas. In addition to its central work on education, for example, the **United Nations Educational, Scientific and Cultural Organization (UNESCO)** (*www.unesco.org*) carries out activities in the fields of science and culture, fostering the advancement, transfer and sharing of knowledge.

Natural and social and human sciences

UNESCO's international and intergovernmental programmes in the natural sciences include the Man and the Biosphere Programme; the Intergovernmental Oceanographic Commission; the Management of Social Transformations Programme; the International Hydrological Programme; the International Basic Sciences Programme; and the International Geoscience Programme. Through science education and capacity-building initiatives, UNESCO also helps increase the scientific capacity of developing countries for sustainable development.

In the wake of the 1997 *Universal Declaration on the Human Genome and Human Rights*—the first international text on the ethics of genetic research and practice—UNESCO's General Conference adopted the *International Declaration on Human Genetic Data* in 2003, and the *Universal Declaration on Bioethics and Human Rights* in 2005.

In its efforts to facilitate social transformations conducive to the universal values of justice, freedom and human dignity, UNESCO focuses on philosophy and social sciences research, including the ethics of science and technology; promoting and teaching human rights and democracy; combating all forms of discrimination, including those related to illnesses such as HIV/AIDS; and improving the status of women. Central to the work of UNESCO on these issues is its intergovernmental programme on the Management of Social Transformations. In 2005, the UNESCO General Conference adopted the *International Convention against Doping in Sport*, which seeks the elimination of doping in sport as a means to promote education, health, development and peace.

Culture and development

UNESCO's cultural activities are concentrated on promoting tangible and intangible heritage to help achieve sustainable development and social cohesion; protecting and promoting the diversity of cultural expressions and the dialogue of cultures, to foster a culture of peace; and building upon cultural factors for reconciliation and reconstruction in post-conflict and post-natural disaster countries.

In 2003, the UNESCO General Conference adopted the *UNESCO Declaration concerning the Intentional Destruction of Cultural Heritage*, mainly in response to the destruction of the Buddhas of Bamiyan in Afghanistan in 2001. The 2003 *Convention for the Safeguarding of the Intangible Cultural Heritage* covers oral traditions, customs, languages, performing arts, social practices, rituals, festive events, traditional knowledge, traditional crafts, endangered languages and the promotion of linguistic diversity. The 2005 *Convention on the Protection and Promotion of the Diversity of Cultural Expressions* recognizes cultural goods and services as vehicles of identity and values, and seeks to strengthen their creation, production, distribution and enjoyment, particularly by supporting related industries in developing countries.

Alliance of Civilizations

The **Alliance of Civilizations (UNAOC)** (*www.unaoc.org*) was launched by Secretary-General Kofi Annan in 2005 as a coalition to advance mutual respect for religious beliefs and traditions, and to reaffirm humanity's increasing interdependence in all areas. Its primary mission is to forge collective political will and mobilize concerted action to improve cross-cultural understanding and cooperation among countries, peoples and communities. UNAOC focuses on strengthening relations within and between Western and Muslim societies and addressing persistent tensions and divides. The High Representative for the Alliance of Civilizations is appointed by the Secretary-General. UNAOC works predominantly in four priority areas: education, youth, media and migration. In 2013, the Alliance held its fifth Global Forum in Vienna, focusing on the promotion of "Responsible Leadership in Diversity and Dialogue".

Sport for development and peace

The **United Nations Office on Sport for Development and Peace (UNOSDP)** (*www.un.org/wcm/content/site/sport/*), based in Geneva, assists the Special Adviser to the United Nations Secretary-General on Sport for Development and Peace in his worldwide activities as an advocate, facilitator and representative of the social purposes of sport. The Office brings the worlds of sport and development together, in particular through the engagement of sport organizations, civil society, athletes and the private sector. Through dialogue, knowledge-sharing and partnerships, UNOSDP encourages cross-cutting and interdisciplinary exchanges between all stakeholders interested in using sport as a tool for education and health. The Office and the Special Adviser also raise awareness about the use of physical activity to advance development and peace, including through the MDGs, the promotion of gender equality and the fight against HIV/AIDS. In the lead-up to and during major global sports events such as the FIFA World Cup and the Olympic Games, UNOSDP fosters UN-wide coordination and representation.

Communication and information

UNESCO promotes press freedom and pluralistic, independent media. It works in favour of the free flow of ideas, especially strengthening the communication capacities of developing countries and their access to information and knowledge. It assists member states in adapting their media laws to democratic standards, and in pursuing editorial independence in public and private media. When violations of press freedom occur, UNESCO's Director-General intervenes through diplomatic channels or public statements.

At UNESCO's initiative, 3 May is observed annually as **World Press Freedom Day**. **World Telecommunication and Information Society Day** is celebrated each year on 17 May, at the initiative of ITU, to promote the vision of a people-centred, inclusive and development-oriented information society.

With the aim of reinforcing developing countries' communication infrastructures and human resources, UNESCO provides training and technical expertise and helps develop national and regional media projects, especially through its International Programme for the Development of Communication.

The **Internet Governance Forum** (*www.intgovforum.org*) brings together governments, the private sector, NGOs and the technical and academic community to discuss Internet governance issues.

Sustainable development

In the first decades of the United Nations, environmental concerns rarely appeared on the international agenda. The related work of the Organization emphasized the exploration and use of natural resources, while seeking to ensure that developing countries in particular would maintain control over their own resources. During the 1960s, agreements were made concerning marine pollution, especially oil spills. Since then, there has been increasing evidence of the deterioration of the environment on a global scale, and the international community has shown increasing alarm over the impact of development on the ecology of the planet and on human well-being. The United Nations has been a leading advocate for environmental concerns, and a leading proponent of 'sustainable development'.

The relationship between economic development and environmental degradation was first placed on the international agenda in 1972, at the United Nations Conference on the Human Environment, held in Stockholm, Sweden. After the Conference, governments set up the **United Nations Environment Programme (UNEP)** (*www.unep.org*), which has become the world's leading environmental agency.

In 1973, the United Nations Sudano-Sahelian Office—now the Drylands Development Centre of the United Nations Development Programme—was set up to spearhead efforts to reverse the spread of desertification in West Africa. The Centre later took on a global mandate. In 1996, the entry into force of the *United Nations Convention to Combat Desertification in those Countries Experiencing Serious Drought and/or Desertification, Particularly in Africa* gave added impetus to the Centre's work.

The 1980s witnessed landmark negotiations among member states on environmental issues, including treaties protecting the ozone layer and controlling the movement of toxic wastes. The World Commission on Environment and Development, established in 1983 by the General Assembly, brought a new understanding and sense of urgency to the need for another kind of development that would ensure economic well-being for present and future generations, while protecting the environmental resources on which all development depends. The Commission's 1987 report to the General Assembly put forward the concept of sustainable development as an alternative to development based simply on unconstrained economic growth. After considering the report, the Assembly called for the United Nations Conference on Environment and Development—the Earth Summit, held in Rio de Janeiro, Brazil, in 1992. Unprecedented in its size, scope and influence, the Earth Summit linked sustainable development with issues of human rights, population, social development and human settlements.

Today, awareness of the need to support and sustain the environment is reflected in virtually all areas of UN work. Dynamic partnerships between the United Nations and governments, NGOs, the scientific community and the private sector are bringing new knowledge and specific action to global environmental problems. For the United Nations, economic and social development are inextricably linked to protection of the environment. Achieving sustainable development requires integrating economic, environmental and social concerns at all levels.

Agenda 21

Governments took a historic step towards ensuring the future of the planet when the Earth Summit adopted *Agenda 21,* a comprehensive plan for global action in all areas of sustainable development. Its implementation and related commitments were reaffirmed at the World Summit on Sustainable Development held in Johannesburg, South Africa, in 2002. In *Agenda 21,* governments outlined actions that could move the world away from an unsustainable model of economic growth towards activities that will protect and renew the environmental resources on which growth and development depend. Areas for action include: protecting the atmosphere; combating deforestation, soil loss and desertification; preventing air and water pollution; halting the depletion of fish stocks; and promoting the safe management of toxic wastes.

Agenda 21 also addresses patterns of development that cause stress to the environment, including: poverty and external debt in developing countries; unsustainable patterns of production and consumption; demographic stress; and the structure of the international economy. The action programme recommends ways to strengthen the part played by major groups—women, trade unions, farmers, children and young people, indigenous people, the scientific community, local authorities, business, industry and NGOs—in achieving sustainable development.

The United Nations has acted to integrate the concept of sustainable development in all relevant policies and programmes. Income-generating projects increasingly take environmental consequences into account. Development assistance programmes are more than ever directed towards women, in view of their roles as producers of goods, services and food, and as caretakers of the environment. The moral and social imperatives for alleviating poverty are given additional urgency by the recognition that poverty eradication and environmental quality go hand-in-hand.

To ensure full support for *Agenda 21*, the General Assembly, in 1992, established the **Commission on Sustainable Development**. A functional commission of ECOSOC, the 53-member body monitors the implementation of *Agenda 21* and the other Earth Summit agreements, as well as the outcomes of the 2002 World Summit on Sustainable Development. It also addresses cross-cutting issues in the context of sustainable development, including those related to poverty eradication; changing patterns of consumption and production; protecting and managing the natural resource base of economic and social development; globalization; health; small island developing states; Africa; gender equality; and education.

The **Division for Sustainable Development** of the UN Department of Economic and Social Affairs (*sustaimabledevelopment.un.org*)—the secretariat for the Commission—provides technical services for capacity-building in sustainable development, as well as other analytical and information services.

World Summit on Sustainable Development

The 2002 World Summit on Sustainable Development was held in Johannesburg, South Africa, to take stock of achievements, challenges and new issues since the 1992 Earth Summit. The Summit brought together a wide range of interests. Member states agreed to the *Johannesburg Declaration on Sustainable Development* and *Plan of Implementation* detailing the priorities for action. The Summit reaffirmed sustainable development as a central element of the international agenda. Paving the way for measures addressing some of the world's most pressing challenges, it emphasized the links between economic and social development and the conservation of natural resources. The Summit's internationally agreed commitments were complemented by a range of voluntary partnership initiatives for sustainable development.

UN Conference on Sustainable Development

The United Nations Conference on Sustainable Development—or Rio+20—took place in Rio de Janeiro, Brazil, in June 2012. It marked the twentieth anniversary of the 1992 Earth Summit, also held in Rio de Janeiro; and the tenth anniversary of the 2002 World Summit on Sustainable Development, held in Johannesburg. The Conference, devoted to the theme "The Future We Want", adopted an outcome document containing practical measures for implementing sustainable development. Member states launched a process to develop a set of Sustainable Development Goals (SDGs), which would build on the MDGs and converge with the post-2015 development agenda. The Conference also adopted guidelines on green economy policies.

An intergovernmental process was established under the General Assembly to prepare options for a sustainable development financing strategy. Governments agreed to strengthen UNEP in several areas and establish a high-level political forum for sustainable development. They also adopted the 10-year framework of programmes on sustainable consumption and production patterns. The Rio+20 conference resulted in over 700 voluntary commitments to deliver concrete results for sustainable development—initiating a new bottom-up approach to advancing sustainable development. The registry of partnerships to advance sustainable development and enhance international cooperation included over 200 such mechanisms.

Financing sustainable development

At the 1992 Earth Summit, it was agreed that most financing for *Agenda 21* would come from each country's public and private sectors. However, additional external funds were deemed necessary to support developing countries' efforts to implement sustainable development practices and protect the global environment.

The Global Environment Facility (GEF) (*www.thegef.org/gef*), established in 1991, helps developing countries fund projects that protect the global environment and promote sustainable livelihoods in local communities. Over the years, it has provided more than $11.5 billion in grants and generated over $57 billion in cofinancing from recipient governments, international development agencies, private industry and NGOs to support 3,215 projects in 165 developing countries and economies in transition. GEF funds are the primary means for achieving the goals of the conventions on biological diversity, climate change, desertification and persistent organic pollutants. In line with those goals, GEF projects—principally carried out by UNDP, UNEP and the World Bank—are aimed at conserving and making sustainable use of biological diversity; addressing global climate change; reversing the degradation of international waters; phasing out substances that deplete the ozone layer; combating land degradation and drought; and reducing and eliminating the production and use of certain persistent organic pollutants.

The following agencies also contribute to the management and execution of GEF projects: the **African Development Bank** (*www.afdb.org*), the **Asian Development Bank** (*www.adb.org*), the **European Bank for Reconstruction and Development** (*www.ebrd.org*), **FAO** (*www.fao.org*), the **Inter-American Development Bank** (*www.iadb.org*), the **International Fund for Agricultural Development** (*www.ifad.org*) and **the United Nations Industrial Development Organization** (*www.unido.org*)

Action for the environment

The entire United Nations system is engaged in environmental protection in diverse ways. Its lead agency in this area is the **United Nations Environment Programme (UNEP)** (*www.unep.org*). UNEP assesses the state of the world's environment and identifies issues requiring international cooperation. It helps formulate international environmental law and integrate environmental considerations in the social and economic policies and programmes of the UN system. UNEP helps solve problems that cannot be handled by countries acting alone. It provides a forum for building consensus and forging international agreements. In doing so, it strives to enhance the participation of business and industry, the scientific and academic communities, NGOs, community groups and others in achieving sustainable development. UNEP's six priority areas are: climate change, disasters and conflicts, ecosystem management, environmental governance, harmful substances, and resource efficiency.

Scientific research promoted and coordinated by UNEP has generated a variety of reports on the state of the environment. Reports such as the *Global Environment Outlook* (*www.unep.org/geo*) have created worldwide awareness of emerging environmental problems and even triggered international negotiations on environmental conventions. UNEP has a growing network of centres of excellence, including the UNEP World Conservation Monitoring Centre; the Global Resource Information Database; the UNEP Risø Centre on Energy, Climate and Sustainable Development; the UNEP Collaborating Centre on Water and Environment; the Global Reporting Initiative; and the Basel Agency for Sustainable Energy.

UNEP's **Division of Technology, Industry and Economics** (*www.unep.org/dtie*) is active in UN efforts to encourage decision makers in government, industry and business to adopt policies, strategies and practices that are cleaner and safer, use natural resources more efficiently, and reduce pollution risks to people and the environment. The Division facilitates the transfer of safer, cleaner and environmentally sound technologies, especially those that deal with urban and freshwater management; helps countries build capacities for the sound management of chemicals and the improvement of chemical safety worldwide; supports the phase-out of ozone-depleting substances in developing countries and countries with economies in transition; assists decision makers to make better, more informed energy choices;

and works with governments and the private sector to integrate environmental considerations into activities, practices, products and services.

UNEP Chemicals (*www.chem.unep.ch*)—the Division's chemicals branch—provides countries with access to information about toxic chemicals; assists countries in building their capacities to produce, use and dispose of chemicals safely; and supports international and regional actions for reducing or eliminating chemical risks. In 2001, UNEP facilitated the completion of the *Stockholm Convention on Persistent Organic Pollutants*, a treaty to reduce and eliminate releases of certain chemicals that remain intact in the environment for long periods, become widely distributed geographically, collect in the fatty tissue of living organisms and are toxic to humans and wildlife. These include pesticides, industrial chemicals and by-products.

Over the years, UNEP has been the catalyst for the negotiation of other international agreements that form the cornerstone of UN efforts to halt and reverse damage to the planet. The historic 1987 *Montreal Protocol* and its subsequent amendments seek to preserve the ozone layer in the upper atmosphere. The 1989 *Basel Convention on the Control of Hazardous Wastes and their Disposal* has reduced the danger of pollution from toxic waste. In collaboration with FAO, UNEP facilitated the negotiation of the 1998 *Rotterdam Convention on the Prior Informed Consent Procedure for Certain Hazardous Chemicals and Pesticides in International Trade*, which gives importing countries the power to decide which chemicals they want to receive and to exclude those they cannot manage safely.

In January 2013, over 140 nations agreed on the text of a legally binding treaty to prevent emissions and releases of mercury. The *Minamata Convention on Mercury* would be opened for signature in Japan in October 2013.

The 1973 *Convention on International Trade in Endangered Species* is universally recognized for its contribution to controlling trade in wildlife products. UNEP assisted African governments in developing the 1994 *Lusaka Agreement on Cooperative Enforcement Operations Directed at Illegal Trade in Wild Fauna and Flora*. The 1992 *Convention on Biological Diversity* and the 2000 *Cartagena Protocol on Biosafety* seek to conserve and encourage the sustainable and equitable use of the planet's wide variety of plants, animals and micro-organisms. UNEP has also helped negotiate and implement conventions on desertification and climate change.

Climate change and global warming

Since the dawn of the industrial age, there has been a steady—and now dangerously increasing—build-up of greenhouse gases in the earth's atmosphere, leading to a continuing rise in global temperatures. When fossil fuels are burned to generate energy, or when forests are cut down and burned, carbon dioxide is released. Greenhouse gases—including methane, nitrous oxide and others—have accumulated in the atmosphere to such an extent that the planet now faces the prospect of massive and potentially destructive consequences. The UN system is meeting this challenge head-on through its work on climate change (*www.un.org/climatechange*).

In 1988, at a time when the best research available was beginning to indicate the possible severity of the problem, two UN bodies—UNEP and the World Meteorological Organization (WMO)—came together to establish the **Intergovern-mental Panel on Climate Change (IPCC)** (*www.ipcc.ch*) to assemble the current knowledge on climate change and its potential environmental and socio-economic impact, and to point the way forward. The Panel, a worldwide network of thousands of leading scientists and experts contributing on a voluntary basis, reviews scientific research on the issue, with a view to developing a legally binding and coordinated approach to the problem. In recognition of its work, the Panel was awarded the 2007 Nobel Peace Prize, together with former United States Vice President Albert Arnold (Al) Gore, Jr.

Heeding the warnings of scientists worldwide, the nations of the world came together in Rio de Janeiro in 1992 to sign the *United Nations Framework Convention on Climate Change* (*www.unfccc.int*). To date, 195 countries have joined in this international treaty, by which developed countries agreed to reduce to 1990 levels emissions of carbon dioxide and other greenhouse gases they release into the atmosphere. They also agreed to transfer to developing countries the technology and information needed to help them respond to the challenges of climate change.

In 1995, evidence presented by IPCC scientists made it clear that the 1992 target would not be enough to prevent global warming and its associated problems. Therefore, in 1997, countries that had ratified the *Convention* met in Kyoto, Japan, and agreed on a protocol under which developed countries were to reduce their collective emissions of six greenhouse gases by 5.2 per cent between 2008 and 2012.

The *Protocol* entered into force in 2005. Of the six gases it sought to control, carbon dioxide, methane and nitrous oxide occur naturally in the atmosphere, but human activities have increased their levels dramatically. Through the *Protocol*'s **Clean Development Mechanism** (*www.cdmbazaar.net*), projects that reduce greenhouse gas emissions in developing countries and contribute to sustainable development can earn certified emission reduction credits, which can be bought by industrialized countries to cover a portion of their emission reduction commitments.

The *Protocol*'s first commitment period ended in 2012. Under the *Doha Amendment* to the *Protocol*, adopted in December 2012, 37 industrialized countries and the European Community committed to reduce greenhouse gas emissions to an average of five per cent against 1990 levels. During the second commitment period, the parties committed to reduce emissions by at least 18 per cent from 2013 to 2020.

When the United Nations first began to mobilize world public opinion to address the threat posed by climate change, many people remained unconvinced that such change was taking place. In 2007, however, IPCC, making use of major advances in climate modelling and the collection and analysis of data, and based on a review of the most up-to-date, peer-reviewed scientific literature, reported with 90 per cent certainty that significant global warming was in process and increasing, to a degree that was directly attributable to human activity and that would worsen unless major corrective actions were taken. The Panel's report—*Climate Change 2007*—represents a consensus agreement of climate scientists and experts from 40 countries and has been endorsed by 113 governments. It indicates that the world faces an average temperature rise of around 3 degrees Celsius by the end of this century if greenhouse gas emissions continue to rise at their current pace. The results of such an increase would include more extreme temperatures; heat waves; new wind patterns; worsening drought in some regions and heavier precipitation in others; melting glaciers and Arctic ice; and rising sea levels worldwide. While the number of tropical cyclones (typhoons and hurricanes) is projected to decline, their intensity is expected to increase, with higher peak wind speeds and more intense precipitation due to warmer ocean waters.

The *Hyogo Framework for Action, 2005–2015*, adopted by 168 nations at the 2005 UN World Conference on Disaster Reduction in Kobe, Japan, includes recommendations that can be effective in reducing the disaster risks caused by climate-related hazards. Ultimately, however, the only effective course is to combat the tide of global warming by restoring the sustainability of the atmosphere. Fortunately, the means to do so have been outlined, and the goal can be accomplished if the people of the world come together to make it happen. In addition to action contemplated in such international agreements as the *Framework Convention on Climate Change* and its *Kyoto Protocol*, the United Nations recognizes that individuals, municipalities, NGOs and other bodies all have a part to play. For example, the UNEP Plant for the Planet: Billion Tree Campaign, a worldwide tree-planting initiative launched in 2006 to help mitigate the build-up of carbon dioxide, resulted in more than 12 billion trees planted.

In 2007, the Security Council, highlighting the urgent need for concerted international action to deal with the problem of climate change, held an unprecedented, open debate on energy, security and climate. Addressing that debate, Secretary-General Ban Ki-moon called for "a long-term global response, in line with the latest scientific findings, and compatible with economic and social development". Describing climate change as "a defining issue of our era", he identified it as one of his top priorities, and named a number of special envoys to discuss the issue with the world's national leaders.

Ozone depletion

The ozone layer is a thin layer of gas in the stratosphere, more than 10 kilometres (6 miles) above the ground, that shields the earth's surface from the sun's damaging ultraviolet rays. In the mid-1970s, it was discovered that certain man-made chemicals, including the chlorofluorocarbons (CFCs) used for refrigeration, air conditioning and industrial cleaning, were destroying atmospheric ozone and depleting the ozone layer. This became a matter of increasing international concern, since greater exposure to ultraviolet radiation results in skin cancer, eye cataracts and suppression of the human immune system; it also causes unpredictable damage to the global ecosystem.

In response to this challenge, UNEP helped negotiate the historic 1985 *Vienna Convention for the Protection of the Ozone Layer*, along with the 1987 *Montreal Protocol* and its amendments. Under these agreements, administered by UNEP, developed countries banned the production and sale of CFCs, and developing countries were required to stop their production by 2010. Schedules were also put in place to phase out other ozone-depleting substances. **UNEP's Ozone Secretariat** (*ozone.unep.org*) has documented clear evidence of a recent decrease in ozone-depleting substances in the lower atmosphere and in the stratosphere, as well as early signs of the expected ozone recovery of the stratosphere. In its view, continued elimination of all emissions of ozone-depleting substances should help restore the global ozone layer to pre-1980 levels by 2035.

Small islands

Small islands share specific disadvantages and vulnerabilities. Their ecological fragility, small size, limited resources and isolation from markets limit their ability to take advantage of globalization, posing a major obstacle to their socio-economic development. This makes sustainable development a unique challenge for them (see *www.un.org/ohrlls*). At present, 52 small island developing states and territories are included in the list used by the UN Department of Economic and Social Affairs in monitoring progress towards the implementation of the *Barbados Programme of Action*, adopted in 1994 at the Global Conference on the Sustainable Development of Small Island Developing States. The *Programme of Action* sets forth policies, actions and measures at all levels to promote sustainable development in these states.

In 2005, the international community, meeting at Mauritius to conduct a 10-year review of the *Programme of Action*, approved a wide-ranging set of further recommendations, known as the *Mauritius Strategy*. The *Strategy* addresses such issues as climate change and rising sea levels; natural and environmental disasters; waste management; coastal, marine, freshwater, land, energy, tourism and biodiversity resources; transportation and communication; science and technology; globalization and trade liberalization; sustainable production and consumption, capacity-building and education for sustainable development; health; culture; and knowledge management and information for decision-making.

Sustainable forest management

With international trade in forest products generating hundreds of billions of dollars annually, more than 1.6 billion people around the world rely on forests for their livelihoods. As the foundation of indigenous knowledge, forests provide profound socio-cultural benefits. As ecosystems, they play a critical role in mitigating the effects of climate change and protecting biodiversity. While the rate of net forest loss is slowing down, thanks to new planting and natural expansion of existing forests, every year some 13 million hectares of the world's forests are lost to deforestation, which accounts for up to 20 per cent of global greenhouse gas emissions. The world's forests and forest soils store more than one trillion tons of carbon— twice the amount found in the atmosphere.

The most common causes of deforestation are unsustainable timber harvesting, the conversion of forests to agricultural land, unsound land management practices, and the creation of human settlements. The UN has been at the forefront of the movement towards sustainable forest management since the 1992 Earth Summit, which adopted a non-binding statement of forest principles.

From 1995 to 2000, the Intergovernmental Panel on Forests and the Intergovernmental Forum on Forests, acting under the UN Commission on Sustainable Development, were the main intergovernmental forums for the development of forest policy. In 2000, the Economic and Social Council established the **United Nations Forum on Forests** (*www.un.org/esa/forests*), a high-level intergovernmental body charged with strengthening long-term political commitment for sustainable forest management.

In 2007, the Forum adopted a landmark agreement on international forest policy and cooperation: the *Non-Legally Binding Instrument on All Types of Forests*, adopted by the General Assembly the same year. Although the agreement is nonbinding and includes a voluntary global financing mechanism, it nevertheless sets a standard in forest management aimed at reducing deforestation, preventing forest degradation, promoting sustainable livelihoods and reducing poverty for all forest-dependent peoples.

At the invitation of ECOSOC, the heads of relevant international organizations have also formed a 14-member **Collaborative Partnership on Forests**, which fosters cooperation and coordination in support of the goals of the UN Forum on Forests and the implementation of sustainable forest management worldwide.

Desertification

Deserts are harsh, dry environments where few people live. Drylands, which cover about 41 per cent of the earth's land area, are characterized by low rainfall and high rates of evaporation. They are home to more than 2 billion people, including half of all those living in poverty worldwide. Some 1.8 billion of these people live in developing countries.

Desertification is land degradation in arid, semi-arid and dry, sub-humid areas resulting from various factors, including climatic variations and human activities. Land degradation in drylands is the reduction or loss of biological or economic productivity in such areas. Its main human causes are overcultivation, overgrazing, deforestation and poor irrigation. UNEP has estimated that it affects one third of the earth's surface and more than 1 billion people in more than 110 countries. Sub-Saharan Africa, where two thirds of the land is either desert or dryland, is particularly at risk.

The consequences of desertification and drought include food insecurity, famine and poverty. Ensuing social, economic and political tensions can create conflicts, cause more impoverishment and further increase land degradation. Growing desertification worldwide threatens to increase by millions the number of poor people forced to seek new homes and livelihoods.

The 1994 *United Nations Convention to Combat Desertification in those Countries Experiencing Serious Drought and/or Desertification, Particularly in Africa* (*www. unccd.int*) seeks to address this problem. It focuses on rehabilitation of land, improving productivity, and the conservation and management of land and water resources. The *Convention* emphasizes the establishment of an enabling environment for local people to help reverse land degradation. It also sets out criteria for the preparation by affected countries of national action programmes and gives an unprecedented role to NGOs in preparing and carrying out such programmes. The *Convention*, which entered into force in 1996, has 195 states parties.

Many UN bodies provide assistance to combat desertification. UNDP funds antidesertification activities through its Nairobi-based **Drylands Development Centre** (*www.undp.org/drylands*). IFAD has committed more than $3.5 billion over the last three decades to support dryland development. The World Bank funds programmes aimed at protecting drylands and increasing their agricultural productivity. FAO provides practical help to governments for sustainable agricultural development. UNEP supports regional action programmes, data assessment, capacity-building and public awareness of the problem.

Biodiversity, pollution and overfishing

Biodiversity—the world's resplendent variety of plant and animal species—is essential for human survival. The protection and conservation of the diverse species of animal and plant life and their habitats is the aim of the 1992 *United Nations Convention on Biological Diversity* (*www.cbd.int*), to which 192 states and the European Union (EU) are party. The *Convention* obligates states to conserve biodiversity, ensure its sustainable development, and provide for the fair and equitable sharing of benefits from the use of genetic resources. Its *Cartagena Protocol on Biosafety*, which entered into force in 2003, aims to ensure the safe use of genetically modified organisms. It has 166 parties.

Protection of endangered species is also enforced under the 1973 *Convention on International Trade in Endangered Species* (*www.cites.org*), administered by UNEP. The 178 states parties to the *Convention* meet periodically to update the list of plant and animal species or products, such as ivory, that should be protected by quotas or outright bans. The 1979 *Bonn Convention on the Conservation of Migratory Species of Wild Animals* (*www.cms.int*), along with a series of associated agreements, aims to conserve terrestrial, marine and avian migratory species and their habitats, especially those threatened with extinction; the treaty has 119 parties. UNESCO's **Man and the Biosphere Programme** (*www.unesco.org/mab*) concerns itself with the sustainable use and conservation of biological diversity, as well as the improvement of the relationship between people and their environment worldwide. The Programme combines natural and social sciences, economics and education to improve livelihoods and safeguard natural ecosystems, and so promote innovative approaches to economic development that are socially and culturally appropriate, as well as environmentally sustainable.

Acid rain, caused by emissions of sulphur dioxide from industrial manufacturing processes, has been significantly reduced in much of Europe and North America, thanks to the 1979 *Convention on Long-Range Transboundary Air Pollution* (*www. unece.org/env/lrtap*). The *Convention*, to which 50 states and the EU are party, is administered by the United Nations Economic Commission for Europe. Its scope has been extended by eight specific protocols addressing such issues as ground-level ozone, persistent organic pollutants, heavy metals, further reduction of sulphur emissions, volatile organic compounds and nitrogen oxides.

Hazardous wastes and chemicals. To regulate the millions of tons of toxic waste that cross national borders each year, member states negotiated, in 1989, the *Basel Convention on the Control of Transboundary Movements of Hazardous Wastes and their Disposal* (*www.basel.int*), administered by UNEP. The *Convention*, to which 179 states and the EU are party, was strengthened in 1995 to ban the export of toxic waste to developing countries, which often do not have the technology for safe disposal. In 1999, governments adopted the *Basel Protocol on Liability and Compensation* to deal with the question of financial responsibility in the event of the illegal dumping or accidental spills of hazardous wastes.

High-seas fishing. Overfishing and the near exhaustion of many species of commercially valuable fish, along with the increasing incidence of illegal, unregulated and unreported fishing, have led governments to call for measures to conserve and sustainably manage fish resources—especially those that migrate across broad areas of the ocean or move through the economic zone of more than one country. The 1995 *Agreement for the Implementation of the Provisions of the United Nations Convention on the Law of the Sea of 10 December 1982 relating to the Conservation and Management of Straddling Fish Stocks and Highly Migratory Fish Stocks,* which entered into force in 2001, provides a regime for the conservation and management of these stocks, with a view to ensuring their long-term conservation and sustainable use. It has 79 parties, including the European Union.

Protecting the marine environment

Coastal and marine areas cover some 70 per cent of the earth's surface and are vital to the planet's life support system. Protecting the marine environment has become a primary concern of the United Nations, and UNEP has worked hard to focus the world's attention on oceans and seas.

Most water pollution comes from industrial wastes, mining, agricultural activities and emissions from motor vehicles; some of these forms of pollution occur thousands of miles inland. The **Global Programme of Action for the Protection of the Marine Environment from Land-based Activities** (*www.gpa.unep.org*), adopted in 1995 under UNEP auspices, is considered a milestone in international efforts to protect oceans, estuaries and coastal waters from such pollution.

Under its **Regional Seas Programme** (*www.unep.org/regionalseas*), which now covers more than 140 countries, UNEP addresses the accelerating degradation of the world's oceans and coastal areas. The Programme works to protect shared marine and water resources through 13 conventions or action plans. Regional programmes, established under the auspices of UNEP, cover the Black Sea, East Asian Seas, Eastern Africa, the Regional Organization for the Protection of the Marine Environment Sea Area, the Mediterranean, the North-East Pacific, the North-West Pacific, the Red Sea and the Gulf of Aden, the South Asian Seas, the Pacific, the South-East Pacific, Western Africa and the Wider Caribbean.

Despite the dramatic expansion of world shipping, oil pollution from ships was reduced by around 60 per cent during the 1980s, and has continued to decline since then. This has been due partly to the introduction of better methods of controlling the disposal of wastes and partly to the tightening of controls through international conventions (*http://oils.gpa.unep.org*). The **International Maritime Organization (IMO)** (*www.imo.org*) is the UN specialized agency responsible for measures to help prevent marine pollution from ships and improve the safety of international shipping. The pioneering *International Convention for the Prevention of Pollution of the Sea by Oil* was adopted in 1954, and IMO took over responsibility for it five years later. In the late 1960s, a number of major tanker accidents led to further action. Since then, IMO has developed many measures to help prevent accidents at sea and oil spills; minimize the consequences of accidents and spills; and combat marine pollution, including that generated by land-based activities.

Among the main international treaties in this area are: the 1969 *International Convention Relating to Intervention on the High Seas in Cases of Oil Pollution Casualties*; the 1972 *Convention on the Prevention of Marine Pollution by Dumping of Wastes and Other Matter*; and the 1990 *International Convention on Oil Pollution Preparedness, Response and Cooperation*.

IMO has also tackled environmental threats caused by such routine operations as the cleaning of oil cargo tanks and the disposal of engine-room wastes, which, in terms of tonnage, constitute a bigger menace than accidents. The most important of related measures is the *International Convention for the Prevention of Marine Pollution from Ships, 1973, as modified by the Protocol of 1978 relating thereto*. It covers not only accidental and operational oil pollution, but also pollution by chemicals, packaged goods, sewage and garbage; a 1997 Annex addresses the prevention of air pollution from ships. Amendments to the *Convention* adopted in 1992 oblige all new oil tankers to be fitted with double hulls, or a design that provides equivalent cargo protection in the event of a collision or grounding, phasing out existing single-hull tankers by 2010, with certain exceptions.

Two IMO treaties—the 1969 *International Convention on Civil Liability for Oil Pollution Damage* and the 1971 *International Convention on the Establishment of an International Fund for Oil Pollution Damage*—established a system for providing compensation to those who have suffered financially as a result of pollution. The treaties, revised in 1992, enable victims of oil pollution to obtain compensation much more simply and quickly than had been possible before.

Weather, climate and water

From weather prediction to climate change research and early warning on natural hazards, the **World Meteorological Organization (WMO)** (*www.wmo. int*) coordinates global scientific efforts to provide timely and accurate information on the state and behaviour of the Earth's atmosphere, its interaction with the oceans, the climate it produces and the resulting distribution of water resources. In the UN system, WMO organizes and facilitates international cooperation in establishing and operating networks of stations for making meteorological, hydrological and related observations. It promotes the rapid exchange of meteorological information, standardization of meteorological observations, and uniform publication of observations and statistics. It also extends the application of meteorology to aviation, shipping, agriculture and other weather-sensitive socio-economic activities; promotes water resources development; and encourages research and training.

The World Weather Watch is the backbone of WMO activities. It offers up-to the-minute worldwide weather information through observation systems and telecommunication links operated by member states and territories, employing satellites, aircraft, land observation stations, ship stations, moored buoys and drifting buoys carrying automatic weather stations. The resulting data, analysis and forecasts are exchanged every day, freely and without restriction, between WMO centres and weather offices in every country. As a result, a five-day weather forecast today is as reliable as a two-day forecast was 20 years ago.

WMO makes it possible for complex international agreements on weather standards, codes, measurements and communications to be established. The Tropical Cyclone Programme helps countries vulnerable to cyclones minimize destruction and loss of life by improving forecasting and warning systems and disaster preparedness. The WMO Natural Disaster Prevention and Mitigation Programme ensures the integration of various WMO programme activities in this area. It coordinates them with related activities of international, regional and national organizations, including civil defence bodies, particularly with respect to risk assessment, early warning systems, and capacity-building. It also provides scientific and technical support for WMO's response to disaster situations.

The World Climate Programme collects and preserves climate data, helping governments plan for climate change. The Programme can also warn governments of impending climate variations (such as the El Niño and La Niña phenomena) and their impact several months ahead of time, as well as of changes—natural or man-made—that could affect critical human activities. To assess all available information on climate change, WMO and UNEP established in 1988 the Intergovernmental Panel on Climate Change (IPCC) (*www.ipcc.ch*).

The Atmospheric Research and Environment Programme coordinates research on the structure and composition of the atmosphere, the physics and chemistry of clouds, weather modification, tropical meteorology, and weather forecasting. It helps member states conduct research projects, disseminate scientific information, and incorporate the results of research into forecasting and other techniques. Under the Global Atmosphere Watch, a network of global and regional monitoring stations and satellites assesses the levels of greenhouse gases, ozone, radionuclides and other traces of gases and particles in the atmosphere.

The Applications of Meteorology Programme helps countries apply meteorology to the protection of life and property and to social and economic development. It seeks to improve public weather services; increase the safety of sea and air travel; reduce the impact of desertification; and improve agriculture and the management of water, energy and other resources. In agriculture, for instance, prompt meteorological advice can mean a substantial reduction in losses caused by droughts, pests and disease.

The Hydrology and Water Resources Programme helps assess, manage and conserve global water resources. It promotes global cooperation in evaluating water resources and developing hydrological networks and services, including data collection and processing, hydrological forecasting and warning, and the supply of meteorological and hydrological data for design purposes. It facilitates cooperation with respect to water basins shared between countries, and provides specialized forecasting in flood-prone areas, thus helping preserve life and property.

The WMO Space Programme contributes to the Global Observing System of the World Weather Watch and other WMO-supported programmes and associated observing systems. The Education and Training Programme and the Technical Cooperation Programme encourage the exchange of scientific knowledge, the development of technical expertise and the transfer of technology.

Natural resources and energy

The United Nations has long assisted countries in managing their natural resources. As early as 1952, the General Assembly declared that developing countries had "the right to determine freely the use of their natural resources" and that they should use such resources towards realizing economic development plans in accordance with their national interests.

Water resources. It has been estimated that 768 million people lack basic access to a sufficient water supply, defined as a source likely to provide 20 litres per person per day at a distance no greater than 1 kilometre (a 30-minute round-trip journey). Such sources would include household connections, public standpipes, boreholes, protected dug wells, protected springs and rainwater collections. The United Nations has long been addressing the global crisis caused by growing demands on the world's water resources to meet human, commercial and agricultural needs, as well as the need for basic sanitation. The United Nations Water Conference (1977), the International Drinking Water Supply and Sanitation Decade (1981–1990), the International Conference on Water and the Environment (1992) and the Earth Summit (1992) all focused on this vital resource. The Decade, in particular, helped some 1.3 billion people in developing countries gain access to safe drinking water.

Causes of inadequate water supply include inefficient use, degradation of water by pollution, and over-exploitation of groundwater reserves. Corrective action aims at achieving better management of scarce freshwater resources, with a particular focus on supply and demand, quantity and quality. UN system activities focus on the sustainable development of fragile and finite freshwater resources, which are under increasing stress from population growth, pollution and the demands of agricultural and industrial uses. The crucial importance of water to so many aspects of health, development and well-being also led to specific water-related targets in support of every one of the MDGs.

To help raise public awareness of the importance of intelligent development of freshwater resources, the General Assembly declared 2003 the UN International Year of Freshwater. Also that year, the United Nations System Chief Executives Board for Coordination (CEB) established **UN-Water** (*www.unwater.org*)—an inter-agency mechanism to coordinate UN system actions to achieve the water-related goals of the *Millennium Declaration* and the 2002 World Summit on Sustainable Development. To further strengthen global action to meet the water-related MDG targets, the Assembly proclaimed the period 2005–2015 the International Decade for Action "Water for Life"; the Decade began on 22 March 2005, observed annually as **World Water Day**. In 2012, UNESCO published the fourth edition of the triennial *United Nations World Water Development Report* on the theme "Managing water under uncertainty and risk".

Sanitation. According to the *Millennium Development Goals Report 2012*, the MDG target on water and sanitation, as it pertains to access to safe drinking water, was met in 2010, but remained out of reach as it pertains to sanitation. Some 2.5 billion people still lack access to basic sanitation, defined as connection to a public sewer or septic system, a pour-flush latrine, a simple pit latrine, or a ventilated and improved pit latrine.

Energy. About one quarter of the world's population lives without electricity, and even more people lack access to modern fuels for cooking and heating. Yet while an adequate supply of energy is essential to economic advancement and poverty eradication, the environmental and health effects of conventional energy systems are a matter of concern. Moreover, the increasing demand for energy per capita, coupled with the rising global population, is resulting in consumption levels that cannot be sustained using current energy systems.

UN system activities on energy help developing countries in many ways, including through education, training and capacity-building, assistance in policy reforms, and the provision of energy services. However, while efforts are being made to move towards renewable sources of energy that are significantly less polluting, additional demand still outpaces the introduction of new capacity. Further effort is needed to improve energy efficiency and move towards cleaner fossil fuel technologies in the transition towards sustainable development.

In 2004, CEB established **UN-Energy** (*esa.un.org/un-energy*) as the principal inter-agency mechanism in the field of energy. Its task is to help ensure coherence in the UN system's response to the 2002 World Summit on Sustainable Development, as well as the engagement of major actors from the private sector and the NGO community for implementing the Summit's energy-related decisions.

Nuclear safety

At the end of 2012, 437 nuclear power reactors were in operation around the world. In five countries, over 40 per cent of energy production comes from nuclear power. The **International Atomic Energy Agency (IAEA)** (*www.iaea.org*), a member of the United Nations family, fosters the development of the safe, secure and peaceful uses of atomic energy, playing a prominent role in international efforts to ensure the use of nuclear technology for sustainable development. In the current debate on energy options to curb carbon dioxide emissions, which contribute to global warming, IAEA has stressed the benefits of nuclear power as an energy source free of greenhouse and other toxic gas emissions. IAEA serves as the world's central intergovernmental forum for scientific and technical cooperation in the nuclear field. It is a focal point for the exchange of information and the formulation of guidelines and norms in the area of nuclear safety, as well as for the provision of advice to governments, at their request, on ways to improve the safety of reactors and avoid the risk of accidents.

The Agency's responsibility in the area of nuclear safety has increased as nuclear-power programmes have grown and the public has focused its attention on safety aspects. The IAEA formulates basic standards for radiation protection and issues, regulations and codes of practice on specific types of operations, including the safe transport of radioactive materials. Acting under the *Convention on Assistance in the Case of a Nuclear Accident or Radiological Emergency* and the *Convention on Early Notification of a Nuclear Accident*, both adopted in 1986, the Agency facilitates emergency assistance to member states in the event of a radiation accident.

Other international treaties for which the IAEA is the depositary include the 1987 *Convention on the Physical Protection of Nuclear Material*, the 1963 *Vienna Convention on Civil Liability for Nuclear Damage*, the 1994 *Convention on Nuclear Safety*, and the 1997 *Joint Convention on the Safety of Spent Fuel Management and on the Safety of Radioactive Waste Management*.

IAEA's technical cooperation programme provides assistance in the form of in-country projects, experts, and training in the application of peaceful nuclear techniques. These help countries in such critical areas as water, health, nutrition, medicine and food production. Examples include work related to mutation breeding, through which beneficial varieties of crops have been developed using radiation-based technology, thereby improving food production. Another is the use of isotope hydrology to map underground aquifers, manage ground and surface water, detect and control pollution, and monitor dam leakage and safety, thus improving access to safe drinking water. The Agency also supplies radiotherapy equipment for use in medical treatment and trains staff to safely treat cancer patients in developing and middle-income countries.

IAEA collects and disseminates information on virtually every aspect of nuclear science and technology through its International Nuclear Information System, based in Vienna. With UNESCO, it operates the International Centre for Theoretical Physics in Trieste, Italy (*www.ictp.trieste.it*), and maintains several laboratories. IAEA works with FAO in research on atomic energy in food and agriculture, and with WHO on radiation in medicine and biology. Its Marine Environment Laboratory in Monaco carries out worldwide marine pollution studies with UNEP and UNESCO.

The **United Nations Scientific Committee on the Effects of Atomic Radiation (UNSCEAR)** (*www.unscear.org*), established in 1955, assesses and reports on the levels and effects of exposure to ionizing radiation. Governments and organizations worldwide rely on its estimates as the scientific basis for evaluating radiation risk, establishing radiation protection and safety standards, and regulating radiation sources.

IV.   HUMAN RIGHTS

On her sixteenth birthday, Malala Yousafzai spoke at the "Malala Day" UN Youth Assembly. The Secretary-General presented her with a leather-bound copy of the Charter of the United Nations, which is normally given only to heads of state. (12 July 2013, UN Photo/Eskinder Debebe)

One of the most significant achievements of the United Nations is the creation of a comprehensive body of human rights law (see *www.un.org/rights*)—a universal and internationally protected code to which all nations can subscribe and all people aspire. The United Nations has defined a broad range of internationally accepted rights, including civil, cultural, economic, political and social rights. It has also established mechanisms to promote and protect these rights and to assist states in carrying out their responsibilities.

The foundations of this body of law are the *Charter of the United Nations* and the *Universal Declaration of Human Rights*, adopted by the General Assembly in 1945 and 1948, respectively. Since then, the United Nations has gradually expanded human rights law to encompass specific standards for women, children, persons with disabilities, minorities and other vulnerable groups, who now possess rights that protect them from discrimination that had long been common in many societies.

Rights have been extended through groundbreaking General Assembly decisions that have gradually established their universality, indivisibility and interrelatedness with development and democracy. Education campaigns have informed the world's public of their inalienable rights, while numerous national judicial and penal systems have been enhanced through UN training programmes and technical advice. The UN machinery for monitoring compliance with human rights treaties has acquired a remarkable cohesiveness and weight among member states.

The United Nations High Commissioner for Human Rights works to strengthen and coordinate UN efforts for the protection and promotion of the human rights of all persons around the world. Human rights, however, is a central theme that unifies the Organization's work in the key areas of peace and security, development, humanitarian assistance, and economic and social affairs. As a result, virtually every UN body and specialized agency is involved to some degree in the protection of human rights.

Human rights instruments

At the San Francisco Conference in 1945 that established the United Nations, some 40 non-governmental organizations representing women, trade unions, ethnic organizations and religious groups joined forces with government delegations, mostly from smaller countries, and pressed for more specific language on human rights than had been proposed by other states. Their determined lobbying resulted in the inclusion of some provisions on human rights in the *Charter of the United Nations*, laying the foundation for the post-1945 era of international lawmaking.

Thus, the Preamble to the *Charter* explicitly reaffirms "faith in fundamental human rights, in the dignity and worth of the human person, in the equal rights of men and women and of nations large and small". Article 1 establishes that one of the four principal tasks of the United Nations is to promote and encourage "respect for human rights and for fundamental freedoms for all without distinction as to race, sex, language, or religion". Other provisions commit states to take action in cooperation with the United Nations to achieve universal respect for human rights.

International Bill of Human Rights

Three years after the United Nations was created, the General Assembly laid the cornerstone of contemporary human rights law: the *Universal Declaration of Human Rights (www.ohchr.org/EN/UDHR/Pages/UDHRIndex.aspx)*, intended as a "common standard of achievement for all peoples". It was adopted on 10 December 1948, the day now observed worldwide as **International Human Rights Day**. Its 30 articles spell out basic civil, cultural, economic, political and social rights that all human beings in every country must enjoy.

Articles 1 and 2 state that "all human beings are born equal in dignity and rights" and are entitled to all the rights and freedoms set forth in the *Declaration* "without distinction of any kind such as race, colour, sex, language, religion, political or other opinion, national or social origin, property, birth or other status".

Articles 3 to 21 set forth the civil and political rights to which all human beings are entitled, including:

- the right to life, liberty and security;
- freedom from slavery and servitude;
- freedom from torture or cruel, inhuman or degrading treatment or punishment;
- the right to recognition as a person before the law, the right to judicial remedy; freedom from arbitrary arrest, detention or exile; the right to a fair trial and public hearing by an independent and impartial tribunal; the right to be presumed innocent until proved guilty;
- freedom from arbitrary interference with privacy, family, home or correspondence; freedom from attacks upon honour and reputation; the right to protection of the law against such attacks;
- freedom of movement; the right to seek asylum; the right to a nationality;
- the right to marry and to found a family; the right to own property;
- freedom of thought, conscience and religion; freedom of opinion and expression;
- the right to peaceful assembly and association;
- the right to take part in government and to equal access to public service.

Articles 22 to 27 set forth the economic, social and cultural rights to which all human beings are entitled, including:

- the right to social security;
- the right to work; the right to equal pay for equal work; the right to form and join trade unions;
- the right to rest and leisure;
- the right to a standard of living adequate for health and well-being;
- the right to education;
- the right to participate in the cultural life of the community.

Finally, Articles 28 to 30 recognize that everyone is entitled to a social and international order in which the human rights set forth in the *Declaration* may be fully realized; that these rights may only be limited for the sole purpose of securing recognition and respect of the rights and freedoms of others and of meeting the requirements of morality, public order and the general welfare in a democratic society; and that each person has duties to the community in which she or he lives.

The provisions of the *Universal Declaration* are considered by scholars to have the weight of customary international law because they are so widely accepted and used to measure the conduct of states. Newly independent countries have cited the *Universal Declaration* or included its provisions in their basic laws or constitutions.

The broadest legally binding human rights agreements negotiated under UN auspices are the *International Covenant on Economic, Social and Cultural Rights* and the *International Covenant on Civil and Political Rights*. These agreements, adopted by the General Assembly in 1966, take the provisions of the *Universal Declaration* a step further by translating these rights into legally binding commitments, while committees of experts (treaty bodies) monitor compliance of states parties.

Together, the *Universal Declaration*, the *International Covenants* and the *First* and *Second Optional Protocols to the International Covenant on Civil and Political Rights* constitute the *International Bill of Human Rights*.

Economic, social and cultural rights

The *International Covenant on Economic, Social and Cultural Rights* entered into force in 1976, and had 160 states parties as of 31 May 2013. The human rights that the *Covenant* seeks to promote and protect include:

*   the right to work in just and favourable conditions;
*   the right to social protection, to an adequate standard of living and to the highest attainable standards of physical and mental well-being;
*   the right to education and the enjoyment of benefits of cultural freedom and scientific progress.

The *Covenant* provides for the realization of these rights without discrimination of any kind. The **Committee on Economic, Social and Cultural Rights** (*www2.ohchr.org/english/bodies/cescr*) was established in 1985 by the Economic and Social Council to monitor implementation of the *Covenant* by states parties. This 18-member body of experts studies reports periodically submitted by states parties in accordance with article 16 of the *Covenant* and discusses them with representatives of the states concerned. The Committee makes recommendations to states based on its review of their reports. It also adopts general comments which seek to outline the meaning of human rights or cross-cutting themes.

In 2008, a major new development occurred with regard to individual complaints. That year the General Assembly unanimously adopted an *Optional Protocol* to the *Covenant*, which provides the Committee on Economic, Social and Cultural Rights competence to receive and consider communications. The *Optional Protocol* entered into force on 5 May 2013; it had 10 states parties and 42 signatories.

Civil and political rights

The *International Covenant on Civil and Political Rights* and its *First Optional Protocol* entered into force in 1976. The *Covenant* had 167 states parties at the end of May 2013. The *Second Optional Protocol* was adopted in 1989.

The *Covenant* deals with such rights as freedom of movement; equality before the law; the right to a fair trial and presumption of innocence; freedom of thought, conscience and religion; freedom of opinion and expression; peaceful assembly; freedom of association; participation in public affairs and elections; and protection of minority rights. It prohibits arbitrary deprivation of life; torture, cruel or degrading treatment or punishment; slavery and forced labour; arbitrary arrest or detention; arbitrary interference with privacy; war propaganda; discrimination; and advocacy of racial or religious hatred.

The *Covenant* has two optional protocols. The *First Optional Protocol* (1966) provides the right of petition to individuals who claim to be victims of a violation of a right contained in the *Covenant*; it had 114 states parties as of 31 May 2013. The *Second Optional Protocol* (1989) establishes substantive obligations towards abolition of the death penalty; it had 76 states parties at the end of May 2013.

The *Covenant* established an 18-member **Human Rights Committee** *(www2. ohchr.org/english/bodies/hrc/index.htm)* which considers reports submitted periodically by states parties on measures taken in their countries to implement the provisions of the *Covenant*. For states parties to the *First Optional Protocol*, the Committee also considers communications from individuals who claim to be victims of violations of any of the rights set forth in the *Covenant*. The Committee considers such communications in closed meetings; all related communications and documents remain confidential. The findings of the Committee, however, are made public and are reproduced in its annual report to the General Assembly. The Committee also publishes its interpretation of the content of human rights provisions, known as 'general comments', on thematic issues or its methods of work.

Other conventions

The *Universal Declaration of Human Rights* has served as the inspiration for some 80 conventions and declarations that have been concluded within the United Nations on a wide range of issues. Among the earliest of these were conventions on the crime of genocide and on the status of refugees called for at the time, as the world had just emerged from the horrors of the Second World War, the Holocaust and the uprooting of millions of people. They have remained just as pertinent in the new millennium.

- The *Convention on the Prevention and Punishment of the Crime of Genocide* (1948), a direct response to the atrocities of the Second World War, defines the crime of genocide as the commission of certain acts with intent to destroy a national, ethnic, racial or religious group, and commits states to bringing to justice alleged perpetrators. It has 142 states parties.

- The *Convention relating to the Status of Refugees* (1951), also a direct response to the Second World War, defines the rights of refugees, especially their right not to be forcibly returned to countries where they are at risk. It also provides for their everyday lives, including their right to work, education, public assistance and social security, and their right to travel documents. The *Protocol relating to the Status of Refugees* (1967) ensures the universal application of the Convention, which was originally designed for people who became refugees as a result of the Second World War. At the end of May 2013, the *Convention* had 145 states parties and the *Protocol* had 146 states parties.

In parallel to the *International Covenants*, seven more so-called 'core' international human rights treaties (*http://www.ohchr.org/EN/ProfessionalInterest/Pages/CoreInstruments.aspx*) are monitored for compliance by states parties. Each of the treaties described below has established a committee of experts—usually referred to as a 'treaty body'—to monitor implementation of treaty provisions. Some of these treaties are supplemented by optional protocols dealing with specific concerns, including the possibility for individual persons to file a complaint if they believe they have been a victim of a human rights violation.

- The *International Convention on the Elimination of All Forms of Racial Discrimination* (1966) is accepted by 176 states parties. Based on the premise that any policy of superiority based on racial differences is unjustifiable, scientifically false and morally and legally condemnable, it defines 'racial discrimination' and commits states parties to take measures to abolish it in both law and practice. The *Convention* established a treaty body, the **Committee on the Elimination of Racial Discrimination**, to consider reports from states parties, as well as petitions from individuals alleging a violation of the *Convention*, if the state concerned has accepted this optional procedure of the *Convention*.

- The *Convention on the Elimination of All Forms of Discrimination against Women* (1979), with 187 states parties, guarantees women's equality before the law and specifies measures to eliminate discrimination against women with respect to political and public life, nationality, education, employment, health, marriage and the family. The **Committee on the Elimination of Discrimination against Women** is the treaty body that monitors implementation and considers reports from states parties. The *Optional Protocol* to the *Convention* (1999), with 104 states parties, allows individuals to submit to the Committee complaints on violations and provides the Committee with a mandate to conduct inquiries if information indicates grave or systematic violations of the *Convention*.

- The *Convention against Torture and Other Inhuman or Degrading Treatment or Punishment* (1984), with 153 states parties, defines torture as an international crime, holds states parties accountable for preventing it and requires them to punish perpetrators. No exceptional circumstances may be invoked to justify torture, nor may a torturer offer a defence of having acted under orders. The *Convention's* monitoring treaty body is the **Committee against Torture**. It reviews reports of states parties, receives and considers petitions from individuals whose states have accepted this procedure, and initiates investigations regarding countries where it believes that torture is serious and systematic. *The Optional Protocol* to the *Convention* (2002) created the **Subcommittee on Prevention of Torture** and allows in-country inspections of places of detention. The *Protocol* also provides for the establishment of national preventive mechanisms. It has 68 states parties.

- The *Convention on the Rights of the Child* (1989) recognizes the particular vulnerability of children. It brings together in one comprehensive code protections for children in all categories of human rights. The *Convention* guarantees non-discrimination and recognizes that the best interests of the child must guide all actions. Special attention is paid to children who are refugees or members of minorities. States parties are to provide guarantees for children's survival, development, protection and participation. The *Convention* is the most broadly ratified treaty, with 193 states parties. The **Committee on the Rights of the Child**, established by the *Convention*, oversees implementation and considers reports submitted by states parties. The *Convention* has three optional proto-cols: one on the involvement of children in armed conflict; another on the sale of children, child prostitution and child pornography; and another on a com-munications procedure that will allow children to submit complaints regarding violations of their rights under the *Convention*.

- The *International Convention on the Protection of the Rights of All Migrant Work-ers and Members of Their Families* (1990) defines basic rights of, and meas-ures to protect, migrant workers, whether documented or undocumented, throughout the process of migration. It entered into force in 2003 and has 46 states parties. Its monitoring treaty body is the **Committee on Migrant Workers**.

- The *Convention on the Rights of Persons with Disabilities* (2006) outlaws discrimi-nation against the world's 650 million persons with disabilities in all areas of life, including employment, education, health services, transportation and access to justice. It entered into force in 2008; as of 15 June 2013, 131 states and the European Union (EU) were parties to the *Convention*. Its monitoring body is the **Committee on the Rights of Persons with Disabilities**. An *Optional Protocol* to the *Convention* gives individuals recourse to that Committee when all national options have been exhausted. The *Optional Protocol* had 77 parties as of 15 June 2013.

- The *International Convention for the Protection of All Persons from Enforced Disappearance* (2006) prohibits the practice of enforced disappearance and calls on states parties to make it an offence under law. It also affirms the right of victims and their families to know the circumstances of such disappear-ances and the fate of the disappeared person, as well as to claim reparations. It entered into force in 2010; at the end of May 2013 it had 38 states parties.

The *Universal Declaration* and other UN instruments have also formed part of the background to several regional agreements, such as the *European Conven-tion on Human Rights,* the *American Convention on Human Rights* and the *African Charter of Human and Peoples' Rights.*

Other standards

The United Nations has adopted many other standards and rules on the protec-tion of human rights. These 'declarations', 'codes of conduct' and 'principles' are not treaties to which states become party. Nevertheless, they have a profound influ-ence, not least because they are carefully drafted by states and adopted by con-sensus. Some of the most important of these are described:

- The *Declaration on the Elimination of All Forms of Intolerance and of Discrimina-tion Based on Religion and Belief* (1981) affirms the right of everyone to freedom of thought, conscience and religion and the right not to be subject to discrimi-nation on the grounds of religion or other beliefs.

- The *Declaration on the Right to Development* (1986) established that right as "an inalienable human right by virtue of which each person and all peoples are entitled to participate in, contribute to and enjoy economic, social, cultural and political development in which all human rights and fundamental freedoms can be fully realized". It adds that "equality of opportunity for development is a prerogative both of nations and of individuals".

- The *Declaration on the Rights of Persons Belonging to National or Ethnic, Religious and Linguistic Minorities* (1992) proclaims the right of minorities to enjoy their own culture; to profess and practise their own religion; to use their own language; and to leave any country, including their own, and to return to their country. The *Declaration* calls for action by states to promote and protect these rights.
- The *Declaration on Human Rights Defenders* (1998) seeks to recognize, promote and protect the work of human rights activists all over the world. It enshrines the right of everyone—individually and in association with others—to promote and strive to protect human rights at the national and international levels, and to participate in peaceful activities against human rights violations. States are to take all necessary measures to protect human rights defenders against any violence, threat, retaliation, pressure or other arbitrary action.
- *The Declaration on the Rights of Indigenous Peoples* (2007) sets out the individual and collective rights of indigenous peoples, as well as their rights to culture, identity, language, employment, health, education and other benefits. It emphasizes the rights of indigenous peoples to maintain and strengthen their own institutions, cultures and traditions, and models of development. It prohibits discrimination against them and promotes their participation in public affairs.

Other important non-treaty standards include the *Standard Minimum Rules for the Treatment of Prisoners* (1957), the *Basic Principles on the Independence of the Judiciary* (1985), the *Basic Principles on the Role of Lawyers* (1990) and the *Body of Principles for the Protection of All Persons under Any Form of Detention or Imprisonment* (1988), among many others.

Human rights machinery

Human Rights Council

The **Human Rights Council** (*www.ohchr.org/EN/HRBodies/HRC*) is the main United Nations intergovernmental body responsible for promoting and protecting all human rights and fundamental freedoms. It was established by the General Assembly in 2006 to replace the 60-year-old Commission on Human Rights. The Council addresses human rights violations and makes corresponding recommendations. It responds to human rights emergencies, works to prevent abuses, provides overall policy guidance, develops new international norms, monitors the observance of human rights around the world, and assists states in fulfilling their human rights obligations. It provides an international forum where states (members and observers), intergovernmental organizations, national human rights institutions and NGOs can voice their concerns about human rights issues.

The Council's 47 members are elected directly and individually by secret ballot by the majority of the 193 members of the UN General Assembly. They serve for a three-year renewable term and cannot seek immediate re-election after two consecutive terms. The membership is based on equitable geographical distribution. Thirteen seats each are devoted to the Group of African States and the Group of Asian States; eight to the Group of Latin American and Caribbean States; seven to the Group of Western European and other States; and six to the Group of Eastern European States.

The Council meets regularly throughout the year. It holds no fewer than three sessions per year, for no less than 10 weeks in total. Special sessions can be requested at any time by a member state with the support of one third of the Council's members. In 2012, one special session was held to address the deteriorating human rights situation in the Syrian Arab Republic, where armed conflict between government and rebel forces continues unabated.

The most innovative feature of the Human Rights Council is the **Universal Periodic Review**. This unique mechanism involves a review of the human rights records of all 193 UN member states once every four years. The Review is a cooperative, state-driven process, under the auspices of the Council, which provides the opportunity for each state to present measures taken and challenges to be met to improve the human rights situation in their country and to meet their international obligations. The Review is designed to ensure universality and equality of treatment for every country.

The Council can rely on the independence and expertise of a wide range of experts and working groups. It can set up fact-finding missions to investigate alleged violations of human rights, provide assistance to states, engage in dialogue with governments to bring about needed improvements and condemn abuses. Through its complaint procedure, it can be seized of gross and systematic human rights violations by individuals, groups or NGOs.

The work of the Human Rights Council is also supported by the **Advisory Committee**. Composed of 18 experts, the Committee serves as the Council's 'think-tank' and provides it with expertise and advice on human rights issues such as missing persons, the right to food, leprosy-related discrimination and human rights education and training. In the performance of its mandate, the Committee interacts with states, intergovernmental organizations, national human rights institutions, NGOs and other civil society entities.

UN High Commissioner for Human Rights

The **United Nations High Commissioner for Human Rights** exercises principal responsibility for UN human rights activities. Appointed for a four-year term, the High Commissioner is charged with many tasks, including: promoting and protecting the effective enjoyment by all of all human rights; promoting international cooperation for human rights; stimulating and coordinating action on human rights in the UN system; assisting in the development of new human rights standards; and promoting the ratification of human rights treaties. The High Commissioner is also mandated to respond to serious violations of human rights and to undertake preventive action.

Under the direction and authority of the Secretary-General, the High Commissioner reports to the Human Rights Council and the General Assembly. With the aim of securing respect for human rights and preventing violations, the High Commissioner engages in dialogue with governments. Within the UN system, the High Commissioner works to strengthen and streamline the United Nations human rights machinery to make it more efficient and effective.

The **Office of the High Commissioner for Human Rights (OHCHR)** (*www.ohchr.org*) is the focal point for United Nations human rights activities. It serves as the secretariat for the Human Rights Council, the treaty bodies (expert committees that monitor treaty compliance) and other UN human rights organs. It also undertakes human rights field activities, and provides advisory services and technical assistance. In addition to its regular budget, some of the Office's activities are financed through extrabudgetary resources. The High Commissioner has taken specific steps to institutionalize cooperation and coordination with other UN bodies involved in human rights, such as the United Nations Children's Fund, the United Nations Educational, Scientific and Cultural Organization, the United Nations Development Programme, the Office of the United Nations High Commissioner for Refugees and the United Nations Volunteers programme. Similarly, the Office works in the area of peace and security in close cooperation with the corresponding departments of the UN Secretariat. The Office is also part of the Inter-Agency Standing Committee, which oversees the international response to humanitarian emergencies.

Special rapporteurs and working groups

The special rapporteurs and working groups on human rights (*www.ohchr.org/EN/ HRBodies/SP*) are on the front lines in the protection of human rights. They investigate violations and intervene in individual cases and emergency situations, in what are referred to as 'special procedures'. Human rights experts are independent. They serve in their personal capacity for a maximum of six years and are not remunerated. The number of such experts has grown steadily over the years. As of April 2013, there were 36 thematic and 13 country-specific special procedure mandates.

In preparing their reports to the Human Rights Council and the General Assembly, these experts use all reliable resources, including individual complaints and information from NGOs. They may also initiate 'urgent-action procedures' to intercede with governments at the highest level. A significant portion of their research is done in the field, where they meet with both authorities and victims, and gather on-site evidence. Their reports are made public, thus helping publicize violations and emphasize the responsibility of governments for the protection of human rights.

Country-specific special rapporteurs, independent experts and representatives currently report on Belarus, Cambodia, Côte d'Ivoire, Eritrea, the Democratic People's Republic of Korea, Haiti, Iran, Mali, Myanmar, Palestinian territories occupied since 1967, Somalia, the Sudan and Syria.

Thematic special rapporteurs, representatives and working groups currently report on adequate housing; people of African descent; arbitrary detention; the sale of children, child prostitution and child pornography; cultural rights; the promotion of a democratic and equitable international order; education; the environment; enforced or involuntary disappearances; summary executions; extreme poverty; the right to food; the effects of foreign debt on human rights; freedom of peaceful assembly and association; freedom of opinion and expression; freedom of religion or belief; physical and mental health; human rights defenders; independence of the judiciary; indigenous people; internally displaced persons; mercenaries; migrants; minority issues; the promotion of truth, justice, reparation and guarantees of non-recurrence; racism and racial discrimination; slavery; international solidarity and human rights; terrorism; torture; the management and disposal of hazardous substances and waste; trafficking in persons; transnational corporations; water and sanitation; discrimination against women; and violence against women.

Promoting and protecting human rights

The role and scope of UN action in promoting and protecting human rights continue to expand. The central mandate of the Organization is to ensure full respect for the human dignity of the "peoples of the United Nations", in whose name the *Charter of the United Nations* was written.

For the United Nations, education is a fundamental human right and one of the most effective instruments for the promotion of human rights. Human rights education, whether in formal or non-formal settings, seeks to advance a universal culture of human rights through innovative teaching methods, the spreading of knowledge and the modification of attitudes. During the United Nations Decade for Human Rights Education (1995–2004), for example, efforts were made to increase global awareness and foster a universal culture of human rights. The Decade led many countries to promote human rights education by including it in their school curricula and adopting national action plans.

Through its international machinery, the UN is working on many fronts:

• as *global conscience*—setting the pace in establishing international standards of acceptable behaviour by nations. It has kept the world's attention focused on practices that threaten to undermine human rights standards. The General Assembly, through a wide range of declarations and conventions, has underscored the universality of human rights principles.

• as *lawmaker*—giving impetus to an unprecedented codification of international law. Human rights pertaining to women, children, prisoners, detainees and persons with mental disabilities, as well as to such violations as genocide, racial discrimination and torture, are now a major feature of international law, which once focused almost exclusively on inter-state relations.

• as *monitor*—playing a central role in ensuring that human rights are not only defined but also protected. The *International Covenant on Civil and Political Rights* and that on *Economic, Social and Cultural Rights* (1966) are among the earliest examples of treaties that empower international bodies to monitor how states live up to their commitments. Treaty bodies, special rapporteurs and working groups of the Human Rights Council each have procedures and mechanisms to monitor compliance with international standards and to investigate alleged violations. Their decisions on specific cases carry a moral weight that few governments are willing to defy.

• as *nerve centre*—OHCHR receives communications from groups and individuals claiming violations of their human rights. More than 100,000 complaints are received every year. OHCHR refers these communications to the appropriate UN bodies and mechanisms, taking into account the implementation procedures established by conventions and resolutions. Requests for urgent intervention can be addressed to OHCHR by fax (41-22-917-9022) and e-mail (*petitions@ohchr.org*).

• as *defender*—when a rapporteur or the chairman of a working group learns that a serious human rights violation, such as torture or imminent extrajudicial execution, is about to occur, he or she may address an urgent message to the state concerned, requesting clarification and seeking guarantees that the alleged victim's rights will be protected.

- as *researcher*—compiling data that are indispensable to the development and application of human rights law. Studies and reports prepared by OHCHR at the request of UN bodies point the way towards new policies, practices and institutions to enhance respect for human rights.

- as *forum of appeal*—under the *First Optional Protocol to the International Covenant on Civil and Political Rights*, as well as the *International Convention on the Elimination of All Forms of Racial Discrimination*, the *Convention Against Torture*, the *Optional Protocol to the Convention on the Elimination of All Forms of Discrimination against Women*, the *Optional Protocol to the Convention on the Rights of Persons with Disabilities*, the *International Convention for the Protection of All Persons from Enforced Disappearance* and the *Optional Protocol to the International Covenant on Economic, Social and Cultural Rights*, individuals can bring complaints against states that have accepted the relevant appeal procedure, once all domestic remedies have been exhausted. The same will be possible in the future for children when the *Optional Protocol to the Convention on the Rights of the Child on a communications procedure* enters into force. In addition, the special procedures of the Human Rights Council deal with numerous complaints submitted annually by NGOs or individuals.

- as *fact-finder*—the Human Rights Council has mechanisms to monitor and report on the incidence of certain kinds of abuses, as well as on violations in a specific country. The special rapporteurs, representatives and working groups are entrusted with this politically sensitive, humanitarian and sometimes dangerous task. They gather facts, keep contact with local groups and government authorities, conduct on-site visits when governments permit, and make recommendations on how respect for human rights might be strengthened.

- as *discreet* diplomat—the Secretary-General and the UN High Commissioner for Human Rights raise human rights concerns with member states on a confidential basis on such issues as the release of prisoners and the commutation of death sentences. The Human Rights Council may ask the Secretary-General to intervene or send an expert to examine a specific human rights situation, with a view to preventing flagrant violations. The Secretary-General may also undertake quiet diplomacy in the exercise of his good offices to communicate the United Nations' legitimate concerns and curb abuses.

The right to development

The principle of equality of opportunity for development is deeply embedded in the *Charter of the United Nations* and the *Universal Declaration on Human Rights*. The *Declaration on the Right to Development,* adopted by the General Assembly in 1986, marked a turning point by proclaiming this an inalienable human right, by which each person and all peoples are entitled to participate in, contribute to and enjoy economic, social, cultural and political development. The right to development is given prominence in the 1993 *Vienna Declaration and Programme of Action* of the Second World Conference on Human Rights, and is cited in the outcomes of other major UN summits and conferences as well, including the 2000 *Millennium Declaration*. In 1998, the Commission on Human Rights established a working group to monitor progress, analyse obstacles and develop strategies for implementing the right to development.

The right to food

The right to food is a particular focus of the **Food and Agriculture Organization of the United Nations (FAO)** (*www.fao.org*). In support of that right, the FAO Council, in 2004, adopted its *Voluntary Guidelines to Support the Progressive Realisation of the Right to Adequate Food in the Context of National Food Security*. These 'Right to Food Guidelines' cover the full range of actions governments can consider in creating an environment that enables people to feed themselves in dignity—and to establish safety nets for those who are unable to do so. They also recommend measures to strengthen government accountability, while promoting integration of the human rights dimension in the work of agencies dealing with food and agriculture.

Labour rights

The **International Labour Organization (ILO)** (*www.ilo.org*) is the UN specialized agency entrusted with defining and protecting the rights of labour. Its tripartite **International Labour Conference**—made up of government, employer and worker representatives—had adopted 189 conventions and 202 recommendations as of 15 June 2013 on all aspects of work life, comprising a system of international labour law. While its recommendations provide guidance on policy, legislation and practice, its conventions create binding obligations for those states that ratify them.

Conventions and recommendations have been adopted on such matters as labour administration, industrial relations, employment policy, working conditions, social security, occupational safety and health. Some seek to ensure basic human rights in the workplace, while others address such issues as the employment of women and children, and such special categories as migrant workers and persons with disabilities (see *www.ilo.org/ilolex/english/index.htm*).

ILO's supervisory procedure to ensure that its conventions are applied both in law and in practice is based on objective evaluations by independent experts, and on the examination of cases by ILO's tripartite bodies. There is also a special procedure for investigating complaints of infringement of the freedom of association.

ILO has brought about many landmark conventions, including the following:

- *on forced labour* (1930); requires the suppression of forced or compulsory labour in all its forms;
- *on freedom of association and protection of the right to organize* (1948); establishes the right of workers and employers to form and join organizations without prior authorization, and lays down guarantees for the free functioning of such organizations;
- *on the right to organize and collective bargaining* (1949); provides for protection against anti-union discrimination, protection of workers' and employers' organizations, and measures to promote collective bargaining;
- *on equal remuneration* (1951); calls for equal pay and benefits for work of equal value;
- *on discrimination* (1958); calls for national policies to promote equality of opportunity and treatment, and to eliminate discrimination in the workplace on grounds of race, colour, sex, religion, political opinion, extraction or social origin;

- *on minimum age* (1973); aims at the abolition of child labour, stipulating that the minimum age for employment shall not be less than the age of completion of compulsory schooling;
- *on the worst forms of child labour* (1999); prohibits child slavery, debt bondage, prostitution and pornography, dangerous work, and forcible recruitment for armed conflict;
- *on maternity protection* (2000); provides standards for maternity leave, employment protection, medical benefits and breaks for breastfeeding.

In 2010, the ILO Conference adopted a groundbreaking international labour standard on HIV/AIDS, the first international human rights instrument to focus specifically on this issue in the world of work. It provides for antidiscrimination measures and emphasizes the importance of employment and income-generating activities for workers and people living with HIV.

The General Assembly has also taken a number of measures to protect the rights of migrant workers.

The struggle against discrimination

Apartheid

One of the great successes of the United Nations was the abolition of apartheid in South Africa, which demonstrated ways in which it can bring an end to major injustices in the world. Practically from its inception, the UN was involved in the struggle against apartheid, a system of institutionalized racial segregation and discrimination imposed by the South African government from 1948 until the early 1990s.

Apartheid was condemned by the UN in 1966 as a "crime against humanity" incompatible with the *Charter* and the *Universal Declaration of Human Rights*, and it remained on the General Assembly's agenda until its demise:

- During the 1950s, the General Assembly repeatedly appealed to the South African government to abandon apartheid in light of the principles of the *Charter*.
- In 1962, it established the United Nations Special Committee against Apartheid, to keep the racial policies of South Africa under review. The Special Committee became the focal point of international efforts to promote a comprehensive programme of action against apartheid.
- In 1963, the Security Council instituted a voluntary arms embargo against South Africa.
- The Assembly refused to accept South Africa's credentials to its regular sessions from 1970 through 1974. Following this ban, South Africa did not participate in further proceedings of the Assembly until the end of apartheid in 1994.
- In 1971, the Assembly called for a sports boycott of South Africa, a move that had strong impact on public opinion within the country and abroad.
- In 1973, the Assembly adopted the *International Convention on the Suppression and Punishment of the Crime of Apartheid*.
- In 1977, the Council made its arms embargo against South Africa mandatory, after determining that the country's aggressions against its neighbours and its potential nuclear capability constituted a threat to international peace and security. This was the first such action by the Council against a member state.

- In 1985, the Assembly adopted the *International Convention Against Apartheid in Sports*.
- Also in 1985, when the South African government proclaimed a state of emergency and escalated repression, the Security Council, for the first time, called on governments to take significant economic measures against South Africa under Chapter VII of the *Charter*.

The transition from the apartheid government to a non-racial democracy was facilitated by a 1990 national peace accord between the government and major political parties, with the full support of the UN. Two Security Council resolutions in 1992 emphasized the involvement of the international community in that transition. In 1992, the Security Council deployed the United Nations Observer Mission in South Africa (UNOMSA) to strengthen the structures of the accord. UNOMSA observed the 1994 elections that led to the establishment of a non-racial, democratic government. With the installation of that government and the adoption of the country's first non-racial, democratic constitution, apartheid came to an end.

When the newly elected President, Nelson Mandela, addressed the General Assembly in 1994, he noted that it was the first time in its 49 years that the Assembly had been addressed by a South African head of state drawn from among the African majority. Welcoming the vanquishing of apartheid, he observed: "That historic change has come about not least because of the great efforts in which the United Nations engaged to ensure the suppression of the apartheid crime against humanity."

Racism

In 1963, the General Assembly adopted the *United Nations Declaration on the Elimination of All Forms of Racial Discrimination*. The *Declaration* affirms the fundamental equality of all persons and confirms that discrimination between human beings on the grounds of race, colour or ethnic origin is a violation of the human rights proclaimed in the *Universal Declaration* and an obstacle to friendly and peaceful relations among nations and peoples. Two years later, the Assembly adopted the *International Convention on the Elimination of All Forms of Racial Discrimination*, which obliges states parties to adopt legislative, judicial, administrative and other measures to prevent and punish racial discrimination.

In 1993, the General Assembly proclaimed the Third Decade to Combat Racism and Racial Discrimination (1993–2003) and called on all states to take measures to combat new forms of racism, especially through laws, administrative measures, education and information. Also in 1993, the Commission on Human Rights appointed a special rapporteur on contemporary forms of racism, racial discrimination, xenophobia and related intolerance. The special rapporteur's mandate is to examine incidents of contemporary forms of racism worldwide; racial discrimination; any form of discrimination against Arabs, Muslims, Africans and people of African descent; xenophobia; antisemitism; and related expressions of intolerance, as well as governmental measures to overcome them.

The third World Conference against Racism, Racial Discrimination, Xenophobia and Related Intolerance, held in 2001, focused on practical measures to eradicate racism, including measures of prevention, education and protection; and adopted the *Durban Declaration and Programme of Action*. The Durban Review Conference, held in 2009, resulted in a 143-point declaration to combat racism and discrimination against minorities. It also warned against stereotyping people based on their religion and condemned antisemitism, islamophobia and christianophobia. On 22 September 2011, the General Assembly held a one-day high-level meeting at UN Headquarters in New York to commemorate the tenth anniversary of the adoption of the *Declaration and Programme of Action*. In a political declaration adopted at the meeting, world leaders proclaimed their determination to make the fight against racism, racial discrimination, xenophobia and related intolerance a high priority for their countries.

The rights of women

Equality for women has been a focus of the work of the United Nations since its founding in 1945. The UN has played a leading role in the global struggle for the promotion and protection of women's human rights; the elimination of all forms of discrimination and violence against women; and efforts to ensure that women have full and equal access to, and opportunities for participation in, politics and public life, including all aspects of economic and social development and decision-making.

In 2010, the General Assembly created **UN-Women** (*www.unwomen.org*), the **United Nations Entity for Gender Equality and the Empowerment of Women**. The move came as part of the UN reform agenda, bringing together resources and mandates for greater impact. UN-Women aims to significantly boost UN efforts to expand opportunities for women and girls and to tackle discrimination around the globe. Involvement in the formulation of global standards and norms is one of UN-Women's principal roles.

The **Commission on the Status of Women** has elaborated international guidelines and laws for women's equality and non-discrimination—notably, the 1979 *Convention on the Elimination of Discrimination against Women* and the 1999 *Optional Protocol* to the *Convention*. It also prepared the *Declaration on the Elimination of All Forms of Violence against Women,* adopted by the General Assembly in 1993, which, among other things, defined violence against women as physical, sexual or psychological violence occurring in the family or the community and perpetrated or condoned by the state.

The **Committee on the Elimination of Discrimination against Women**, a body made up of 23 independent experts, monitors implementation of the 1979 *Convention on the Elimination of Discrimination against Women* by states parties. It considers reports submitted by states parties to assess their progress in giving form to the principle of equality of women and men. The Committee can also examine individual communications and carry out inquiries under the provisions of the *Convention's Optional Protocol*. It makes recommendations on any issues affecting women to which it believes states parties should devote more attention, such as violence against women.

In line with international human rights standards, the Secretary-General's **UNiTE to End Violence against Women** campaign (*http://www.un.org/en/women/ endviolence/index.shtml*) works to raise public awareness and increase political will and resources for preventing and ending all forms of violence against women and girls in all parts of the world. UNiTE supports the efforts of women's and civil society organizations and engages the private sector to achieve five goals by the end of the campaign in 2015: the adoption and enforcement of national laws to address and punish all forms of violence against women and girls; the adoption of national action plans; the establishment of data collection on the prevalence of various forms of violence against women and girls; the establishment of national and local campaigns on preventing violence and in supporting women and girls who have been abused; and addressing the problem of sexual violence in conflict situations.

The rights of children

Millions of children die every year from malnutrition and disease. Countless others become victims of war, natural disaster, HIV/AIDS and extreme forms of violence, exploitation and abuse. Millions of children, especially girls, do not have access to quality education. The **United Nations Children's Fund (UNICEF)**, as well as OHCHR and other UN agencies, strive to sustain global commitment to the *Convention on the Rights of the Child*, which embodies universal ethical principles and international legal standards of behaviour towards children.

The **Committee on the Rights of the Child**, established under the *Convention*, is a body of 18 independent experts that meets regularly to monitor the progress made by states parties in fulfilling their obligations under the *Convention* and makes recommendations to governments on ways to meet those obligations. The Committee also issues its interpretation of the *Convention's* provisions in the form of general comments.

The General Assembly in 2000 adopted two *Optional Protocols* to the *Convention*: one prohibits the recruitment of children under 18 into armed forces or their participation in hostilities; the other strengthens prohibitions and penalties concerning the sale of children, child prostitution and child pornography. A third *Optional Protocol*, adopted by the Assembly in 2011, provides a communications procedure that will allow individual children to submit complaints regarding violations of their rights under the *Convention* and the first two *Protocols*. The *Optional Protocol* on a communications procedure has 36 signatories and 6 states parties; it will enter into force after 10 UN member states have become parties.

Concerning child labour, the UN seeks to protect children from exploitation and hazardous conditions that endanger their physical and mental development; to ensure children's access to quality education, nutrition and health care; and, in the long term, progressively eliminate child labour. The **International Programme on the Elimination of Child Labour**, an ILO initiative, seeks to raise awareness and mobilize action through the provision of technical cooperation. Direct interventions focus on the prevention of child labour; the search for alternatives, including decent employment for parents; and rehabilitation, education and vocational training for children. UNICEF supports programmes providing education, counselling and care to children working in very hazardous or abusive conditions, and vigorously advocates against the violation of their rights.

Both the General Assembly and the Human Rights Council have urged governments to take action to protect and promote the rights of children, particularly children in difficult situations. They have called on states to implement programmes and measures that provide children with special protection and assistance, including access to health care, education and social services, as well as (where appropriate) voluntary repatriation, reintegration, family tracing and family reunification, in particular for children who are unaccompanied. The two bodies have also called on states to ensure that the best interests of the child are accorded primary consideration.

The special rapporteur on the sale of children, child prostitution and child pornography, as well as the special representatives of the Secretary-General on violence against children and for children and armed conflict, report regularly to the General Assembly and to the Human Rights Council. The latter also reports to the Security Council.

The post of special representative of the Secretary-General on violence against children was established in 2007, in the wake of the *World Report on Violence against Children*, which was presented to the General Assembly the previous year. The *Report* exposed for the first time the horrendous scale and impact of all forms of violence against children, highlighting the universality and magnitude of the problem in different settings: the home and family; schools; care and justice institutions; the workplace; and the community. Its 12 overarching recommendations and a number of specific recommendations have provided a comprehensive framework for follow-up action. The mandate of the special representative of the Secretary-General for children and armed conflict, established in 1996 by the Assembly for a period of three years, has been renewed ever since, most recently in 2012, for a further three-year period.

The rights of minorities

Some 1 billion people worldwide belong to minority groups, many of which are subject to discrimination and exclusion, and are often the victims of conflict. Meeting the legitimate aspirations of national, ethnic, religious and linguistic groups strengthens the protection of basic human rights, protects and accommodates cultural diversity, and increases the stability of society as a whole. The United Nations has from its inception placed minority rights high on its human rights agenda. The protection of the human rights of members of minority groups is guaranteed specifically in article 27 of the *International Covenant on Civil and Political Rights*, as well as in the principles of non-discrimination and participation, which are basic to all United Nations human rights law. The adoption of the *Declaration on the Rights of Persons Belonging to National or Ethnic, Religious and Linguistic Minorities* by the General Assembly in 1992 gave new impetus to the UN human rights agenda.

The **Forum on Minority Issues** was established in 2007 to provide a platform for promoting dialogue and cooperation on issues pertaining to national or ethnic, religious and linguistic minorities, and to provide thematic contributions and expertise to the work of the Independent Expert on minority issues. The Forum identifies and analyses best practices, challenges, opportunities and initiatives for the further implementation of the *Declaration*. It meets annually for two days of thematic discussions. The independent expert on minority issues guides the work of the Forum and reports its recommendations to the Human Rights Council. The president of the Human Rights Council appoints for each session, on the basis of regional rotation and in consultation with regional groups, a Forum chairperson selected from experts on minority issues.

Indigenous peoples

The United Nations has increasingly taken up the cause of indigenous peoples, who constitute one of the world's most disadvantaged groups. Indigenous peoples are also called first peoples, tribal peoples, aboriginal peoples and autochthons. There are at least 5,000 indigenous peoples, made up of some 370 million individuals living in over 70 countries on five continents. Often excluded from decision-making processes, many have been marginalized, exploited, forcefully assimilated, and subjected to repression, torture and murder when they speak out in defence of their rights. Fearing persecution, they often become refugees and sometimes must hide their identity, abandoning their languages and traditional way of life.

In 1982, the Subcommission on Human Rights established a working group on indigenous populations, which prepared a draft *Declaration on the Rights of Indigenous Peoples*. In 1992, the Earth Summit heard the collective voice of indigenous peoples as they expressed their concerns about the deteriorating state of their lands, territories and environment. Various UN bodies—including UNDP, UNICEF, IFAD, UNESCO, the World Bank and WHO—developed programmes to improve their health and literacy and combat degradation of their ancestral lands and territories. Subsequently, the General Assembly proclaimed 1993 the International Year of the World's Indigenous People, followed by the International Decade of the World's Indigenous People (1995–2004) and the **Second International Decade of the World's Indigenous People** (2005–2015) (*social.un.org/index/Indigenous-Peoples/SecondDecade.aspx*).

This increased focus on indigenous issues led, in 2000, to the establishment of the **Permanent Forum on Indigenous Issues** (*social.un.org/index/Indigenous-Peoples.aspx*) as a subsidiary organ of ECOSOC. The 16-expert forum, composed of an equal number of governmental and indigenous experts, advises ECOSOC; helps coordinate related UN activities; and considers indigenous concerns relating to economic and social development, culture, education, the environment, health and human rights. In addition, an Inter-Agency Support Group on Indigenous Issues was established.

The landmark *Declaration on the Rights of Indigenous Peoples* was adopted by the General Assembly in 2007. The *Declaration* sets out the individual and collective rights of indigenous peoples, including their rights to culture, identity, language, employment, health and education. It emphasizes their rights to maintain and strengthen their own institutions, cultures and traditions, and to pursue their development in keeping with their own needs and aspirations. It also prohibits discrimination against them, and promotes their full and effective participation in all matters that concern them, including their right to remain distinct and to pursue their own visions of economic and social development.

OHCHR has played a pivotal role in these developments, and the implementation of the *Declaration* remains a priority for the Office. It contributes actively to the UN Inter-Agency Support Group on Indigenous Issues. It conducts training on indigenous issues for UN country teams and for OHCHR field presences. OHCHR builds capacities among indigenous peoples and services the Board of Trustees of the Voluntary Fund for Indigenous Populations. The Fund, composed of five representatives of indigenous communities, supports the participation of indigenous communities and organizations in the annual sessions of the Permanent Forum on Indigenous Issues and the **Expert Mechanism on the Rights of Indigenous Peoples**. Established in 2007, the five-expert Mechanism assists the Human Rights Council on issues related to indigenous rights. OHCHR also supports the Expert Mechanism and assists the special rapporteur on the situation of human rights and fundamental freedoms of indigenous peoples. It carries out country-specific and regional activities to advance the rights of indigenous peoples. The Office provides support for legislative initiatives and pursues thematic work on issues such as extractive industries and the rights of isolated indigenous peoples.

Persons with disabilities

Some 650 million persons—approximately 10 per cent of the world's population—have some type of physical, mental or sensory impairment. Around 80 per cent of persons with disabilities live in developing countries. They are often excluded from the mainstream of society. Discrimination takes various forms, ranging from the denial of education or work opportunities to more subtle forms, such as segregation and isolation through the imposition of physical and social barriers. Society also suffers, as the loss of their enormous potential impoverishes the world. Changing the perception and concept of disability requires changing values and increasing understanding at all levels of society.

Since its inception, the United Nations has sought to advance the status of persons with disabilities and to improve their lives (see *www.un.org/disabilities*). Its concern for the well-being and rights of persons with disabilities is rooted in its founding principles of human rights, fundamental freedoms and equality of all human beings.

In the 1970s, the concept of human rights for persons with disabilities gained wider international acceptance. Through its adoption of the *Declaration on the Rights of Mentally Retarded Persons* (1971) and the *Declaration on the Rights of Disabled Persons* (1975), the General Assembly established the standards for equal treatment and equal access to services, thus accelerating the social integration of persons with disabilities. The International Year of Disabled Persons (1981) led to the adoption by the General Assembly of the *World Programme of Action Concerning Disabled Persons,* a policy framework for promoting the rights of persons with disabilities. The programme identifies two goals for international cooperation: equality of opportunity, and full participation of persons with disabilities in social life and development.

A major outcome of the United Nations Decade of Disabled Persons (1983–1992) was the adoption by the General Assembly in 1993 of the *Standard Rules on the Equalization of Opportunities for Persons with Disabilities,* which serve as an instrument for policymaking and provide a basis for technical and economic co-operation. A special rapporteur monitors the implementation of the *Rules* and reports annually to the **Commission for Social Development**, a subsidiary body of ECOSOC.

A further set of standards for the protection of people with mental illness—the *Principles for the Protection of Persons with Mental Illness and the Improvement of Health Care*—was adopted by the General Assembly in 1991. Three years later, the Assembly endorsed a long-term strategy to further the implementation of the *World Programme of Action*, with the goal of "a society for all".

The *Convention on the Rights of Persons with Disabilities* and its *Optional Protocol* were adopted in 2006 and opened for signature in 2007. As of 15 June 2013, there were 155 signatories to the *Convention*, 91 signatories to the *Optional Protocol*, 132 parties to the *Convention* and 77 to the *Optional Protocol*. This is the highest number in history of signatures and ratifications to a UN convention since its opening day. The *Convention* entered into force in 2008. It is the first comprehensive human rights treaty of the 21st century and the first human rights convention to be open for signature by regional integration organizations.

The *Convention* marks a paradigm shift in attitudes and approaches to persons with disabilities. It takes the movement to new heights from viewing persons with disabilities as 'objects' of charity, medical treatment and social protection towards viewing them as 'subjects' with rights, who are capable of making decisions based on their free and informed consent, as well as being active members of society. The secretariat for the *Convention's* international monitoring mechanisms, including the **Committee on the Rights of Persons with Disabilities**, lies with OHCHR, while the UN Department for Economic and Social Affairs organizes the conference of states parties in New York.

A growing body of data reveals the need to address disability issues in the context of national development, within the broad framework of human rights. The UN works with governments, NGOs, academic institutions and professional societies to promote awareness and build national capacities for broad human rights approaches to persons with disabilities. In doing so, it links disability issues with the international development agenda, including the MDGs. Growing public support for disability action has focused on the need to improve information services, outreach and institutional mechanisms to promote equal opportunity. The UN is involved in helping countries strengthen their national capacities to promote such action in their overall development plans.

Migrant workers

More than 175 million people—including migrant workers, refugees, asylum-seekers, permanent immigrants and others—live and work in a country other than that of their birth or citizenship. Many of them are migrant workers. The term 'migrant worker' is defined in article 2 of the *International Convention on the Protection of the Rights of All Migrant Workers and Members of Their Families (Migrant Workers Convention)* as "a person who is to be engaged or has been engaged in a remunerated activity in a State of which he or she is not a national". The *Convention* breaks new ground in defining those rights that apply to certain categories of migrant workers and their families, including: frontier workers; seasonal workers; seafarers; workers on offshore installations; itinerant workers; migrants employed for a specific project; and self-employed workers.

The *Migrant Workers Convention* was adopted by the General Assembly in 1990, following 10 years of negotiations. It covers the rights of both documented and undocumented migrant workers and their families. It makes it illegal to expel migrant workers on a collective basis or to destroy their identity documents, work permits or passports. It entitles migrant workers to receive the same remuneration, social benefits and medical care as nationals; to join or take part in trade unions; and, upon ending their employment, to transfer earnings, savings and personal belongings. It also grants children of migrant workers the right to registration of birth and nationality, as well as access to education. The *Convention*, which entered into force in 2003, has 35 signatories and 46 parties. States parties monitor implementation of the *Convention* through the **Committee on Migrant Workers**.

The inter-agency **Global Migration Group** brings together 14 partners (12 UN agencies, the World Bank and the International Organization for Migration) to promote the application of international instruments and norms relating to migration, and to encourage the adoption of coherent, comprehensive and better coordinated approaches to international migration.

Administration of justice

The United Nations is committed to strengthening the protection of human rights in the judicial process. When individuals are under investigation by state authorities, or when they are arrested, detained, charged, tried or imprisoned, there is a need to ensure that the law is applied with due regard for the protection of human rights.

The UN has worked to develop standards and codes that serve as models for national legislation. They cover such issues as the treatment of prisoners, the protection of detained juveniles, the use of firearms by police, the conduct of law enforcement officials, the role of lawyers and prosecutors, and the independence of the judiciary. Many of these standards have been developed through the United Nations Commission on Crime Prevention and Criminal Justice and the Centre for International Crime Prevention.

OHCHR has a programme of technical assistance that focuses on human rights training for legislators, judges, lawyers, law enforcement officers, prison officials and the military.

At the end of May 2013, there were 25 international instruments relating to the administration of justice. These include: *Standard Minimum Rules for the Treatment of Prisoners; Basic Principles for the Treatment of Prisoners; Body of Principles for the Protection of All Persons under Any Form of Detention or Imprisonment; United Nations Rules for the Protection of Juveniles Deprived of their Liberty; Safeguards Guaranteeing Protection of the Rights of those Facing the Death Penalty; Code of Conduct for Law Enforcement Officials; Basic Principles on the Use of Force and Firearms by Law Enforcement Officials; Basic Principles on the Role of Lawyers; Guidelines on the Role of Prosecutors; Basic Principles and Guidelines on the Right to a Remedy and Reparation;* and the *International Convention for the Protection of All Persons from Enforced Disappearance.* (For a complete list, see *www.ohchr.org/EN/Professional-Interest/Pages/UniversalHumanRightsInstruments.aspx.*)

OHCHR priorities

Despite the efforts of the United Nations, massive and widespread violations of human rights continue worldwide. More than six decades after the adoption of the *Universal Declaration of Human Rights*, violations across the broad spectrum of human rights still dominate the news. At least part of this can be attributed to the heightened awareness of human rights and the stepped-up monitoring of problem areas. Particular examples are child abuse, violence against women and abuses that until only recently were considered acceptable behaviour by traditional standards.

Indeed, measures to promote and protect human rights are stronger than ever, and are increasingly linked to the fight for social justice, economic development and democracy. Human rights has become a cross-cutting theme in all UN policies and programmes. The vigorous actions taken by OHCHR, together with enhanced cooperation and coordination among UN partners, are tangible expressions of the strengthened ability of the UN system to fight for human rights.

The **Programme of Technical Cooperation for Human Rights**, supervised by OHCHR, manages a range of projects to promote democracy, development and human rights, and strengthen the capacity of states to advance such rights in their laws and practice. It encourages the ratification and supports the implementation of international human rights instruments. The Programme focuses on four core areas: the administration of justice, human rights education, national institutions and national plans of action. It is funded primarily by contributions from the Voluntary Fund for Technical Cooperation in the Field of Human Rights (*www2. ohchr.org/English/about/funds/coop*).

OHCHR's Management Plan for 2012–2013 contains the following thematic priorities:

- countering discrimination, in particular racial discrimination, discrimination on the grounds of sex, religion and against others who are marginalized;
- combating impunity and strengthening accountability, the rule of law and democratic society;
- pursuing economic, social and cultural rights, and combating inequalities and poverty, including in the context of the economic, food and climate crises;
- protecting human rights in the context of migration;
- protecting human rights in situations of violence and insecurity;
- strengthening human rights mechanisms and the progressive development of international human rights law.

V. HUMANITARIAN ACTION

Boys receive food aid from the World Food Programme in Al-Shaddadi, Syrian Arab Republic, a contested hotspot in that country's internal armed conflict. (5 February 2013, WFP/Abeer Etefa)

S ince it first coordinated humanitarian relief operations in Europe following the devastation and massive displacement of people in the Second World War, the United Nations has led the international community in responding to natural and man-made disasters that are beyond the capacity of national authorities alone. Today, the Organization is a major provider of emergency relief and longer-term assistance, a catalyst for action by governments and relief agencies, and an advocate for people affected by emergencies (see *www.un.org/en/humanitarian/index.shtml*).

Man-made disasters and natural calamities have driven millions from their homes in recent years. The displacement of entire populations as a result of war and insurgency in Afghanistan, Somalia, the Syrian Arab Republic and other countries continues to concern the international community. Moreover, 3 of the 10 deadliest natural disasters of the last 100 years occurred in the past decade alone—the 2004 Indian Ocean tsunami, the 2008 Nargis cyclone in Myanmar, and the 2010 earthquake in Haiti. Together, these calamities claimed over 600,000 lives. More than 98 per cent of those killed in natural disasters in the last decade were in developing countries—an overwhelming figure that indicates how poverty, population pressures and environmental degradation exacerbate human suffering.

Confronted with conflict and the escalating human and financial cost of natural disasters, the UN engages on two fronts. On one hand, it brings immediate relief to those who have been affected, primarily through its operational agencies; on the other hand, it seeks more effective strategies to prevent emergencies from arising in the first place.

When disaster strikes, the UN and its agencies rush to deliver humanitarian assistance. The January 2010 earthquake in Haiti killed 220,000 people and rendered 1.5 million others homeless. Despite its own loss of 102 staff members, the United Nations completed a needs assessment within 72 hours and deployed relief teams to the field. The UN and its Stabilization Mission in Haiti (MINUSTAH), working with international humanitarian partners, helped provide shelter for the homeless, as well as food, water and medical assistance for millions. As of December 2012, 80 per cent of those displaced into camps following the earthquake had left, but some 350,000 people continued to live in the camps. MINSUTAH also mobilizes logistical resources to assist the Haitian government and its UN system partners in their efforts to contain and reverse the devastating cholera epidemic that began in 2010.

In Pakistan at the end of 2010, hundreds of thousands people displaced after the summer's floods remained in camps, and thousands more were cut off from assistance. The United Nations Children's Fund (UNICEF) and its partners provided clean water to 2.8 million people daily, as well as sanitation facilities for 1.5 million. UNICEF also set up 1,550 temporary learning centres to educate children. Together with the World Health Organization (WHO), it supplied vaccines for more than 9 million children, while the United Nations Population Fund (UNFPA) coordinated interventions to prevent and respond to gender-based violence among the affected population.

The UN sent a disaster team to assist the Japanese government with relief efforts following the earthquake and tsunami that struck Japan and caused catastrophic damage to the Fukushima nuclear plant in March 2011. WFP supported government delivery of relief items, while FAO, WHO and the International Atomic Energy Agency (IAEA) moved to address related food safety issues. IAEA helped monitor radiation near the plant, and continues to support the Fukushima Prefecture in remediation and decontamination, management of waste generated during remediation activities, radiological mapping and radiation monitoring.

In 2012, the Central Emergency Response Fund, managed by the Office for the Coordination of Humanitarian Affairs, allocated $319 million for rapid response operations. More than $40 million was allocated to South Sudan to address a worsening humanitarian situation resulting from armed conflict, displacement and food insecurity. Through other means, such as the **Humanitarian Early Warning Service** (*www.hewsweb.org*) and the **United Nations International Strategy for Disaster Reduction (ISDR)** (*www.unisdr.org*), the UN works to prevent humanitarian crises and mitigate their effects. FAO monitors impending famines, as well as other food and agricultural concerns, while the World Meteorological Organization carries out tropical cyclone forecasting and drought monitoring. The United Nations Development Programme assists disaster-prone countries in developing contingency planning and other preparedness measures.

Coordinating humanitarian action

Since the 1990s, the world has seen an upsurge in the number and intensity of civil wars. These have caused large-scale humanitarian crises—with extensive loss of life, massive displacements of people and widespread damage to societies in complicated political and military environments. To address these complex emergencies, the United Nations has considerably upgraded its capacity to respond quickly and effectively. In 1991, the General Assembly established an inter-agency standing committee to coordinate the international response to humanitarian crises. The **United Nations Emergency Relief Coordinator** is the Organization's focal point for this endeavour, acting as the system's principal policy adviser, coordinator and advocate on humanitarian emergencies. The Emergency Relief Coordinator heads the **Office for the Coordination of Humanitarian Affairs (OCHA)** (*www.ochaonline.un.org*), which coordinates assistance in humanitarian crises that go beyond the capacity and mandate of any single agency.

Usually there are many actors in the international community—including governments, non-governmental organizations (NGOs) and UN agencies—who seek to respond simultaneously to complex emergencies. OCHA works with them to ensure that there is a coherent framework within which everyone can contribute promptly and effectively to the overall effort. When an emergency strikes, OCHA coordinates the international response. It determines priorities for action through consultations with member states and with the **Inter-Agency Standing Committee (IASC)** (*www.humanitarianinfo.org/iasc*) at Headquarters and in the field. As the primary mechanism for the inter-agency coordination of humanitarian assistance, the IASC engages key UN and non-UN humanitarian partners in the international community. OCHA then provides support for the coordination of activities in the affected country. For example, OCHA ensures that military resources—when available and appropriate—are effectively used to respond to humanitarian emergencies.

OCHA maintains an in-house emergency response capacity, supported by a 24-hour monitoring and alert system. UN disaster assessment and coordination teams can be dispatched within 12 to 24 hours of a natural disaster or sudden-onset emergency to gather information, assess needs and coordinate international assistance. It also operates through a network of regional offices and field offices, humanitarian coordinators and country teams. The humanitarian coordinator has overall responsibility for ensuring coherence of relief efforts in the field. By bringing together needs assessments, contingency planning and the formulation of programmes, OCHA supports the humanitarian coordinator and the operational agencies that deliver assistance.

The Office also helps its IASC partners and the humanitarian coordinator to mobilize resources by launching consolidated inter-agency appeals for contributions. It organizes donor meetings and follow-up arrangements, monitors the status of contributions in response to its appeals, and issues situation reports to keep donors and others updated on developments. Between 1992 and 2012, OCHA raised more than $42 billion for emergency assistance, through a total of 330 consolidated and flash appeals.

OCHA's **Central Emergency Response Fund (CERF)** was launched in March 2006 as an improved financing mechanism to facilitate immediate response to humanitarian emergencies. It was established in the aftermath of a string of extremely destructive recent natural disasters that occurred with little warning and demanded rapid response for emergency relief and recovery. These included the December 2004 Indian Ocean earthquake-tsunami, the October 2005 South Asian earthquake, a record-breaking hurricane season, and a major landslide in the Philippines in February 2006. More than 40 UN member states, together with other public and private donors, pledged more than $384 million for 2013 during the annual CERF High-Level Conference in December 2012. Since its establishment in 2006, CERF has allocated nearly $3 billion to humanitarian agencies operating in 87 countries.

OCHA also works with its partners in the humanitarian community to build consensus around policies, and to identify specific humanitarian issues arising from operational experiences in the field. It tries to ensure that major humanitarian issues are addressed—including those that fall between the mandates of humanitarian bodies. By advocating on humanitarian issues, OCHA gives voice to otherwise unheard victims of crises, and ensures that the views and concerns of the humanitarian community are reflected in overall efforts towards recovery and peacebuilding. In this way, OCHA also promotes greater respect for humanitarian norms and principles, and draws attention to such specific issues as access to affected populations; the humanitarian impact of sanctions; anti-personnel landmines; and the unchecked proliferation of small arms.

To support humanitarian advocacy, policymaking and emergency coordination, OCHA has developed a robust set of online tools. OCHA manages **ReliefWeb** (*www.reliefweb.int*)—the world's foremost humanitarian website—providing the latest information on emergencies worldwide. It also hosts IRIN (*www.irinnews.org*), a news service that offers accurate and impartial reporting and analysis about sub-Saharan Africa, the Middle East, Asia and the Americas.

Humanitarian assistance and protection

Three United Nations entities—UNICEF, WFP and UNHCR—have primary roles in providing protection and assistance in humanitarian crises.

Children and women constitute the majority of refugees and displaced persons. In acute emergencies, the **United Nations Children's Fund (UNICEF)** works alongside other relief agencies to help re-establish basic services such as water and sanitation; set up schools; and provide immunization services, medicines and other supplies to uprooted populations. UNICEF also consistently urges governments and warring parties to act more effectively to protect children. Its programmes in conflict zones have included the negotiation of ceasefires to facilitate the provision of key services such as child immunization. To this end, UNICEF has pioneered the concept of 'children as zones of peace' and created 'days of tranquillity' and 'corridors of peace' in war-affected regions. Special programmes assist traumatized children and help reunite unaccompanied children with parents or extended families. UNICEF responded to 286 humanitarian situations in 79 countries in 2012, and organizational spending on humanitarian action totalled $809 million.

The **World Food Programme (WFP)** provides fast, efficient relief to millions of people who are victims of natural or man-made disasters, including most of the world's refugees and internally displaced persons. Such crises consume the largest part of WFP's financial and human resources. A decade ago, two thirds of food aid provided by WFP was used to help people become self-reliant. Today, three quarters of WFP resources go to victims of humanitarian crises. In 2012, WFP delivered 3.5 million metric tons of food assistance to 97.2 million people in 80 countries. Beneficiaries included internally displaced persons, refugees, children orphaned by AIDS, and victims of conflict and natural disasters such as floods, drought and earthquakes. When war or disaster strikes, WFP responds quickly with emergency relief, then mounts programmes to facilitate smooth and effective recovery aimed at rebuilding lives and livelihoods. WFP is also responsible for mobilizing food and funds for all large-scale refugee-feeding operations managed by the Office of the United Nations High Commissioner for Refugees.

Rural populations in the developing world are often the most vulnerable to disasters, with most of these communities dependent on agriculture for their food security and livelihoods. The expertise of the **Food and Agriculture Organization of the United Nations (FAO)** in farming, livestock, fisheries and forestry is crucial in emergency relief and rehabilitation. FAO assists countries in preventing, mitigating, preparing for and responding to disasters. Its **Global Information and Early Warning System** (*www.fao.org/giews/english/index.htm*) provides regular and updated information on the global food situation. Together with WFP, FAO carries out assessments of the food situation in food-insecure countries following man-made or natural disasters. Based on these assessments, emergency food aid operations are prepared and jointly approved. Its work in post-disaster and complex emergency situations emphasizes the protection and rehabilitation of agricultural livelihoods. FAO aims to restore local food production, providing an exit from food aid and other forms of assistance, bolstering self-reliance and reducing the need for relief and coping strategies.

The **World Health Organization (WHO)** focuses on assessing the health needs of those affected by emergencies and disasters, providing health information and assisting in coordination and planning. WHO carries out emergency programmes in such areas as nutritional and epidemiological surveillance, control of epidemics, immunizations, management of essential drugs and medical supplies, reproductive health and mental health. It makes special efforts to eradicate polio and to control tuberculosis and malaria in countries affected by emergencies.

The **United Nations Population Fund (UNFPA)** also moves quickly when emergency strikes. Pregnancy-related deaths and sexual violence soar in times of upheaval, while reproductive health services often become unavailable. Young people become more vulnerable to HIV infection and sexual exploitation, and many women lose access to family planning services. In emergencies, UNFPA acts to protect the reproductive health of communities in crisis, and continues to provide assistance as these communities move beyond the acute phase into reconstruction efforts.

The **United Nations Development Programme (UNDP)** is the agency responsible for coordinating activities for natural disaster mitigation, prevention and preparedness. Governments frequently call on UNDP to help design rehabilitation programmes and direct donor aid. UNDP and humanitarian agencies work together to integrate concern for recovery and transitional and long-term development in their relief operations. UNDP also supports programmes for the demobilization of former combatants, comprehensive mine action, the return and reintegration of refugees and internally displaced persons, and the restoration of the institutions of governance.

To ensure that resources provided have maximum impact, each project is carried out in consultation with local and national government officials. UNDP offers rapid assistance to entire communities, while helping to establish the social and economic foundations for lasting peace, development, and the alleviation of poverty. This community-based approach has helped provide urgent and lasting relief for hundreds of thousands of victims of war and civil upheaval. Today, many conflict-scarred communities have improved their living standards thanks to UN-led training programmes, credit schemes and infrastructure projects.

Protecting humanitarian workers

United Nations personnel and other humanitarian workers in the field are all too often subject to violent attacks. Over the years, scores have been killed, taken hostage or detained while working in conflict areas (*www.un.org/en/memorial*). Violent incidents against UN staff have included armed robbery, assault and rape. The heightened visibility of UN personnel places them at substantial risk of being targeted. In the past ten years, this danger was made real on 19 August 2003, when terrorists bombed UN headquarters in Baghdad, leaving 22 dead and 150 injured. Among those killed was UN High Commissioner for Human Rights Sergio Vieira de Mello, on assignment as head of the mission there. It was the most devastating single attack on UN civilian staff in the Organization's history.

On 11 December 2007, a bomb attack in Algiers claimed the lives of 17 UN staff members and injured 40. The Secretary-General set up an independent panel to investigate the atrocity—the second deadliest attack against UN staff—and make recommendations to improve the security of UN employees around the world.

The 1994 *Convention on the Safety of United Nations and Associated Personnel* obliges the governments of countries in which the UN is working to safeguard its staff, and to take preventive measures against murders and abductions. Despite those obligations, too many UN staff, peacekeepers and associated personnel lose their lives each year in service to the world's poorest and most vulnerable.

Protecting and assisting refugees

In 2012, the **Office of the United Nations High Commissioner for Refugees (UNHCR)** (*www.unhcr.org*) counted 42.5 million forcibly displaced people worldwide. This included 26.4 million internally displaced persons (IDPs), 15.2 million refugees and 895,000 asylum-seekers. UNHCR had identified some 3.5 million stateless persons in 64 countries, but estimated that the overall number of stateless persons worldwide could be far higher, at around 12 million.

More than 26 million people—10.4 million refugees and 15.5 million IDPs—were receiving protection or assistance from UNHCR at the end of 2011—700,000 more than in 2010. Another 4.8 million Palestine refugees were assisted under the mandate of the United Nations Relief and Works Agency for Palestine Refugees in the Near East (UNRWA).

Of the 10.4 million refugees, there were some 3.6 million in the Asian and Pacific region; 2.7 million in Africa (excluding North Africa); 1.7 million in the Middle East and North Africa (not including Palestinians assisted by UNRWA); 1.6 million in Europe; and 807,400 in the Americas. Developing countries were host to four fifths of the world's refugees. Women and girls represented, on average, 49 per cent of persons of concern to UNHCR. They constituted 47 per cent of refugees and asylum-seekers, and half of all IDPs and returnees (former refugees). Forty-six per cent of refugees and asylum-seekers were children less than 18 years of age.

In 2011, Afghanistan remained the leading country of origin of refugees, with close to 2.7 million in 79 countries. On average, one out of four refugees in the world originated in Afghanistan. Major refugee populations at the end of 2011 included Palestinians (4.8 million); Iraqis (1.4 million); Somalis (1 million); Sudanese, including some citizens of South Sudan (500,000); Congolese (491,500); Myanmarese (415,000); and Colombians (396,000). As of July 2013, UNHCR and its partners were addressing the needs of more than 1.8 million refugees fleeing violent conflict in Syria.

UNHCR has been one of the lead humanitarian agencies for some of the major emergencies in post-war history—in the Balkans, which produced the largest refugee flows in Europe since the Second World War; in the aftermath of the Gulf War; in the Great Lakes region of Africa; in the massive exoduses in Kosovo and Timor-Leste; in repatriation in Afghanistan; and, more recently, in the exodus from conflict-ridden Iraq and from southern and central Somalia.

Refugees are defined as those who have fled their countries because of a well-founded fear of persecution due to their race, religion, nationality, political opinion or membership in a particular social group, and who cannot or do not want to return. It also includes persons who have fled war or other violence. The legal status of refugees is defined in two international treaties, the 1951 *Convention Relating to the Status of Refugees* and its 1967 *Protocol*, which spell out their rights and obligations. There are 147 states parties to one or both of these instruments.

UNHCR's most important function is international protection—trying to ensure respect for refugees' basic human rights, including their ability to seek asylum, and to ensure that no one is returned involuntarily to a country where he or she has reason to fear persecution. Other types of assistance include:

- help during major emergencies involving the movement of large numbers of refugees;
- regular programmes in such fields as education, health and shelter;
- assistance to promote the self-sufficiency of refugees and their integration in host countries;
- voluntary repatriation; and
- resettlement in third countries for refugees who cannot return to their homes and who face protection problems in the country where they first sought asylum.

As a result of enhanced efforts to provide durable solutions, 532,000 refugees were repatriated voluntarily, more than double the figure for 2010, but still the third lowest number of voluntarily repatriated refugees in a decade. The three main durable solutions for refugees are voluntary repatriation to their home country in safety and dignity; local integration in the country of asylum, where feasible; or resettlement in a third country. Voluntary repatriation is generally considered the preferred option. The sudden return of large numbers of people to their home country, however, can quickly overwhelm fragile economic and social infrastructures. To ensure that returnees can rebuild their lives after they return home, UNHCR works with a range of organizations to facilitate their reintegration. This requires emergency assistance for those in need, development programmes for the areas that have been devastated, and job-creation schemes. For all of these reasons, the development of effective links between peace, stability, security, respect for human rights and sustainable development is increasingly seen as crucial for the achievement of durable solutions to the refugee problem.

Although UNHCR's mandate is to protect and assist refugees, it has increasingly been called upon to come to the aid of a wider range of people living in refugee-like situations. These include people displaced within their own countries, former refugees who may need UNHCR monitoring and assistance once they have returned home, stateless persons, and those who receive temporary protection outside their home countries but do not receive the full legal status of refugees. Today, refugees comprise the second largest group of people of concern to UNHCR, after IDPs. IDPs are people who have been forced to flee their homes to escape war, general violence, human rights violations or natural and man-made disasters, but have not crossed an international border. During 2011, some 3.2 million IDPs were able to return home—the highest number in more than a decade.

Asylum-seekers are persons who have left their countries of origin and have applied for recognition as refugees in other countries, and whose applications are still pending. In 2011, some 876,100 individual applications for asylum or refugee status were submitted to governments or UNHCR offices in 171 countries or territories. South Africa was the main destination for asylum-seekers, with some 107,000 new claims, followed by the United States, Kenya, France, Canada, the United Kingdom and Germany. The highest number of new asylum claims filed by individuals with UNHCR or with states originated from Zimbabwe (52,500), Afghanistan (43,000), Somalia (35,900), Côte d'Ivoire (33,000), the Democratic Republic of the Congo (31,500), Myanmar (29,800) and Iraq (29,100).

Palestine refugees

Since 1950, the **United Nations Relief and Works Agency for Palestine Refugees in the Near East (UNRWA)** has been providing education, health, relief and social services to Palestine refugees. The General Assembly created UNRWA to provide emergency relief to some 750,000 Palestine refugees who had lost their homes and livelihoods as a result of the 1948 Arab-Israeli conflict. At the end of 2012, UNRWA was providing essential basic services to assist some 5 million registered Palestine refugees in Jordan, Lebanon, Syria, and the occupied Palestinian territory, which comprises the Gaza Strip and the West Bank, including East Jerusalem. In the past decade, the need for UNRWA's humanitarian role has been reinforced by recurrent conflicts in the region.

Education is UNRWA's largest area of activity, accounting for nearly 60 per cent of its regular budget. The Agency operates one of the largest school systems in the Middle East, with 703 schools, 22,885 educational staff, 491,641 enrolled pupils (an average of 51.4 per cent female), 9 vocational and technical training centres, 7,024 training sites, 2 educational science faculties and 891 teachers in training. The Agency's network of 139 health care centres performed 9.6 million medical consultations in 2012. Its environmental health programme controls the quality of drinking water, provides sanitation, and carries out vector and rodent control in refugee camps.

In 2011, the UNRWA microfinance programme issued a record 17,717 loans, valued at $12.4 million. Between 1991 and 2011, UNRWA extended 265,561 loans, valued at $302.65 million, across all of its fields of operation. As of 1 January 2013, 292,259 of the poorest refugees had received special hardship assistance, including the provision of food and shelter rehabilitation.

The Agency continues to help upgrade infrastructure, create employment and improve socio-economic conditions. Unlike other UN organizations that may work through local authorities or executing agencies, UNRWA provides its services directly to refugees. It plans and carries out its own activities and projects, and builds and administers facilities such as schools and clinics. The international community considers UNRWA a stabilizing factor in the Middle East. The refugees themselves look upon its programmes as a symbol of the international community's commitment to attaining a lasting solution of the Palestine refugee issue.

VI. INTERNATIONAL LAW

The Great Hall of Justice of the Peace Palace in The Hague (the Netherlands) at the opening of hearings in the case *Nicaragua* v. *Colombia*. (24 April 2012, UN Photo/ICJ-CIJ/ANP-in-Opdracht/Frank van Beek)

Among the most wide-reaching results of the United Nations is the development of a body of international law (*www.un.org/law*)—conventions, treaties and standards—central to promoting economic and social development, as well as to advancing international peace and security. Many of the treaties brought about by the United Nations form the basis of the law that governs relations among nations. While the work of the UN in this area does not always receive attention, it has a daily impact on the lives of people everywhere.

The *Charter of the United Nations* specifically calls on the Organization to help in the settlement of international disputes by peaceful means, including arbitration and judicial settlement (Article 33), and to encourage the progressive development of international law and its codification (Article 13). Over the years, the United Nations has sponsored over 500 multilateral agreements that treat a broad range of common concerns among states and are legally binding for the countries that ratify them.

In many areas, the legal work of the United Nations has been pioneering, addressing problems as they take on an international dimension. The UN has been in the forefront of efforts to establish a legal framework in such areas as protecting the environment, regulating migrant labour, curbing drug trafficking and combating terrorism. This work continues today, as international law assumes a more central role across a wider spectrum of issues, including human rights law and international humanitarian law.

Judicial settlement of disputes

The primary United Nations organ for the settlement of disputes is its principal judicial organ, the **International Court of Justice (ICJ)** (*www.icj-cij.org*). Also known as the "World Court", ICJ is the only court of a universal character with general jurisdiction; this is reflected by the wide range of states parties appearing before it, and of the issues it has been asked to address. Since its founding in 1946, the Court has considered 152 cases, and issued over 110 judgments and over 100 judicial orders on legal disputes brought to it by UN member states. It has also issued 27 advisory opinions in response to requests by UN organizations.

ICJ has become increasingly busy in recent years. Although the Court has cleared some of its judicial backlog, its docket still comprises 11 active cases originating in disputes from all corners of the globe. States are increasingly turning to the Court to resolve disputes relating to treaty interpretation, land and maritime frontiers, the environment and the conservation of living resources, and other issues. Consequently, the Court has delivered more judgments in the last 22 years than during the first 44 years of its existence.

ICJ has developed a particularly strong reputation in adjudicating land and maritime boundary disputes, in which tensions between states can escalate into open conflict. Parties to such disputes invariably place their confidence in the prospect of the Court reaching an equitable solution that will in turn normalize relations between them.

Although the most obvious effect of ICJ's judgments is the peaceful settlement of disputes, the influence of the Court's jurisprudence is felt more broadly. Its pronouncements are widely perceived as authoritative statements of international law, and are studied closely by other courts and tribunals, legal scholars and advisers to states. Its contribution to the development of international law includes the clarification of specific rules of customary law.

Contentious cases

Contentious cases have represented 80 per cent of ICJ's work since 1946. The Court has delivered judgments on disputes concerning a wide range of issues, including those related to frontiers, maritime boundaries, territorial sovereignty, the non-use of force, violation of international humanitarian law, non-interference in the internal affairs of states, diplomatic relations, hostage-taking, the right of asylum, nationality, guardianship, rights of passage and economic rights.

As to the length of contentious cases, some 71 per cent of cases were dealt with by ICJ within 4 years; 23 per cent were completed within 5–9 years; and 6 per cent (5 cases so far) were completed after 10 years or more. The length of each case varies depending on its complexity, but also on the will of parties to engage in swift proceedings. As the parties to proceedings are sovereign states, ICJ is limited in its ability to expedite its work on cases.

When so requested, the Court can deliver swift decisions. For example, in 1999, it delivered an order for provisional measures 24 hours after an urgent request by Germany in a case against the United States (*LaGrand*) concerning alleged violations of the *Vienna Convention on Consular Relations* in the trial and sentencing for murder of two German nationals. The case itself was dealt with in 28 months.

The procedure followed by the Court in contentious cases includes a written phase as well as an oral phase consisting of public hearings, during which agents and counsels address the Court. Following oral proceedings, the Court deliberates in camera, then delivers its judgment at a public sitting, usually within six months after the end of the oral phase. The judgment is final and without appeal. Should one of the states involved fail to comply, the other party may have recourse to the Security Council. Nearly all ICJ judgments, however, have been implemented.

Recent ICJ cases

In February 2012, ICJ concluded a high-profile case between two European states—Germany and Italy—concerning jurisdictional immunities of the state. The Court found in particular that Italy had violated its obligation to respect the immunity enjoyed by Germany under international law by allowing civil claims to be brought in Italy against Germany based on violations of international humanitarian law committed by the German Reich between 1943 and 1945.

In June 2012, in the case between Guinea and the Democratic Republic of the Congo (DRC), the Court delivered its judgment concerning compensation owed by the DRC to Guinea: it decided that the amount of $95,000 was due in compensation for injury suffered by a Guinean national.

In July 2012, in the case between Belgium and Senegal concerning questions relating to the obligation to prosecute or extradite the former president of Chad, Hissène Habré, ICJ found that Senegal had to submit the case of Mr. Habré to its competent authorities for the purpose of prosecution, if it did not extradite him.

In a typical case involving territorial rights, ICJ, in December 2012, delivered its judgment in the case concerning the territorial and maritime dispute between Nicaragua and Colombia. It found unanimously that that Colombia had sovereignty over the maritime features in dispute. The Court drew a single maritime boundary that was endorsed unanimously by its 15 judges.

In April 2013, ICJ ended a frontier dispute submitted to it jointly by Burkina Faso and Niger by determining the course of the frontier between the two states in a specific sector. Burkina Faso and Niger made a formal commitment to commence the work of demarcating the frontier within 18 months of the delivery of the Judgment.

As of 28 May 2013, there were 11 pending cases on the Court's docket involving 19 different states: seven Central and South American states (*Peru* v. *Chile, Ecuador* v. *Colombia,* Costa Rica and Nicaragua in two cases, *Bolivia* v. *Chile*); four African states (*Democratic Republic of the Congo* v. *Uganda, Burkina Faso and Niger*); four states of the Asia-Pacific region (*Cambodia* v. *Thailand, Australia* v. *Japan*); and four European states (*Hungary/Slovakia, Croatia* v. *Serbia*).

Advisory opinions

Another role of the Court is to respond to any legal questions put to it by certain UN organs and institutions. This procedure culminates in advisory opinions, which represent 20 per cent of ICJ's workload. Since 1946, the Court has given 27 advisory opinions, of which the majority—55 per cent, or 15 opinions—were requested by the General Assembly.

Unlike judgments, advisory opinions are not binding per se: it is for the UN organs or specialized agencies that request an opinion to give effect to it or not, by the means at their disposal. On occasion, a state and an international organization agree that the organization will request an advisory opinion of the Court in the event of dispute, and that the two parties will treat the opinion as conclusive. The consideration given to the Court's opinions by states and international organizations in their legal practice fosters the development of international law.

ICJ advisory opinions have covered various issues, including the legality of the threat or use of nuclear weapons (1996); the status of human rights rapporteurs (1999); the legal consequences of the construction of a wall in the Occupied Palestinian Territory (2004); and the accordance with international law of the unilateral declaration of independence in respect of Kosovo (2010). Other opinions have addressed admission to UN membership (1948); reparation for injuries suffered in the service of the UN (1949); questions concerning South West Africa (Namibia, in 1950, 1955, 1956 and 1971); the territorial status of Western Sahara (1975); expenses of certain UN operations (1962); and the applicability of the UN Headquarters Agreement (1988). ICJ has also given advisory opinions on judgments rendered by international administrative tribunals, most recently on a request by the Administrative Tribunal of the International Labour Organisation in 2012.

So far, the Security Council has only requested one advisory opinion: in July 1970 on the legal consequences for states of the continued presence of South Africa in Namibia. In its advisory opinion of June 1971, the Court found, inter alia, that the continued presence of South Africa in Namibia was illegal and that the former was obligated to withdraw its administration immediately.

Development and codification of international law

The **International Law Commission** (*www.un.org/law/ilc*) was established by the General Assembly in 1947 to promote the progressive development of international law and its codification. The Commission, which meets annually, is composed of 34 members elected by the General Assembly for five-year terms. Collectively, the members represent the world's principal legal systems and serve as experts in their individual capacity, not as representatives of their governments. They address a wide range of issues relevant to the regulation of relations among states, and frequently consult with the International Committee of the Red Cross, the International Court of Justice and UN specialized agencies, depending on the subject being examined.

Most of the Commission's work involves the preparation of drafts on aspects of international law. Some topics are chosen by the Commission, others are referred to it by the General Assembly. When the Commission completes work on a topic, the General Assembly sometimes convenes an international conference of plenipotentiaries to incorporate the draft into a convention. The convention is then opened to states to become parties—countries that agree to be bound by the provisions of a convention. Some of these conventions form the foundation of the law governing relations among states. Examples include:

- the *Convention on Diplomatic Relations* and the *Convention on Consular Relations*, adopted at conferences held in Vienna in 1961 and 1963, respectively;
- the *Convention on the Law of Treaties*, adopted at a conference in Vienna in 1969;
- the *Convention on the Prevention and Punishment of Crimes against Internationally Protected Persons, including Diplomatic Agents*, adopted by the General Assembly in 1973;
- the *Convention on the Succession of States in Respect of State Property, Archives and Debts*, adopted at a conference in Vienna in 1983;
- the *Convention on the Law of Treaties between States and International Organizations or between International Organizations*, adopted at a conference in Vienna in 1986;
- the *Convention on the Non-navigational Uses of International Watercourses*, adopted by the General Assembly in 1997, which regulates the equitable and reasonable utilization of watercourses shared by two or more countries.

State responsibility has been a major subject of study by the Commission since 1949. In 1999, the Commission adopted a draft declaration aimed at preventing people from becoming stateless in such situations as dissolution of a state or separation of a territory. In 2001, the Commission adopted draft articles on the prevention of transboundary damage resulting from hazardous activities.

In 2008, the Commission adopted two sets of draft articles—on reservations to treaties and on the law of transboundary aquifers. In 2009, the Commission adopted a set of draft articles on the responsibility of international organizations. In 2011, it adopted the Guide to Practice on Reservations to Treaties, as well as sets of draft articles on the responsibility of international organizations and on the effects of armed conflicts on treaties. Topics considered by the Commission in 2012 included the expulsion of aliens; obligation to extradite or prosecute; protection of persons in the event of disasters; immunity of state officials from foreign criminal jurisdiction; treaties over time; and the most-favoured-nation clause.

International trade law

The **United Nations Commission on International Trade Law (UNCITRAL)** (*www. uncitral.org*) facilitates world trade by developing conventions, model laws, rules and legal guides designed to harmonize international trade law. Established by the General Assembly in 1966, UNCITRAL has become the core legal body of the UN system in the field of international trade law. The international trade law division of the UN Office of Legal Affairs serves as its secretariat. The Commission is composed of 60 member state representatives elected by the General Assembly. Membership is structured to represent the world's various geographic regions and its principal economic and legal systems. Members of the Commission are elected for six-year terms. The terms of half the members expire every three years.

In the past 47 years, the Commission has developed texts that are viewed as landmarks in various fields of law. These include the *UNCITRAL Arbitration Rules* (1976); the *UNCITRAL Conciliation Rules* (1980); the *United Nations Convention on Contracts for the International Sale of Goods* (1980); the *UNCITRAL Model Law on International Commercial Arbitration* (1985); the *Model Law on Electronic Commerce* (1996); the *United Nations Convention on Contracts for the International Carriage of Goods Wholly or Partly by Sea* (2008); and the revisions of the *UNCITRAL Arbitration Rules* (2010) and the *UNCITRAL Model Law on Public Procurement* (2011).

At its most recent session in 2012, the Commission considered the issues of arbitration and conciliation; online dispute resolution; electronic commerce insolvency law; and security interests. Its work on the compilation and publication of Case Law on UNCITRAL Texts is ongoing.

Environmental law

The UN has pioneered the development of international environmental law, brokering major treaties that have advanced environmental protection everywhere. The **United Nations Environment Programme (UNEP)** (*www.unep.org*) administers many of these treaties, while the rest are administered by other bodies, including treaty secretariats:

- The *Convention on Wetlands of International Importance Especially as Waterfowl Habitat* (1971) obligates states parties to use wisely all wetlands under their jurisdiction (promoted by UNESCO).
- The *Convention Concerning the Protection of the World Cultural and Natural Heritage* (1972) obligates states parties to protect unique natural and cultural areas (promoted by UNESCO).
- The *Convention on International Trade in Endangered Species of Wild Fauna and Flora* (1973) controls international trade in selected wild animal and plant species or products through quotas or outright bans, to ensure their survival.
- The *Bonn Convention on the Conservation of Migratory Species of Wild Animals* (1979) and a series of associated regional and species-specific agreements aim to conserve terrestrial, marine and avian migratory species and their habitats.
- The *Convention on Long-range Transboundary Air Pollution (Acid Rain Convention)* (1979) and its protocols, negotiated under the auspices of the United Nations Economic Commission for Europe, provide for the control and reduction of air pollution in Europe and North America.

- The *United Nations Convention on the Law of the Sea* (1982) regulates in a comprehensive way numerous maritime issues, including the protection and preservation of coasts and the marine environment; the prevention and control of marine pollution; rights to living and non-living resources; and the management and conservation of living resources.
- The *Vienna Convention for the Protection of the Ozone Layer* (1985) and the *Montreal Protocol* (1987) and its amendments seek to reduce damage to the ozone layer, which shields life from the sun's harmful ultraviolet radiation.
- The *Basel Convention on the Control of Transboundary Movement of Hazardous Wastes and their Disposal* (1989) and its amendments, along with its 1999 *Protocol* on liability and compensation resulting from cross-border movement of hazardous wastes, obligate states parties to reduce shipping and dumping of dangerous wastes across borders and minimize their toxic potential.
- The *Agreement on the Conservation of Small Cetaceans of the Baltic and North Seas* (1991) aims to promote cooperation among parties for the conservation of small cetaceans and their habitats.
- The *Convention on Biological Diversity* (1992) seeks to conserve biological diversity, promote the sustainable use of its components, and encourage equitable sharing of the benefits arising from the use of genetic resources. Its *Cartagena Protocol* on biosafety (2000) seeks to protect biological diversity from potential risks posed by living modified organisms.
- The *Framework Convention on Climate Change* (1992) obligates states parties to reduce emissions of greenhouse gases that cause global warming and related atmospheric problems. The Convention's *Kyoto Protocol* (1997) strengthened the international response to climate change by setting legally binding emission targets for the period 2008–2012.
- The *International Convention to Combat Desertification in those Countries Experiencing Serious Drought and/or Desertification, Particularly in Africa* (1994) seeks to promote international cooperation to combat desertification and to mitigate the effects of drought.
- The *Agreement on the Conservation of Cetaceans in the Black Sea, Mediterranean Sea and Contiguous Atlantic Area* (1996) seeks to reduce the threat to cetaceans in Mediterranean and Black Sea waters, and requires that states ban the deliberate capture of cetaceans and create protected zones.
- The *Rotterdam Convention on the Prior Informed Consent Procedure for Certain Hazardous Chemicals and Pesticides in International Trade* (1998) obligates exporters of hazardous chemicals or pesticides to inform importing states on the potential dangers of these substances.
- The *Stockholm Convention on Persistent Organic Pollutants* (2001) aims to reduce and eliminate releases of certain highly toxic pesticides, industrial chemicals and by-products—such as DDT, PCBs and dioxin—that are highly mobile and accumulate in the food chain.
- The *Kyiv Protocol on Strategic Environmental Assessment* (2003) requires states parties to evaluate the environmental consequences of their draft plans and programmes.

Law of the sea

The *United Nations Convention on the Law of the Sea* (www.un.org/depts/los) is one of the world's most comprehensive instruments of international law. Its 320 articles and nine annexes contain an all-encompassing legal regime for our oceans and seas, establishing rules governing all activities in the oceans and the use of their resources—including navigation and overflight, exploration and exploitation of minerals, conservation and management of living resources, protection of the marine environment, and marine scientific research. It enshrines the notion that all problems of ocean space are interrelated and need to be addressed as a whole. It embodies in one instrument the codification of traditional rules for the use of the oceans, as well as the development of new rules governing emerging concerns. It is a unique instrument, often referred to as a 'constitution for the oceans'.

It is now almost universally accepted that all activities in the oceans and the seas must be carried out in conformity with the provisions of the *Convention*. Like other such instruments, its authority resides in its acceptance. As of June 2013, the *Convention* had 165 parties, including states, the European Union and two non-independent territories. Other states are in the process of becoming party to it. Nearly all states recognize and adhere to its provisions.

Impact of the Convention

Through national and international legislation and related decision-making, states have consistently upheld the *Convention* as the pre-eminent international legal instrument in the field. Its authority is found in the near-universal acceptance of some of its key provisions, including: 12 nautical miles as the limit of the territorial sea; coastal states' sovereign rights and jurisdiction in an "exclusive economic zone" up to the limit of 200 nautical miles; and their sovereign rights over the continental shelf extending up to a distance of 200 nautical miles or, under certain circumstances, beyond that limit. The *Convention* has also brought stability in the area of navigation, establishing the rights of innocent passage through the territorial sea; transit passage through narrow straits used for international navigation; sea lanes passage through archipelagic waters; and freedom of navigation in the exclusive economic zone.

The near-universal acceptance of the *Convention* was facilitated in 1994 by the General Assembly's adoption of the *Agreement Relating to the Implementation of Part XI of the Convention*, which removed certain obstacles relating to the seabed area that had prevented mainly industrialized countries from signing the *Convention*. The Part XI Agreement is now widely accepted, with 144 parties as of June 2013.

The *Convention* has also been acknowledged for its provisions on the rights of coastal states, in the exercise of their jurisdiction, to regulate, authorize and conduct marine scientific research, as well as their duties relating to the prevention, reduction and control of pollution of the marine environment, and on the rights of landlocked states to participate in the exploitation of the living marine resources of the exclusive economic zones of coastal states. Moreover, the *Convention* is recognized as the framework and foundation for any future instruments that seek to further clarify the rights and obligations of states with regard to the oceans.

One such instrument, the 1995 *Agreement on Straddling Fish Stocks and Highly Migratory Fish Stocks*, implements provisions in the *Convention* relating to these fish stocks, setting out the legal regime for their conservation and management. It requires states to cooperate in adopting measures to ensure their long-term sustainability and to promote their optimum utilization. States are also required to cooperate to achieve compatibility of measures with respect to these stocks for areas under national jurisdiction and the adjacent high seas. As of June 2013, the *Agreement* had 80 parties.

Bodies established under the Convention

The *Convention* established three specific organs to deal with various aspects of the law of the sea.

Through the **International Seabed Authority** (*www.isa.org.jm*), states parties organize and control activities relating to the deep seabed's mineral resources in the International Seabed Area, defined as "the seabed and ocean floor and the subsoil therof, beyond the limits of national jurisdiction". Inaugurated in 1994, it is located in Kingston, Jamaica. In 2002, the Authority adopted regulations on prospecting and exploration for polymetallic nodules in the Area.

Following adoption of these regulations, which include standard clauses for exploration contracts, the first 15-year contracts for exploration for polymetallic nodules in the deep seabed were signed in 2001 with the registered pioneer investors from various countries. These pioneer investors are state-owned enterprises or multinational consortia that—having undertaken prospecting activities and having located economically exploitable deposits of polymetallic nodules in the Area before the adoption of the *Convention*—were accorded preferential treatment in the granting of production authorizations over other applicants, with the exception of 'the Enterprise'. The Enterprise is the organ of the International Seabed Authority that carries out activities in the Area as enumerated in the *Convention*, as well as the transport, processing and marketing of minerals recovered from the Area—functions currently being carried out by the Authority's Legal and Technical Commission.

The **International Tribunal for the Law of the Sea** (*www.itlos.org*), operational since 1996, was established to settle disputes relating to the interpretation or application of the *Convention*. Composed of 21 judges elected by the states parties, it is located in the German seaport of Hamburg. It received its first application instituting a case in 2001.

As of June 2013, 21 cases had been submitted to the Tribunal, most of them seeking the prompt release of vessels and crews allegedly arrested in breach of the *Convention*. Some, such as *New Zealand* v. *Japan* and *Australia* v. *Japan*, concerning southern blue-fin tuna stocks, have dealt with the conservation of living resources. Another case, *Ireland* v. *United Kingdom*, dealt with the prevention of land-based pollution from a plant designed to reprocess spent nuclear fuel. Of these 21 cases, two were still on the court's docket in June 2013: one concerning a dispute between Panama and Guinea-Bissau regarding an oil tanker, the other dealing with a request for an advisory opinion from the Sub-Regional Fisheries Commission.

The purpose of the **Commission on the Limits of the Continental Shelf** (*www.un.org/depts/los/clcs_new/clcs_home.htm*) is to facilitate implementation of the *Convention* with respect to delineation of the outer limits of the continental shelf when that submerged portion of the land territory of a coastal state extends beyond the 200 nautical miles from its coastline—established as the minimal legal distance under the *Convention*. Under its article 76, the coastal state may establish the outer limits of its *juridical* continental shelf in such cases through the application of specified scientific and technical formulas. The Commission held its first session at United Nations Headquarters in 1997. Its 21 members, elected by the states parties to the *Convention*, serve in their personal capacity. They are experts in geology, geophysics, hydrography and geodesy. The Commission received its first submission by a state party, the Russian Federation, in December 2001.

Meetings of states parties and General Assembly processes

Although the *Convention* does not provide for a periodic conference of states parties, the annual meeting of states parties, which is convened by the UN Secretary-General, has served as a forum where issues of concern have been discussed. This is in addition to its assigned administrative functions, such as election of members of the Tribunal and the Commission, as well as other budgetary and administrative actions. The Secretary-General has also convened annual informal consultations of the states parties to the *Fish Stocks Agreement* since its entry into force in 2001, to monitor its implementation.

The General Assembly performs an oversight function with respect to ocean affairs and the law of the sea. In 2000, it established an open-ended, informal, consultative process to facilitate its own annual review of developments in the field. That process, convened annually, makes suggestions to the Assembly on particular issues, with an emphasis on identifying areas where coordination and cooperation among governments and agencies should be enhanced. Such topics have included safety of navigation and the protection of vulnerable marine ecosystems. The consultative process has been repeatedly extended because of the positive results it has achieved. In 2004, the General Assembly also established an open-ended, informal, ad hoc working group to study issues relating to the conservation and sustainable use of marine biological diversity beyond areas of national jurisdiction.

International humanitarian law

International humanitarian law encompasses the principles and rules that regulate the means and methods of warfare, as well as the humanitarian protection of civilian populations, sick and wounded combatants, and prisoners of war. Major instruments include the 1949 *Geneva Conventions for the Protection of War Victims* and two additional protocols concluded in 1977 under the auspices of the International Committee of the Red Cross.

The United Nations has taken a leading role in efforts to advance international humanitarian law. The Security Council has become increasingly involved in protecting civilians in armed conflict, promoting human rights and protecting children in wars. The establishment of the **International Criminal Tribunals for the former Yugoslavia** (1993) and **for Rwanda** (1994) have served both to ensure accountability, and to strengthen and enhance the wider appreciation of humanitarian law.

This applies as well to three courts established by the states concerned but with substantial UN support: the **Special Court for Sierra Leone** (2002), the **Extraordinary Chambers in the Courts of Cambodia** (2006) and the **Special Tribunal for Lebanon** (2007). Sometimes referred to as 'hybrid' courts, they are non-permanent institutions which will cease to exist once all their cases have been heard.

The General Assembly, as a political forum of the United Nations, has contributed to elaborating a number of instruments that have significantly advanced the scope and application of international humanitarian law. Among them are the *Convention on the Prevention and Punishment of the Crime of Genocide* (1948); the *Convention on the Non-Applicability of Statutory Limitations to War Crimes and Crimes Against Humanity* (1968); the *Convention on Prohibition and Restrictions on the Use of Certain Conventional Weapons which may be deemed to be Excessively Injurious or to have Indiscriminate Effects* (1980) and its five protocols; the *Principles of International Cooperation in the Detection, Arrest, Extradition and Punishment of Persons Guilty of War Crimes and Crimes Against Humanity,* which the Assembly adopted in 1973; and the *Convention on Cluster Munitions* (2008).

The Assembly also facilitated the convening of the diplomatic conference that adopted the *Rome Statute of the International Criminal Court* in 1998. Even prior to this landmark event, the preparatory commission for the Court had elaborated the "elements of crimes" with respect to genocide, war crimes and crimes against humanity—a major contribution to international humanitarian law.

International terrorism

The United Nations has consistently addressed the problem of terrorism in both its legal and political dimensions. The UN has also been the target of terrorism. From Afghanistan to Algeria, from Iraq to Pakistan, UN staff members have lost their lives in the line of duty, in the service of peace, human rights and development.

Since 1963, the international community—under the auspices of the UN, its specialized agencies and the International Atomic Energy Agency—has elaborated 14 universal legal instruments and four amendments to prevent terrorist acts:

- *Convention on Offences and Certain Other Acts Committed on Board Aircraft* (Tokyo, 1963);
- *Convention for the Suppression of Unlawful Seizure of Aircraft* (The Hague, 1970) and its supplementary Protocol (2010);
- *Convention for the Suppression of Unlawful Acts against the Safety of Civil Aviation* (Montreal, 1971);
- *Convention on the Prevention and Punishment of Crimes against Internationally Protected Persons, including Diplomatic Agents* (New York, 1973);
- *International Convention against the Taking of Hostages* (New York, 1979);
- *Convention on the Physical Protection of Nuclear Material* (Vienna, 1980) and its amendments (2005);
- *Protocol for the Suppression of Unlawful Acts of Violence at Airports Serving International Civil Aviation* (Montreal, 1988);
- *Convention for the Suppression of Unlawful Acts against the Safety of Maritime Navigation* (Rome, 1988) and its Protocol (2005);

- *Protocol for the Suppression of Unlawful Acts against the Safety of Fixed Platforms Located on the Continental Shelf* (Rome, 1988) and its Protocol (2005);
- *Convention on the Marking of Plastic Explosives for the Purpose of Detection* (Montreal, 1991).
- *International Convention for the Suppression of Terrorist Bombings* (1997);
- *International Convention for the Suppression of the Financing of Terrorism* (1999);
- *International Convention for the Suppression of Acts of Nuclear Terrorism* (2005);
- *Convention on the Suppression of Unlawful Acts Relating to International Civil Aviation* (2010).

In 1994, the General Assembly adopted a *Declaration on Measures to Eliminate International Terrorism*. In 1996, in a *Declaration to Supplement the 1994 Declaration*, the Assembly condemned all acts and practices of terrorism as criminal and unjustifiable, wherever and by whomever committed. It also urged states to take measures at the national and international levels to eliminate terrorism. An *ad hoc* committee established by the Assembly in 1996 is currently negotiating a comprehensive convention against terrorism to address gaps left by existing treaties.

Soon after the 11 September 2001 terrorist attacks on the United States, the Security Council established its **Counter-Terrorism Committee** (*www.un.org/sc/ctc*). Among its functions, the Committee monitors implementation of Council resolutions 1373(2001) and 1624(2005), which imposed certain obligations on member states. These include: criminalization of terrorism-related activities, including the provision of assistance to carry them out; denial of funding and safe haven to terrorists; and the exchange of information on terrorist groups.

At the 2005 World Summit, world leaders unequivocally condemned terrorism in all its forms and manifestations. The Summit also requested member states to work through the General Assembly to adopt a counter-terrorism strategy based on recommendations from the UN Secretary-General.

In 2006, the **United Nations Global Counter-Terrorism Strategy** (*www. un.org/ terrorism*) was launched, following its unanimous adoption by the General Assembly. Based on the fundamental conviction that terrorism in all its forms is unacceptable and can never be justified, the Strategy outlines a range of measures to address terrorism in all its aspects at the national, regional and international levels. In 2010, in its second biennial review of the Strategy, the Assembly reaffirmed the primary responsibility of member states for its implementation. Member states also emphasized the need to promote worldwide solidarity in support of the victims of terrorist acts and highlighted the role that they can play in countering the appeal of terrorism.

International Criminal Court

The International Criminal Court (ICC) (*www.icc-cpi.int*) is an independent, permanent court that tries persons accused of the most serious crimes of international concern, namely genocide, crimes against humanity and war crimes. It will also have jurisdiction over the crime of aggression when agreement is reached on the definition of such a crime. The Court was established by the *Rome Statute of the International Criminal Court* (*www.un.org/law/icc*), adopted at a plenipotentiary conference held in Rome on 17 July 1998. The *Statute* entered into force on 1 July 2002. As of June 2013, it had 122 states parties.

ICC is legally and functionally independent of the United Nations, and is not a part of the UN system. Cooperation between the UN and ICC is governed by a Negotiated Relationship Agreement. The Security Council can initiate proceedings before ICC, and can refer to ICC situations that would not otherwise fall under the Court's jurisdiction. The Court has 18 judges, elected by the states parties for a term limited to nine years; judges can, however, remain in office to complete any trial or appeal that has already begun. No two judges can be from the same country.

To date, four states parties to the *Rome Statute*—Uganda, the Democratic Republic of the Congo, the Central African Republic and Mali—have referred situations occurring in their territories to the Court. In addition, the Security Council referred to ICC the situations in Darfur in the Sudan, the Sudan, and in Libya, both non-state parties. After a thorough analysis of available information, the ICC Prosecutor opened and was conducting investigations in all of these situations. In 2010 and 2011, the Court's Pre-Trial Chambers II and III authorized the Prosecution to open investigations *proprio motu* (on its own initiative) in the situations of Kenya and Côte d'Ivoire, respectively. Eighteen cases have been brought before the Court.

Other legal questions

The General Assembly has adopted legal instruments on various other questions concerning the international community and the peoples of the world. Among these are the *International Convention against the Recruitment, Use, Financing and Training of Mercenaries* (1989); the *Body of Principles for the Protection of All Persons under Any Form of Detention or Imprisonment* (1988); and the *Declaration on the Enhancement of the Effectiveness of the Principle of Refraining from the Threat or Use of Force in International Relations* (1987).

The Assembly has adopted many international instruments having to do with the work of the UN itself on the recommendation of the **Special Committee on the Charter of the United Nations and on the Strengthening of the Role of the Organization**, established by the Assembly in 1974. These include the *Declaration on the Peaceful Settlement of International Disputes* (1982); the *Declaration on the Prevention and Removal of Disputes and Situations Which May Threaten International Peace and Security and on the Role of the United Nations in this Field* (1988); the *Declaration on Fact-finding by the United Nations in the Field of the Maintenance of International Peace and Security* (1991); the *Declaration on the Enhancement of Cooperation between the United Nations and Regional Arrangements or Agencies in the Maintenance of International Peace and Security* (1994); and the *United Nations Model Rules for the Conciliation of Disputes between States* (1995).

Under Article 102 of the *Charter of the United Nations*, every international agreement entered into by any member state shall be registered with the United Nations Secretariat and published by it. The United Nations Office of Legal Affairs is responsible for the registration and publication of treaties. It publishes the *United Nations Treaty Series,* which contains the texts of more than 180,000 treaties and related subsequent actions. It also discharges the functions of the Secretary-General as depository of multilateral treaties. In that role, the Office maintains the status of over 500 major multilateral treaties updated daily in electronic format and available in the United Nations Treaty Collection on the Internet (*http://treaties.un.org*).

APPENDICES

A young girl is engaged in a drawing activity as part of a programme organized by the UN Relief and Works Agency for Palestine Refugees in the Near East to encourage creativity and psychosocial well-being. (3 July 2013, UN Photo/Shareef Sarhan)

I.   UNITED NATIONS MEMBER STATES

Total membership: 193

Member state	Date of admission	Scale of assessments for 2013 (per cent)	Net contributions* (US dollars)
Afghanistan	19 November 1946	0.005	127,414
Albania	14 December 1955	0.010	254,828
Algeria	8 October 1962	0.137	3,491,146
Andorra	28 July 1993	0.008	203,862
Angola	1 December 1976	0.010	254,828
Antigua and Barbuda	11 November 1981	0.002	50,966
Argentina	24 October 1945	0.432	11,008,578
Armenia	2 March 1992	0.007	178,379
Australia	1 November 1945	2.074	52,851,369
Austria	4 December 1955	0.798	20,335,290
Azerbaijan	2 March 1992	0.040	1,019,313
Bahamas	18 September 1973	0.017	433,208
Bahrain	21 September 1971	0.039	993,830
Bangladesh	17 September 1974	0.010	254,828
Barbados	9 December 1966	0.008	203,862
Belarus[1]	24 October 1945	0.056	1,427,038
Belgium	27 December 1945	0.998	25,431,854
Belize	25 September 1981	0.001	25,483
Benin	20 September 1960	0.003	76,448
Bhutan	21 September 1971	0.001	25,483
Bolivia (Plurinational State of)	14 November 1945	0.009	229,345
Bosnia and Herzegovina[2]	22 May 1992	0.017	433,208
Botswana	17 October 1966	0.017	433,208
Brazil	24 October 1945	2.934	74,766,593
Brunei Darussalam	21 September 1984	0.026	662,553
Bulgaria	14 December 1955	0.047	1,197,693
Burkina Faso	20 September 1960	0.003	76,448
Burundi	18 September 1962	0.001	25,483
Cambodia	14 December 1955	0.004	101,931
Cameroon	20 September 1960	0.012	305,794
Canada	9 November 1945	2.984	76,040,734
Cape Verde	16 September 1975	0.001	25,483
Central African Republic	20 September 1960	0.001	25,483
Chad	20 September 1960	0.002	50,966
Chile	24 October 1945	0.334	8,511,262
China	24 October 1945	5.148	131,185,558
Colombia	5 November 1945	0.259	6,600,050
Comoros	12 November 1975	0.001	25,483
Congo	20 September 1960	0.005	127,414
Costa Rica	2 November 1945	0.038	968,348
Côte d'Ivoire	20 September 1960	0.011	280,311
Croatia[2]	22 May 1992	0.126	3,210,835
Cuba	24 October 1945	0.069	1,758,315

Member state	Date of admission	Scale of assessments for 2013 (per cent)	Net contributions* (US dollars)
Cyprus	20 September 1960	0.047	1,197,693
Czech Republic[3]	19 January 1993	0.386	9,836,368
Democratic People's Republic of Korea	17 September 1991	0.006	152,897
Democratic Republic of the Congo[4]	20 September 1960	0.003	76,448
Denmark	24 October 1945	0.675	17,200,903
Djibouti	20 September 1977	0.001	25,483
Dominica	18 December 1978	0.001	25,483
Dominican Republic	24 October 1945	0.045	1,146,727
Ecuador	21 December 1945	0.044	1,121,244
Egypt[5]	24 October 1945	0.134	3,414,698
El Salvador	24 October 1945	0.016	407,725
Equatorial Guinea	12 November 1968	0.010	254,828
Eritrea	28 May 1993	0.001	25,483
Estonia	17 September 1991	0.040	1,019,313
Ethiopia	13 November 1945	0.010	254,828
Fiji	13 October 1970	0.003	76,448
Finland	14 December 1955	0.519	13,225,583
France	24 October 1945	5.593	142,525,412
Gabon	20 September 1960	0.020	509,657
Gambia	21 September 1965	0.001	25,483
Georgia	31 July 1992	0.007	178,379
Germany[6]	18 September 1973	7.141	181,972,818
Ghana	8 March 1957	0.014	356,760
Greece	25 October 1945	0.638	16,258,039
Grenada	17 September 1974	0.001	25,483
Guatemala	21 November 1945	0.027	688,036
Guinea	12 December 1958	0.001	25,483
Guinea-Bissau	17 September 1974	0.001	25,483
Guyana	20 September 1966	0.001	25,483
Haiti	24 October 1945	0.003	76,448
Honduras	17 December 1945	0.008	203,862
Hungary	14 December 1955	0.266	6,778,430
Iceland	19 November 1946	0.027	688,036
India	30 October 1945	0.666	16,971,558
Indonesia[7]	28 September 1950	0.346	8,817,056
Iran (Islamic Republic of)	24 October 1945	0.356	9,071,884
Iraq	21 December 1945	0.068	1,732,832
Ireland	14 December 1955	0.418	10,651,818
Israel	11 May 1949	0.396	10,091,197
Italy	14 December 1955	4.448	113,347,584
Jamaica	18 September 1962	0.011	280,311
Japan	18 December 1956	10.833	276,055,389
Jordan	14 December 1955	0.022	560,622
Kazakhstan	2 March 1992	0.121	3,083,421
Kenya	16 December 1963	0.013	331,277
Kiribati	14 September 1999	0.001	25,483
Kuwait	14 May 1963	0.273	6,956,810

Member state	Date of admission	Scale of assessments for 2013 (per cent)	Net contributions* (US dollars)
Kyrgyzstan	2 March 1992	0.002	50,966
Lao People's Democratic Republic	14 December 1955	0.002	50,966
Latvia	17 September 1991	0.047	1,197,693
Lebanon	24 October 1945	0.042	1,070,279
Lesotho	17 October 1966	0.001	25,483
Liberia	2 November 1945	0.001	25,483
Libyan Arab Jamahiriya	14 December 1955	0.142	3,618,561
Liechtenstein	18 September 1990	0.009	229,345
Lithuania	17 September 1991	0.073	1,860,246
Luxembourg	24 October 1945	0.081	2,064,108
Madagascar	20 September 1960	0.003	76,448
Malawi	1 December 1964	0.002	50,966
Malaysia[8]	17 September 1957	0.281	7,160,672
Maldives	21 September 1965	0.001	25,483
Mali	28 September 1960	0.004	101,931
Malta	1 December 1964	0.016	407,725
Marshall Islands	17 September 1991	0.001	25,483
Mauritania	27 October 1961	0.002	50,966
Mauritius	24 April 1968	0.013	331,277
Mexico	7 November 1945	1.842	46,939,355
Micronesia (Federated States of)	17 September 1991	0.001	25,483
Monaco	28 May 1993	0.012	305,794
Mongolia	27 October 1961	0.003	76,448
Montenegro[2]	28 June 2006	0.005	127,414
Morocco	12 November 1956	0.062	1,579,934
Mozambique	16 September 1975	0.003	76,448
Myanmar	19 April 1948	0.010	254,828
Namibia	23 April 1990	0.010	254,828
Nauru	14 September 1999	0.001	25,483
Nepal	14 December 1955	0.006	152,897
Netherlands	10 December 1945	1.654	42,148,585
New Zealand	24 October 1945	0.253	6,447,154
Nicaragua	24 October 1945	0.003	76,448
Niger	20 September 1960	0.002	50,966
Nigeria	7 October 1960	0.090	2,293,454
Norway	27 November 1945	0.851	21,685,880
Oman	7 October 1971	0.102	2,599,248
Pakistan	30 September 1947	0.085	2,166,039
Palau	15 December 1994	0.001	25,483
Panama	13 November 1945	0.026	662,553
Papua New Guinea	10 October 1975	0.004	101,931
Paraguay	24 October 1945	0.010	254,828
Peru	31 October 1945	0.117	2,981,490
Philippines	24 October 1945	0.154	3,924,354
Poland	24 October 1945	0.921	23,469,677
Portugal	14 December 1955	0.474	12,078,857
Qatar	21 September 1971	0.209	5,325,909
Republic of Korea	17 September 1991	1.994	50,812,743

Member state	Date of admission	Scale of assessments for 2013 (per cent)	Net contributions* (US dollars)
Republic of Moldova	2 March 1992	0.003	76,448
Romania	14 December 1955	0.226	5,759,117
Russian Federation[9]	24 October 1945	2.438	62,127,115
Rwanda	18 September 1962	0.002	50,966
Saint Kitts and Nevis	23 September 1983	0.001	25,483
Saint Lucia	18 September 1979	0.001	25,483
Saint Vincent and the Grenadines	16 September 1980	0.001	25,483
Samoa	15 December 1976	0.001	25,483
San Marino	2 March 1992	0.003	76,448
Sao Tome and Principe	16 September 1975	0.001	25,483
Saudi Arabia	24 October 1945	0.864	22,017,157
Senegal	28 September 1960	0.006	152,897
Serbia[2]	1 November 2000	0.040	1,019,313
Seychelles	21 September 1976	0.001	25,483
Sierra Leone	27 September 1961	0.001	25,483
Singapore[8]	21 September 1965	0.384	9,785,403
Slovakia[3]	19 January 1993	0.171	4,357,562
Slovenia[2]	22 May 1992	0.100	2,548,282
Solomon Islands	19 September 1978	0.001	25,483
Somalia	20 September 1960	0.001	25,483
South Africa	7 November 1945	0.372	9,479,609
South Sudan[12]	14 July 2011	0.004	101,931
Spain	14 December 1955	2.973	75,760,424
Sri Lanka	14 December 1955	0.025	637,070
Sudan	12 November 1956	0.010	254,828
Suriname	4 December 1975	0.004	101,931
Swaziland	24 September 1968	0.003	76,448
Sweden	19 November 1946	0.960	24,463,508
Switzerland	10 September 2002	1.047	26,680,513
Syrian Arab Republic[5]	24 October 1945	0.036	917,381
Tajikistan	2 March 1992	0.003	76,448
Thailand	16 December 1946	0.239	6,090,394
The former Yugoslav Republic of Macedonia[2]	8 April 1993	0.008	203,862
Timor-Leste	27 September 2002	0.002	50,966
Togo	20 September 1960	0.001	25,483
Tonga	14 September 1999	0.001	25,483
Trinidad and Tobago	18 September 1962	0.044	1,121,244
Tunisia	12 November 1956	0.036	917,381
Turkey	24 October 1945	1.328	33,841,185
Turkmenistan	2 March 1992	0.019	484,174
Tuvalu	5 September 2000	0.001	25,483
Uganda	25 October 1962	0.006	152,897
Ukraine	24 October 1945	0.099	2,522,799
United Arab Emirates	9 December 1971	0.595	15,162,278
United Kingdom of Great Britain and Northern Ireland	24 October 1945	5.179	131,975,525
United Republic of Tanzania[10]	14 December 1961	0.009	229,345

Member state	Date of admission	Scale of assessments for 2013 (per cent)	Net contributions* (US dollars)
United States of America	24 October 1945	22.000	618,481,182
Uruguay	18 December 1945	0.052	1,325,107
Uzbekistan	2 March 1992	0.015	382,243
Vanuatu	15 September 1981	0.001	25,483
Venezuela (Bolivarian Republic of)	15 November 1945	0.627	15,977,729
Viet Nam	20 September 1977	0.042	1,070,279
Yemen[11]	30 September 1947	0.010	254,828
Zambia	1 December 1964	0.006	152,897
Zimbabwe	25 August 1980	0.002	50,966

Non-member states

The following states are not members of the United Nations but have been invited to participate as observers in the sessions and the work of the General Assembly, and maintain permanent observer missions at Headquarters:

Holy See
State of Palestine

The Holy See contributes towards the expenses of the Organization based on a scale of assessment of 0.001 per cent.

---

* Net contributions are equal to gross contributions less total staff assessment amounts for each country. The staff assessment is an amount deducted from all UN staff members' gross pay and credited to the Tax Equalization Fund, which is used to resolve issues related to staff members' taxes.

NOTES

[1] On 19 September 1991, the Byelorussian Soviet Socialist Republic informed the United Nations that it had changed its name to Belarus.

[2] The Socialist Federal Republic of Yugoslavia was an original member of the United Nations, the *Charter* having been signed on its behalf on 26 June 1945 and ratified 19 October 1945, until its dissolution following the establishment and subsequent admission, as new members, of Bosnia and Herzegovina, the Republic of Croatia, the Republic of Slovenia, The former Yugoslav Republic of Macedonia, and the Federal Republic of Yugoslavia. The Republic of Bosnia and Herzegovina, the Republic of Croatia and the Republic of Slovenia were admitted as members of the United Nations on 22 May 1992. On 8 April 1993, the General Assembly decided to admit as a member of the United Nations the state provisionally referred to for all purposes within the United Nations as 'The former Yugoslav Republic of Macedonia' pending settlement of the difference that had arisen over its name. The Federal Republic of Yugoslavia was admitted as a member of the United Nations on 1 November 2000. On 12 February 2003, it informed the United Nations that it had changed its name to Serbia and Montenegro, effective 4 February 2003. In a letter dated 3 June 2006, the President of the Republic of Serbia informed the Secretary-General that the membership of Serbia and Montenegro was being continued by the Republic of Serbia following Montenegro's declaration of

independence from Serbia on 3 June 2006. On 28 June 2006, Montenegro was accepted as a United Nations member state by the General Assembly.

[3] Czechoslovakia, an original member of the United Nations from 24 October 1945, changed its name to the Czech and Slovak Federal Republic on 20 April 1990. It was dissolved on 1 January 1993 and succeeded by the Czech Republic and Slovakia, both of which became members of the United Nations on 19 January 1993.

[4] The Republic of Zaire informed the United Nations that, effective 17 May 1997, it had changed its name to the Democratic Republic of the Congo.

[5] Egypt and Syria were original members of the United Nations from 24 October 1945. Following a plebiscite on 21 February 1958, the United Arab Republic was established by a union of Egypt and Syria and continued as a single member. On 13 October 1961, Syria, having resumed its status as an independent state, resumed its separate membership in the United Nations; it changed its name to the Syrian Arab Republic on 14 September 1971. On 2 September 1971, the United Arab Republic changed its name to the Arab Republic of Egypt.

[6] The Federal Republic of Germany and the German Democratic Republic were admitted to membership in the United Nations on 18 September 1973. Through the accession of the German Democratic Republic to the Federal Republic of Germany, effective 3 October 1990, the two German states united to form one sovereign state. As of that date, the Federal Republic of Germany has acted in the United Nations under the designation Germany.

[7] By a letter of 20 January 1965, Indonesia announced its decision to withdraw from the United Nations "at this stage and under the present circumstances". By a telegram of 19 September 1966, it announced its decision "to resume full cooperation with the United Nations and to resume participation in its activities". On 28 September 1966, the General Assembly took note of this decision, and the President invited representatives of Indonesia to take their seats in the Assembly.

[8] The Federation of Malaya joined the United Nations on 17 September 1957. On 16 September 1963, its name was changed to Malaysia, following the admission to the new federation of Sabah (North Borneo), Sarawak and Singapore. Singapore became an independent state on 9 August 1965 and a member of the United Nations on 21 September 1965.

[9] The Union of Soviet Socialist Republics was an original member of the United Nations from 24 October 1945. On 24 December 1991, the President of the Russian Federation informed the Secretary-General that the membership of the Soviet Union in the Security Council and all other UN organs was being continued by the Russian Federation with the support of the 11 member countries of the Commonwealth of Independent States.

[10] Tanganyika was a member of the United Nations from 14 December 1961 and Zanzibar from 16 December 1963. Following the ratification on 26 April 1964 of Articles of Union between Tanganyika and Zanzibar, the United Republic of Tanganyika and Zanzibar continued as a single member, changing its name to the United Republic of Tanzania on 1 November 1964.

[11] Yemen was admitted to membership in the United Nations on 30 September 1947 and Democratic Yemen on 14 December 1967. On 22 May 1990, the two countries merged and have since been represented as one member of the United Nations with the name Yemen.

[12] The Republic of South Sudan formally seceded from Sudan on 9 July 2011 as a result of an internationally monitored referendum held in January 2011, and was admitted as a new United Nations member state on 14 July 2011.

II.   PEACEKEEPING OPERATIONS: PAST AND PRESENT

UNTSO*	United Nations Truce Supervision Organization (Jerusalem)	May 1948–present
UNMOGIP*	United Nations Military Observer Group in India and Pakistan	January 1949–present
UNEF I	First United Nations Emergency Force (Gaza)	November 1956–June 1967
UNOGIL	United Nations Observation Group in Lebanon	June–December 1958
ONUC	United Nations Operation in the Congo	July 1960–June 1964
UNSF	United Nations Security Force in West New Guinea (West Irian)	October 1962–April 1963
UNYOM	United Nations Yemen Observation Mission	July 1963–September 1964
UNFICYP*	United Nations Peacekeeping Force in Cyprus	March 1964–present
DOMREP	Mission of the Special Representative of the Secretary-General in the Dominican Republic	May 1965–October 1966
UNIPOM	United Nations India-Pakistan Observation Mission	September 1965–March 1966
UNEF II	Second United Nations Emergency Force (Suez Canal and later Sinai Peninsula)	October 1973–July 1979
UNDOF*	United Nations Disengagement Observer Force (Syrian Golan Heights)	May 1974–present
UNIFIL*	United Nations Interim Force in Lebanon	March 1978–present
UNGOMAP	United Nations Good Offices Mission in Afghanistan and Pakistan	May 1988–March 1990
UNIIMOG	United Nations Iran-Iraq Military Observer Group	August 1988–February 1991
UNAVEM I	United Nations Angola Verification Mission I	December 1988–June 1991
UNTAG	United Nations Transition Assistance Group (Namibia and Angola)	April 1989–March 1990
ONUCA	United Nations Observer Group in Central America	November 1989–January 1992
MINURSO*	United Nations Mission for the Referendum in Western Sahara	April 1991–present
UNIKOM	United Nations Iraq-Kuwait Observation Mission	April 1991–October 2003
UNAVEM II	United Nations Angola Verification Mission II	May 1991–February 1995
ONUSAL	United Nations Observer Mission in El Salvador	July 1991–April 1995
UNAMIC	United Nations Advance Mission in Cambodia	October 1991–March 1992
UNPROFOR	United Nations Protection Force (former Yugoslavia)	February 1992–December 1995
UNTAC	United Nations Transitional Authority in Cambodia	March 1992–September 1993

UNOSOM I	United Nations Operation in Somalia I	April 1992–March 1993
ONUMOZ	United Nations Operation in Mozambique	December 1992–December 1994
UNOSOM II	United Nations Operation in Somalia II	March 1993–March 1995
UNOMUR	United Nations Observer Mission Uganda–Rwanda	June 1993–September 1994
UNOMIG	United Nations Observer Mission in Georgia	August 1993–June 2009
UNOMIL	United Nations Observer Mission in Liberia	September 1993–September 1997
UNMIH	United Nations Mission in Haiti	September 1993–June 1996
UNAMIR	United Nations Assistance Mission for Rwanda	October 1993–March 1996
UNASOG	United Nations Aouzou Strip Observer Group (Chad/Libya)	May–June 1994
UNMOT	United Nations Mission of Observers in Tajikistan	December 1994–May 2000
UNAVEM III	United Nations Angola Verification Mission III	February 1995–June 1997
UNCRO	United Nations Confidence Restoration Operation in Croatia	March 1995–January 1996
UNPREDEP	United Nations Preventive Deployment Force (The former Yugoslav Republic of Macedonia)	March 1995–February 1999
UNMIBH	United Nations Mission in Bosnia and Herzegovina	December 1995–December 2002
UNTAES	United Nations Transitional Administration for Eastern Slavonia, Baranja and Western Sirmium (Croatia)	January 1996–January 1998
UNMOP	United Nations Mission of Observers in Prevlaka	February 1996–December 2002
UNSMIH	United Nations Support Mission in Haiti	July 1996–June 1997
MINUGUA	United Nations Verification Mission in Guatemala	January–May 1997
MONUA	United Nations Observer Mission in Angola	June 1997–February 1999
UNTMIH	United Nations Transition Mission in Haiti	August–November 1997
MIPONUH	United Nations Civilian Police Mission in Haiti	December 1997–March 2000
UNPSG	United Nations Civilian Police Support Group (Croatia)	January–October 1998
MINURCA	United Nations Mission in the Central African Republic	April 1998–February 2000
UNOMSIL	United Nations Observer Mission in Sierra Leone	July 1998–October 1999
UNMIK*	United Nations Interim Administration Mission in Kosovo	June 1999–present
UNAMSIL	United Nations Mission in Sierra Leone	October 1999–December 2005
UNTAET	United Nations Transitional Administration in East Timor	October 1999–May 2002

MONUC	United Nations Observer Mission in the Democratic Republic of the Congo	December 1999–June 2010
UNMEE	United Nations Mission in Ethiopia and Eritrea	July 2000–July 2008
UNAMA**	United Nations Assistance Mission in Afghanistan	March 2002–present
UNMISET	United Nations Mission of Support in East Timor	May 2002–May 2005
MINUCI	United Nations Mission in Côte d'Ivoire	May 2003–April 2004
UNMIL*	United Nations Mission in Liberia	September 2003–present
UNOCI*	United Nations Operation in Côte d'Ivoire	April 2004–present
MINUSTAH*	United Nations Stabilization Mission in Haiti	April 2004–present
UNMIS	United Nations Mission in the Sudan	March 2005–July 2011
ONUB	United Nations Operation in Burundi	May 2004–31 December 2006
UNMIT	United Nations Integrated Mission in Timor-Leste	August 2006–December 2012
BINUB	United Nations Integrated Office in Burundi	January 2007–December 2010
UNAMID*	African Union/United Nations Hybrid Operation in Darfur	July 2007–present
MINURCAT	United Nations Mission in the Central African Republic and Chad	September 2007–December 2010
MONUSCO*	United Nations Organization Stabilization Mission in the Democratic Republic of the Congo	July 2010–present
UNISFA*	United Nations Interim Security Force for Abyei	June 2011–present
UNMISS*	United Nations Mission in the Republic of South Sudan	July 2011–present
UNSMIS	United Nations Supervision Mission in Syria	April 2012–August 2012
MINUSMA*	United Nations Multidimensional Integrated Stabilization Mission in Mali	April 2013–present

---

* Current operation.
** Current political mission directed and supported by DPKO.

For the most up-to-date listing of United Nations Peacekeeping Operations, please visit the website: *www.un.org/en/peacekeeping*.

III. DECOLONIZATION

Trust and Non-Self-Governing Territories that have achieved independence since the adoption of the _Declaration on the Granting of Independence to Colonial Countries and Peoples_ on 14 December 1960

AFRICA	Date of UN admission
Algeria	8 October 1962
Angola	1 December 1976
Botswana	17 October 1966
Burundi	18 September 1962
Cape Verde	16 September 1975
Comoros	12 November 1975
Djibouti	20 September 1977
Equatorial Guinea	12 November 1968
Gambia	21 September 1965
Guinea-Bissau	17 September 1974
Kenya	16 December 1963
Lesotho	17 October 1966
Malawi	1 December 1964
Mauritius	24 April 1968
Mozambique	16 September 1975
Namibia	23 April 1990
Rwanda	18 September 1962
Sao Tome and Principe	26 September 1975
Seychelles	21 September 1976
Sierra Leone	27 September 1961
Swaziland	24 September 1968
Uganda	25 October 1962
United Republic of Tanzania[1]	14 December 1961
Zambia	1 December 1964
Zimbabwe	18 April 1980

ASIA	
Brunei Darussalam	21 September 1984
Democratic Yemen	14 December 1967
Oman	7 October 1971
Singapore	21 September 1965

CARIBBEAN	
Antigua and Barbuda	11 November 1981
Bahamas	18 September 1973
Barbados	9 December 1966
Belize	25 September 1981
Dominica	18 December 1978
Grenada	17 December 1974
Guyana	20 September 1966
Jamaica	18 September 1962
Saint Kitts and Nevis	23 September 1983
Saint Lucia	18 September 1979
Saint Vincent and the Grenadines	16 September 1980

Suriname[2]	4 December 1975
Trinidad and Tobago	18 September 1962
EUROPE	
Malta	1 December 1964
PACIFIC	
Federated States of Micronesia	17 September 1991
Fiji	13 October 1970
Kiribati	14 September 1999
Marshall Islands	17 September 1991
Nauru	14 September 1999
Palau	15 December 1994
Papua New Guinea	10 October 1975
Samoa	15 December 1976
Solomon Islands	19 September 1978
Timor-Leste	27 September 2002
Tuvalu	5 September 2000

Notes

[1] The former Trust Territory of Tanganyika, which became independent in December 1961, and the former Protectorate of Zanzibar, which achieved independence in December 1963, united into a single state in April 1964.

[2] By resolution 945(X), the General Assembly accepted the cessation of the transmission of information regarding Suriname following constitutional changes in the relationship between the Netherlands, Suriname and the Netherlands Antilles.

Dependent Territories that have become integrated or associated with independent states since the adoption of the *Declaration on the Granting of Independence to Colonial Countries and Peoples* on 14 December 1960

Territory

Cameroons (under British administration)	The northern part of the Trust Territory joined the Federation of Nigeria on 1 June 1961 and the southern part joined the Republic of Cameroon on 1 October 1961.
Cook Islands	Fully self-governing in free association with New Zealand since August 1965.
Ifni	Returned to Morocco in June 1969.
Niue	Fully self-governing in free association with New Zealand since August 1974.
North Borneo	North Borneo and Sarawak joined the Federation of Malaya in 1963 to form the Federation of Malaysia.
São Joao Batista de Ajuda	Nationally united with Dahomey (now Benin) in August 1961.
Sarawak	Sarawak and North Borneo joined the Federation of Malaya in 1963 to form the Federation of Malaysia.
West New Guinea (West Irian)	United with Indonesia in 1963.
Cocos (Keeling) Islands	Integrated with Australia in 1984.

Trust Territories that have achieved self-determination

Territory

Togoland (under British administration)	United with the Gold Coast (Colony and Protectorate), a Non-Self-Governing Territory administered by the United Kingdom, in 1957 to form Ghana.
Somaliland (under Italian administration)	United with British Somaliland Protectorate in 1960 to form Somalia.
Togoland (under French administration)	Became independent as Togo in 1960.
Cameroons (under French administration)	Became independent as Cameroon in 1960.
Tanganyika (under British administration)	Became independent in 1961 (in 1964, Tanganyika and the former Protectorate of Zanzibar, which had become independent in 1963, united as a single state under the name of the United Republic of Tanzania).
Ruanda-Urundi (under Belgian administration)	Voted to divide into the two sovereign states of Rwanda and Burundi in 1962.
Western Samoa (under New Zealand administration)	Became independent as Samoa in 1962.
Nauru (administered by Australia on behalf of Australia, New Zealand and the United Kingdom)	Became independent in 1968.
New Guinea (administered by Australia)	United with the Non-Self-Governing Territory of Papua, also administered by Australia, to become the independent state of Papua New Guinea in 1975.

Trust Territories of the Pacific Islands

Territory

Federated States of Micronesia	Became fully self-governing in free Association with the United States in 1990.
Republic of the Marshall Islands	Became fully self-governing in free Association with the United States in 1990.
Commonwealth of the Northern Mariana Islands	Became fully self-governing as a Commonwealth of the United States in 1990.
Palau	Became fully self-governing in free Association with the United States in 1994.

IV. UNITED NATIONS OBSERVANCES

International Decades

2014–2024	United Nations Decade of Sustainable Energy for All
2011–2020	Third International Decade for the Eradication of Colonialism
	United Nations Decade on Biodiversity
	Decade of Action for Road Safety
2010–2020	United Nations Decade for Deserts and the Fight against Desertification
2008–2017	Second United Nations Decade for the Eradication of Poverty
2006–2016	Decade of Recovery and Sustainable Development of the Affected Regions (third decade after the Chernobyl disaster)
2005–2015	International Decade for Action, "Water for Life" (from 22 March 2005)
2005–2014	Second International Decade of the World's Indigenous People
	United Nations Decade of Education for Sustainable Development

International Years

2014	International Year of Small Island Developing States
	International Year of Crystallography
	International Year of Family Farming
2013	International Year of Water Cooperation
	International Year of Quinoa

Annual Weeks

First week of February	World Interfaith Harmony Week
21–27 March	Week of Solidarity with the Peoples Struggling against Racism and Racial Discrimination
6–12 May	United Nations Global Road Safety Week
25–31 May	Week of Solidarity with the Peoples of Non-Self-Governing Territories
1–7 August	World Breastfeeding Week (WHO)
4–10 October	World Space Week
24–30 October	Disarmament Week
The week of 11 November	International Week of Science and Peace

Annual Days

27 January	International Day of Commemoration in Memory of the Victims of the Holocaust
4 February	World Cancer Day (WHO)
6 February	International Day of Zero Tolerance to Female Genital Mutilation (WHO)
13 February	World Radio Day (UNESCO)
20 February	World Day of Social Justice
21 February	International Mother Language Day (UNESCO)
8 March	International Women's Day
20 March	International Day of Happiness
21 March	International Day for the Elimination of Racial Discrimination
	International Day of Nowruz
	World Down Syndrome Day

	International Day of Forests and the Tree
	World Poetry Day (UNESCO)
22 March	World Water Day
23 March	World Meteorological Day (WMO)
24 March	International Day for the Right to the Truth concerning Gross Human Rights Violations and for the Dignity of Victims
	World Tuberculosis Day (WHO)
25 March	International Day of Remembrance of the Victims of Slavery and the Transatlantic Slave Trade
	International Day of Solidarity with Detained and Missing Staff Members
2 April	World Autism Awareness Day
4 April	International Day for Mine Awareness and Assistance in Mine Action
7 April	World Health Day (WHO)
	Day of Remembrance of the Victims in Rwanda Genocide
12 April	International Day of Human Space Flight
22 April	International Mother Earth Day
23 April	World Book and Copyright Day (UNESCO)
25 April	World Malaria Day (WHO)
26 April	World Intellectual Property Day (WIPO)
28 April	World Day for Safety and Health at Work (ILO)
29 April	Day of Remembrance for all Victims of Chemical Warfare
30 April	International Jazz Day
Day of full moon in May	Day of Vesak
3 May	World Press Freedom Day
8–9 May	Time of Remembrance and Reconciliation for Those Who Lost Their Lives during the Second World War
12–13 May	World Migratory Bird Day (UNEP)
15 May	International Day of Families
17 May	World Telecommunication and Information Society Day (ITU)
21 May	World Day for Cultural Diversity for Dialogue and Development
22 May	International Day for Biological Diversity
23 May	International Day to End Obstetric Fistula
29 May	International Day of UN Peacekeepers
31 May	World No-Tobacco Day (WHO)
1 June	Global Day of Parents
4 June	International Day of Innocent Children Victims of Aggression
5 June	World Environment Day (UNEP)
8 June	World Oceans Day
12 June	World Day Against Child Labour (ILO)
14 June	World Blood Donor Day (WHO)
15 June	World Elder Abuse Awareness Day
17 June	World Day to Combat Desertification and Drought
20 June	World Refugee Day
23 June	International Widows' Day
	United Nations Public Service Day
25 June	Day of the Seafarer (IMO)
26 June	International Day against Drug Abuse and Illicit Trafficking

	United Nations International Day in Support of Victims of Torture
First Saturday of July	International Day of Cooperatives
11 July	World Population Day
18 July	Nelson Mandela International Day
28 July	World Hepatitis Day (WHO)
30 July	International Day of Friendship
9 August	International Day of the World's Indigenous People
12 August	International Youth Day
19 August	World Humanitarian Day
23 August	International Day for the Remembrance of the Slave Trade and Its Abolition (UNESCO)
29 August	International Day against Nuclear Tests
30 August	International Day of the Victims of Enforced Disappearances
5 September	International Day of Charity
8 September	International Literacy Day (UNESCO)
10 September	World Suicide Prevention Day (WHO)
12 September	United Nations Day for South-South Cooperation
15 September	International Day of Democracy
16 September	International Day for the Preservation of the Ozone Layer
21 September	International Day of Peace
27 September	World Tourism Day (UNWTO)
28 September	World Rabies Day (WHO)
Last Saturday in September	World Heart Day (WHO)
Last week of September	World Maritime Day (IMO)
1 October	International Day of Older Persons
2 October	International Day of Non-Violence
First Monday in October	World Habitat Day
5 October	World Teachers' Day (UNESCO)
9 October	World Post Day (UPU)
10 October	World Mental Health Day (WHO)
11 October	International Day of the Girl Child
13 October	International Day for Disaster Reduction
Second Thursday in October	World Sight Day (WHO)
15 October	International Day of Rural Women
16 October	World Food Day (FAO)
17 October	International Day for the Eradication of Poverty
24 October	United Nations Day
	World Development Information Day
27 October	World Day for Audiovisual Heritage (UNESCO)
6 November	International Day for Preventing the Exploitation of the Environment in War and Armed Conflict
10 November	World Science Day for Peace and Development (UNESCO)
12 November	World Pneumonia Day (WHO)
14 November	World Diabetes Day (WHO)
16 November	International Day for Tolerance
	World Chronic Obstructive Pulmonary Disease Day (WHO)
Third Thursday in November	World Philosophy Day (UNESCO)
Third Sunday in November	World Day of Remembrance for Road Traffic Victims (WHO)
19 November	World Toilet Day

20 November	Africa Industrialization Day
	Universal Children's Day
21 November	World Television Day
25 November	International Day for the Elimination of Violence against Women
29 November	International Day of Solidarity with the Palestinian People
1 December	World AIDS Day
2 December	International Day for the Abolition of Slavery
3 December	International Day of Persons with Disabilities
5 December	International Volunteer Day for Economic and Social Development
7 December	International Civil Aviation Day (ICAO)
9 December	International Anti-Corruption Day
10 December	Human Rights Day
11 December	International Mountain Day
18 December	International Migrants Day
20 December	International Human Solidarity Day

For the most up-to-date listing of United Nations Observances, please visit the website: *www.un.org/observances.*

V. UN INFORMATION CENTRES, SERVICES AND OFFICES

AFRICA

Accra
United Nations Information Centre
Gamal Abdel Nasser/Liberia Roads
(P.O. Box GP 2339)
Accra, Ghana
Tel.: (233) 30 2 665511
Fax: (233) 30 2 701 0943
E-mail: unic.accra@unic.org
Website: *http://accra.unic.org*
Serving: Ghana, Sierra Leone

Algiers
United Nations Information Centre
41 rue Mohamed Khoudi, El Biar
El Biar, 16030 El Biar, Alger
(Boîte Postale 444, Hydra-Alger 16035)
Algiers, Algeria
Tel.: (213 21) 92 54 42
Fax: (213 21) 92 54 42
E-mail: unic.dz@undp.org
Website: *http://algiers.unic.org*
Serving: Algeria

Antananarivo
United Nations Information Centre
159, Rue Damantsoa, Amkorahotra
(Boîte Postale, 1348)
Antananarivo, Madagascar
Tel.: (261 20) 22 330 50
Fax: (261 20) 22 367 94
E-mail: unic.ant@moov.mg
Website: *http://antananarivo.unic.org*
Serving: Madagascar

Asmara
United Nations Information Centre
Hiday Street, Airport Road
(P.O. Box 5366)
Asmara, Eritrea
Tel.: (291 1) 15 11 66, Ext. 311
Fax: (291 1) 15 10 81
E-mail: dpi.er@undp.org
Website: *http://asmara.unic.org*
Serving: Eritrea

Brazzaville
United Nations Information Centre
Avenue Foch, Case ortf 15
(Boîte Postale 13210)
Brazzaville, Congo
Tel.: (242) 06 661 20 68
E-mail: unic.brazzaville@unic.org
Website: *http://brazzaville.unic.org*
Serving: Congo

Bujumbura
United Nations Information Centre
117 Avenue de la Révolution
(Boîte Postale 2160)
Bujumbura, Burundi
Tel.: (257) 22 50 18
Fax: (257) 24 17 98
E-mail: unic.bujumbura@unic.org
Website: *http://bujumbura.unic.org*
Serving: Burundi

Cairo
United Nations Information Centre
1 Osiris Street, Garden City
(P.O. Box 262)
Cairo, Egypt
Tel.: (202) 27959861
Fax: (202) 27953705
E-mail: info@unic-eg.org
Website: *http://www.unic-eg.org*
Serving: Egypt, Saudi Arabia

Dakar
United Nations Information Centre
Immeuble Soumex–3ème Etage,
    Mamelles-Almadies
(Boîte Postale 154)
Dakar, Senegal
Tel.: (221) 33 869 99 11
Fax: (221) 33 860 51 48
E-mail: unic.dakar@unic.org
Website: *http://dakar.unic.org*
Serving: Cape Verde, Côte d'Ivoire,
    Gambia, Guinea-Bissau, Mauritania,
    Senegal

Dar es Salaam
United Nations Information Centre
Garden Avenue/Shaaban Robert Street
6th Floor International House
(P.O. Box 9224)
Dar es Salaam, United Republic of Tanzania
E-mail: unic.daressalaam@unic.org
Website: *http://daressalaam.unic.org*
Serving: United Republic of Tanzania

Harare
United Nations Information Centre
Sanders House (2nd floor), cnr. First Street
   Jason Moyo Avenue
(P.O. Box 4408)
Harare, Zimbabwe
Tel.: (263 4) 777 060
Fax: (263 4) 750 476
E-mail: unic.harare@unic.org
Website: *http://harare.unic.org*
Serving: Zimbabwe

Khartoum
United Nations Information Centre
United Nations Compound House #7, Blk 5
Gamma'a Avenue
(P.O. Box 1992)
Khartoum, Sudan
Tel.: (249 183) 783 755
Fax: (249 183) 773 772
E-mail: unic.sd@undp.org
Website: *http://khartoum.unic.org*
Serving: Somalia, Sudan

Lagos
United Nations Information Centre
17 Alfred Rewane Road
   (formely Kingsway Road), Ikoyi
(P.O. Box 1068), Lagos, Nigeria
Tel.: (234 1) 775 5989
Fax: (234 1) 463 0916
E-mail: lagos@unic.org
Website: *http://lagos.unic.org*
Serving: Nigeria

Lomé
United Nations Information Centre
468, Angle rue Atime
Avenue de la Libération
(Boîte Postale 911)
Lomé, Togo
Tel.: (228) 22 21 23 06
Fax: (228) 22 21 11 65
E-mail: unic.lome@unic.org
Website: *http://lome.unic.org*
Serving: Benin, Togo

Lusaka
United Nations Information Centre
Revenue House (Ground floor)
Cnr. Great North and Kalambo Roads
(P.O. Box 32905, Lusaka 10101)
Lusaka, Zambia
Tel.: (260 211) 228 487

Fax: (260 211) 222 958
E-mail: unic.lusaka@unic.org
Website: *http://lusaka.unic.org*
Serving: Malawi,
   Swaziland, Zambia

Maseru
United Nations Information Centre
United Nations Road
UN House
(P.O. Box 301, Maseru 100)
Maseru, Lesotho
Tel.: (266 22) 313 790
Fax: (266 22) 310 042
E-mail: unic.maseru@unic.org
Website: *http://maseru.unic.org*
Serving: Lesotho

Nairobi
United Nations Information Centre
United Nations Office, Gigiri
(P.O. Box 67578-00200)
Nairobi, Kenya
Tel.: (254 20) 762 25421
Fax: (254 20) 762 24349
E-mail: nairobi.unic@unon.org
Website: *http://unicnairobi.org*
Serving: Kenya,
   Seychelles, Uganda

Ouagadougou
United Nations Information Centre
14 Avenue de la Grande Chancellerie
Secteur no. 4
(Bôite postale 135, Ougadougou 01)
Ougadougou, Burkina Faso
Tel.: (226) 5030 6076
Fax: (226) 5031 1322
E-mail: unic.ouagadougou@unic.org
Website: *http://ouagadougou.unic.org*
Serving: Burkina Faso,
   Chad, Mali, Niger

Pretoria
United Nations Information Centre
Metropark Building
351 Francis Baard Street
(P.O. Box 12677, Tramshed)
Pretoria, South Africa 0126
Tel.: (27 12) 3548 506
Fax: (27 12) 3548 501
E-mail: unic.pretoria@unic.org
Website: *http://pretoria.unic.org*
Serving: South Africa

Rabat
United Nations Information Centre
13 Avenue Ahmed Balafrej
(Boîte postale 601), Casier ONU
  Rabat-Chellah
Rabat, Morocco
Tel.: (212 537) 75 03 93
Fax: (212 37) 75 03 82
E-mail: cinu.rabat@unic.org
Website: *http://www.unicmor.ma*
Serving: Morocco

Tripoli
United Nations Information Centre
Khair Aldeen Baybers Street
Hay El-Andalous
(P.O. Box 286, Hay El-Andalous)
Tripoli, Libyan Arab Jamahiriya
Tel.: (218 21) 4770 251
Fax: (218 21) 4777 343
E-mail: tripoli@un.org
Website: *http://tripoli.unic.org*
Serving: Libyan Arab Jamahiriya

Tunis
United Nations Information Centre
41 Bis, Av. Louis Braille, Cité El Khadra
(Boîte postale 863)
1003 Tunis, Tunisia
Tel.: (216 71) 902203
Fax: (216 71) 906811
E-mail: unic.tunis@unic.org
Website: *http://www.unictunis.org.tn*
Serving: Tunisia

Windhoek
United Nations Information Centre
UN House, 38–44 Stein Street, Klein
(Private Bag 13351)
Windhoek, Namibia
Tel.: (264 61) 2046111
Fax: (264 61) 2046521
E-mail: unic.windhoek@unic.org
Website: *tunis.sites.unicnetwork.org*
Serving: Namibia

Yaoundé
United Nations Information Centre
Immeuble Tchinda
Rue 2044
Derrière camp SIC TSINGA
(Boîte postale 836)
Yaoundé, Cameroon

Tel.: (237) 2 221 23 67
Fax: (237) 2 221 23 68
E-mail: unic.yaounde@unic.org
Website: *http://yaounde.unic.org*
Serving: Cameroon, Central African Republic,
  Gabon

THE AMERICAS

Asunción
United Nations Information Centre
Avda. Mariscal López esq. Guillermo Saraví
Edificio Naciones Unidas
(Casilla de Correo 1107)
Asunción, Paraguay
Tel.: (595 21) 614 443
Fax: (595 21) 611 988
E-mail: unic.asuncion@unic.org
Website: *http://asuncion.unic.org*
Serving: Paraguay

Bogotá
United Nations Information Centre
Calle 100 No. 8A-55 Piso 10
Edificio World Trade Center-Torre "C"
(Apartado, Aéro 058964)
Bogotá 2, Colombia
Tel.: (57 1) 257 6044
Fax: (57 1) 257 6244
E-mail: unic.bogota@unic.org
Website: *http://www.nacionesunidas.org.co*
Serving: Colombia, Ecuador, Venezuela

Buenos Aires
United Nations Information Centre
Junín 1940, 1er piso
1113 Buenos Aires, Argentina
Tel.: (54 11) 4803 7671
Fax: (54 11) 4804 7545
E-mail: unic.buenosaires@unic.org
Website: *http://www.unic.org.ar*
Serving: Argentina, Uruguay

La Paz
United Nations Information Centre
Calle 14 esq. S. Bustamante
Edificio Metrobol II, Calacoto
(Apartado Postal 9072)
La Paz, Bolivia
Tel.: (591 2) 262 4512
Fax: (591 2) 279 5820
E-mail: unic.lapaz@unic.org
Website: *http://www.nu.org.bo*
Serving: Bolivia

Lima
United Nations Information Centre
Av. Perez Aranibar 750
Magdalena
(P.O. Box 14-0199)
Lima 17, Peru
Tel.: (511) 625 9140
Fax: (511) 625 9100
E-mail: unic.lima@unic.org
Website: *http://www.uniclima.org.pe*
Serving: Peru

Mexico City
United Nations Information Centre
Montes Urales 440, 3rd floor
Colonia Lomas de Chapultepec
Mexico City, D.F. 11000, Mexico
Tel.: (52 55) 4000 9717
Fax: (52 55) 5203 8638
E-mail: infounic@un.org.mx
Website: *http://www.cinu.mx*
Serving: Cuba, Dominican Republic,
Mexico

Panama City
United Nations Information Centre
UN House Bldg 128, 1st Floor
Ciudad del Saber, Clayton
(P.O. Box 0819-01082)
Panama City, Panama
Tel.: (507) 301 0035/0036
Fax: (507) 301 0037
E-mail: unic.panama@unic.org
Website: *http://www.cinup.org*
Serving: Panama

Port of Spain
United Nations Information Centre
2nd floor, Bretton Hall
16 Victoria Avenue
(P.O. Box 130)
Port of Spain, Trinidad and Tobago, W.I.
Tel.: (868) 623 4813
Fax: (868) 623 4332
E-mail: unic.portofspain@unic.org
Website: *http://portofspain.unicnetwork.org*
Serving: Antigua and Barbuda,
Aruba, Bahamas, Barbados, Belize,
Dominica, Grenada, Guyana, Jamaica,
Netherlands Antilles, Saint Kitts and
Nevis, Saint Lucia, Saint Vincent and
the Grenadines, Suriname, Trinidad
and Tobago

Rio de Janeiro
United Nations Information Centre
Palácio Itamaraty
Av. Marechal Floriano 196
20080-002 Rio de Janeiro RJ, Brazil
Tel.: (55 21) 2253 2211
Fax: (55 21) 2233 5753
E-mail: unic.brazil@unic.org
Website: *http://unicrio.org.br*
Serving: Brazil

Santiago
United Nations Information Service,
    Economic Commission for
    Latin America and the Caribbean
Edificio Naciones Unidas
Avenida Dag Hammarskjöld 3477
Vitacura (Casilla 179-D)
Santiago, Chile
Tel.: (56 2) 210 2040
Fax: (56 2) 208 1947
E-mail: dpisantiago@eclac.cl
Website: *http://www.eclac.org/prensa*
Serving: Chile, ECLAC

Washington D.C.
United Nations Information Center
1775 K Street, N.W., Suite 400
Washington, D.C. 20006
United States of America
Tel.: (202) 331 8670
Fax: (202) 331 9191
E-mail: unicdc@unicwash.org
Website: *http://www.unicwash.org*
Serving: United States of America

ASIA AND THE PACIFIC

Bangkok
United Nations Information Service,
    Economic and Social Commission
    for Asia and the Pacific
United Nations Building
Rajdamnern Nok Avenue
Bangkok 10200, Thailand
Tel.: (66 2) 288 1865
Fax: (66 2) 288 1052
E-mail: unisbkk.unescap@un.org
Website: *http://www.unescap.org/unis*
Serving: Cambodia, Lao People's
    Democratic Republic, Malaysia,
    Singapore, Thailand,
    Viet Nam, ESCAP

Beirut
United Nations Information Centre
United Nations Information Service,
  Economic and Social Commission
  for Western Asia
UN House, Riad El-Sohl Square
(P.O. Box 11-8575-4656)
Beirut, Lebanon
Tel.: (961 1) 981 301, Ext. 1828
Fax: (961 1) 97 04 24
E-mail: unic-beirut@un.org
Website: *http://www.unicbeirut.org*
Serving: Jordan, Kuwait, Lebanon,
  Syrian Arab Republic, ESCWA

Canberra
United Nations Information Centre
Level 1, 7 National Circuit, Barton
(P.O. Box 5366, Kingston, ACT 2604)
Canberra ACT 2600, Australia
Tel.: (61 2) 627 09200
Fax: (61 2) 627 38206
E-mail: unic.canberra@unic.org
Website: *http://www.un.org.au*
Serving: Australia, Fiji, Kiribati, Nauru, New
  Zealand, Samoa, Tonga, Tuvalu, Vanuatu

Colombo
United Nations Information Centre
202/204 Bauddhaloka Mawatha
(P.O. Box 1505, Colombo)
Colombo 7, Sri Lanka
Tel.: (94 112) 580 791
Fax: (94 112) 581 116
E-mail: unic.lk@undp.org
Website: *http://colombo.sites.unicnetwork.org*
Serving: Sri Lanka

Dhaka
United Nations Information Centre
IDB Bhaban (8th floor), Sher-e-Banglanagar
(G.P.O. Box 3658, Dhaka-1000)
Dhaka-1207, Bangladesh
Tel.: (880 2) 9183 086 (library)
Fax: (880 2) 9183 106
E-mail: unic.dhaka@undp.org
Website: *http://www.unicdhaka.org*
Serving: Bangladesh

Islamabad
United Nations Information Centre
Serena Business Complex 2nd Floor, Sector G-5/1
Khayaban e Suharwardy
(P.O. Box 1107)

Islamabad, Pakistan
Tel.: (0092) 51 835 5719
Fax: (0092) 51 2271 856
E-mail: unic.islamabad@unic.org
Website: *http://www.un.org.pk/unic*
Serving: Pakistan

Jakarta
United Nations Information Centre
Menara Thamrin Building, 3A floor
Jalan MH Thamrin, Kav. 3
Jakarta 10250, Indonesia
Tel.: (62 21) 3983 1011
Fax: (62 21) 3983 1014
E-mail: unic.jakarta@unic.org
Website: *http://www.unic-jakarta.org*
Serving: Indonesia

Kathmandu
United Nations Information Centre
Harihar Bhavan Pulchowk
(P.O. Box 107, UN House)
Kathmandu, Nepal
Tel.: (977 1) 55 23 200, Ext. 1600
Fax: (977 1) 55 43 723
E-mail: unic.np@undp.org
Website: *http://kathmandu.unic.org*
Serving: Nepal

Manama
United Nations Information Centre
United Nations House
Bldg. 69, Road 1901, Block 319
(P.O. Box 26004, Manama), Manama, Bahrain
Tel.: (973) 1731 1676
Fax: (973) 1731 1692
E-mail: unic.manama@unic.org
Website: *http://manama.unic.org*
Serving: Bahrain, Qatar, United Arab Emirates

Manila
United Nations Information Centre
GC Corporate Plaza (ex Jaka II Building)
5th floor, 150 Legaspi Street, Legaspi Village
(P.O. Box 7285 ADC (DAPO), 1300 Domestic
  Road Pasay City)
Makati City
1229 Metro Manila, Philippines
Tel.: (63 2) 338 5521
Fax: (63 2) 339 0177
E-mail: unic.manila@unic.org
Website: *http://www.unicmanila.org*
Serving: Papua New Guinea, Philippines,
  Solomon Islands

New Delhi
United Nations Information Centre
55 Lodi Estate, New Delhi 110 003, India
Tel.: (91 11) 4653 2242
Fax: (91 11) 2462 8508
E-mail: unicindia@unicindia.org
Website: *http://www.unic.org.in*
Serving: Bhutan, India

Sana'a
United Nations Information Centre
Street 5, Off Abawnya Area
Handhel Zone, beside Handhal Mosque
(P.O. Box 237)
Sana'a, Yemen
Tel.: (967 1) 274 000
Fax: (967 1) 274 043
E-mail: unicyem@y.net.ye
Website: *http://www.unicyemen.org*
Serving: Yemen

Tehran
United Nations Information Centre
No. 8, Shahrzad Blvd., Darrous
(P.O. Box 15875-4557)
Tehran, Iran
Tel.: (98 21) 2 286 0694
Fax: (98 21) 2 287 3395
E-mail: unic.tehran@unic.org
Website: *http://www.unic-ir.org*
Serving: Iran

Tokyo
United Nations Information Centre
UNU Building (8th floor)
53–70 Jingumae 5-Chome, Shibuya-Ku
Tokyo 150-0001, Japan
Tel.: (81 3) 5467 4454
Fax: (81 3) 5467 4455
E-mail: unic.tokyo@unic.org
Website: *http://www.unic.or.jp*
Serving: Japan

Yangon
United Nations Information Centre
6 Natmauk Road
Tamwe Township
(P.O. Box 230)
Yangon, Myanmar
Tel.: (95 1) 542 911
Fax: (95 1) 545 634
E-mail: unic.myanmar@undp.org
Website: *http://yangon.unic.org*
Serving: Myanmar

EUROPE AND THE COMMMONWEALTH OF INDEPENDENT STATES

Almaty
United Nations Information Centre
67 Tole Bi Street, 050000 Almaty
Republic of Kazakhstan
Tel.: (7 727) 258 2643
Fax: (7 727) 258 2645
E-mail: kazakhstan@unic.org
Website: *http://kazakhstan.unic.org*
Serving: Kazakhstan

Ankara
United Nations Information Centre
Birlik Mahallesi, 415 Cadde No. 11
06610 Cankaya
Ankara, Turkey
Tel.: (90 312) 454-1052
Fax: (90 312) 496-1499
E-mail: unic.ankara@unic.org
Website: *http://www.unicankara.org.tr*
Serving: Turkey

Baku
United Nations Office
UN 50th Anniversary Street, 3
Baku, AZ1001
Azerbaijan
Tel.: (994 12) 498 98 88
Fax: (994 12) 498 32 35
E-mail: un-dpi@un-az.org
Website: *http://bakusites.unicnetwork.org*
Serving: Azerbaijan

Brussels
Regional United Nations Information Centre
Residence Palace
Rue de la Loi/Westraat 155
Quartier Rubens, Block C2
1040 Brussels, Belgium
Tel.: (32 2) 788 84 84
Fax: (32 2) 788 84 85
E-mail: info@unric.org
Website: *http://www.unric.org*
Serving: Belgium, Cyprus,
    Denmark, Finland, France,
    Germany, Greece, Holy See,
    Iceland, Ireland, Italy, Luxembourg,
    Malta, Monaco, Netherlands,
    Norway, Portugal, San Marino,
    Spain, Sweden, United Kingdom,
    European Union

Geneva
United Nations Information Service
United Nations Office at Geneva
Palais des Nations
1211 Geneva 10, Switzerland
Tel.: (41 22) 917 2302
Fax: (41 22) 917 0030
E-mail: press_geneva@unog.ch
Website: *http://www.unog.ch*
Serving: Switzerland

Kyiv
United Nations Office
Klovskiy Uzviz, 1, Kyiv, Ukraine
Tel.: (380 44) 253 9363
Fax: (380 44) 253 2607
E-mail: registry@un.org.ua
Website: *http://www.un.org.ua*
Serving: Ukraine

Minsk
United Nations Office
Kirov Street, 17, 6th Floor, 220030
Minsk, Belarus
Tel.: (375 17) 327 3817
Fax: (375 17) 226 0340
E-mail: dpi.staff.by@undp.org
Website: *http://www.un.by*
Serving: Belarus

Moscow
United Nations Information Centre
Glazovsky Pereulok, 4/16
Moscow, 119002 Russian Federation
Tel.: (7 499) 241 28 94
Fax: (7 495) 695 21 38
E-mail: dpi-moscow@unic.ru
Website: *http://www.unic.ru*
Serving: Russian Federation

Prague
United Nations Information Centre
Zeleza 24
11000 Prague 1, Czech Republic
Tel.: (420) 2557 11645
Fax: (420) 2573 16761
E-mail: info@osn.cz
Website: *http://www.osn.cz*
Serving: Czech Republic

Tashkent
United Nations Office
Mirabad Str. 41/3

Tashkent, Uzbekistan 100015
Tel.: (998 71) 1203 450
Fax: (998 71) 1203 485
E-mail: registry.uz@undp.org
Website: *http://www.un.uz*
Serving: Uzbekistan

Tbilisi
United Nations Office
9, Eristavi Street
0179 Tbilisi, Georgia
Tel.: 995 32 225 11 26
Fax: 995 32 225 02 71
E-mail: uno.tbilisi@unic.org
Website: *http://ungeorgia.ge*
Serving: Georgia

Vienna
United Nations Information Service
United Nations Office at Vienna
Vienna International Centre
Wagramer Strasse 5
(P.O. Box 500, 1400 Vienna)
1220 Vienna, Austria
Tel.: (43 1) 26060 4666
Fax: (43 1) 26060 5899
E-mail: unis@unvienna.org
Website: *http://www.unis.unvienna.org*
Serving: Austria, Hungary, Slovakia, Slovenia

Warsaw
United Nations Information Centre
Al. Niedpodleglosci 186
00-608 Warsaw, Poland
Tel.: (48 22) 825 57 84
Fax: (48 22) 825 77 06
E-mail: unic.poland@unic.org
Website: *http://www.unic.un.org.pl*
Serving: Poland

Yerevan
United Nations Office
14 Petros Adamyan Street, 1st Floor
0010 Yerevan, Armenia
Tel.: (374 10) 560 212
Fax: (374 10) 560 212
E-mail: uno.yerevan@unic.org
Website: *http://www.un.am*
Serving: Armenia

VI. SELECTED UNITED NATIONS WEBSITES

United Nations	*www.un.org*
United Nations system	*www.unsystem.org*

Principal Organs

Economic and Social Council	*www.un.org/en/ecosoc*
General Assembly	*www.un.org/en/ga*
International Court of Justice	*www.icj-cij.org*
Secretariat	*www.un.org/en/mainbodies/secretariat*
Security Council	*www.un.org/docs/sc*
Trusteeship Council	*www.un.org/en/mainbodies/trusteeship*

Programmes and Funds

International Trade Center (ITC)	*www.intracen.org*
Office of the United Nations High Commissioner for Refugees (UNHCR)	*www.unhcr.org*
United Nations Capital Development Fund (UNCDF)	*www.uncdf.org*
United Nations Children's Fund (UNICEF)	*www.unicef.org*
United Nations Conference on Trade and Development (UNCTAD)	*www.unctad.org*
United Nations Development Programme (UNDP)	*www.undp.org*
United Nations Entity for Gender Equality and the Empowerment of Women (UN-Women)	*www.unwomen.org*
United Nations Environment Programme (UNEP)	*www.unep.org*
United Nations Human Settlements Programme (UN-HABITAT)	*www.unhabitat.org*
United Nations Office on Drugs and Crime (UNODC)	*www.unodc.org*
United Nations Population Fund (UNFPA)	*www.unfpa.org*
United Nations Relief and Works Agency for Palestine Refugees in the Near East (UNRWA)	*www.unrwa.org*
United Nations Volunteers (UNV)	*www.unv.org*
World Food Programme (WFP)	*www.wfp.org*

Research and Training Institutes

United Nations Institute for Disarmament Research (UNIDIR)	*www.unidir.org*
United Nations Institute for Training and Research (UNITAR)	*www.unitar.org*
United Nations Interregional Crime and Justice Research Institute (UNICRI)	*www.unicri.it*
United Nations Research Institute for Social Development (UNRISD)	*www.unrisd.org*
United Nations System Staff College (UNSSC)	*www.unssc.org*
United Nations University (UNU)	*www.unu.edu*

Other Entities

Joint United Nations Programme on HIV/AIDS (UNAIDS)	*www.unaids.org*
United Nations International Strategy for Disaster Reduction (UNISDR)	*www.unisdr.org*
United Nations Office for Project Services (UNOPS)	*www.unops.org*

Subsidiary Bodies and Functional Commissions

Commission on Crime Prevention
and Criminal Justice   *www.unodc.org/unodc/en/commissions/CCPCJ/index.html*

Commission on Narcotic Drugs   *www.unodc.org/unodc/en/commissions/CND/index.html*

Commission on Population
and Development   *www.un.org/esa/population/cpd/aboutcom.htm*

Commission on Science
and Technology for Development   *www.unctad.org/cstd*

Commission on Social Development   *www.un.org/esa/socdev/csd/index.html*

Commission on the Status of Women   *www.un.org/womenwatch/daw/csw*

Commission on Sustainable
Development   *www.un.org/esa/dsd/csd/csd_aboucsd.shtml*

Counter-Terrorism Committee (CTC)   *www.un.org/en/sc/ctc*

Disarmament Commission (UNDC)   *www.un.org/Depts/ddar/discomm/undc*

Human Rights Council (HRC)   *www2.ohchr.org/english/bodies/hrcouncil*

International Criminal Tribunal for Rwanda (ICTR)   *www.unictr.org*

International Criminal Tribunal for the former Yugoslavia (ICTY)   *www.icty.org*

International Law Commission (ILC)   *www.un.org/law/ilc*

Peacekeeping operations
and political missions   *www.un.org/en/peacekeeping*

Permanent Forum on Indigenous Issues   *www.un.org/esa/socdev/unpfii*

Statistical Commission   *unstats.un.org/unsd/statcom/commission.htm*

United Nations Forum on Forests   *www.un.org/esa/forests*

United Nations Peacebuilding Commission   *www.un.org/peace/peacebuilding*

Regional Commissions

Economic Commission for Africa (ECA)   *www.uneca.org*

Economic Commission for Europe (ECE)   *www.unece.org*

Economic Commission for Latin America
and the Caribbean (ECLAC)   *www.eclac.org*

Economic and Social Commission for Asia and the Pacific (ESCAP)   *www.unescap.org*

Economic and Social Commission for Western Asia (ESCWA)   *www.escwa.un.org*

Specialized Agencies

Food and Agriculture Organization of the United Nations (FAO)   *www.fao.org*

International Civil Aviation Organization (ICAO)   *www.icao.int*

International Fund for Agricultural Development (IFAD)   *www.ifad.org*

International Labour Organization (ILO)   *www.ilo.org*

International Maritime Organization (IMO)   *www.imo.org*

International Monetary Fund (IMF)   *www.imf.org*

International Telecommunication Union (ITU)   *www.itu.int*

United Nations Educational, Scientific
and Cultural Organization (UNESCO)   *www.unesco.org*

United Nations Industrial Development Organization (UNIDO)   *www.unido.org*

Universal Postal Union (UPU)   *www.upu.int*

World Bank Group   *www.worldbank.org*

World Health Organization (WHO)	*www.who.int*
World Intellectual Property Organization (WIPO)	*www.wipo.int*
World Meteorological Organization (WMO)	*www.wmo.ch*
World Tourism Organization (UNWTO)	*www.unwto.org*

Related Organizations

International Atomic Energy Agency (IAEA)	*www.iaea.org*
Organization for the Prohibition of Chemical Weapons (OPCW)	*www.opcw.org*
Preparatory Committee for the Comprehensive Nuclear-Test-Ban Treaty Organization (CTBTO)	*www.ctbto.org*
World Trade Organization (WTO)	*www.wto.org*

INDEX